DEAREST MAMA

Edited by Roger Fulford

Dearest Child
Letters Between Queen Victoria
and the Princess Royal
1858–1861

Dearest Mama
Letters Between Queen Victoria
and the Crown Princess of Prussia
1861–1864

Queen Victoria with *(left to right)* Princess Alice, the Crown Princess, and Prince Alfred. The photograph bears an inscription by the Queen.

DEAREST MAMA

*Letters Between Queen Victoria and the Crown Princess
of Prussia*

1861-1864

Edited by

ROGER FULFORD

HOLT, RINEHART AND WINSTON
New York   Chicago   San Francisco

Library of Congress Catalog Card Number: 69-16185

First published in the United States, May, 1969

FIRST EDITION

The frontispiece and Plates 2, 7, 9, 10, 12,
13, 15, 16, 17, 18, 19, 20, 21, 22, 23, 24, 25, 26,
27, and 28 are reproduced by gracious permission of Her Majesty Queen Elizabeth II.
Plates 8 and 14 are from the private collection of Prince Wolfgang of Hesse and Plate
11 is from the collection of Her Majesty
Queen Victoria Eugenia of Spain.
Plates 1, 3, 4, 5, and 6 are reproduced by
permission of the Radio Times Hulton Picture Library.

SBN: 03-076425-4

PRINTED IN THE UNITED STATES OF AMERICA

CONTENTS

Two sixteen-page inserts of black and white
photographs follow pages 116 and 244.

v

PREFACE

I acknowledge the gracious permission of Her Majesty the Queen, as owner of the copyright, to print the letters of Queen Victoria in this book and also the letters of the Crown Princess of Prussia which are in Her Majesty's possession in the Royal Archives at Windsor. I respectfully thank Prince Philip, Landgrave of Hesse, who owns the letters of Queen Victoria in this book, and his brothers Prince Wolfgang and Prince Richard, for giving me the opportunity to edit the correspondence and for helping me throughout.

Over the problems which necessarily arise in a correspondence of this kind I have depended completely on the friendliness and sagacity of Mr. Robin Mackworth-Young, the Queen's Librarian. Not the least of his many kindnesses lay in arranging for a member of his staff, Miss Julia Gandy, to transcribe Queen Victoria's letters for me in her spare time. Anyone with experience of the Queen's handwriting, which was flowing rather than legible, vehement rather than considered, will realise the extent of my debt to Miss Gandy. In addition to providing me with accurate working-copies of the text she has helped me to disentangle many difficult readings and obscure allusions.

The handwriting of the Crown Princess was remarkably clear, quite unlike that of her mother and somewhat similar to the controlled hand of the Prince Consort. I was therefore able to use photostat copies of her letters and I am particularly grateful to Miss Kay Hallett, who made a first-class job of typing the manuscript from these photographs.

Prince Clary, with kindness and deep knowledge of genealogies, explained to me about the descendants of Graf von Mensdorff-Pouilly who married Queen Victoria's aunt; for some reason this family (though nearly related to our Royal Family) seems to bow themselves out from genealogical trees in English. They are alluded to on page 63.

The identity of the author whose prize poem on the death of the Prince Consort charmed the Queen and her daughter (see page 80) proved a hard problem as he seems to have been only known to the royal correspondents as "the Cambridge undergraduate". His name was revealed to me by the kindness of the sub-librarian of Trinity College, Cambridge, Mr. Halcrow, who tells me that the poem consists of 49 stanzas. The author, Mr. James Rhoades, would not seem to have won distinction in later life but let us hope that he knew of the comfort which his song had brought to Windsor and Berlin.

I was puzzled by the whereabouts of the Prince Consort's favourite Raphael, the Madonna of the Candelabras—a version of which was reputedly in the National Gallery (see page 32). I am ashamed to remember my scornful incredulity when the attendant at the Gallery looked completely blank when I asked him to show me the painting. Mr. Cecil Gould, the Deputy Keeper of the Gallery, has told me that one version of the painting is in the United States and that the other, whose whereabouts are obscure, was, contrary to rumour, never in the Gallery.

For the most part an editor must be left to fight his own battles; he must decide whether, when the Queen says "Augusta", she means the Queen of Prussia, the Grand-Duchess of Mecklenburg-Strelitz or Lady Augusta Stanley; he must search diligently till he finds Tennyson's lines written for the Duchess of Kent's mausoleum; he must unravel the true meaning of the Crown Princess's terrible partiality for nicknames. I have found the answers to these and to almost all points of difficulty in the London Library, and to the Librarian and his staff I offer my warmest thanks for all their help.

I should like to thank the firm of Norma Skemp and in particular Miss Lunniss and Mrs. Lanner for their help with urgent transcriptions and translations from German schrift.

Many of the illustrations for this book are taken from the private collections at Windsor, and I should like to acknowledge the gracious permission of the Queen to use this material.

If I leave to the last Miss Audrey White of Evans it is only to emphasise what the final version of the book has gained from her meticulous reading of the text and from her mastery of the persons and issues brought to life by it. To her and to my publishers I am deeply indebted.

ROGER FULFORD

May 1968

FAMILIAR NAMES USED IN THE CORRESPONDENCE

ABBAT. Prince Albrecht of Prussia, nephew to the King.

ADA. Princess Adelaide of Hohenlohe-Langenburg, married to Prince Frederick of Schleswig-Holstein.

ADDY. Princess Alexandrine of Prussia, niece to the King.

AFFIE. Prince Alfred, later Duke of Edinburgh.

ALEXANDRINE. See ADDY.

ALICE. Princess Alice, the Queen's second daughter, married to Prince Louis of Hesse-Darmstadt.

ALIX. Princess of Wales, formerly Princess Alexandra of Schleswig-Holstein-Sonderburg-Glücksburg.

ARTHUR. Prince Arthur, afterwards Duke of Connaught.

AUNT or AUNT FEODORA. The Queen's half-sister, Princess Feodora of Hohenlohe-Langenburg.

AUNT ALEXANDRINE. The Duchess of Saxe-Coburg—the Queen's sister-in-law.

AUGUSTA or COUSIN AUGUSTA or AUGUSTA STRELITZ. See FRITZ STRELITZ. Sometimes, according to context Augusta is Augusta Bruce afterwards Stanley—the Queen's Woman of the Bedchamber.

AUGUSTUS. Prince Augustus of Saxe-Coburg, first cousin to the Queen and the Prince Consort.

BABY. Princess Beatrice.

THE OLD, GOOD or BELOVED BARON. Christian Frederick Stockmar.

THE YOUNG or MY BARON or BARON E. Ernest Stockmar, son of above.

BERTIE or B. The Prince of Wales.

LADY CAROLINE. Daughter of 2nd Lord Grey and widow

of Captain George Barrington, R.N. Woman of the Bedchamber to the Queen.

PRINCE CHRISTIAN. See following entry.

PRINCESS C. or PRINCESS CHRISTIAN. Wife of Prince Christian of Schleswig-Holstein-Sonderburg-Glücksburg, afterwards King Christian IX of Denmark—the parents of the Princess of Wales.

CHARLOTTE. Daughter of King Leopold of the Belgians and wife of the Archduke Maximilian.

AUNT CLEMENTINE. Daughter of Louis Philippe and wife of Prince Augustus of Saxe-Coburg.

THE COUNTESS, THE DEAR or THE BELOVED COUNTESS. Madeline Dallas, wife of Count Blücher.

DAGMAR. Princess Dagmar, second daughter of Prince and Princess Christian.

DITTA. Princess Charlotte of Prussia, eldest daughter of the Crown Prince.

UNCLE ERNEST or UNCLE E. Ernest II, Duke of Saxe-Coburg. Brother of the Prince Consort.

ERNEST or ERNEST L. The Prince of Leiningen, son of the Queen's half-brother.

AUNT FEODORA. See AUNT.

UNCLE FERDINAND. The King-Consort of Portugal.

FRITZ. The Crown Prince of Prussia.

FRITZ AUGUSTENBURG. Prince Frederick, hereditary Prince of Schleswig-Holstein-Sonderburg-Augustenburg, married to the Queen's niece, Princess Adelaide of Hohenlohe-Langenburg.

FRITZ OF BADEN. The Grand-Duke, married to the Crown Prince's sister.

FRITZ CARL. Prince Frederick Charles of Prussia, first cousin to the Crown Prince.

FRITZ SCHLESWIG-HOLSTEIN. See FRITZ AUGUSTENBURG.

FRITZ or FRITZ STRELITZ or FRITZ AND AUGUSTA. Grand-Duke of Mecklenburg-Strelitz married to Princess Augusta of Cambridge, first cousin to the Queen.

THE GENERAL. General Charles Grey, son of 2nd Lord Grey; private secretary to the Prince Consort and afterwards to the Queen.

UNCLE GEORGE. The 2nd Duke of Cambridge, first cousin
to the Queen.

HEDWIG. Countess Brühl.

HENRY. Prince Henry of Prussia, second son of the Crown
Prince.

KATHERINE. Widow of General Bruce, Governor to the
Prince of Wales, and sister-in-law of Lady Augusta
Stanley.

THE KING. The King of Prussia.

LENCHEN. Princess Helena.

LEOPOLD or LEO. Prince Leopold afterwards Duke of
Albany.

UNCLE LEOPOLD. See UNCLE.

LEOPOLD or LEOPOLD B. King Leopold's elder son—the
Duc de Brabant.

LOUIS. Prince Louis of Hesse-Darmstadt, married to Princess Alice—the Queen's second daughter.

LOUISE. According to context, either the Queen's fourth
daughter or Louise of Baden.

LOUISE OF BADEN. The Grand-Duchess, sister to the Crown
Prince.

MARIANNE. Princess Marie Anne of Anhalt, married to
Prince Frederick Charles of Prussia.

MARIE BRABANT. Archduchess of Austria, married to the
elder son of King Leopold.

MARIE or MARIE L. Sister of the Grand-Duke of Baden and
wife of the Prince of Leiningen.

MARIECHEN. Princess Marie of the Netherlands, niece of
the King of Prussia.

MAROUSSY. Great-niece of the King of Prussia, married to
Prince William of Baden.

MARY. Princess Mary of Cambridge, first cousin to the
Queen.

MAX. Archduke Maximilian of Austria, afterwards Emperor of Mexico.

PHILIP. Count of Flanders, younger son of King Leopold.

THE QUEEN. The Queen of Prussia.

THE QUEEN DOWAGER. Elizabeth, widow of Frederick
William IV of Prussia.

xi

SANNY. Princess Alexandra of Saxe-Altenburg, wife of the Grand-Duke Constantine of Russia.

TIS. Charles, son of the Grand-Duke of Saxe-Weimar.

UNCLE or UNCLE LEOPOLD. Leopold I, King of the Belgians.

VALERIE. Countess Hohenthal.

AUNT VICTOIRE. Daughter of Prince Ferdinand of Saxe-Coburg, married the Duc de Nemours. Died 1857.

WALLY. Walburga, Lady Paget.

WILLIAM. Prince William of Baden.

WILLIE OF HOLSTEIN. Prince William of Schleswig-Holstein-Sonderburg-Glücksburg, brother to the Princess of Wales.

WILLY. Eldest child of the Crown Prince—the future Kaiser.

INTRODUCTION

For forty years Queen Victoria and her eldest daughter, the Princess Royal, afterwards Crown Princess of Prussia and German Empress, maintained a massive correspondence. It began in 1858 when the Princess married, and it ended in 1901—the year in which mother and daughter died. The Princess's letters are in the Royal Archives at Windsor and are kept in sixty bound volumes, each of approximately 400 pages. The Queen's letters, likewise bound and even more voluminous, belong to her great-grandson, Prince Philip of Hesse. They are kept at Friedrichshof, the house near Frankfort which the Princess built to the memory of her husband.

After her husband's death in 1888 the Princess asked the Queen whether she might have extracts made from her letters to provide the material for a biography of her husband. The letters themselves were sent to her, and therefore both sides of the correspondence were at Friedrichshof when she was dying. The letters were sent back to Windsor shortly before her death. After the Princess's death Queen Victoria's letters remained at Friedrichshof until 1945. In that year King George VI asked his librarian, Sir Owen Morshead, to go to Germany and bring back the letters to Windsor for safe custody. They were returned to Friedrichshof in 1952.

But whatever their past history the letters have survived —bringing with them a remarkably detailed picture, drawn from inside, of royal life in Europe with all its gaiety and sorrow, its personal and political problems. During the period covered by this book there was some tampering with letters (even with royal ones) in the continental post-offices. Consequently the Queen frequently used a messenger who, on the return journey from Berlin, would bring a letter from the Crown Princess. Letters going through the post were written with somewhat guarded comments on individuals.

This selection from their correspondence opens at a disastrous time for each writer. The death of the Prince Consort on 14 December 1861 at the age of 42, which was to the Queen at once inexplicable and annihilating, fell on her, her children and the English court with a weight of sorrow which was all-pervading. The black-edged writing-paper on which henceforth she always wrote, the widow's weeds which henceforth she always wore out of doors, and the white cap and veil—'the sad cap' as her youngest child called it—which was part of her dress indoors for the rest of her life were the insignia of grief. Her feelings matched them. Indeed the appurtenances of mourning were, in her case, unnecessary for she felt to the depths of her being what the symbols proclaimed. Queen Victoria—had it been possible—would have wished to remain immovable in the happy, family life which she had known and loved for the twenty years before 1861. Everything was done to preserve the impression of the Prince's presence, to prevent new persons, new surroundings, new problems and even new ideas from varying that world which once the Prince had known and adorned. The fascination of the Queen's letters lies in her realisation (often expressed with much lamentation and tartness of language) that she could not preserve the past inviolate from the pressure of the present. Nobody else except herself could make the final decisions about the marriage of her second daughter, Princess Alice; nobody except she could finally overcome the personal and political obstacles confronting the Prince of Wales's marriage. When she had to receive the King of Prussia, or the Emperor of Austria, while she was staying at Coburg, she had to rely on herself for what she should say. No whisper of guidance could break from the shadows of 1861. In the mounting crisis with Prussia, which began at the end of 1863 and reached its height in the summer of 1864, she may have been influenced by what the Prince Consort thought in 1852 but each new event, each new swirl in that complicated stream of history, carried her further from 1852, further from Prince Albert's world to dangers which called for her own foresight and her exertions alone. We can see how the complexities of Schleswig-Holstein and the Prusso-Danish war pulled her away from her struggle to petrify herself in the past.

On her side the Crown Princess was anguished by her father's death. Gifted with the same kind of intellectual interests which had marked him, she had developed an absorbing admiration for him so that a remarkable understanding was established between father and daughter. When she married at the age of 17 in 1858 she wrote to her father, after they parted on the royal yacht, "You know, dear Papa, how entirely you possess the deep confidence, reverence and affection of your child, who is proud to call herself such." The letters, which follow, show that these were no idle words. The Crown Princess was only 21 when her father died and no one, not even the Queen, would have expected her to live her life in the twilight of old memories and old loyalties. Once or twice the Queen noticed that her daughter seemed to forget the Prince and she remarked on her daughter's wonderful high spirits. Wonderful, in the Queen's vocabulary, was not a word of praise.

The Queen is of course the more accomplished and the more graphic of the two letter-writers. A somewhat irreverent Victorian, Wilfrid Blunt, once wrote: "The old Queen has the power of conveying her meaning in a few simple, not to say common-place words so as to give the impression of true feeling—more than most women." Almost every letter confirms the truth of that remark. The Crown Princess, who read and thought more widely and deeply than her mother, was much concerned with intellectual and political movements and perhaps less capable than her mother of giving a vivid picture of persons and events surrounding her. But her letters, moving more slowly than those of the Queen, set off and enhance the vigour of the Queen's mind.

When the Princess married in 1858, her husband, Prince Frederick William of Prussia, was 26—nearly ten years older than she was. He was nephew to the King of Prussia, Frederick William IV, who was childless and afflicted by a disorder of the brain. The Prince's father, Prince William, was recognised as heir to his brother and dignified with the title—The Prince of Prussia. At the beginning of 1861 King Frederick William died, the Prince of Prussia became King William I and Prince Frederick William became Crown Prince. The world into which the Crown Princess moved on her marriage was a curious one. Her husband's family was large and his uncles and aunts and cousins seem to have moved in a stately phalanx, the ladies a little faded and talkative, the gentlemen with the stiff back and courteous bearing of a military family. The winter was spent in their palaces at Berlin, the summer in their country houses at Potsdam. Conventional behaviour counted greatly with them all. No Prussian sovereign or his heir had ever before married outside Germany, and the Royal Family, confident of their own superiority, courageous and worldly, looked at the English Princess with curiosity tinged with apprehension. So much is clear from her comments on them to the Queen in this correspondence.

There is a further important point. All the reigning Princes of Germany, including of course Prussia, had been greatly alarmed by the events of 1848. In step with the great revolutionary outbreak in France, the German populace had demonstrated, had clamoured for reform and secured concessions from their rulers. The King of Bavaria was forced to abdicate and all the states of Germany had to make gestures towards constitutional government. King Frederick William IV had the humiliation of walking through the streets of Berlin under a great red, black and gold flag—the symbol of nationalism. The Prince of Prussia had to fly to England and it was suggested that his son, Prince Frederick William, should become King under a regency. To the Prussian Royal Family those had been terrible days: after 1848 the conservatism of the Hohenzollerns which had been a preference became a stubborn conviction.

At the same time a handful of German thinkers was contemplating the unity of their nation within a framework of liberalism and constitutionalism. Prominent in all these idealistic schemes was the Prince Consort: much of his correspondence with his brother, the reigning Duke of Saxe-Coburg-Gotha and with his confidential adviser, Baron Stockmar,[1] is concerned with them. In correspondence with King Frederick William IV, who was much alarmed by the march of radicalism, he wrote "The only way to deal with this onrush, threatening destruction, is to bind that part of the people which has means and intelligence (i.e. the real people) to the Government by trustfully admitting it to participation in the administration of its own life."[2] He believed neither in the closed minds of the church nor in the privileged outlook of an aristocracy: as he says, he believed that a Government should disentangle itself from such influences and rely instead on an educated democracy. In almost the last letter which she wrote to her father (16 November 1861) the Crown Princess warned him that her father-in-law, the King of Prussia, was incapable of taking in the principles of constitutional government. She went on "My daily prayer and my first wish, the labour of my life, is that Fritz should make those principles his own, which are the only ones which can alone be the saving—not only of Prussia's position in Europe and in Germany—but of the Prussian monarchy."[3] Such views were not acceptable to

---

[1] Christian Frederick Stockmar, born at Coburg in 1787, was trained as a doctor and in that capacity served King Leopold of the Belgians. He subsequently became confidential and political adviser to the Coburg family including Queen Victoria and the Prince Consort. Though subject to the curiosity and criticism which attach themselves to all who exercise power from behind the scenes, Stockmar was not only an adviser of penetration and capacity but was disinterested and completely loyal. He was liberal in his political opinions and worked for the unity of Germany based on the confederation of states. His son Ernest (1823–86), who shared his father's views but was perhaps less effective than he in spreading them, was the Crown Princess's secretary and general adviser to her and her husband.

[2] Frank Eyck, *The Prince Consort*, Chatto and Windus, 1959.

[3] Royal Archives.

the Hohenzollerns. They looked rather to the autocratic principles of the Russian dynasty to whom they were closely allied by marriage. Before her marriage, the Crown Princess had spent many evenings alone with her father when he expounded to her these and kindred views. They were inherited from him and inculcated by him: in her new surroundings she preached them and developed them, with the fervour of a disciple. Unhappily Germany (and especially Prussia) moved rapidly away from such thoughtful ideals: rather the aim of a united Germany was to be achieved not by constitutions but by conquest. As this correspondence develops it becomes clear that the Danish duchies of Schleswig and Holstein were far more tempting to the Prussian mind than fancies about a constitution. There lay the misfortune for the Crown Princess: there lay the cause of her unpopularity with her husband's family: in a world of blood and iron she stood for liberalism and moderation.

But in her desolation she had the satisfaction of having made one whole-hearted convert—her husband the Crown Prince. He figures in this correspondence—as we may be sure he did to contemporaries in life—a gentle, charming character fond of his family but easily swayed by them. Primed by the Crown Princess about his words and actions he was yet inclined to forget his promptings when confronted by his father the King. These family and political complications were all magnified by the quarrels and growlings of the Crown Prince's parents—the King and Queen. Certainly not an easy character and perhaps not an agreeable one, the Queen was a political ally of the Crown Princess—but it was an alliance weakened by an absence of understanding and of any deep, mutual affection. But if we are inclined to view the Queen of Prussia through the eyes of her daughter-in-law, the Queen of England in her letters corrects the impression. Walburga Lady Paget, whose comments on people are often quoted in some of the notes to this correspondence, said of Queen Augusta: "I suppose that no woman had a sadder youth and middle age than hers." The King, who as a youth had fallen in love with Princess Elisa Radziwill whose rank was insufficient to permit of marriage, had been forced to marry the Queen—then a princess of Saxe-Weimar. Their life together was miserable.

After four years of marriage, when this book begins, the Crown Princess was therefore encompassed by great sorrows and difficulties. She was bowed down by her father's death and by the knowledge of her mother's abandoned grief: she was made unhappy by the persisting squabbles in her husband's family and she was genuinely alarmed by the drift to reaction in Prussian politics, with which the King was allowing himself to move. Only in her husband and children did she find happiness and consolation. Often held up to us as a severe and Roman matron, she emerges from this correspondence as a sensitive and warmhearted mother. Her two children are Willy (the future Kaiser) and "Ditta" (Princess Charlotte): Henry was born in the period covered by this book. Some of the most revealing letters—revealing both her tenacity and tenderness—are those which she writes to her mother describing her battles with the doctors over the various experiments attempted to correct the deformities of the future Kaiser. But the sorrows and anxieties of her life have to be set against the background of a domestic life of unruffled happiness. From the battlefield in Schleswig the Crown Prince wrote to her: "In spite of all the serious and shattering experiences we have had in our young married life, never has even a little cloud disturbed our own family happiness."[1]

The letters between the Queen and the Crown Princess for the first year of this selection are dominated by the majesty of death. The letters between mother and daughter give the reader the opportunity to see in detail how the Victorians faced bereavement, how they were absorbed by their indulgence in grief which seemed to them to soothe it, and how they showed their confidence—sometimes hesitant but never far below the surface—that there was for them a certain if incomprehensible prospect of reunion with the dead—with "adored, angel Papa"—to quote the Queen. Each may have felt that "wind-dispersed and vain" their

---

[1] Count Corti, *The English Empress*, page 123, Cassell, 1957.

words of sorrow may have been but that by giving "their grief its hour" they were keeping the memory of the Prince alive and, by keeping their minds fixed on him and free from the encroachments of the world, they were preparing themselves for a speedy reunion with him on whom their hearts were fixed.

Here, in an aside, one point may be emphasised. The reason why the Queen preserved the Prince's rooms exactly as when he left them, with fires burning and all the appurtenances of existence continuing, was not, as is sometimes stupidly said, because she expected that he would step back to life, but because all these outward symbols kept her association with him alive. This was also the reason, as Lord Clarendon noticed, why she was ever anxious to be in Osborne or Balmoral. There was nothing in either house which the Prince and she had not collected or arranged together. She felt with her innermost being that the way to a speedy reunion after her death lay in keeping fragrant, not only his memory, but the whole of their associated life together.

To us, reading what mother and daughter wrote after the passage of a century, such analysis of sorrow, such probing of the future, such confidence in what it was to bring may seem not only incomprehensible but almost irritating. This reaction is perfectly understandable. But if we wish to understand Victorian England, if we wish to understand (so far as we can) the inner feelings of people who lived then and if we wish to calculate those explanations of behaviour which lie below the surface, we should be wholly wrong to try to conceal the outpourings of the Queen—or to dismiss them as merely morbid indulgences because they happen to be different from the turn of mind of the mid-twentieth century—because her revelation of herself strikes no chord in the iron heart of the 1960's.

There are therefore certain things which need to be said in explanation or, if the reader so wishes it, in defence of the tone of the Queen's letters—a tone most marked in the beginning of the correspondence but prevailing thereafter throughout it. The first and perhaps the most important is to dispel the false impression that the Queen set the fashion for extravagant grief or for everlasting mourning or for a climax of sorrow as the years brought round each melancholy anniversary. Naturally there were widows in Victorian England such as Lady Eustace in Trollope's *The Eustace Diamonds* who found in the death of their husbands a release, and looked forward less to reunion with the departed than to a new and happier marriage. "In two years from Sir Florian's death she will be married again," said Lady Eustace's mother. There were of course also countless widows in nineteenth-century England, immortalised in no diaries or chronicles, who were left to battle for mere existence and lacked the leisure essential for the display of grief. But though there are exceptions, it is broadly true that the widow in Victorian England, enjoying affluence or comfortable circumstances, faced her tribulation in somewhat the same way as the Queen did. At most the Queen was emphasising a fashion—not setting it. The following trifling episode shows how the nineteenth century relished a becoming show of feeling and would have been horrified had it been lacking. In a letter written before the death of the Prince Consort, an allusion was made by the Queen to the sentiments of Lady Waterford whose husband was killed in the hunting field. A rough, Northern Irish baronet, Sir John Leslie, who attended the funeral, wrote of the widow—"the grief that was written in her face I shall never forget: and I like to remember it, for I have seen nothing to equal it". Nor will the reader suppose that there was anything idiosyncratic about the Queen's preoccupation with pictures, relics and statuary of her dead husband. Here is Lady Charlotte Guest, a little older than the Queen, not especially happy in marriage and a woman of remarkable gifts and capacity, describing her first visit to her country house after her husband's death: "I went straight to the Library, where luckily there was a light. A slight veil had been thrown over his bust, which at once I removed and then I flung my arms around it, and remained clasping it for some minutes, kissing the cold lips—not colder than his own when I kissed them last—and shedding torrents of passionate tears. And this cold marble is now all that is left to me." Nor would it be right to imagine that feelings such as these left the intellectual Victorians unscathed—even the most eminent of them. Leslie Stephen, the rock on which the fraternity of Bloomsbury was built, was almost morbidly sentimental over bereavement so that his distinguished biographer (Lord Annan) excuses such displays of feeling by his "fear of the future, desire to remain in the past, to remember what had been happiness because he could never know happiness again: and this was inflicted upon his wife and children". At least in this particular he did not differ from Queen Victoria.

Are we then to believe that the Victorians felt more deeply or—to use the words of the most perceptive authority on the age, G. M. Young—were more easily touched than are we their descendants? Such questions are perhaps impossible to answer. Certainly no answer will be forthcoming from those who merely close their eyes to manifestations of feeling which may seem almost laughable in the 1960's but were searingly felt in 1860.

Nor will the reader for one moment suppose that there was anything out of the ordinary, here or abroad, in the Queen's preoccupation with the royal mausoleum and its ornamentation. Reasonable objection could be made that the Queen instead of glorifying the royal vaults, where lay some of the great names in English royal history, chose, as Lord Clarendon tartly remarked, "to set up insignificant tombs in that morass at Frogmore which is constantly flooded". But that is a different point. Her absorption in an appropriate refuge for the remains of the Prince Consort differed only in degree from the absorption with the same problem shared by many of her subjects. Anyone doubting this has only to wander through the 218 acres of the cemetery at Kensal Green to realise the concern of Victorian England with weighty habitations for the eminent dead; some of those in Kensal Green are complete with double doors and knockers as though many of the occupiers lay expecting individual attention when the last trump was blown.

In justice to Queen Victoria one further point, and its particular impact on her, needs to be stated and remembered. Victorian widowhood, with its lugubrious trappings, is explained not only by sentimental indulgence: the real explanation for it lies deeper. In that masculine world the great majority of women depended on their husbands as an automaton on its clockwork. Bereft and broken by the deaths of their husbands, they were pitiful spectacles left to tread the measure of existence guided only by recollections of what once had been. This is the point made by the Queen in the first letter which follows—"How I, who leant on him for all and everything—without whom I did nothing, moved not a finger, arranged not a print or photograph, didn't put on a gown or bonnet if he didn't approve it, shall be able to go on, to live, to move, to help myself in difficult moments . . .!" Such was surely the heartbroken cry of many a Victorian widow, but the Queen's position was made infinitely more melancholy by the intrusion of public business. Lord Clarendon, who perhaps understood her better than any of her ministers, observed that "the mass of business which she can not escape" compels her to think of something other than her sorrow. That is perfectly true. Many people would have found consolation and stimulus in the burden of work. But to the Queen the business of sovereignty—the study of papers and policies—did not come readily: we know that in the earliest days she was completely guided by Melbourne in all these matters and thereafter by the Prince. She told Lord Clarendon "the Prince used to read and arrange everything for her, to save her all trouble, to bring her things she merely had to sign, and explain them to her and tell her what to do about them and that now she had to do all this herself". She then added the ominous words "her mind was strained to the uttermost . . . she was afraid of going mad".[1] Although such fears may have been ill-founded they were felt.

---

[1] George Villiers, *A Vanished Victorian*, Eyre and Spottiswoode, 1938.

A final point remains. Reading the Queen's letters in the shadow of sorrow we might suppose that the same lamentations made themselves felt when she was compelled to see her ministers, members of the court or other personages. This was not the case. Gladstone had his first interview with her three months after the Prince's death. For a quarter of an hour they discussed affairs: then putting her head down the Queen said "the nation has been very good to me in my time of sorrow". At much the same time Lord Clarendon watched the Queen laying the foundation-stone of the mausoleum—"laying the mortar and knocking the stone three times with the mallet . . . with wonderful calmness, not shedding a tear". The Bishop of Oxford, who saw her at the time of the first anniversary of the Prince's death, noticed—and was struck by—her resignation and calm. These impressions were however never made without a struggle on the Queen's part, and she would have thought it disloyal to the memory of the Prince if her family had not been made to realise what these things cost her. Some may feel that she ought not to have poured out these innermost feelings of anguish to her daughter who from nearly a thousand miles away could do little to assuage them. But her particular turn of mind and character made these outpourings inevitable. Only a few weeks before he died the Prince told her: "My advice to be less occupied with yourself and your own feelings is really the kindest I can give." She bravely struggled to carry out that advice when he was no more. But nature triumphed over intention. Yet in a sense it was a measure of the confidence between mother and daughter that she could write as she did. Nor will the reader overlook the remarkable character of the youthful recipient of these confidences. Faced with the problems of her own small family, with the brusque and difficult personalities of her husband's family and with mounting problems in the Government of Prussia she never fails in patience, sympathy and devotion towards her remarkable mother. Almost every letter ends with or contains the words "kissing your dear hands"—an allusion to the mark of respect paid by members of the Royal Family to its head. Occasionally the mother is severe but the daughter never answers with acrimony: her letters flow on loving and unruffled.

During 1862 there are a few allusions to political difficulties in Prussia: these become more frequent in 1863 and dominate the letters in 1864. The reader may be helped by a broad outline of the developments in Prussia and of the Schleswig-Holstein problem which brought with it the prospect—highly alarming to both correspondents—of war between England and Prussia.

King William of Prussia, whose political interests were predominantly military, was a natural conservative. In his case this was modified by a realisation that change was inherent to the nineteenth century and—unlike most men of moderate abilities—he was content to be guided by men whose capacity he rated higher than his own. He had become regent in 1858 and almost his first act was to install a government, with strong, liberal elements, under the Prince of Hohenzollern-Sigmaringen who comes frequently into the correspondence. In 1861 the King, as he had now become, drifted apart from his Government, following disputes over the recruitment for the army, and he increased the conservative elements in the Government—Prince Hohenzollern was superseded by Prince Hohenlohe. When the correspondence opens there was a general election, as a result of which the Prussian parliament or Landtag swung decisively to the left. Another general election was held a few months later in which the swing to the left was more pronounced. By September 1862 the deadlock between Government and Landtag was complete. By the end of that month Bismarck had become Minister-President at the head of a conservative Government. The disputes between Government and Landtag grew sharper and at the end of the Government's first year a further general election was held: in spite of severe pressure from Bismarck and the Government the electors continued to show preference for the liberals. But the truth was that the liberals were fired by two contradictory motives—they wished to curb Bismarck but at the same time they supported the main element in his policy—Prussian self-assertion. This contradiction is apparent in much of the Crown Princess's correspondence in 1864.[1] Although the Prussian Royal Family was overwhelmingly conservative it is curious that the three most powerful members after the King—the Crown Prince, the Crown Princess and the Queen—were all three strongly opposed to Bismarck and the King's conservative leanings. This is of course the principal explanation for the difficulties between the King and Queen which made things disagreeable for her and the Crown Princess within the family circle. Queen Augusta, as Queen Victoria consistently maintained, was endowed with gifts of intellect and a sympathy with progressive causes which distinguished her from the family into which she had married. A princess of Saxe-Weimar, she brought an aroma of liberalism from her native land, and she was fortified by a faith in constitutional rule long exemplified in that thoughtful duchy.

Although in the events that were to happen Prussia was to seize the headship of the German nation, many of the influential people in the smaller states believed in the emergence of a German nation through the Confederation of nearly forty German states formed after the defeat of Napoleon. This met in the Diet at Frankfort but had no power though a little influence. At best it was a league of independent countries—never the United States of Germany. The deficiencies are revealed in the letters of the summer of 1863, and they were illustrated forcefully in the issue of Schleswig-Holstein which dominates the correspondence from the autumn of 1863 until the end of this selection. The Schleswig-Holstein question was, in its essentials, not especially complex or difficult except to those who wish to avoid unravelling them. No doubt those who try to disentangle exactly where the sovereignty of the duchies lay and have to bemuse their minds with the companionship of agnates and the lex regia of Denmark may find themselves in a morass, but on this point it is sufficient to say that

---

[1] For a fuller account of this see Agatha Ramm, *Germany 1789–1919: A Political History*, Methuen, 1967.

a member of the royal house of Schleswig-Holstein-Sonder-burg-Glücksburg was recognised as heir to the throne of Denmark although the family of Schleswig-Holstein-Sonderburg-Augustenburg made a strong *de jure* claim. Holstein was in population largely German; Schleswig was not. There Germans and Danes were mixed.

In a shrewd and highly entertaining analysis[1] of the question the future Prime Minister (Lord Salisbury) had this to say on this problem of the mixed population in Schleswig. In the northern part of the duchy 119 parishes were wholly Danish: in the southern part there were 110 parishes assumed to be wholly German. There were 49 remaining parishes in which the population was mixed: in these parishes both languages were taught in the schools. The author adds that as the peasants spoke a kind of patois composed of bad dialects of both languages they had "no room for indulging any sentiment about their native tongue". Both duchies were part of the Danish kingdom: both were united to one another: Holstein was a member of the Germanic Confederation; Schleswig was not. Then in the widespread disorder in Germany in 1848 the two duchies established a provisional Government of their own and appealed to the Diet. The Danes announced the annexation of Schleswig, and the Diet replied by recognising the provisional Government and admitting Schleswig to the Germanic Confederation. After some years of desultory fighting and confusion, Great Britain, Sweden and Russia effected a compromise. By the Treaty of London of 1852 they recognised the territorial integrity of the Danish kingdom, including the Duchies. For the following years there was much simmering of the question with the German minority in Schleswig loudly proclaiming their grievances. In November 1863 King Christian IX, father of the Princess of Wales, came to the throne of Denmark and published a fresh constitution. The Augustenburg prince immediately organised a provisional Government for the Duchies. He was not recognised by either Austria or Prussia. In defiance of the

---

[1] Essay by the late Marquess of Salisbury, *The Danish Duchies.*

Germanic Confederation—to which of course both countries belonged—Austria and Prussia declared war on Denmark. The course of events and the war becomes clear from the correspondence.

Not the least of the Queen's trials was that the Schleswig-Holstein problem made its difficult presence felt in the family circle. The Prince and Princess of Wales were reasonably and naturally rabid in their support for Denmark. The Crown Prince and Princess were staying at Windsor when the crisis broke—with the death of King Frederick VII of Denmark. The Queen reported to her Uncle Leopold that "Fritz is very violent" but "that Vicky is sensible". The matter was additionally complicated because the Queen's niece had married the Augustenburg claimant. The niece's mother, Princess Feodora, was also in the family party at Windsor and was described by the Queen as "very anxious and at times violent, but much distressed for me". She went on "no respect is paid to my opinion now and it makes visits like Fritz and Vicky's very painful and trying". Replying, her wise uncle told her "The North Germans are quite mad on this unfortunate question. You must forbid it in your rooms."

There is however one point which, for those concerned with the personality of Queen Victoria, is here of importance. The Prince Consort—whose ideas on the development of Germany broadly corresponded with those of his brother, Queen Augusta, and Stockmar—strongly disapproved the modus vivendi achieved by the Powers in the 1850's. In a letter to Stockmar he had stated fairly the English point of view—namely that Germany wished to separate Holstein and Schleswig from Denmark so as to draw them from the English into the Prussian commercial system. He admitted that the British resentment at this was a perfectly tenable view but went on "assuredly this affords no ground for doing violence to law, to honour, to equity and to morality, in order to defeat an eventuality which has not been brought about by ambition or caprice, but by the nature of things. Schleswig is entitled to insist on union with Holstein; Holstein belongs to Germany, and the Augustenburgs are the heirs. How is it possible to get over these things?"[1] He even went so far as to argue that Lord Palmerston, who was Foreign Secretary at the time, had sacrificed "the rights of the poor people of Schleswig and Holstein in order to re-purchase the good-will of France and Russia".[2]

During the development of the Prussian–Danish crisis of 1863 and 1864, the Queen turned up the Prince's papers of the 1850's, regarded them in her own words as "gospel now", and guided herself by them. The two dreadful old men—as she called the Prime Minister (Palmerston) and the Foreign Secretary (Russell)—were lukewarm partisans of Denmark while the Conservative party and public opinion generally became increasingly and vociferously Danish. In his book on the *Political Influence of Queen Victoria*, Mr. Frank Hardie states—and he is surely right—that the Queen's opinions and the pressure she was able to exert were important factors (though whether they were decisive factors is difficult to say for certain) in the pacific policy pursued by England. But whether the Queen's intervention was decisive or not, this crisis is of cardinal importance to an understanding of her personality. By acting as she did she felt that she had carried out the wishes of the Prince; she derived confidence in her own powers; and it marked the beginning of the end of her complete seclusion, of the complete indulgence of grief, and of her attempt to live her life "dreaming through the twilight".

Note on the method of editing

I should like to explain to the reader the method of editing which I have followed. This selection of the correspondence covers only two and half years, but they are important years in the history of the family and of the two countries, for they mark the slow—the pitiably slow—emergence of

---

[1] Martin, *Life of the Prince Consort*, Vol. II, page 315.
[2] Frank Eyck, *The Prince Consort*, page 145.

the Queen from the shadows of sorrow and the alarmingly rapid development of Prussia, bringing in its train the beginning of the rivalry between England and Germany which was to last for eighty years. But even in this short period a great weight of material has had to be dropped, in order to fit the selection into one reasonable-sized volume, and I have left out what struck me as the less interesting parts of the correspondence though recognising that this was an individual preference with which others might disagree. Broadly speaking I was governed by a wish that my selection should reflect—though in miniature but in proportion —the topics which dominated the complete correspondence. I have left out whole letters, several paragraphs of a letter and constantly one or two sentences. The reader will appreciate that in a correspondence on this scale there is inevitably much repetition, and that often explains the smaller cuts of a few sentences as distinguished from the larger excisions. Where cuts in any text are made on a limited scale it is reasonable to indicate where they have been made, but it seemed to me that where, as in this case, there are as many cuts as text there was no advantage to the reader in indicating where they were made. Readers, I felt, would be confused by the persistent breaking up of the page.

With regard to punctuation I have not followed the text: both the Queen and her daughter had a great partiality for the dash and a certain unconventionality in their use of all forms of stop. Though claiming no superiority I have, where changing punctuation, been guided by the convenience of the reader. Similarly I have expanded all abbreviations—& to and, wd. to would, shd. to should, Pce to Prince and so on. Since neither correspondent always used these abbreviations it seemed that uniformity was best. Both correspondents occasionally wrote words or short phrases in German schrift: I have translated them but not indicated where they were used, as they seem to have been used for convenience and not for significance. The Queen throughout and the Crown Princess very much less frequently underlined passages and were partial to exclamation marks. The latter I have left: the former I have deleted. Occasionally the Queen underlines a sentence to draw attention to a concealed meaning: where this is used I have tried to explain the point in a footnote. While there is certainly room for two opinions on the reproduction of the nineteenth-century habit of underlining, there was nothing singular or peculiar to the Queen about it. She probably caught the habit from her uncle, the King of the Belgians, who was greatly addicted to it. But on a printed page the constant sprinkling of italics or of capitals (to indicate double underlinings) could become an irritant to the reader—especially as in the Queen's usage it indicates vehemence rather than emphasis.

I have always felt that in all these matters the editor has a duty to explain to the reader the methods by which he has been guided; once explained the methods should not be varied. Some two years ago *The Times Literary Supplement* (27 October 1966) pointed out the unsuitability of treating family-letters with the full paraphernalia of scholarship— the brackets, the square brackets, the braces, the writer's slips corrected by *sic*, the scratched-out word reproduced with the scratch and so forth. The writer of that article explained that the visual effect in print of such elaboration is to distract appreciation from the flow of sense.

A more difficult problem lay in the number of members of royal families who figure largely in the letters. An instance from the article already quoted shows how easy it is to be over-meticulous in the problems of identification which must face any editor. "Dear Aunt M.[1] Papa[2] has bought two shawls for Maria[3] and Christina.[4]" In order to overcome a similar proliferation of footnotes I have included a list of familiar names used by the Queen and her daughter. For example Abbat is Prince Albrecht. A very brief description of Prince Albrecht will then be found in the index before the page references to him. Here and there a footnote may be necessary to explain the allusion to an individual in the particular context. For example a footnote explains that the Queen's vexation that Lady Augusta Bruce had married was the reason why she writes "Dear Augusta (Stanley—I can't bear to call her so) . . ." 13 January 1864.

A part of five letters from the Princess—those for 8 June

1863, 21 June 1863, 13 April 1864, 11 May 1864 and 26 May 1864—are published in *Queen Victoria's Letters* (Second Series, Vol. 1, 1926) and also a part of three of the Queen's letters—those for 27 January 1864, 31 May 1864 and 6 July 1864. The originals of the correspondence between the Princess and her mother were not available to the editors of the Queen's letters and these particular letters were clearly made from copies. A few sentences from the correspondence will be found in *The English Empress* by Count Corti which was published by Cassell and Company in 1957. Parts of the letters mentioned above, together with those of the Princess of 5 January 1864 and 8 February 1864 are published in Sir Frederick Ponsonby's book *Letters of the Empress Frederick*, published by Macmillan's in 1928. Fragments from the correspondence will also be found in the important royal biographies of Queen Victoria by Lady Longford, of King Edward VII by Sir Philip Magnus and of Queen Mary by Mr. Pope-Hennessy. With these exceptions the correspondence has been unpublished.

THE CORRESPONDENCE

1861

From the Queen

Bless you for your beautiful letter of Sunday received yesterday! Oh! my poor child, indeed "Why may the earth not swallow us up?" Why not? How am I alive after witnessing what I have done? Oh! I who prayed daily that we might die together and I never survive him! I who felt, when in those blessed arms clasped and held tight in the sacred hours at night, when the world seemed only to be ourselves, that nothing could part us. I felt so very secure. I always repeated: "And God will protect us!" though trembling always for his safety when he was a moment out of my sight. I never dreamt of the physical possibility of such a calamity— such an awful catastrophe for me—for all. What is to become of us all? Of the unhappy country, of Europe, of all? For you all, the loss of such a father is totally irreparable! I will do all I can to follow out all his wishes—to live for you all and for my duties. But how I, who leant on him for all and every-thing—without whom I did nothing, moved not a finger, arranged not a print or photograph, didn't put on a gown or bonnet if he didn't approve it shall be able to go on, to live, to move, to help myself in difficult moments? How I shall long to ask his advice! Oh! it is too, too weary! The day—the night (above all the night) is too sad and weary. The days never pass! I try to feel and think that I am living on with him, and that his pure and perfect spirit is guiding and leading me and inspiring me! But my own dear child, so worthy of him, so like him in mind, my life as I con-sidered it is gone, past, closed! Pleasure, joy—all is for ever gone. Think of Osborne, of the Highlands, of—oh! of Christ-mas—the 10th of February—all, all belong to a precious past which will for ever and ever be engraven on my dreary heart![1] But you, his children, his flesh and blood can cheer

---

[1] 10th February was the wedding-day of the Prince and Queen. Writing in her journal on the anniversary of the Prince's birthday in August

your wretched mother's crushed and bruised heart with your tender love and in trying to be like him! One alone (who does his best and feels his loss most deeply) is utterly unlike him and this is a cross.[1] Alice has behaved and is behaving in a manner which commands the respect and admiration of all, while she is a real support to me. She is quite my right hand. All the others are most tender—Arthur (who is so like dearest Papa) touchingly so. Sweet little Beatrice comes to lie in my bed every morning which is a comfort. I long so to cling to and clasp a loving being. Oh! how I admired Papa! How in love I was with him! How everything about him was beautiful and precious in my eyes! Oh! how, how I miss all, all! Oh! Oh! the bitterness of this—of this woe! I saw him twice on Sunday—beautiful as marble—and the features so perfect, though grown very thin. He was surrounded with flowers. I did not go again. I felt I would rather (as I know he wished) keep the impression given of life and health than have this one sad though lovely image imprinted too strongly in my mind! I do hope you will come in two or three weeks; it will be such a blessing then.[2] I shall need your taste to help me in carrying out works to his memory which I shall want his aid to render at all worthy of him! You know his taste. You have inherited it. I chose this morning a spot in Frogmore Gardens for a mausoleum for us.

Now God bless and protect you. Kindest remembrance and thanks to the King and Queen. How the Queen admired my own darling!

From the Crown Princess

BERLIN, DECEMBER 21, 1861

Today is a whole week since we began our new life of sorrow and desolation! And when I look back upon it—dark,

---

1900 the Queen rather curiously repeats these words "all, all is engraven on my mind and in my heart". *Letters of Queen Victoria*, Third series.
[1] The Prince of Wales.
[2] The Crown Princess, being pregnant, was forbidden to come for a time.

frightful and cruel—yet I have reason to be thankful. Papa's memory, Papa's love shines like a bright star in our darkness and God's almighty hand has poured his heavenly peace into our crushed souls and broken hearts! None of us thought we could have survived this and yet we live, we love, we trust—and we hope still! Your two letters are jewels and treasures to me. I am sure I did not thank you enough for them.

Papa read to me from the "Idylls of a King"[1] at Osborne and wished me to draw something for him, and it has been my occupation for weeks—thinking of him, whether the drawings would please him, whether he would think them right. Do you wish to have them—shall I send or bring them? They are the last I shall ever take pleasure in doing; as he ordered them I consider they belong to you!

I am so glad you have chosen a spot in Frogmore Gardens—how happy I shall be to think you mean to make use of me in any way for helping you. I knew Papa's taste so well. As he was the most perfect model of all that was pure, good, virtuous and great—so was his judgement in all things concerning art—unerring.

This letter will be put into your hands on a dreadful day.[2] Oh how I tremble for you! How I pray that God may support you through it as he has done through the rest! How I shall bear it I do not know. I will think of you and of what Papa said to me when I spoke to him of death, and of the form left to us when the soul had fled; he said: "this is not the human being". It is so true—it says all—and it is so difficult to remember and yet it is our only real comfort!

---

[1] The Crown Prince and Princess, with their children, had stayed at Osborne for several weeks in the summer of 1861. *The Idylls of the King* were first published in the autumn of 1859. The second edition was published early in 1862 with a prefatory dedication ("These to his memory—since he held them dear") to the Prince Consort. The Crown Princess wrote to Tennyson in February 1862 saying that her father had read to her the last two or three pages of *Guinivere*. She added "I can not separate the idea of King Arthur from the image of him whom I most revered on earth." *Alfred Lord Tennyson, A Memoir*, 1897, Vol. I, page 481.
[2] By the Crown Prince on the day of the funeral—Monday, 23 December 1861.

How I long to be with you, to be near you, to speak to you and see you. I hope it will not be long before they let me come. My darling is with you—I like to think it; only I dread Monday—a heart like his that feels so deeply and warmly, and nerves that are not strong, always make me dread strong emotion for him, and he says this has been the first grief in his life.

I hope my letters do not harrow your feelings; tell me if they do, dearest Mama, and I will try and write only what you wish.

I like to think Papa loved my children and saw them and carried them. Poor little things they do not know what they have lost. I always thought that if I died Papa would help Fritz to educate them, and I looked to Papa's advice for educating William which is such a difficult task and so important. His spirit will guide me now in that task I feel sure. Poor poor Bertie, how my heart warms in pity and affection towards him!

I will not say more for fear of tiring you. Dear, dear Mama, goodbye—and oh may God's everlasting blessing rest on your beloved and precious head.

From the Queen

OSBORNE, DECEMBER 23, 1861

It is one o'clock and all, all is over! But I don't feel that worse than what I have lived through! Your letters are very dear—most beautiful—like beloved Papa! They fill me with the same feeling—which fills you! They give me often power to feel I can follow in his footsteps—but oh! only to have feelings of utter broken-heartedness, utter despair at the life I am to lead—but I trust not for very long! Fritz— dear, kind, excellent Fritz—to whom I talked very fully, very openly, can tell you all, and all about adored Papa's dreadful illness! It was to be, else he ought to have got through it so well. He can and will tell you how peculiarly sad and dreadful some of the circumstances are![1]

I trust that in three or four weeks, or perhaps five or six

[1] The Queen went to Osborne on 19 December and here the Crown

you will be able to come quietly and stay with me, for you can understand all I feel, all I suffer, and all he was, better than any one on earth. You have his mind, and therefore I long so to have you, by and by, with me to help me in all my great plans for a mausoleum (which I have chosen the place for at Frogmore) for statues, monuments, etc. Mr. Gruner[1] is sent for to help and advise; Winterhalter[2] is here; Marochetti[3] has been here and is to do a sleeping statue. There is a group of us together and also one in Highland dress for Balmoral! And then I shall dedicate the room to him not as a Sterbe-Zimmer [death chamber]—but as a living beautiful monument. In all this I want your help, your advice, your taste. The Badge or Order you wear, I think of founding as an Order, in double remembrance, for our descendants.[4] All this is now a great, I might say my only interest. Think of Christmas Eve and all!!! It shall never be spent at Windsor again—for he left us in those rooms!

God bless and preserve you!

Uncle Ernest is wretched—but very trying, and I must watch over his children's interests.[5] Dear Fritz brings you precious hair and relics.

Prince joined her, writing to his wife of the Queen's "greatness of soul", *The English Empress* by Count Corti, 1957, page 76.

The "circumstances" were the behaviour of the Prince of Wales, whose escapade with a woman greatly distressed the Prince, and was thought by the Queen to have magnified his illness.

[1] Ludwig Gruner, the designer of the frescoes in the garden-pavilion in Buckingham Palace. This became spoiled, and was demolished in 1928. See *Consort of Taste* by John Steegman, Sidgwick and Jackson, 1950.

[2] Franz Winterhalter (1805–73), court painter.

[3] Carlo Marochetti (1805–67). Perhaps best known for his statue of Richard Cœur de Lion at Westminster. He did recumbent statues of the Prince and the Queen at this time for the tomb in the mausoleum.

[4] This is the Royal Order of Victoria and Albert founded on 10 February 1862—the anniversary of the Queen's marriage. This was a private order for members of the family. In the decoration worn by the Queen, the cameo was cut with the Prince's head in front of the Queen's head. See G. P. L. James, *Royal Family Orders*, Spring Grange, 1951.

[5] i.e. the Prince Consort's children. Uncle Ernest was the Prince's elder brother and Duke of Saxe-Coburg-Gotha. The Queen is referring to the succession to the Duchy of Saxe-Coburg-Gotha to which the Prince had been heir presumptive, his brother having no children.

From the Crown Princess

This day has so completely annihilated me—I feel so crushed, so bowed down by the weight of sorrow which seemed to me more awful even than before.

Prayers and tears are my only relief. I sit with all dear, darling, blessed Papa's photographs on my knees, devouring them with my eyes, kissing them and feeling as if my heart would break. Oh how hard I try to do what you do, to be like you to struggle and wrestle with these feelings of despair, think of beloved Papa, now so happy, of God's goodness—and peace does after a while come over me; it is like a lull after a storm! Thrice happy are the blessed souls of the just in heaven, for whom there is no agony or misery of grief.

Dear Mama, how I wish I could have been near you on this terrible day, how I envy all the others who have had this privilege, how cut off I feel so far away out here! The last, sad consolation has been denied me, all my life this will be a bitter thought to me! Fritz writes to me, so overwhelmed with your kindness and so touchingly; he says you are so brave, so courageous his loving heart is so attached to you, he would do anything for you. He loved Papa as his own father, admired him as he does no one else, and loves you as tenderly as his own mother. Any kindness of yours is not thrown away on that best and kindest of hearts.

From the Crown Princess

Dearest Fritz arrived at a quarter past 8! What a meeting it was—you can imagine! All the sad and interesting details of course rent my heart, while I was anxiously listening. The dear precious relics and hair—how can I thank you enough for them? But you knew in sending them what they would be to me. What Fritz told me of B. was no surprise. When Papa wrote to me in his last letter of the 27th of November: "I have one deep heart-sore about which do not ask me, please", I knew directly what it was, as more than one rumour had reached me. My grief then was great, as it is now that Fritz gave me the sad confirmation of my fears. I will not speak about my feelings on this subject in this letter (which would not be prudent) but when we meet which God grant may be before long, we can talk on all these subjects which weigh so heavily on my heart—and which are more than one.

For the dear mausoleum of which you speak I have made two sketches which I shall send you as soon as possible, as perhaps you might think it worth your while to consider them.

All your other plans I think so good; I am so sure they would have pleased beloved, adored Papa.

I feel so discouraged at times. It is very wrong but it is human; all the efforts that I made for doing my duty here in this position, which is no easy one, were made in hopes of pleasing Papa. A word of satisfaction from him was more to me than the praise of any one else and for that I could have done anything. I felt so full of determination and courage and high spirits. I did not care what I went through, I knew Papa would be satisfied, and now I feel I don't care about anything any more. It is not right I know—he would not approve it—and in time the thought of him will enable me to get over it—but at present I confess it to you, hoping you will not think the worse of me for it, and that you who are setting a better example will pity me!

I am but beginning life and the unerring judgement on which I built with so much security and so much confidence for now and for the future is gone! Where shall I look to for advice? I am only 21 and things here wear a threatening aspect! God will help; He will not desert us. "Seek and ye shall find, knock and it shall be opened unto you". I believe that—it must be so! Grief must have its own way and must have its own time. God has mercifully ordered our nature so that in time those feelings, which we need to go through life, return. Now we feel they will never come back. We feel, by the death of one dear to us, to have tasted of the bitterness of death, to have passed its dark waters, we feel detached from earth and from life, ready to go and pleased to go. When people come and speak to me of comfort it makes me feel worse than when they are silent! Dear Papa's large picture has arrived; it was agony at first to look at it but when I look longer I feel so soothed; it is so beautiful, so like; it will be the dearest treasure in my possession—and I like to think he sent it and wished me to have it. Dear, blessed Papa how beautiful he was! But I shall be tiring you so I will end. God bless you dear, beloved Mama, kissing your dear hand for the kind letter you wrote me by Fritz and for all your kindness to him of which he cannot say enough.

From the Queen

OSBORNE, DECEMBER 27, 1861

I feel his love is ever, ever present and that I understand even every wish of his better than before! Dreadfully as you will miss him—awfully, fearfully, ever in this world—as you should—you will find me more like him than I used to be—less unworthy. Think also (which perhaps you did not know) how very little he clung to life. He often told me: "Ich hänge gar nicht am Leben; du hängst sehr daran,"[1] and that if he knew that those he loved were well cared for he should be ready to go at once, ready to stay and ready to go! He also said: "I feel that I should make no struggle if I were ill—that I should give it up at once"—which made me shudder. But he said that often with the greatest cheerfulness, in the midst of happiness and health—oh! what a blessed state—what a mind, ripe for what he now enjoys! He sees all now and understands it and will not worry himself as he did—oh! so sorely! The wickedness of the world was too much for him to bear. Thank dear Fritz (who was a great comfort) for his dear letter and all he did and said to poor, unhappy Bertie. Tell him that Bertie (oh! that boy— much as I pity I never can or shall look at him without a shudder as you may imagine) does not know, that I know all, (beloved Papa told him that I could not be told "the disgusting details") that I try to employ and use him—but I

---

[1] I do not cling to life: but you do.

am not hopeful. I believe firmly in all Papa foresaw.[1] I am very fond of Lord Granville[2] and Lord Clarendon[3]—but I should not like them to be his moral guides, for dearest Papa said to me that neither of them would understand what we felt upon Bertie's "fall". Lord Russell,[4] Sir G. Lewis,[5] Mr Gladstone[6]—the Duke of Argyll[7]—and Sir G. Grey[8] he said would. Hardly any of the others.

I never thought of Christmas and put all those recollections, as well as on Monday all the harrowing thoughts of what was passing, away from my mind. And this carried me through.

I send you the copy of a beautiful letter from Tennyson, also a photograph done by Heath and Murray[9] and you shall have another. Can't you think of allegorical pictures and decorations? The sacred room[10] is to be dedicated to him—and I wish it to be very beautiful and put some Raphaels on china perhaps into it and busts etc. Mr. Gruner will be here in three or four days and then we shall talk all over! Now, goodbye and God bless you all!

From the Crown Princess

BERLIN, DECEMBER 29, 1861

How often dear Papa and I talked about death when I was sitting with him of an evening in '56 and '57. He

---

[1] The consequences for the country and the world of a debauched Prince of Wales.
[2] 2nd Earl (1815–91), Foreign Secretary and statesman. President of the Council at this time.
[3] 4th Earl (1800–70), diplomat and Foreign Secretary, out of office at this time.
[4] 1st Earl (1792–1878), statesman and Prime Minister, familiar as Lord John Russell. Foreign Secretary at this time.
[5] Sir George Cornewall Lewis (1806–63), politician. Secretary for War at this time.
[6] W. E. Gladstone (1809–98), statesman and Prime Minister. Chancellor of the Exchequer at this time.
[7] 8th Duke (1823–1900), politician. Lord Privy Seal at this time.
[8] 2nd Baronet of Fallodon (1799–1882), politician. Home Secretary at this time.
[9] Heath and Murray, a firm of photographers in Piccadilly.
[10] The Blue Room at Windsor in which the Prince died.

always said he would not care if God took him that moment, he always felt ready.

I have so often longed to talk with you about eternity, about our souls and about death—these subjects are so constantly occupying me—and I find the more one thinks on them and the deeper one tries to penetrate their nature the more comforted and relieved and calm and courageous one feels!

Poor Bertie, how I pity him!—but what sorrow he does cause. Perhaps you do not even know how much I grieve over his "fall". It was the first step to sin and whether it will be the last no one knows. I fear not! How right you are in what you say about Lord Clarendon and Lord Granville; they were my very words to the Queen when she named those two as people who might be good advisers for Bertie. The education of sons is an awful responsibility and a great anxiety and it is bitter indeed if they do not repay one for one's care and trouble—it makes me tremble when I think of my little William and the future! Christmas passed by quite unobserved by me and so will New Year—this letter will arrive about that time. Wish you joy I cannot, for that cannot be yours but pray to God most earnestly and fervently to bless, preserve, comfort and guide you I can, and that I do, with all my heart.

Tomorrow I shall see Mr. Gruner—I shall explain all my ideas to him and I shall give him my sketches which I have had corrected by our first architect here. I have bought a very fine china picture of the "Madonna del Candelabre",[1] which dearest Papa was so very fond of and which he had not got, as I do not believe it existed on china. I thought it would do for the sad but sacred room which you think of dedicating to him. You will say when you wish me to send it.

---

[1] Raphael's picture "La Vierge aux candèlabres". There are two versions of this painting. One is in the Walters Gallery at Baltimore, the other was reputed (incorrectly) to be in the National Gallery.

1862

From the Queen

I am so agitated by news which concerns our family so nearly and will I know agitate you very much too that I hardly know how to write, or what else to write about. I tell it you but beg no one but Fritz to know a word about it. Uncle Ferdinand refuses to go to G.[1] The G——s will have a near relation of ours, and the English Government most earnestly advise that Uncle E. should go, and Affie become at once Duke. Dear Uncle Leopold originally suggested this, and now it is most earnestly pressed. You can imagine how this agitates me, how in my state of desolation, I feel the importance of this event. What Uncle E. will say and do I know not (Uncle L. is sounding him). I think he would like it. For dear Affie I think and so do most of our friends, that it may be an immense blessing; I say to him in my letter today: "If Uncle E. accepts I see nothing to regret in it! That beautiful country is now not well governed—the people are good, devoted."[2]

---

[1] Ferdinand, Prince of Saxe-Coburg, 1816–85. He was first cousin to Queen Victoria and married the Queen of Portugal in 1836 and received the title of King in 1837. By 1862 his wife was dead, his son was reigning and he was consequently available for Greece. He was notoriously fond of women; his decision not to go to Greece much distressed his uncle, King Leopold, who said that in urging his nephew to accept the Greek throne "I even went so far as to say that the beauty of the Levantine women was known to be very great". *Memoirs of the Duke of Saxe-Coburg-Gotha*, Vol. IV, page 146.

[2] This letter is incomplete and deals with Greece where the Bavarian, King Otho, was childless and insecure on the throne. The Greek throne had a curious fascination for the Coburg family; King Leopold once told the Queen that he sometimes thought that, unlike the sun, his career would close in the Orient as King of Greece. But by this time he was too old.

From the Queen

Your dear, beautiful letters are a great consolation and satisfaction. God bless you for them, dearest child, the worthy child of my own, dear darling. You speak of my calmness and courage and goodness! Oh! those who speak of that know not the depth of utter misery and desolation which dwells in that pierced, bleeding heart! I alone have no hope of comfort in my wretched existence here till the blessed moment, the glorious one when I may go to him, and be really less unworthy of him. You all have or will have, D.V., that loving heart, that bosom to lean against and pour out all to, and the support and stay which made my life what it was, and that I have lost for ever here; no not entirely for I feel he is near and loving and supporting me and cheering me!

From the Queen

Thousand thanks for your dear, dear letter of the 4th. Oh! weary, weary is the poor head which has no longer the blessed precious shoulder to rest on in this wretched life! My misery—my despair increase daily, hourly.[1]

I have no rest, no real rest or peace by day or by night; I sleep—but in such a way as to be more tired of a morning than at night and waken constantly with a dreamy, dreadful confusion of something having happened and crushed me! Oh! it is too awful, too dreadful! And a sickness and icy coldness bordering on the wildest despair comes over me— which is more than a human being can bear!

Oh! why, why, has such an awful cross been put upon a back so far too weak to bear it? I can only think because it is to draw me up to him, to be purified, to be less earthly,

---

[1] In her letter of 4 January the Crown Princess had described herself laying her head on Fritz's shoulder and thinking "my own dear Mama has no shoulder on which to lay her weary head".

and to be ready to leave this world to which (I deny it not) I cling most tenaciously for his sake.

I send you a most beautiful little book by Tennyson which is a great comfort to me, which Dr. Jenner spoke of to me—which is as if made for my misery.[1] Alice has marked all the passages which I love.

Thousand thanks to dear Fritz for his letter and to the Queen! She speaks of "Trost".[2] Ah! she little knows that there is none for a broken heart like mine. On Saturday it was three weeks that he left me. Oh—Oh! I can't bear to live on so! I never shall live on! God cannot mean to tear me alive into pieces! Forgive my grieving you, dearest, good child—but my misery is fearfully great!

From the Crown Princess

BERLIN, JANUARY 8, 1862

I have just received your dear letter of the 6th. Oh how sad it is—but still what a comfort to me to have!

I can so well understand that you wish to die, dearest Mama, to be with him again, but who then would carry out his wishes, would work out all he has begun with so much trouble and so much love? You know, beloved Mama, what would most likely be the fate of the nation if God were to remove you now. In 20 years time all that causes us such alarm with Bertie may be changed and softened. But Heaven forbid beloved Papa's work of 20 years should be in vain. God requires immense sacrifices of you and has imposed most difficult duties on you but He has given you adored Papa for a pattern. His bright example will be your guide! And who can know his feelings and opinions on all things as well as you, beloved Mama! Who could carry out his plans better? Your children and your people have need of you—you would not have them doubly bereaved when this blow is already as much as they can bear.

Forgive me for speaking so but I know dear Papa would

---

[1] Presumably *In Memoriam*.
[2] Consolation.

say the same! The struggle between feelings and reason, between wishes and duty is very, very hard and the warmer and deeper the heart the harder the battle is. Though I am not tried as you are—yet I know those struggles too and I think my nature is like yours!

But is not the reward of the knowledge you will be doing what Papa wishes, something? Every day brings you nearer to the one on which you will again be reunited.

Poor human nature has much to suffer, but it has glorious ends to work for and great powers by the side of great weakness.

I do not think I can bring either of the children, dearest Mama, because I should be leaving poor Fritz in an empty house, which I do not think I can do. He has so much to annoy and worry him all day out of the house that he needs something at home to cheer him—or else he gets so low spirited, and as he is so fond of having the children about him and is so sad when I am not with him I think it would hardly be fair perhaps.

And Mrs. Hobbs[1] would cry her eyes out at the mere idea of Charlotte's going without her. William has inflamed eyes and is shut up in his room which makes him look like a cheese. His eyes discharge a good deal of matter and are much swollen; he had this once before in the summer—but it was only one eye then and now it is both. Wegner[2] says it proceeds from cold. Thank you for letting me know about the mausoleum. I am sure you are right in wishing it to be like the one at Coburg;[3] it was my first idea too, but then I did not know whether you had heard dear Papa express any other wish. I hope I may be allowed to contribute in some measure to beautifying it.

I have had some disagreeable but very necessary duties to perform these last few days in which I have missed dearest Papa's advice so much. It has been necessary to settle some-

---

[1] The nurse to the Crown Princess's children.
[2] Doctor to the Crown Prince and his family.
[3] Erected by the Prince Consort and his brother for their parents and family. The Queen described it as "beautiful and so cheerful". Martin's *Life of the Prince Consort*, Vol. V, page 199.

thing in case of Fritz's death before William is of age as Prince C¹ would be Regent and guardian—both if some means are not taken to prevent it—and we are not sure that the King will consent to our wishes. Luckily I did talk all possibilities over with dearest Papa this summer at Osborne and he approved my ideas.

Still the whole thing is trying—difficult and delicate, and requires prudence and tact besides firmness.

Please, dear Mama, keep this quite to yourself—as of course if it got about and came to Prince C's ears all our exertions would be fruitless. I will bring you the papers when I come. Beloved Papa urged me not to let another year pass without having this important point settled. I have also now to change my will—which is also difficult.

I am as well as I can be in such sorrow and better than I have ever been in this condition.

Forgive me for writing on other subjects—but they are all serious, and therefore do not I hope come amiss.

From the Queen

OSBORNE, JANUARY 11, 1862

Don't talk of 20 years longer, it is enough to drive me wild. On my knees do I implore God it may be very, very few, even though it may be some! But I have the feeling that I am getting on in my journey. I must work and work, and can't rest and the amount of work which comes upon me is more than I can bear! I who always hated business, have now nothing but that![2] Public and private, it falls upon me! He, my own darling, lightened all and every thing, spared every trouble and anxiety and now I must labour alone!

I am very glad you are busying yourself with arrangements which shall be necessary and which dearest Papa

---

[1] Prince Charles—the rather disreputable uncle of the Crown Prince.
[2] When she came to England a few weeks later the Crown Princess wrote to her husband "Mama never says a word about politics and we may not even mention them because she dislikes them". Count Corti, *The English Empress*, Cassell, 1957.

thought very necessary and it is most important. I have likewise been very busy with my poor Will which from having been the most simple one, leaving all in dearest Papa's hands, must now be very complicated in order to secure all I wish. There will be instructions of many kinds too—to you all. In case of my death before all the young ones are grown up though the eldest brother will have the guardianship (I believe) you and Alice I intend to ask to take charge of them and direct their education, marriages etc. in strict accordance with our wishes. This will all be written to you both and to Bertie or the eldest son for the time being. I shall then be quite at rest—come what may.

B's journey is all settled. Many wished to shake my resolution and to keep him here—to force a constant contact which is more than ever unbearable to me you can well imagine. And though the intentions are good, the tact, the head, the heart all are lamentably weak. The marriage is the thing and beloved Papa was most anxious for it. The old Baron's letter gave him a dreadful shock and added to his sad illness![1] I can't deny it. But there was and is but one feeling: he must marry early and this he feels now and wishes for. So when you come, we must fully talk it over and see what can be done, and now I feel it is a sacred duty he, our darling angel, left us to perform.

From Baron Stockmar

This is a translation of the letter from Stockmar, the confidential friend of the English Royal Family at Coburg, to which the Queen referred in the preceding letter.

NOVEMBER 20, 1861

I understand that a certain family affair has recently

---

[1] Princess Alexandra, whose engagement to the Prince of Wales was canvassed at the end of the Prince Consort's life, was the daughter of Prince Christian of Schleswig-Holstein, heir to the throne of Denmark. Owing to the smouldering dispute between the German Confederation and Denmark over the duchies of Schleswig-Holstein any strengthening of the Danish dynasty was bound to be unpopular in Germany. This explains the Prince Consort's remark "We take the Princess but not her relations." See the following letter.

been completely suspended by the irresolution of one of the parties concerned.

The reasons that were given to me some time ago for intention and venture had satisfied my reasoning and my feelings so little that my heart was relieved by the fact that the intention and decision was kept as a secret before me. Not only the choice itself would have had to appear to me as highly dubious but I would have had to declare the authorisation of the guardians to suggest an object for the choice as impermissible. The mere suggestion and supplying the opportunity has a predetermining power and makes that person unfree who is exposed to it. The person whom one wishes in fact to follow his own free will must not be exposed to predetermination. The opinion of the guardians therefore that X for certain reasons should marry early and that this should be promoted seems to be more due to mere opinion than consideration and genuine interest.

As main reason for this affair was given to me that it is hoped that the defects of spirit and mind of the one person should be made up by the strength of the other person. How daring would it be to take part in this lottery of possibilities.

Since the affair is based on the condition that one party has the solid features of character that the other party is missing, the certainty of the existence of such features would have to be a "conditio sine qua non". What we know for certain however is only youth and beauty. I am wondering whether the important moral powers that we need are available as well? And if they are, may we assume from the up-bringing and the family conditions, that they have brought about development and fundamental satisfaction? This is very doubtful indeed!!! The general reputation denies it. One of the heads of the family is supposed to be insignificant and imbecile and the other head is of lax principles and has the characteristic of an intriguer. One member of the family is almost of doubtful standing. How do these facts fit to the principles that have hitherto been applied in dealing with such cases?

Although my topic is far from being exhausted I must

conclude this letter because I am personally exhausted. I only hope that nothing will come out of this affair because the facts that are not unknown and that have been reported to me recently oblige every honest man to exclaim "Not a step further otherwise a disaster can occur whose consequences cannot be foreseen."[1]

From the Queen

Yes, dearest child, you can well preach to me to live and work! I may drag on an utterly extinguished life but it will be death in life. For you dear children I will try my best—the devotion of your sisters, and your love for me, as the remaining, poor half of what was our light, our life, our sun-shine, touches me most deeply. I send you here Tennyson's Idyll which is glorious and beautiful. It will cheer you very much.[2] I am so thankful the dear Countess is coming; it will be a real comfort and a comfort to Fritz to know her with you. Could the good Baron come,[3] if but for a few days? I think it would be very useful. I hope the old Baron knows the real truth about B.? If he does not would Fritz kindly ask Baron E. to put him in possession of the sad truth, and of the awful fact of its having made beloved Papa so ill—for there must be no illusion about that—it was so; he was struck down—and I never can see B.—without a shudder! Oh! that bitterness—oh! that cross! B. will go for a night to Coburg to see the old Baron (who has written to me such a touching letter and to B. also) and I don't wish he should be ignorant of the facts, which have assumed so awful a form from the dread result which I fear the old

---

[1] Baron Stockmar is alluding to Princess Alexandra's parents in the passage following "general reputation". The last paragraph almost certainly refers to the affair between the Prince of Wales and a courtesan, which possibly came to his ears through King Leopold or the Duke of Saxe-Coburg.

[2] This is a copy of the dedication to the *Idylls* which Tennyson had sent to Princess Alice two days before.

[3] The Countess Blücher and "the good Baron"—i.e. Ernest Stockmar, son of the old Baron—were coming with the Crown Princess to England.

Baron may ignore, and ought not, if he is to be of any use to B. and to me. We must then when you come here talk his marriage prospects over. B. and every one are most pressing for its settlement as the only "point de salut". I only want your advice—not to get you further mixed up.

Dear Uncle is gone to Town for three nights as he wishes to see people and to be of use to me in my utterly forlorn position.[1]

From the Crown Princess

Poor Bertie and all relating to him is the subject of my constant thought day and night. I feel a double responsibility now that you are so tried, and be assured that no effort or no trouble shall be wanting on my part to relieve you of any part of anxiety on his account. With regard to his marriage, the letter written by the old Baron to beloved Papa which Papa wrote to me about, contained libels against poor Princess Christian.

Of course I never for a moment believed them, for that is impossible after having seen her and her husband and daughter, but knowing so little of the circumstances I could not take it upon myself to contradict them only on the ground of my own personal impressions. The only thing which I could do and which I did without loss of time was to ask what was said of Princess C. and who said it. The old and the young Baron, Fritz and Louise of Baden, M. de Roggenbach,[2] Dr. Meyer,[3] Fritz Holstein,[4] Uncle Ernest, all repeated verbally and by letter the story that Princess C. had had illegitimate children, and Princess Alix had had flirtations with young officers—one of whom had been removed from the neighbourhood in consequence. All these

---

[1] King Leopold came to Osborne on Boxing Day, and stayed with the Queen for some weeks.
[2] Roggenbach had been head of the Ministry in Baden.
[3] The Prince Consort's librarian and German secretary.
[4] Prince of Schleswig-Holstein-Sonderburg-Augustenburg; regarded by the German Confederation as rightful ruler of the duchies.

persons (except Fritz H.) had heard this from Roggenbach, and Roggenbach, when asked, said as a secret he had it from the young Duchess of Nassau![1] Of course this staggered me still more—I thought the Duchess must be either very wicked to blacken her aunt and cousin, or that there must be some most extraordinary "mesentente" which wanted clearing up. I puzzled my brain to think how I could set about it. One way was to beg Countess Blücher to write to Wally Paget, and Stockmar to Mr. Paget—and ask them to find out the truth. They have as yet sent no answers. Another way was to ask Valerie Hohenthal to write to a friend of her's an elderly Danish lady (a very clever woman whom I know)—a Mlle de Wancelle, and ask her whether she knew anything about these reports running all over the world. This lady who is now in Denmark has answered today and I send you a copy of her letter in the Baron's hand, which I think clears up everything most naturally and satisfactorily—particularly the darkest point—the Duchess of Nassau.

This Danish lady has not a notion that the reports can be traced to the Duchess as of course I am bound to keep Roggenbach's secret to all but you.

The mother of the Duchess, Princess C.'s sister is bad and has had an illegitimate child; now either she has told her daughter this child was Princess C.'s or, the Duchess of N. has heard the report about her mother, puts it upon Princess C., her aunt, to screen her mother, which, though inexcusable to me, seems far from unlikely. This one story is enough to invent many others upon. God knows the wickedness of this world passes all belief, and who can screen poor unsuspecting princesses from the breath of scandal? I send you also an extract from Wally's letter to her sister. I think it far from right that a young girl like Valerie should be mixed up in all this but she, like her sister, has been brought up without a mother in the house of a vulgar and worldly minded aunt—widow of the late

---

[1] Adelaide Marie of Anhalt-Dessau married the Duke of Nassau 1851. She was niece to Princess Christian.

Elector of Hesse—and they both as young girls were accustomed to hear what certainly is not good for unmarried people.[1] This is not my fault and it is only a marvel to me how they have remained so modest and nice in every way! I hope this explanation may relieve your mind and remove doubts which, however reluctantly, yet you must have had, since you heard all these lies, and I am sure this would have been a comfort to dear Papa. Marry early Bertie must; I am more convinced of that every day; he has not resisted small temptations, only launch him alone in the London society and you will see what becomes of him. You will regret it only once and that will be for ever, whereas the chances are, if he married a nice wife that he likes, she will keep him straight; and as he is too weak to keep from sin for virtue's sake, he will only keep out of it from other motives and surely a wife will be the strongest.

I don't know whether you may think it advisable to make all this known to General Bruce[2] as I don't know how far he is initiated in this matter and I do not know whom else in the world you can or ought to consult except perhaps Aunt Feodora—who is so clever and good!

I am glad you have not let yourself be talked into keeping poor Bertie now. What earthly good could it do him or you? Later when your poor nerves are in a stronger state it will be much better—he does improve and every journey does him good! I know you will be kind, pitying, forgiving and loving to the poor boy for Papa's sake; for without your love how hard it would be for him. He has no father now—oh! let him feel how great, generous and forgiving a mother's heart can be! He is not like Alfred or Arthur or Leo—or even like us his sisters—he is not like Papa and you—but he cannot help it poor boy, and I assure you he

---

[1] Count Adolph Hohenthal married the widow of the Elector William II of Hesse-Cassel, who was a cousin of Princess Alexandra's parents. This marriage of the elector was morganatic and Walburga, Lady Paget ("Wally") refers to her aunt as considering herself a royalty but looked upon as "half a one". *Embassies of Other Days*, Hutchinson, 1932, Vol. I, page 41.
[2] Son of the 7th Lord Elgin. Born 1813, died 1862, governor to the Prince of Wales.

knows it and he feels it. It has gone to my very heart to hear him say so, for I love him tenderly although I know his faults! We must hope for the best! To give him up as lost at 20, would not be right, it would do him harm and us no good. He has really the best intentions.

I fear you will be very angry with me for saying all this and think I forget who and what I am, but if I err—it is out of love to you and out of fear of evil which might arise if he were "froissé" or set aside!

From the Queen

OSBORNE, JANUARY 18, 1862

Your dear, long and interesting letter of the 13th reached me the day before yesterday and I thank you a thousand times for it. Always speak openly to me and fear not to displease me! All you say is quite true and right, but, darling child, you have that one loving heart still with you to bear all and feel all with you, and you can well speak to me of what he wishes and what he, our darling angel, would expect me to do. But you have not lost all, have not had your life crushed utterly, totally, and for ever destroyed in its holiest, purest, greatest affection. Then, again, you don't know my peculiar character—a pining one, one caring not at all for what is around me, not for any thing of the outer world, unable to rouse myself and only one could shake me out of it—and he is gone, gone from this world!

From the Queen

OSBORNE, JANUARY 24, 1862

As regards B.'s affair, one thing I think very necessary and which has been strongly urged on me by those who wish my comfort—viz. that I should see the girl before B. sees her again so that I could judge, before it is too late, whether she will suit me. That whole affair is our "forlorn hope" and if it were not to be successful, or she not to take to me, all would be lost! You will understand me.

From the Queen

Though this letter only goes on Wednesday I will begin it at once writing in beloved Papa's room, at his table, and let me in both our names—for dear Papa does wish you joy too I know and feel it—wish you joy of our dear, darling, little William's birthday—his 3rd. He loved that dear child so dearly, felt so anxious about him, was so sure he would be so clever—that it only adds to my love for and interest in the sweet child, who you know is my favourite! These poor days all pass to me like nothing, they don't make me sadder for my grief is too deep to be saddened by any day! But it does not lessen my love for those dear objects of our affection and solicitude. I send the dear child a bronze bust of beloved Papa (Marochetti's) thinking you would like that for him.

Baron Marochetti has made a sketch for the monument in the mausoleum, and is now modelling the head here, as I won't allow that sacred cast (which I never have seen, and dare not look at—as I know beloved Papa disliked it) to go out of the house.[1] I think the monument will be very fine! The mausoleum is quite decided upon and they have begun the foundations. I mean to lay the first stone myself in March; you will be able to be there then!

There is to be but one sarcophagus and we shall lie together! Do you remember the discussion upon that subject with dear Papa, Uncle E. and Aunt Alexandrine, in the Erbegräbniss at Coburg and how dear Aunt prayed and begged that she and Uncle should be in one? Yes, she was right and the two shall rest side by side, as they slept in life.[2]

---

[1] A cast of the Prince after death was evidently made. When the Queen writes that the Prince "disliked it" she means the practice of taking a death-mask.
[2] The notorious infidelities of the Duke of Saxe-Coburg give a certain pathos to his wife's request.

From the Queen

How strange, that you and Dr. Becker sang that pretty, melancholy song![1] Yes there are peculiar circumstances which I cannot call coincidences, which show to me very clearly how near the visible and invisible world is! Oh! that we could know more! But that dare not be here, or we should not stay here at all. That absurd fiction you alluded to the other day of being told one was to love God more than any one, was one which Papa always treated as most preposterous! He said that the love for God was quite of a different kind—it was the trust and confidence in and adoration of a great, incomprehensible spirit! Not that love which came from intimate knowledge of one another, as one acquired on earth and which became more and more purified! Yes, I ever did and ever shall love adored Papa more than anything on earth or in heaven and God sees and knows and approves that, for He gave me that heart, that feeling of love and gave me that blessed precious object to gaze only upon, and love beyond all and everything—and keeping him safe for me!

From the Queen

Corbould's[2] drawing I will send in a case with a key —but you must promise not to show it any one but Fritz

---

[1] Dr. Becker had been German secretary to the Prince Consort, and was to be private secretary to Princess Alice. When the telegram came warning the Crown Princess to expect the death of her father she was singing a German duet with Dr. Becker of which the following is a translation:

The last moment already approaches to separate us
The paradise of coming-back!
Back without me
Good-bye now until the dawn of a more beautiful day appears
That, free from earthly worries, will unite us for ever!

[2] E. H. Corbould (1815–1905), water-colour painter. This drawing was evidently made of the Prince after death.

and the dear Queen and don't dwell on their images. Only quite a short while ago, he spoke of that. Always pray for him, as before—never make any difference, I don't and won't and treat him as living, only invisible to us—as he has reached the end of our journey. As I am overwhelmed with business (oh! so new to me) I must end here for today.

From the Queen

WINDSOR CASTLE, MARCH 31, 1862

You are gone from me and those sad days you passed in this house of desolation are past! God bless you. Beloved Papa watches over you better than I can! He is ever near you! Bless you for your love—your helpfulness in so many ways. The remainder of my poor, weary life shall be devoted to you dear children! What I can do for you I will, and strive humbly to do something to make you feel less fearfully the loss of the greatest and best of fathers.

From the Queen

WINDSOR CASTLE, APRIL 2, 1862

It is very rainy and stormy and blows much since you left so that we are all very thankful you had a good passage. Often and often do I think of you, darling, and of all we talked of, thought of, and of my woe—my never ending misery. Your loss is very, very great, nothing can ever replace or make up for it, but you have a husband, whom you can respect and look up to, who is so good, so kind, on whose bosom you can pillow your head when all seems dark, and I—who want it so much more even than you— I have none.

If I can, I will send you some of the excellent ones [photographs] Affie took of me yesterday; they are the best ever taken![1]

---

[1] One of these is reproduced in *Queen Victoria* by H. and A. Gernsheim (Longmans Green) page 166.

From the Queen

What you tell me and the Countess herself tells me about the Z.[1] is inexplicable! I do so grieve for all that awaits you, and wish that my weary shoulders could bear still more! I feel so anxious to try humbly to be of a 100th part of the use adored Papa was to you! Alas! alas! I can be but of very little, but still you have but to tell me and I shall be only too glad to bear any responsibility, any apprehension for any thing. Fritz must not be injured, and tell him from me that I know that beloved Papa would have urged him this in the very strongest manner, not to remain a witness to all that is done. It will do him harm if he is present at things and even tacitly submits to what he must disapprove.

You say, dear, that you feel no one can do me good. Well dear—this is true and not true; take away my grief, help to lighten the load of that agony of longing and yearning you cannot assuredly, but you can and you did help me very much with your sound, good sense, your advice and your wonderful taste and genius; your clever conversation, your sound intellect are so like him—whom you have inherited it from.

From the Crown Princess

BERLIN, APRIL 5, 1862

You can imagine how much there is here to gall my feelings; being among merry people with coloured gowns is a great trial and I feel a great lump in my throat the whole time.

We dined with the King and Queen yesterday, the King was very kind, and full of enquiries after you and the brothers and sisters whom he is really very fond of. The

---

[1] Zeitung. This was the right wing of the Conservative Party; it was founded in 1848, was pro-Russian and preached the salvation of the nation through the improvement of the individual. The organ of the party was the *Kreuzzeitung* which displayed the iron cross on its title page.

Queen was remarkably cold and ungracious and seems quite out of humour.

Going out again is very painful to me, but I must try to get accustomed to it. The more people I see the more I feel the great contrast of all merry faces with my own sad and heavy heart.

From the Queen

OSBORNE, APRIL 9, 1862

Many, many thanks for your dear, affectionate letter of the 5th. Respecting Fritz's coming I hardly know what to say! I won't press for it, though I am anxious to do what I can for the country and the Exhibition! Still it is for Fritz to do what he likes best.[1] I can't write you the long letter I had wished, for I have had many bothers and worries, all arising out of the loss of that one great head! Troubles which annoyed and vexed me—miserable, little misunderstandings—which agitated and distressed me, but I think all is at rest. It was not between Sir C. and the General,[2] but about the tutors—something however which never could have happened in my adored angel's time!

Joining with merry faces must be trying. Still you are much more elastic than I am and therefore you can bear this better.

From the Crown Princess

BERLIN, APRIL 8, 1862

Here is the copy of my letter to Princess C. Valerie has told me a great deal about Princess Alix—nothing but the

---

[1] In her letter of 5 April the Crown Princess spoke of the King's extreme reluctance that the Crown Prince should come to England for the 1862 Exhibition. He did in fact attend the opening on 1 May. He, Prince Oscar of Sweden and the Cambridge family were the only royal persons attending the Exhibition in South Kensington, which had been conceived largely by the Prince Consort to perpetuate the ideals of the Great Exhibition of 1851.
[2] Sir Charles Phipps (1801–66) and General Grey (1804–70)—the Prince Consort's secretaries.

highest praise, saying the more one saw of her the more charming, sweet and amiable she appeared. She seems too to be so universally beloved. Valerie says she observed her much in company and could hardly believe she was so young —so "posée," quiet and self-possessed were her manners, and so full of tact, so little aware of her beauty. I am sure all this will give you pleasure to hear, as it did to me as it exactly tallys with my own observations and impressions.

I told Valerie to ask a great deal about her temper and disposition, all she has heard seems to be of the very best. Alix was said to be very violent and passionate as a child— which she is not at all now though she is naturally lively and can be quick. I was glad to hear it—as I was a little afraid she might have been too gentle—and not have enough firmness and will of her own, but from what I hear this does not seem to be the case.

Valerie says she does not think her very clever—but she had never heard her make one "bévue"—or say what she should not say—and that she was particularly gifted with tact, and "esprit de conduite" and had plenty of sense, which is just the thing we want. What on earth is the use of ever so much cleverness with an absence of the above named qualities! This was what struck me with E. W—d.[1] She had plenty of cleverness, but all the rest was completely wanting; she kept one on coals all the time she was talking, which I think for Bertie's wife would be a serious disadvantage.

Alix has no more lessons except music lessons; she is well-informed, and no pains have been spared in her education.

From the Crown Princess

I have heard a good deal more about the Danish family —which may be interesting to you to hear. The old Land-

---

[1] Princess Elizabeth of Wied. She subsequently married the King of Roumania, and achieved some literary distinction as Carmen Silva.

gravine, Princess C.'s mother, is said to be wicked and very intriguing—besides not being at all respectable; she is said to have in a great measure contributed to the divorce of the King of Denmark from his wife Princess Caroline of Strelitz, because she wanted him to marry her own daughter Princess Augusta.[1] The story which was so infamously laid to poor Princess Christian's charge belongs to her sister the Princess of Dessau[2] and happened at Copenhagen in the Landgravine's house, who encouraged her daughter's passion for one of her grooms in her stables. It seems too horrid to be true, but it is affirmed from so good a source (Wally Paget) that I fear one can hardly doubt it. The old Landgrave is not ill-natured, but weak and dreadfully mean and avaricious.

Prince and Princess Christian are very poor indeed which I did not know. Fritz of Hesse—Anna's husband you know—worthy son of his parents having inherited both their faults and I do not know whether any one good quality.[3] Princess Augusta married to M. Blixen,[4] and departed from him, is not at all respectable; her husband as you know is an adventurer and the worst enemy Prince and Princess Christian have. The old Queen of Denmark is said to be a most excellent person.[5] You know all about her better than I do. I think it is good to know all this about Princess Alix's relations so as to be able later to caution Bertie against those who are not recommendable though I do not think he is very likely ever to come in contact with

---

[1] King Frederick VII of Denmark (1808–63) was married three times—first to the daughter of King Frederick VI, then to Princess Caroline of Mecklenburg-Strelitz and finally morganatically to the Countess of Danner. Princess Louise Charlotte, the "old" Landgravine of Hesse-Cassel and mother of Princess Christian, was King Frederick VII's aunt. Her husband (1787–1867) was William; he was brother to the Duchess of Cambridge. Her daughter, Augusta, see later in this letter.
[2] Marie married, in 1832, Prince Frederick of Anhalt-Dessau.
[3] Prince Frederick of Hesse-Cassel married secondly in 1853 Princess Anna of Prussia, daughter of Prince Charles. Their son was to marry the Crown Princess's youngest daughter.
[4] Augusta married in 1854 Baron Blixen-Fineke.
[5] Widow of King Christian VIII and the youngest sister of the Landgravine.

them; he may just meet them when on the continent, that is all.

You did not tell me that Bertie had met Uncle Ernest at Thebes. M. de Reuter[1] wrote to his sister Mlle de Habe who is the Queen's maid that they had seen Bertie, and it is in all the newspapers. Did you know it? I was quite surprised to hear it. I am always alarmed when I think of Uncle Ernest and Bertie being together as I know the former will do all he can to set Bertie against the marriage with Princess Alix.[2]

Today I have to see all the new Ministers at which I do not rejoice—so I must already end my letter.

From the Queen

It is today 7 years that the Emperor and Empress[3] arrived at Windsor, that there was all that excitement and now beloved, adored Papa is no more here, dear Uncle Charles[4] gone, poor Lady Canning[5] also—all those were with us then, and:

> But I remain'd, whose hopes were dim,
>   Whose life, whose thoughts were little worth,
>   To wander on a darken'd earth,
>   Where all things round me breathed of him. [6]

Were ever words more true?

Many, many thanks for your dear long letter of the 11th.

---

[1] Not identified.

[2] The Prince, accompanied by General Bruce and Arthur Stanley, started for a tour of the Holy Land on 5 February. On the way the party travelled down the Nile as far as Assuan. Of Thebes the Prince wrote that it contained "wonderful antiquities". Sidney Lee, *Life of King Edward VII*, Vol. I, page 133 (Macmillan). Although the Duke of Coburg (Uncle Ernest) may have often pained the Queen and the Crown Princess he was an extremely intelligent man. An account of his journey to Egypt and Abyssinia in 1862 was subsequently published.

[3] Napoleon and Eugénie.

[4] The Queen's half-brother, Prince Charles of Leiningen, who was staying at Windsor for the visit.

[5] Lady of the Bedchamber at the time. See note on page 78.

[6] *In Memoriam*, LXXXV.

Has perhaps Princess Christian heard of poor, wretched Bertie's miserable escapade—and thinks him a regular "mauvais sujet"? The Aunt here[1] may have written in that way? I fear we can say no more. The meeting must be at Laeken,[2] and can't be before the 2nd or 3rd Sept:. I will however let Bertie know that she is much sought after; but more we cannot do. Your account of the family is certainly as bad as possible, and that is the weak point in the whole affair, but dearest Papa said we could not help it. Oh! the whole thing is so disheartening to me! Alone! to do all this, and with B.! If he turns obstinate I will withdraw myself altogether and wash my hands of him, for I cannot educate him, and the country must make him feel what they think. Affie would be ready to take her at once, and really if B. refused I would recommend Affie's engaging to marry her in three years. He will be very comfortably off—and has a fine prospect, and is very charming! I never heard of Bertie's having met Uncle Ernest till I saw it in the papers, and it is a month since we heard a word from Bertie or the General and never heard how they came to see him at all. I therefore could not tell what I did not know. I don't care the least to hear what Bertie saw— for all that is sad and trying to me now. But I wish to know how B. is going on and how they came to see Uncle E. Coburg matters become more and more "brouillé".[3]

Tomorrow is poor dear Lenchen's confirmation; it will be an awful day! It is to be at 12. I and the brothers and sisters will be close to the altar. Behind the rails—only the Bishop of Winchester,[4] the Dean[5] and Mr. Prothero.[6] The

---

[1] Duchess of Cambridge who had married the Queen's uncle, Adolphus, Duke of Cambridge. She was Princess Christian's aunt.
[2] The palace outside Brussels, where the Prince of Wales and Princess Alexandra were to meet.
[3] Duke Ernest was childless; the Queen is referring to the succession. Prince Alfred was heir-presumptive, the Prince of Wales as heir to the English throne being excluded.
[4] Charles Richard Sumner, Bishop of Winchester from 1827. The favourite of George IV.
[5] Gerald Valerian Wellesley (1809–92), Dean of Windsor.
[6] George Prothero, Rector of Whippingham, in which parish Osborne was.

Dean examined her a little before me (alone) yesterday morning in dear Papa's room. On Monday (dearest Baby's birthday and a very trying day for me) I saw Tennyson. He is very peculiar looking and very shy, but it is a fine head and you soon recognise when you talk to him—the intellect and the kind heart! I hope to see him again.

One word about Princess Alix; don't encourage too much dressing or smartness; great quietness and simplicity going to the opposite of loud or fast dress, like our foolish English girls. For God's sake don't let Wally try to encourage them to catch the poor boy by that fashionable dress! Anything but that.

From the Crown Princess

BERLIN, APRIL 15, 1862

I hear that the Emperor of Russia has not given up his intention of asking for Alix or Dagmar for his son. Princess C. feels very nervous now for fear that Bertie should not be in earnest after all, and for that case she would still wish to have the Cesarewitch in reserve. I should be very sorry if any thing were decided for Dagmar before you had seen her as it would be one chance less for Affie—and it is surely to be desired he should have as large a choice as possible.

Here is also a letter from Prince Hohenzollern[1] in answer to mine, by which you will see that poor Louis[2] must give up all thoughts of Marie Hohenzollern.[3] I cannot but say that all Prince H.'s remarks are most sensible and plausible, which they were sure to be—as he is a wise man and an excellent father.

Fritz has been obliged much "contre son gre"—to give up all thoughts of going to the opening of the Exhibition. The King would not send him and his coming in a private way on his own account would be of no good. He has written to Lord Granville[4] to explain this and to say that

---

[1] Prince Hohenzollern-Sigmaringen.
[2] The King of Portugal; succeeded his brother in 1861.
[3] Younger daughter of Prince Hohenzollern. She married in 1867 Prince Philip of the Belgians and was the mother of King Albert.
[4] Chairman of the Commissioners for the 1862 Exhibition.

he means to stay several days in London for the purpose of visiting the Exhibition (in June), and showing all the interest he takes in it. The Commissioners are very anxious for visits of royal personages during the whole time the Exhibition is open, and I think Fritz's paying several visits there would be of use to them also and would tend towards keeping up the interest. I am sorry it cannot be done as we had wished at first—but I see myself that it was not possible.

I do not hear very much of politics now as we keep out of it as much as ever we can and never mention the subject with the King. What else is to be done while such a distressing state of things last?

From the Queen

OSBORNE, APRIL 19, 1862

Many, many thanks for your dear long letter of the 15th. First of all let me say how glad I am dear Fritz is coming;[1] I hope we might get a glimpse of him on the 30th at Windsor! We only start at half past six that evening on our dreadful journey,[2] and if he could manage to arrive in the day so that I could get a glimpse of that dear, trim face, which is so pure, it would be a real comfort. Do let me know.

Now with respect to Princess C.'s anxiety—I quite feel for her as we should do the same, if it regarded our child. All I can now do is to tell B. that he is in great danger of losing far the best—indeed the only one—fit wife for him, and that we must encourage the mother to hope that he will choose her daughter. This is all we can do at present. Respecting Dagmar, I do not wish her to be kept for Affie; let the Emperor have her. I spoke openly to the good Dean[3] about all these things—and he said that even

---

[1] For the 1862 Exhibition.
[2] To Balmoral. The journey was undertaken so that the Queen could be far removed from the opening of the Exhibition with its memories of 1851.
[3] Of Windsor.

for B. he deeply regretted the family being so bad, for that it was a great disadvantage; still as there was hardly any choice for B. and the young lady in question was so charming and dear Papa wished it we were right to try and get her for him. But that on no account should one take a second daughter from that family; besides which he thought two sisters marrying two brothers hardly ever answered even in private life, and in a position like our one, it was most undesirable. Considering the outcry there is in Germany about this marriage—the alliance itself being so repugnant to all Germany, the connection so objectionable as regards the family—that to go and make Affie, the future Duke of Coburg, take the other sister would be really courting abuse and enmity. Another reason against the thought of it is that dear Papa, even in A. of H.'s[1] case (before he had seen her, and before he knew she would not suit) thought her being Louis' sister an objection as too much of one family. And yet a brother and sister is a very different thing to two sisters.

I think therefore, dearest, Dagmar should be entirely dropped and the mother encouraged to give her to the future Czar if that will secure Alix. Show this to the Baron, who I am sure will agree with me. The young Princess of Altenburg[2] would be a very good match for dear Affie—as well as the Hanoverian[3] and possibly the eldest Weimar may turn out less ugly.[4] There is also the young Princess of Württemberg for him; never mind equality of age.[5] How many marry people of the same age?

---

[1] Anne of Hesse, sister of Prince Louis to whom Princess Alice was then engaged.
[2] Princess Marie, born 1845, daughter of Prince Edward of Saxe-Altenburg.
[3] Princess Frederica, born 1848, daughter of George V of Hanover.
[4] Marie, born 1849, daughter of the Grand-Duke of Saxe-Weimar and niece to the Queen of Prussia. The Crown Princess had told her mother that the King of Prussia "did not think her ugly—only delicate-looking".
[5] Probably one of the daughters of Duke Eugene of Württemberg.

From the Queen

The letter I received (at length) from Bertie on Saturday is so favourable that I write a line to extract what he said to me—"Before I close I must thank you so much for the trouble you and dear Vicky have been taking about my future prospects, and I only trust that every thing will succeed according to your wishes, and that you will be pleased with the young Princess when you see her."

You may, I think safely, tell the mother that you know your brother's feelings have not changed and that you hope all will end as we could wish. This you may safely do. Tell me what he says to you.

From the Crown Princess

BERLIN, APRIL 19, 1862

The King has written to you to say that Fritz is to go to the opening of the Exhibition. After everybody had said it was impossible and I had written to tell you so, the King consulted Bernstorff[1] and Schleinitz[2] and decided in favour of the plan. But the King refuses to pay for the journey and it has all to come out of poor Fritz's pocket. I send you an Easter egg, dear Mama, painted by Mlle Schrödter[3] which I hope you will like—the words upon it are so very pretty.

About Princess Alix you need not fear that they will think of overdressing her or making her fashionable. I think nothing is further from Princess Christian who is so simple and quiet in her tastes and has a horror of anything fast or showy. They have it not in their power to spend much on their daughter's dress, which was as simple as it possibly could be when I saw her.

---

[1] Albrecht Bernstorff, the Prussian Ambassador in London.
[2] Baron de Schleinitz, the Foreign Minister.
[3] Probably the daughter of Adolph Schrödter—a German genre painter of note.

From the Queen

I have had a long letter to write to the King of which I send you a copy for you both to see! I cried bitterly in writing it—as you may imagine—as all, all is so fearful to me now.[1] Darling Fritz will be met by Affie at Dover and Col. de Ros[2]—who will remain in attendance on him. Thousand thanks for your dear little letter of the 18th. and the lovely eggs; the one is beautiful and the words dear Fritz wrote to me after dear Grandmama left us—and belong to a lovely poem by Geibel![3]

From the Crown Princess

BERLIN, APRIL 26, 1862

We have had so much worry these last few days. Fritz gets so teased and tormented and the bad party do all they can to intimidate him by telling him he is most unpopular and I don't know what more. The King is terribly suspicious of both Fritz and me, and the Queen much out of humour. We are obliged to be terribly on our guard, and you can imagine what a nice life it is. Augusta Strelitz passes through here today and dines with us. As dear Uncle Leopold is not well and cannot receive Fritz, he leaves on Monday instead of Sunday and will try to see Uncle, on his way back. I feel very sad to lose dearest Fritz as I have so little here, when he is away, which I care for. But still I am so glad that he is able to be at the opening of the Exhibition.

---

[1] This letter was written on the same day and is printed in *Further Letters of Queen Victoria*, edited by Hector Bolitho, Thornton Butterworth, 1938. The Queen wrote to thank the King for allowing Fritz to come "a fresh proof of your friendship and graciousness towards us".
[2] Equerry to the Queen; afterwards 24th Baron de Ros.
[3] Emanuel Geibel (1815–84) the outstanding German lyric poet of the time.

From the Queen

The journey was wonderfully rapid and quiet and easy but oh! the waking to look at where he always lay and to see poor, dear good Alice (who was most attentive and devoted) there instead!![1] Oh! all—all where he is not! And the arrival here in rain—not a soul out—only Dr. Robertson[2] at the door and poor Grant[3] in the hall! Oh! darling child— the agonising sobs as I crawled up with Alice and Affie! The stags heads—the rooms—blessed, darling Papa's room— then his coats—his caps—kilts—all, all convulsed my poor shattered frame!

Princess Alice had been engaged to Prince Louis (afterwards Grand-Duke) of Hesse-Darmstadt in November 1860. The Queen faced the marriage of this devoted daughter with reluctance after the Prince Consort's death. The anxieties of the bridegroom about the date of the marriage are understandable, but the Queen was annoyed by the tone of his letter which she sends to the Crown Princess.

From the Queen

BALMORAL, MAY 6, 1862

Poor good Louis seemed to imagine it is as Alice is not well—I send you his letter to read in answer to one of good advice I wrote him. He doesn't write well good boy! On the other hand your dear excellent Fritz writes so well—and is oh! so dear and good. He wrote me such a dear, affectionate letter yesterday which I received this morning and has given every one such satisfaction. I enclose two copies of letters from Sir C. Phipps and from Lord Palmerston[4] which

---

[1] The Queen first travelled to Scotland by night in 1859.
[2] The factor. "He had from the beginning the entire management of our property at Balmoral." *Journal of Our Life in the Highlands.*
[3] John Grant, born 1810, head-keeper.
[4] 1784–1865. Prime Minister at the time.

will please you. I am so glad, as it would—and will—please beloved Papa (for he knows it all I am sure) and will do so much good. Dearest Fritz, he is now the only male, very near relation I have whom I can rely on, from his high principles and excellence and I do cling to him, with all my heart. I will write to him in a day or two. In the mean time, tell him that when he comes for Alice's wretched marriage (which I wish were years off) he will act as my representative and do the honours for me, which the poor boys cannot and must not (though they can assist him) and with dear Aunt Feodora. How distressed we are to hear of your cold and cough; I always think it is the want of stronger medicine (and nothing else which makes your colds so bad in Germany) and good not very energetic treatment. Please God! it will soon be over.

Extract from Lord Palmerston's letter.

MAY 4, 1862

The Crown Prince of Prussia made a remarkably good speech yesterday evening at the dinner of the Royal Academy, and its effect was not spoiled, but perhaps rather increased, by some little deviations from the accustomed idioms of the English language. But the Prince had great command of words to express excellent ideas and sentiments.

(Copy)

ST. JAMES'S PALACE, MAY 4, 1862

My dear Grey

Nothing could be more successful than the Crown Prince's little speech at the Royal Academy dinner last night. It was very characteristic, earnest, simple and unaffected, and produced a wonderful effect upon his hearers. The audience is not usually a very impressionable one, but he sat down under quite a storm of applause. I am happy to think that his visit to England has certainly been, to him at any rate, very beneficial. His coming is considered as a compliment and his frank manner has given him much popularity. The English were always disposed to like him for the sake of the Princess Royal, but all who have come across him this time speak of the personal, favourable impression that he has made.

Sincerely yours
C. B. Phipps.

From the Queen

BALMORAL, MAY 13, 1862

Though I can see that Princess Alix's photographs are not flattered,[1] they are extremely pretty and look so distinguished. All those which I have shown them to, are in great admiration. Bertie must be hard to please indeed if he is not satisfied. I at once had the extract of Wally's letter translated and put it into the General's hands.[2] It is a great comfort to me, that he should be so clever and quick in framing a letter in the sense I suggest. Really, God has been in that sense very merciful—and who do I owe this (as everything else) to, but my own darling, who chose them and trained them! That M. de Blixen's visit is very disagreeable; fortunately Uncle George and Mary hate him and know what he is worth.

Poor dear Alice is very poorly! She has never held her head up since she came here and though we have now such very warm weather she got a dreadful cold—violent on her chest—and is so sick with it and can't touch anything. It is most vexatious and I live in fear of some further contretemps about that luckless marriage.

---

[1] In sending the photographs the Crown Princess described them as "horrible".

[2] This letter concerned Princess Alexandra's uncle by marriage, Baron Blixen-Finke who was regarded as undesirable. General Grey, son of the Prime Minister, who was the Prince's private secretary, and was acting in that capacity for the Queen. The position of private secretary to the sovereign was jealously viewed by ministers, and his position was not officially recognised by the Government for four more years.

From the Queen

I grieve to hear the state of your politics. It is very disheartening. Dear Fritz's success is in every one's mouth![1] Dear Uncle Leopold is much better; it is most distressing that he will not see any of his children for a moment even, and they feel it so much; poor Charlotte travelled night and day to Brussels and he is furious to hear it (though he knew he was very ill) and forbid her coming to Laeken! But don't say this to any one else. Philip is very unhappy about it. I will send you by the messenger a most interesting but really dreadful account of poor Aunt Alexandrine's stay near Massowa which she wrote me; she has been very unwell since. Uncle E. will I suppose come to Alice's marriage —at least I must ask him as dear Papa wished it, and if Uncle L. can't come he is the only person to give her away; but I will write to him before to tell him plainly that he must make no mention of Bertie's marriage to him—and I think he considers it hopeless.

Dear Baby is the bright spot in this dead home. Poor Louise has an awful sty on her eye.

From the Queen

BALMORAL, MAY 20, 1862

I try to mortify every evil passion (I mean every weakness and frailty, by which I mean selfishness) irritability, which great grief and misery like mine make very difficult to bear! But the life of utter depression, of objectless pleasurelessness is dreadful and wears me away! All is flat and indifferent to me here, though nature is so beautiful! The fresh green of the larch and birch mingled with wild flowers, and the air so very sweet, the highest mountains still tipped with snow—all, all I admire—but otherwise it produces no effect, no pleasure or satisfaction.

I send you merely to look at and beg to have them back

---

[1] At the Academy dinner and International Exhibition.

Uncle Alphonse's photograph, his bride's and his girls. The bride is plain but pleasant-looking and much more so, than Uncle Alexander's.[1]

Now goodbye and God bless and preserve you all four! Remember, darling child, that my life now is solely to devote myself to all of you—his dear children—for, for myself, I know no wish but to die!

From the Queen

I am reading a book, which I read 11 years ago, which is very striking—no one knows by whom—and which is unfortunately out of print; it is called: "New Philosophy", and is all upon the future.[2] When I have finished it I will send it you to read and to tell me what you think of it; but you must let me have it back again soon. I think that you will find that it makes one more at home with that next world than almost any thing has done. You must only let me have it back soon again. I send you Bertie's last letter as I think you will be pleased with it. Show it Fritz and then let me have it back again. The General says that Dr. Stanley has great influence with Bertie.

From the Queen

Every day makes me feel that my position is ruined, for though I may and do struggle on in a manner—and strive

---

[1] These are the two sons of Graf von Mensdorff-Pouilly who married Queen Victoria's aunt, the Duchess Sophie of Saxe-Coburg, and are given the courtesy title of "Uncle" to the Crown Princess. Alphonse, born in 1810, was a favourite cousin of the Prince Consort. He married Marie von Lamberg as his second wife on 31 May 1862. The Queen is alluding to his two daughters by his first marriage. Alexander, born in 1813, married in 1857 the Grafin von Dietrichstein.

[2] A curious book written and published anonymously in 1847. It began from two premises. There are no mysteries in the moral or physical world; and all are soluble by reason. Progression is the law of life and eternity. The heavenly bodies might fit this idea of progression by providing improved abodes for the future enjoyment of human beings after death.

to do whatever he wished in great and small I feel that so much will be left undone and the whole fabric must suffer from the foundation being undermined. A woman in my position and of my nature cannot stand alone, and you will see that a new state of things will in a little while not be looked upon as a misfortune. Your love and affection is a great value, and I can assure you that your dear letters, and the expectation of them are one of the very few things I care for now!

The poor Grand-Duchess of Hesse's death is really very shocking and will throw a great gloom over what is already so sad. I think the Grand-Duke will marry again—and he may have children and then Alice's position will be quite altered, but never mind, she will be quite as happy for this.[1]

From the Crown Princess

NEUES PALAIS, MAY 27, 1862

I was delighted with the little book with extracts from dear Papa's speeches and addresses.[2] I have read it through. Could you be so very kind as to send me some more copies of it? I should like to give them away. I am so glad that a short sketch of his sublime maxims and principles should be brought before the British public in a popular form; it is sure to be immensely read—but I regret that nothing of the kind should exist for Germany. Here people know nothing about him, and a great deal about Uncle Ernest, of what kind you know, and of Papa, I think they know little more than that he is Uncle E.'s brother. I am so

---

[1] The Grand-Duke of Hesse was uncle to Prince Louis—Princess Alice's future husband. He and the Grand-Duchess were childless; she was a daughter of King Louis I of Bavaria.

[2] *Principal Speeches and Addresses of H.R.H. The Prince Consort.* This was published by John Murray and contained an introduction with biographical details based on information given by the Queen and members of the Royal Family. The introduction was written by Sir Arthur Helps (1813–75), Clerk of the Privy Council. His "beautiful, quiet English" was praised by Ruskin. This was published in December 1862, and the Queen here refers to an earlier edition of the Prince's speeches *The Prince Consort's Golden Precepts*. See also page 153.

anxious that he should be better known in the land of his birth, and I think something short is always more likely to be read and to create sensation than a long book in the shape of "memoires" of which such endless numbers come out every month. Will you not consult with Mr. Rulandt[1]—he and Dr. Becker and my Baron might arrange something after the same kind as that little book.

Prince Oscar of Sweden is coming here today. I think him rather a bore.[2]

From the Queen

This is my last letter from here as on Monday the weary wandering begins again, and the poor troubled spirit is again moving and disturbed. I have just heard that Uncle Ernest and Aunt Alexandrine have arrived at Trieste and are well. They must come to Alice's marriage but I shall write quite openly to him about Bertie's concerns. I have asked General Grey to give you an account of the final decision about the Wolsey Chapel.[3] It will be slow but sure and safe. The Government have bungled and been shabby and the House of Commons are most difficult people to have anything to do with. I hope now that next year, the real public memorial will be voted in the right and fitting manner. I just hear by telegraph from Louis that there will be no further delay in the marriage—which I cannot deny, I had hoped, as that will be so dreadful, awful a day for me!

---

[1] The Prince Consort's librarian.

[2] Afterwards King Oscar II (1829–1907). He was a poet and musician of note and became a sovereign who was widely respected.

[3] This is the chapel long known as Wolsey's Chapel or the Wolsey Tombhouse to the east of St. George's at Windsor. The Crown Princess had been anxious that this should be made into a memorial to the Prince. This was settled and it was done up by Sir Gilbert Scott and is now known as The Albert Memorial Chapel. The Queen's father, the Duke of Kent, is buried with other members of George III's family in the crypt below. This was of course a family memorial, not the national one.

From the Crown Princess

You say, dear Mama, in your letter that your position is ruined now dear Papa is gone; undoubtedly it cannot be as secure as it was when he was the head and soul of everything, but think of the 21 years of experience you have (as none have had), then all dear Papa's valuable papers, and you are surrounded with trustworthy and excellent people. This all is a safeguard against your position's ever suffering —though your feeling of loneliness may make you feel desponding about it.

I am so anxious to hear what you have settled about Alice's marriage—I am so often asked and never know what to answer. The Grand-Duke may marry again (but Fritz says it is well known he never could have any children) because that was my first thought on hearing of the Grand-Duchess's illness—that he would marry again, as he was not a very tender or a very faithful husband to her. But now poor man I am sure he is very unhappy.

Uncle Ernest is to return on Tuesday and Samwer,[1] who is here, told me the people at Gotha are making immense preparations for receiving him—and also at Coburg. . . .

From the Crown Princess

NEUES PALAIS, JUNE 3, 1862

By the messenger I will send you a little oil sketch of Princess Alix which is like though not flattering and not well done; it is by an artist at Copenhagen,a Mme Jerichau[2] —but it certainly is like.

What a strange man the Grand-Duke of Hesse is, he is gone to Vienna a week after his wife's death.

We wish and hope so very much that it may be possible

---

[1] Karl Samwer, German diplomat and friend of Baron Stockmar. He was a Schleswig-Holsteiner, much in the confidence of the Duke of Coburg. He has been described as "an ambitious man, in whose brain there was far more cunning than wisdom". Sybel, *Founding of the German Empire.*

[2] The wife of the Danish sculptor Jens Adolf Jerichau.

for Bertie to pass this way on his homeward route. Do you think, dear Mama, that this could be arranged? It would give us both so much pleasure, even if it were only for an hour or two—just to see him, as we have seen all the others since our misfortune except him and Leopold. I really feel quite afraid to ask such a favour, but Fritz encouraged me to ask.

From the Queen

Alice's marriage was just settled to be on the 1st July when the poor Grand-Duchess died, but the Grand-Duke (who goes out to dinner daily!!) wishes no further postponement. Tell dear Fritz—never mind if the Grand-Duke marries again, Alice can live here if there is any difficulty. But I believe what you heard about the Grand-Duke is true.

From the Queen

I received your dear letter of the 3rd yesterday, and thank you much for it. I need not tell you that to give you and dear Fritz pleasure would ever be a great object and great satisfaction to me; but about Bertie's going to see you now, it is impossible. In dear Papa's original plan, it was intended he should come home through Paris stopping only a day in order to have got over his visit to that Sodom and Gomorrah; and for this very reason and because he can get off with a morning visit (his mourning preventing his going to dinners and parties) we decided that this plan should be adhered to. But if he had not gone to Paris he would have gone round by sea, for it was never contemplated that he would return by Germany. But in the autumn when I am in Germany, D.V. he can easily visit you. Poor dear General Bruce has been very, though I believe not dangerously, ill with fever; could not land at Athens and cannot come with Bertie to Paris; so Sir C. Phipps (who is also not well) is going to meet him there to replace General Bruce and come back with him here. I shall be very glad to see the oil painting of Princess Alix by that dreadful Mme Jerichau whom you sent with her awful Britannia![1] It is always hoped and intended that the great memorial will end in the National Gallery being brought to S. Kensington but it is a very vexed question and it would not do to begin with that. Therefore what Sir C. Eastlake[2] mentioned would be the beginning.

It is very troublesome for you, poor dear, to be in that state in the hot weather! It causes such misery. Your sisters and brothers go up most days to the Exhibition—as I felt beloved Papa would have wished it. Six of our dear Balmoral people are here—Duncan, D. Stewart, Mackenzie, Patterson, Robertson (the carpenter) and Thompson (our wood-forester)—son of Thompson the postmaster, an excellent young man, only married four or five months, but he is very unwell threatened with pleurisy and obliged to keep his bed instead of seeing sights etc. as the others are!

I saw Augustus and Aunt Clementine on Wednesday and Cousin Augusta yesterday. Uncle A. and Aunt C. were very affectionate and sight of the former quite overcame me! Beloved Papa's playfellow, cousin, contemporary, with a great "air de famille", a great friend of mine before we married—all, all overwhelmed me, and gave me pain and gave me pleasure! You know what the Coburg family are to me!

From the Crown Princess

NEUES PALAIS, JUNE 7, 1862

Your dear splendid picture has arrived quite safe and I really do not know how to thank you enough for it, it will be one of the greatest treasures I have![3] It is so like I can almost imagine it is going to speak, yet it made me so melancholy to look at it and see you sitting there in your

---

[1] Not identified.
[2] Sir Charles Eastlake (1793–1865). He was president of the Royal Academy, and at this time also Director of the National Gallery.
[3] This is now at Friedrichshof.

youth, beauty and happiness and to think that I shall never see you so again but always in black. It really sometimes seems impossible. Dearest Papa's picture hangs opposite to yours—both in my sitting room, when I look at his I always forget that it is the picture of one no longer on earth, it looks so alive.

They hang here for the present as I did not like losing four months' enjoyment of them but their real place is my drawing room at Berlin. They are beautifully copied.

Today the 7th of June our unfortunate Palais is again turned out at the window and my room filled with horrid musty old furniture; it does make me so cross. I must say I think it so inconsiderate, besides it spoils our things which have to be taken down and shifted and taken to pieces every year for this whim. It really is time this barbarous custom should cease.[1]

The King is going to Baden tomorrow perhaps. The Queen I hear comes here on the 24th, which I regret very much as our peace and quiet and liberty is thus at an end as she leads a life of fidget which quite wears one out, and she does not care for country life but carries all her Berlin habits on here.

The poor Empress of Austria is in a bad way—the Queen Dowager told me it was anaemia, and she even feared a beginning of blood decomposition for which I should think there is no cure. Her relations say it is in consequence of her having stayed in hot climates but I suppose that is not the reason. It is very sad.

From the Crown Princess

NEUES PALAIS, JUNE 10, 1862

Many thanks for your dear letter of the 7th received yesterday.

Of course I understand quite well that the plan of Bertie's journey does not allow his coming here, as you have explained it kindly to me. I am very sorry we shall not have

---

[1] The room was converted into a mausoleum for a family service in memory of King Frederick William III who died on 7 June 1840.

the pleasure of seeing him, as we had wished it so much. I only hope you were not displeased by our having asked this question. In the autumn we shall not be here as we are at your disposal at Reinhardtsbrunn[1] as long as you like to have us—and from there we intend to take a holiday tour and not return to Berlin if possible till after the middle of December. We think a change will do us both good, and it will be a great thing not to spend that terrible beginning of December, which must now for all my life be so sad a time, at Berlin so we should not be able to see Bertie here in the autumn.

Dear Wally is here but looking so thin, just half of her former self—her boy is splendid, he is quite enormous, and such a nice, dear, little fellow. William and Charlotte are ready to devour him. Wally seems very happy, but I think they are very poor and have to pinch a good deal—to make both ends meet, as Mr. Paget's whole private fortune, which is but small, goes to a brother of his who has six children. I think, dear Mama, it is in your power to benefit them greatly—by saying a word to Lord Granville who can give a place which that brother is very anxious to obtain, which would take him and his family off Mr. Paget's hands. Of course Wally has not an idea that I have mentioned this to you, but I thought I could do no harm by telling you of this and that perhaps you would kindly interest yourself in the case.[2]

I have spoken so much about dear Princess Alix with her, and really all is satisfactory that one hears of her. Wally says she has sense, tact and discretion above her years, that she was nothing of a genius or had no brilliancy of wit and talent—but that she never saw her do or heard her say anything which was either wanting in sense or apropos, that her abilities were usually underrated—as she was so diffident and humble about herself, besides being very shy—but that she was never at loss what to do or say, and that her judge-

---

[1] Built by the Prince Consort's father and romantically placed in the hills about eight miles from Gotha.
[2] Stewart Paget died as a police magistrate at Gibraltar—so possibly Lord Granville did as he was asked.

ment was singularly good. Moreover that she was the soul of truth, so that every one in the house had the greatest confidence in her—even much older people—as she was always the one to make peace and set things to rights and do good—performing offices of love right and left as judiciously as unostentatiously! Her dignity of manner in society has struck every one, strangers as well as Danes. Wally says that young as Princess Alix is, she is a person in whom one can place implicit trust, and who—as soon as she knows a thing is her duty or any thing is pointed out to her—will do it unswervingly whether it be pleasant or not, as she is so very conscientious.

She seems to be particularly shy as to showing her feelings or expressing her opinions, so that it is necessary to know her very well before one can form a correct opinion of her. Wally hopes you will not judge her by the first few moments as she is doubly shy before her own Mama.

Wally says she has a heart so full of tenderness and love that she is sure you will find in her one who will cling to you with the truest affection and devotion! Does not all this sound good? If she does marry Bertie, may she be loved and cherished, and may she be happy as she deserves—sweet young creature! He may go far before he finds her equal— that I feel sure! Here is a photograph of her which is better than the last I sent you—though the charm of youth, innocence and goodness of her expression does not appear enough. I fervently wish and hope that God's blessing may rest on this affair and that she may be secured to Bertie! It is not every one, one would wish as a sister-in-law in one's own dear home, at your side as your daughter, when we are gone away from you, but of this one—no one could be jealous, she is so worthy to fill a daughter's place.

We wish so very much that in the winter, in January for instance, provided she was then engaged to Bertie, she should come and stay with us for a little—so as to have seen a little of the world besides Copenhagen before she marries. It would do her good I am sure. Wally thinks there would be no sort of difficulty. Princess Christian would be ready to do any thing you expressed a wish for.

From the Queen

Your dear, affectionate letter of the 3d. reached me on Monday, as well as the pretty little picture of Princess Alexandra, which I recognised at once. I am very anxious that she should not be called by a mere nickname—as if you were called Princess Vicky and Helena Princess Lenchen, and besides it would make such a confusion with Alice. Tell those who know her that, except by her own family, I don't wish a nickname to be perpetuated. I am sure dear Papa would have agreed. Alas! dear Uncle Leopold's state causes us again great anxiety—though he is not in danger. On Friday there was a slight return of congestion of the lungs, and there must still be more operations as the pain continues. With this, the sleep and appetite are again worse, and the weakness is great! This at 72 is very alarming I own—I see very black to use a German phrase. Uncle Ernest comes, which I am (I own) glad of—for if Uncle L. is not able to come, he, as beloved Papa's only brother, is the only person who can give poor Alice away.

The mausoleum is making rapid progress and the interior, as proposed, promises to be very fine. Alice went to see the statue at Marochetti's which is finished and which she says is most beautiful and so like now. It overcame all who saw it. How I long for it to be in its place! It will be such an object and such a comfort to go to and sit by!

You never told me of Bismarck's appointment at Paris whither Budberg is also gone![1] Won't this do a great deal of mischief? And is it true—as the papers say—that the King received the Address so very ungraciously?[2] How sad all this! Altogether all looks very threatening.

Your dear letters from beloved Papa of 59 go back today with many thanks. I have been most particular in never copying a single thing which could implicate any one; but

[1] He was appointed ambassador at Paris in June. The appointment was temporary. Baron Budberg had been Russian ambassador in Berlin.
[2] The King and the Chamber were at cross-purposes over the Army, the latter pressing for a reduction.

how admirable, how perfect all are! From some of the general principles, a German book of "golden precepts" could be framed with the greatest advantage. How every word he wrote was like his precious self. Read them again and again and drink in from them wisdom and virtue to give you strength for the "battle of life". Poor dear child, when I read them, how did I feel what you have lost! What wretched, stupid letters mine are, in comparison to those! No one ever wrote as he did! How you must be bored and grieved by mine which are merely the outpourings of the deepest woe and agony—which is really tearing me to pieces. My poor picture! I am glad you like it. Beauty there never was, and youth had already left me then! But now, I am a sad object—the picture of woe and of a broken heart.

From the Queen

WINDSOR CASTLE, JUNE 14, 1862

Many, many thanks for your dear, long and most satisfactory letter about Princess Alexandra of the 10th. All you say is just what we should like! A daughter-in-law never, in my present position, can be what a daughter is, and I must never, during the few (very few I think) years still remaining, be left without one of you—and with five daughters this will be quite easy. Dear Papa said so himself. Bertie could not cross yesterday from the dreadful gale— but has done so this morning and will be here very shortly. It makes me terribly nervous! I am so weak, so shattered, so terribly excitable that any new hint of anxiety alarms and agitates me. And then he comes without the dear General who, though recovering, is still far too weak to come on here with Bertie, though he has come over with him, and the passage, which was a very rough one, has done him no harm we heard by telegraph. But you may imagine my distress not to see him now—and to hear all! I must trust to good Dr. Stanley[1] who comes with Bertie. By saying that you

---

[1] A. P. Stanley (1815–81), Canon of Christ Church and afterwards Dean of Westminster. He was chosen by the Prince Consort to accompany the Prince of Wales to the Holy Land.

would see Bertie in the autumn, I meant probably at Rein-hardtsbrunn, as he will most likely follow me there. It is most satisfactory to think, D.V., that you will come there for some time, and I am so glad that you mean to be away till after that dreadful time in December. Where do you mean to go to? I suppose, if you mean to travel about, you will not take all the children with you? Well, in that case, I wish much you would let me take dear little Charlotte back here; with one of your various nurses and Thurston[1] and Anne, she would be (under my eye) very safe, and I need not tell you that it would be a little light in my dark-ness, for there is something refreshing, in the midst of misery and anguish like mine even, in an innocent little child. Our baby has that in her, which is so soothing, and Charlotte should be as much taken care of as she is. Mlle Dobeneck[2] could fetch her when you come back or even before. But don't think I shall be annoyed if it can't be; only my dreadful distress makes me ask for things, which I other-wise should not do.

The train is beautiful;[3] it remains here—with all Alice's coloured things. I went down to look at her trousseau, and it is sad to see nothing but black gowns made up!

Your idea (if she should be engaged to Bertie) of getting Princess A. (whose photograph is lovely and this very one much sold in London and engraved in the *Illustrated Times*[4] as B.'s bride!!) to be with you in the winter is a very good plan; then she could come to me perhaps or before. I want her to get to know us without B.—and not through "ses lunettes". But Society she would see none of here—naturally.

I am so terribly nervously affected now; my pulse gets so high, it is constantly between 90 and 100 instead of being

---

[1] Children's nurse to the Queen.
[2] The children's governess who was described by the Kaiser as "a great, gaunt dame of firm character".
[3] This had been made in Berlin and the Crown Princess had written to say how greatly it had been admired.
[4] Edited by the somewhat disreputable Henry Vizetelly and subsequently acquired by the *Illustrated London News*.

at 74! This wears me terribly. It exhausts me so and I am so weak, and then my poor memory fails me so terribly.

Now goodbye and God bless and preserve you! Write to me at length, your letters are never too long—and I wish to hear how affairs go on with you. I fear—badly.

From the Crown Princess

NEUES PALAIS, JUNE 14, 1862

I have found out that Olympia Usedom was one of the people who spread those wicked inventions about Princess Christian and Alix. I do not wonder at it much; first because her husband, together with all liberal Germans, is a great anti-Dane—and then because she herself is so vulgar and ill-natured—and such a chatterbox.[1]

I have not heard a single word from Coburg since Uncle and Aunt's return, they did not even answer our telegram sent on the day of their arrival.

I have many torments to go through at present—neuralgia in my left side and left shoulder which I have had for more than a week, and which keeps me in perpetual pain. Then those dreadful nights when I can hardly sleep at all and do nothing but turn and toss, bathed in perspiration and sometimes almost choked. It is really dreadful and makes me feel so knocked up all day long. Then a great deal of mental anxiety about our unfortunate affairs which really must weigh upon the minds of any one who knows their real state, and our sorrow—the thoughts of you, poor Mama,—and altogether one's only relief is in a good cry now and then. And yet I am so thankful for the prospect of a new little being to love—and new life for all we have lost!

---

[1] She was by birth a Scotchwoman—Olympia Malcolm. She was enormous and, as Walburga Lady Paget explains, her large body was adorned—though not confined—by the most daring creations of Worth's. Her daughter Hildegarde was a giantess. Her husband M. d'Usedom had been in the Prussian diplomatic service in Italy: he was director of the Berlin Museums. *Embassies of Other Days*, Vol. I, page 223.

From the Crown Princess

NEUES PALAIS, JUNE 17, 1862

We do not exactly know where we are going. We had very much wished the north of Italy, but Fritz is afraid the King will never allow it as he refuses to recognise the Kingdom of Italy and it is a very sore subject with him.[1] We do not know either whether he will allow us to take a long journey; he dislikes our going away so very much, particularly now, as he thinks Fritz wishes to avoid being drawn into affairs under the present circumstances, which the King considers disobedience and opposition. I shall say it is good for my health and particularly for my spirits—and then perhaps it will be allowed.

I send you here, dear Mama, a sketch which I have made of Princess Alexandra. I have traced it from a sketch I did of her before which you have not seen. I did not think it worth sending you, only Wally Paget said she thought it so like, and encouraged me to send it.

I think it so very desirable that you should see Wally; she can tell you so much about every thing and she would be such a useful channel of communication between you and Princess Christian when I am laid up and unable to be of use; that will just be the time when you may have a great deal of writing on that subject. Mr. Paget and Wally are going to Gordon Castle in August. Do you think you could send for them over to Balmoral for a day or so?

Wally can tell you all and every thing about the Princess's education, character, habits, etc.—and all the family circumstances, besides any wish of yours she can with ease insinuate to Princess Christian with whom she is always in correspondence.

I think, as you do, it would be the best thing in the world for Alix to be with you for a little while when B. is absent. This could be perhaps after she had been with us. But all this you could talk over so well with Wally if you could only see her.

---

[1] The Kingdom of Italy had been proclaimed in February 1861 and had been recognised by England and France.

— 76 —

From the Queen

As dear Fritz is so kind and affectionate and so ready to help me, I have desired Mr. Rulandt (who really is invaluable) to write to him upon a subject in which he may give our good Louis some good advice. He will not however tell him, but I do you, of the highly improper tone of the letter Louis wrote to poor Alice on this question of the Secretary a letter which I hardly know how to qualify, from its tone. It may have been written in a passion but the worst of it is that (though she says little about it and behaves extremely well) it must have lowered Louis in her eyes; it has (as well as various other things) done so very considerably in mine. However I think it will soon be over; but the stupidity and pettiness of the parents and all (so different to your mother-in-law) is dreadful. I begin to fear that dear Papa saw more clearly than we did about the whole. Louis has however a good and excellent heart and is very honest and unselfish. But he is inexperienced and, I fear, not as refined as I could wish. When your dear Fritz also did not understand the appointment of E. Stockmar he wrote—but how differently! How I wish Fritz would tell Louis that it was of the highest importance that, from the beginning, the tone and manner between the young couple should not only be one of love, affection and confidence, but of mutual regard. This Fritz ever showed you; angel Papa ever showed me. This I ever felt so strongly towards him (I mean in private)—and that that love of boy and girl—which during Louis' last visit shocked Aunt Feodora and Ernest and Marie, should be laid aside, else it will soon end in mutual disgust. Well, dearest, it is so true, and just from the peculiar nature of intimacies between husband and wife so necessary God knows! Beloved Papa would have told all this to him, and it would never have happened very likely; but dear Fritz, with kindness, will I hope speak openly and strongly—for Louis' behaviour the last time and this letter have not been at all what we could wish. I fear Alice dreads her sad marriage, and this unhappy affair, in which Louis has really lowered himself very much, grieves me deeply, for it must add to all her sorrow and anxiety. All this I beg you to read and explain to dear Fritz (and keep to yourselves alone) and beg him to write or talk very openly to that really foolish boy. But you must not say anything to Alice about it. She however begged me to get Fritz to speak to him about it all as she dreads all I have mentioned, and also another thing, which Papa would have been very severe about, viz: that he does not bring his young officer friends into her society and intimacy, for that would be most dangerous. I need not tell you that any want of delicacy in his conduct toward Alice would produce the greatest indignation here.

Oh! how dreadful it is to be here without dearest Papa and to be fighting and struggling, weak and ill, by one self! But we all have such confidence in dearest Fritz. I had meant to write to him, but I feel so tired and am so nervous that I must do it through you and Rulandt. I will see what I can do about the Pagets, but the best would be if you write to Lord Granville. Lord Canning's death is a great loss and yet how touching, how blessed to follow so soon.[1] How it fills me with hope for myself!

I can give you a very good report of Bertie. He is much improved and is ready to do every thing I wish, and we get on very well. He is much less coarse looking and the expression of the eyes is so much better.

Alas! the dear General is still very unwell. There is a very bad state of the liver which will make his recovery tedious—to say the least. He is in London and must be kept quite quiet. Sir C. Phipps acts for him. Dr. Stanley has done great good and is so kind, affectionate, clever and good.

Dear Uncle is decidedly improving. I think under all circumstances the meeting with Princess Alexandra must take place at Laeken.[2] How we miss the assistance and wisdom of your mother-in-law who helped us through all our difficulties before your marriage. You both owe her so much that you must never forget that, when you have little

---

[1] Earl Canning (1812–62), Governor-general of India. Lady Canning had died from jungle-fever shortly before the Prince Consort.
[2] The Queen means the first meeting between herself and the Princess.

difficulties. In Princess C.[1] (excellent and good as she is) we find no help, no assistance, no great and large views and Alice feels this already painfully. I know dear Papa felt this. I mention it because you used to say how easy it would be for her and how difficult it was for you, whereas I fear it will be just as difficult for her, and she will now, more than ever, miss a clever companion.

All I tell you here is for yourself and Fritz alone and for the good Baron—but no one else. I love Louis much, and therefore it annoys me doubly.

I have just had very good accounts from dear Uncle.

I am so sorry you are so uncomfortable—but summer is a dreadful time for these affairs, and spring is the only bearable one. I must end at last.

From the Queen

OSBORNE, JUNE 21, 1862

Dear General Bruce's state is a great sorrow and anxiety in the midst of my terrible grief. God spare him and I have hope—though of course now one thinks there can be none when any one is ill—that he will get well through it. It is a complication with the liver which makes one so anxious and the pulse keeps so high and the weakness is great, and diarrhoea continues. They fear an abscess in the liver, which they cannot speak with certainty of—for some days. However if he has strength he may pull well through it. But he is so valuable that it is a terrible anxiety. In the meantime, Sir C. Phipps, General Grey and Colonel Biddulph[2] have kindly undertaken to act (according to their convenience) for him. I think it would be very important that I should see the Pagets and put them in confidential communication with Sir C. Phipps, General Grey and Augusta. But I might see them here in July, or at Balmoral in August. Just tell me what is best.

---

[1] Of Hesse-Darmstadt. Mother of Prince Louis and first cousin of the King of Prussia.
[2] Colonel afterwards Sir Thomas Biddulph (1809–78), Master of the Queen's Household.

I am so glad that my proposal about Charlotte and dear little William too has not been found unreasonable and that you are inclined to consider it. I would never ask for a thing which would or could do you or the children harm. I am so sorry for the state of your affairs. God knows! we are all in a sad state. Here all is quiet and satisfactory. I send you a beautiful poem by a young student at Cambridge. Please let me have this copy back.[1]

From the Crown Princess

NEUES PALAIS, JUNE 21, 1862

Many thanks for your long letter by messenger—the contents of which have really grieved me very much. I cannot understand what can have possessed Louis to write an uncivil letter or to raise objections to the appointment of a secretary and treasurer for Alice, when he had (I thought) agreed to it, and understood the necessity of having such a person, already a year ago. I am quite astonished. I think you must attribute it to thoughtlessness and want of experience, and you may be sure in a little time hence he will greatly see the benefit of what you wish and be very grateful to you for the very thing he now combats.

Prejudice and jealousy you will find in all small German States and in the large ones too, for heaven knows we had and have enough to do with it here, and the Court of Darmstadt is singularly impregnated with the like absurdities though not more than Meiningen, Hanover, and Mecklenburg.

Fritz will do all he possibly can—he is quite of your opinion and can speak strongly from conviction and experience to Louis. But I am sure you will see what an ennobling and enlightening influence Alice will have over him—and how in a short time you will find those sorts of difficulties disappear of themselves. When I said that Elisabeth[2] would be easier to get on with for Alice than the Queen is for me,

---

[1] A poem by James Rhoades, of Trinity College, which obtained the Chancellor's Medal in this year.
[2] i.e. Princess Charles of Hesse.

I meant that she is not of an imperious and tyrannical disposition and of a violent temper as my mother-in-law is, though we get on so well together. I feel I am sure what I owe to her, and she feels that she has no truer friend, and no one who understands her views and her trials better than I do. I am really from my heart attached to her and should be very ungrateful if I was not. I admire her great qualities and pity her most sincerely, but she has often made my life neither pleasant nor easy.[1] Elisabeth is quite negative—and is happier in her own family and I think loves Alice very much.

As for Louis not being quite so refined as you would wish, I think after his marriage this too will greatly change; he is young of his age, and the feeling of his responsibility will call out all his many good qualities. I am really spoilt in this respect—my own darling Fritz is singularly gifted with refinement, delicacy and tact, so thoroughly noble and gentleman-like in all his feelings, thoughts and actions. This springs from his kind and generous heart, his pure mind, elevated sentiments and strong principles, and also from his sweet and amiable temper. What a blessed thing it is when besides one's deep love, one can give one's whole confidence and esteem as you did and as I do! But how very few there are of whom one can say this! Alice and Louis are so much nearer of an age than Fritz and I are (I was but a child—and he a grown up man) whereas Alice is older of her age than Louis is of his. For this reason it seems to me doubly necessary that they should have a person of experience whom they can place their confidence in and consult upon so many subjects—indeed I think it would be dangerous to let them be without such a person. Fritz will tell Louis that he would not know what to do if we had not so excellent and invaluable a friend as the Baron—though Fritz himself was at first, from the same prejudices and ignorance as Louis, so much against his appointment. Fritz

---

[1] A quarter of a century later, when her mother-in-law died, the Crown Princess wrote, "I will try not to remember all that was so hard and bitter, and all I had to endure in thirty years." *The Empress Frederick writes to Sophie*, edited by A. G. Lee, page 55.

has no prejudices now, and I think if you have patience with Louis, you will see his wear off too by degrees.

Oh if you could but have Dr. Becker for Alice—such an excellent man, and in every way so adapted for this position. Could you not try once more whether you could get him?

I have not yet said what great and sincere pleasure your praise of Bertie gave us! May God prosper his efforts to keep in those right paths, for his and for your real happiness.

I heard from Wally Paget—what annoyed me very much—namely that Uncle George wrote to Princess Christian all about Bertie's unfortunate story, and told her besides that you were very angry with Bertie and that there was complete discord between you and him. Wally found Princess Christian one day in floods of tears with this letter from Uncle George in her hands and in great distress about it, saying she feared her daughter would be unhappy and that you would dislike her too if she became Bertie's wife, and that it would make her daughter's position dreadfully difficult etc. She had not heard a word of all this before. Of course Uncle George did not do this out of ill-nature, but it was foolish and indiscreet, and springs from that insatiable love of gossip which makes the members of that family so dangerous. I was so much provoked when I heard it, and so unnecessary to make the poor Princess so uneasy. Do you not think it would be well to tell this to Bertie? It would put him more on his guard with Uncle George.

I am sure that if you wish to have Dr. Becker for Alice— you can get him now, as he said to me, "if he thought he could be of real material use he would consider it his duty not to refuse—however unwillingly he might quit his profession." I am sure you could have no one better. Perhaps you have some one in view for Alice already? I cannot say how I should regret Dr. Becker leaving Berlin for myself—as he is such a resource.

From the Queen

Your dear, affectionate long letter of the 21st was very soothing to me and I thank you much for it. We are still in such terrible anxiety about our dear and valued General Bruce! God Almighty spare him—but as dear Augusta said that what frightened her was, that—"dear Robert is so good!" Oh! is it not too mysterious? Does it not show us that there must be great and good work to do in another world—else why should all be taken or threatened to be, who are most necessary?

I wrote a few lines to dear Fritz and sent him another letter of poor Louis—a most foolish one. Of course it annoys me and poor dear Alice sadly, but we shall be very patient and very affectionate and the more Louis can be got out of that most benighted set the better. If you think Elisabeth is negative—you err; she is very active and also very grand. I unfortunately know this to be so. All this makes poor Alice not at all look forward to her marriage, which in every thing is so different to yours. About good Becker, I can only say that for a short time we must ask him to help Alice but that—from being a Hessian I hardly think he would do permanently, but this we must wait to see.

Bertie (though no resource or support) goes on being as amiable, good and sensible as anyone of us could wish, and dear Augusta says it is such a comfort to them to feel that her dear brother's anxious efforts and wishes should not have been in vain!—He (B.) is most anxious about his marriage, hopes it may be in March or April (!!) and has bought numbers of pretty things for the young lady.

I showed him what you told me about Uncle George and he is furious. It would be well if Wally could let Princess Christian know the truth; viz. that wicked wretches had led our poor, innocent boy into a scrape which had caused his beloved father and myself the deepest pain (the knowledge of which we only obtained just before the fatal illness) but that both of us had forgiven him this (one) sad mistake, that we had never disagreed, and that I was very confident he would make a steady[1] husband; that quite the contrary I looked to his wife as being his salvation, for that he was very domestic and longed to be at home. That I was exceedingly satisfied and pleased with him since his return and thought him immensely improved.

From the Queen

Two words to send you the copy of the answer I received from Louis. Bertie found him still very foolish but much alarmed and distressed at hearing Alice was so much hurt and annoyed, and so she is—and with right. We are terribly anxious about our dear, dear General Bruce. We can't and mustn't give up hope—but it is a very serious case!

From the Queen

God tries us sorely! We have lost the most dear and valued friend we had—our poor Bertie his second father! Dear, dear General Bruce! he has sacrificed his valued life for our poor dear child! And Bertie is quite overwhelmed by it! Poor, dear child! he is indeed very forlorn. Oh! God! for what purpose is all this? No doubt for the best—but it is hard, hard to bear! Affie—arrived! Those two dear boys look so nice together; it was often my dream to see them grown up, with their adored young father, and now he is gone— and I am alone! But God seems to have blessed them, for they are both so improved! God's blessing will rest on those dear children yet.

This last blow has quite crushed our poor dear Alice, who loved our beloved General with filial affection and she looks wretched. This poor, unhappy marriage is more like a funeral than a wedding! God grant that dear, excellent and most sorely tried child may be as happy as she deserves. She is sadly shaken and far from strong.

---

[1] The Queen originally wrote "excellent".

The marriage is at 1 on Tuesday in the dining room—just under the family picture.[1]

From the Queen

OSBORNE, JULY 2, 1862

Poor Alice's wedding (more like a funeral than a wedding) is over and she is a wife! I say God bless her—though a dagger is plunged in my bleeding, desolate heart when I hear from her this morning that she is "proud and happy" to be Louis' wife! I feel what I had, what I hoped to have for at least 20 years more and what I can only have in another world again. All that has passed since December 14 seems gone—forgotten. What I shall not forget is Alice herself, and her wonderful bearing—such calmness, self-possession and dignity, and how really beautiful she looked, so tall, and graceful, and her voice so sweet. The Archbishop of York read that fine service (purified from its worst coarsenesses) admirably, and himself had tears running down his cheeks—for he too lost his dear partner not long ago.[2] I sat the whole time in an armchair, with our four boys near me; Bertie and Affie led me down stairs. The latter sobbed all through and afterwards—dreadfully.

Dear Uncle Ernest is very low, and sad and was much affected. It was a comfort to me that he, darling Papa's only brother, led her and gave her away! I had rather he than any one else should do it. He was so affectionate at our marriage.

Prince and Princess Charles were much affected—but we none of us like her, and Alice not at all. She was very cold, very grand and not at all affectionate to Alice and most unamiable (and I must call it "de mauvaise foi") about Alice's living a good deal here and about what is right and proper. But she has nothing to say and Louis is all right about it and most amiable. Alice is very determined and from the first has taken her position vis-à-vis of the "mother-in-law". But

---

[1] The family group by Winterhalter.
[2] Charles Longley, shortly afterwards appointed to Canterbury. His wife had died in 1858.

I am sorry it should be so. I shall certainly see the Pagets as soon as possible and put General Grey and Sir C. Phipps (he knows more about Bertie even than the other, General Bruce being so very intimate with him) in communication with them.

I must end for today. Tomorrow I shall go over to see the "Honey-Couple", who return here on Friday and on Tuesday evening, 8th, they embark.[1]

From the Queen

We visited the "Honey-Couple" on Thursday evening with Aunt, your two sisters, and Bertie and found dear Alice and Louis quiet and happy—but oh! it all seemed so sad. And she looks so serious, so unlike the excited bride of 58! But then all is so dreadfully sad! All steeped in mourning and poor dear Alice has gone through so much— the sight of my dreadful grief not being the least of it all— that no wonder she should be melancholy and serious.

Louis is very kind and very affectionate but here also to me, things are different to what they were with adored Papa and Fritz. You know what I mean. But he is so good and kind, so discreet and affectionate, that Alice will be happy. Here, Alice seems far the oldest though he is six years older than her!

I have appointed good Mrs. Bruce,[2] who is very clever, discreet and excellent, Extra Bed-Chamber Woman—and she will assist dear Augusta and take her place, whenever Augusta wants leave. She does want it—and I feel I must have some one constantly.

---

[1] The honeymoon was spent near Ryde.
[2] Katherine, daughter of Sir Michael Shaw-Stewart, 6th Bt., and widow of General Bruce. She was appointed an Extra Bed-Chamber Woman to the Princess of Wales in the following year and Bed-Chamber Woman in Ordinary to the Queen in 1866. She died at Victoria Station in 1889. She was of course sister-in-law to Lady Augusta Bruce and some (including the Crown Princess) regretted that the Queen admitted few outside this family to her intimate circle.

Now goodbye and God bless you. What dear Fritz is to us all, I cannot say! God bless him for it. He is our great main stay now—since we are left without help!

From the Crown Princess

Fritz has just returned and as you can imagine I left him no peace until he had satisfied my curiosity (which had been pent up for a whole week) entirely. How happy I am to hear that all went off so well. How lovely Alice must have looked—but yet how sad and wretched the whole must have been.

Many, many thanks for your dear kind letter by messenger—and for the lovely sketch of the wedding by Thomas[1] which of course gave me a better idea of it than all description however good and accurate. I hope I may keep this sketch as you say nothing about it—at any rate until you ask for it.

Fritz cannot say enough of your kindness and affection to him, really you could not have a son who was more attached to you than he is. What a blessing that Bertie seems to wish his marriage! I rejoice sincerely to hear it.

As our present idea is not to return to Berlin after leaving you at Reinhardtsbrunn but to start from there on our tour and to remain away till two or three days before Christmas (so as not to spend those most terrible days where I did last year) you would perhaps allow Bertie to join us on our journey. We could pay Max and Charlotte[2] a visit, also the Hohenzollerns[3] at the Weinburg in Switzerland—and perhaps see something of the coast along the Mediterranean if there was a possibility of having the "Osborne". But I fear this would be asking too much—and I feel quite afraid to express such a wish.

---

[1] George Housman Thomas (1824–68). His picture of Princess Alice's wedding was exhibited at the Academy in 1863.

[2] Archduke Maximilian, later Emperor of Mexico. He married the only daughter of King Leopold. She was insane for the last 60 years of her life.

[3] Prince of Hohenzollern-Sigmaringen and his family.

I am sorry to hear from Fritz and also to see by your letter that Elisabeth[1] behaved so strangely—and produced an unfavourable impression. What a pity! And what can be the reason?

From the Queen

OSBORNE, JULY 9, 1862

Yesterday was a sad day.[2] Alice, dear, excellent child is an immense loss for she has been a support, a comfort, which no one can sufficiently estimate and in my very reduced state I could not have allowed her marriage for another year—if she were not to return at the end of October or beginning of November. I am quite easy and happy about the young ménage. They are quietly, really happy—and Louis dear boy, is so nice, and very sensible about Alice's health and so unselfish, so affectionate towards me, so little playing the husband or taking possession of her. I wish I felt as easy about darling Alice's health as I do about her happiness! She looks very delicate, and very frail since the last 10 days. We all anxiously hope she may not begin having a family soon and the doctors think it is likely. However all is in God's hands as dearest Papa used always to say—that we must take what comes with resignation and with satisfaction and gratitude, according to what it was.

I hope dear, that your second nurse is not equal to Mrs. Hobbs? We never had a second nurse, but only a head nursery maid, capable to act as nurse, and I hope you will not attempt the contrary or you will entirely fail. Dear Papa always directed our nursery and I believe none was ever better; I therefore should be sorry, if you went upon another system.

The sketch by Thomas is not mine, and was never ordered by me. Thomas told me Count Furstenstein[3]

---

[1] Prince Louis' mother.
[2] Princess Alice and her husband left Osborne for Germany.
[3] Gentleman-in-Waiting to the Crown Prince. He was described by Walburga Lady Paget as "very artistic and a man of the world, although quite young".

ordered it. I know not how that is. Your plans for the autumn sound excellent. I must end in great haste and will write more fully on Saturday.

I feel your love and affection most deeply, darling, and try not to lose courage—but I am disheartened about every thing. Bertie is not improved by Affie's presence, and they both get lowered in tone by constant contact.

From the Queen

OSBORNE, JULY 10, 1862

The messenger did not go yesterday and so I add a few lines today to say that I should like to see the Pagets here on the 17th and they could stay till the 19th. I have decided on General Knollys being our dear General Bruce's successor—though he will not be called Governor any more.[1] He is the only person I know who would at all do, and he came to my mind at once as one who beloved Papa had a very high opinion of and had once thought of putting about Bertie. Poor Bertie feels the loss of his dear General very deeply—and I pity the poor, helpless, forlorn child very much. It is quite touching to see how he clings to Augusta and Fanny[2] who are both here. Dear Augusta is very much shaken.

From the Crown Princess

NEUES PALAIS, JULY 8, 1862

If you were to see me now you would think me so like Mrs. Farquharson.[3] If I had a pair of spectacles on, and a beryl stone with three diamond drops on my forehead, I should look her very image! Our affairs here are in a lamentable state—indecision, confusion and mistakes of

---

[1] Sir William Knollys, a veteran soldier, aged 65. He became Controller and Treasurer to the Prince. His son was to become the Prince's secretary and his daughter Charlotte was the life-long confidante of the Princess of Wales.
[2] The General's sisters. Fanny was Lady Francis Baillie.
[3] Mrs. Farquharson of Invercauld, a neighbour at Balmoral.

all kinds and sorts are "l'ordre du jour". The reactionary party get stronger every day and have the King now completely on their side and in their power they succeed in carrying all their hurtful measures—and injure every true patriot and sensible man by raising suspicions against them. The King has become quite "inabordable" on these subjects; the least allusion to them drives him into a frenzy and excites all the opposition in his nature so that it is totally impossible to argue or reason with him, either for the Queen or us or for any one. The only thing to be done is to remain as passive and keep as much out of the way as possible.

I never thought it would be as bad and as hopeless as all this, though I well knew when the Kreuss party came into office, there was no knowing to what it would not lead! What would darling Papa say to all this? He would be shocked and distressed beyond measure, but I am sure he would pity Fritz who is in a most difficult and painful position—and approve of his conduct.

Who wrote the "New Philosophy"? I admire it and enjoy reading it beyond measure. I should like to translate it—if I were not too stupid.

Could you not manage in any way to see Fritz Holstein and Ada when you are in Germany?[1] I think it would be so very desirable after your meeting with Prince and Princess C. It would show that your feelings are not the least altered towards the Augustenburgs by the union with the others!

From the Queen

OSBORNE, JULY 12, 1862

Your dear affectionate letter of the 8th reached me the day before yesterday and I hasten to thank you for it. Your account of yourself as being like Mrs. Farquharson amused

---

[1] He was the hereditary Prince of Schleswig-Holstein-Sonderburg-Augustenburg, and had married the Queen's niece—daughter of her half-sister Princess Feodora. By "the others" the Princess means the rival branch (Schleswig-Holstein-Sonderburg-Glücksburg) to which Prince Christian belonged.

me very much; I do pity you to be in that state in this weather. Spring is the only bearable time for these "campaigns" and except four—all of you were spring flowers.

Dear Aunt Feodora (who has been confined to her room with a cold since Tuesday) had already—without the very wise reason you suggest—asked me whether I would see dear Ada when I was at Reinhardtsbrunn, and I said yes. Everything must be done to show that the proposed marriage makes no change.

Will you tell the Queen that though I have refused seeing any one—I shall manage to see her brother privately.[1] I mean to do the same for the poor Grand-Duke of Mecklenburg-Schwerin[2] whose relationship to dear Papa, as well as his importance, makes him an object of interest to me.

No one knows who wrote the "New Philosophy" or if the man is dead or alive. A great deal is excellent but it lacks "the love which passeth all understanding" and Christ's blessed doctrine—which is so necessary for this and the next life.

From the Crown Princess

NEUES PALAIS, JULY 12, 1862

Mr. Paget was here yesterday and I talked with him about Princess A. "en long et en large", and about the most unhappy Schleswig Holstein question. He is a very discreet and trustworthy person besides being clever and I think you will be very glad to see him and talk to him. He knows all the circumstances of Prince Christian and his family so very well that he can put you quite "au fait".

Whenever I think of the poor Augustenburgs I feel quite a pang and really quite as if I were a culprit—but it can't be helped. I feel so sure that in trying to be of

---

[1] The reigning Grand-Duke of Saxe-Weimar.
[2] Frederick Grand-Duke of Mecklenburg-Schwerin (1823–83). His wife had died in the previous March. His grandmother was a princess of Saxe-Gotha. "Important" because he was an outstanding advocate of German unity.

use to you in securing this sweet and lovely creature as a wife for Bertie I am doing my duty and have no option left. Besides I so often think Bertie would be just as likely to marry her if Fritz and I did not wish it at all—as I really do not see who else he is to take, and surely that would be worse for all parties then. Whereas now we are all friends —and I cannot see that this should be a misfortune for Germany. It is no political marriage and in treating it as such we should be doing and bringing about the very thing we wish to prevent; at least so it seems to me.

The Baron[1] writes to me from Marienbad: "They have once again considerably upset my father about a certain mark on the neck of a certain young lady but I have written him that this mark has often been discussed before and I hope he will calm down."

You see people wish to prevent the thing "à tout prix". As taking away the reputation of the poor young Princess and of her mother has not succeeded they try to make her out unhealthy and go and frighten the old Baron about it; it is really too bad. I spoke to Mr. Paget about that but he said if that mark on the Princess's neck had been what people say it is (out of mischief) it must have put an end to any thoughts of having her for Bertie at once, but he could assure me he knew it was nothing whatever but a cold on which a stupid doctor had tried experiments and he told me all about it.

I think darling Papa felt quite satisfied by the explanation which I gave on this subject when it was first mentioned last year.

From the Crown Princess

NEUES PALAIS, JULY 15, 1862

Yesterday the anniversary of the "attentat" on the King reminded me so much of last year, when darling Papa was so kind and arranged Fritz's journey for him so quickly and now Fritz's father a grey-headed man is alive

[1] Young Baron Stockmar.

and well and our dear, darling Papa, so young is gone! But "the ripest fruit soonest falls to the ground".

I shall tell the Queen that you are going to see her brother. They say the Grand-Duke of Schwerin has got over his misfortune wonderfully soon. I do not know whether this is so as I have not seen him since; he is a very good man, but possessed of very few wits, and very tiresome; his odious brother is now with his mother and we have the advantage of seeing them very often.[1]

Prince F. of the Netherlands is so kind and sympathetic —he wishes me to say so much to you; he is such an amiable excellent man.[2]

The heat is something awful today. I am in a state which I can not describe—almost suffocated, and everybody else is enjoying it so much, and wonders that I find it warm.

I have been reading Motley's—"United Netherlands".[3] How extremely interesting it is, so clever and so well written. I am sure beloved Papa would have delighted in it. I never read a book or a sentence which pleases me without thinking of him and how he would like it. All things that interest me seem to have only half their interest, as he was so bound up with the idea of everything that was good, great, beautiful, clever or useful. There is nobody ever in this wide world whose opinion is so valuable as his was! How happy he must now be at the source of all the knowledge he so dearly loved the faintest gleam of here! And

---

[1] Duke William of Mecklenburg-Schwerin; he was only brother to the reigning duke whom the Queen refers to on 12 July. They were sons of a sister of the King of Prussia.
[2] Prince Frederick, uncle of the King of Holland, William III, had married another sister of the King of Prussia.
[3] J. L. Motley (1814–77), the American historian. *The United Netherlands* was first published in 1860. When she went to Vienna at the end of this year, the Crown Princess said that Motley was the only person she wished to see outside the Imperial Family. Writing to his mother after they had met Motley said: "She is rather *petite*, has a fresh young face with pretty features, fine teeth, and a frank and agreeable smile and an interested, earnest and intelligent manner. Nothing could be simpler or more natural than her style, which I should say was the perfection of good breeding."

how must we all work while we are left in this world to be fit to share the joys he now has! I feel this more every day, and I think we must be grateful for the time that is left (we know not how long it is) for us to prepare ourselves to come as near his perfection here—that we may be as much as possible on the same footing with him hereafter. I always feel if I were to die now I should not be fit to be where he is—I have done nothing yet to deserve it—but I pray to be more and more fitted for such an end.

I regret that dear Uncle Ernest should have been at Frankfort and have held a speech, as the people now assembled there—if they be patriots at all—are not of the choicest kind.

Is it true that Louis of Portugal is going to marry the King of Italy's daughter? In his letter to you which I saw, he did not seem much inclined that way but the newspapers give his engagement as a "fait accompli".[1]

From the Queen

OSBORNE, JULY 16, 1862

Many, many thanks for your dear letter of the 12th. I shall talk very fully to the Pagets and hope all will be well managed and arranged. We have done right and God will bless us though, dear child, I own that my courage, my strength—all, all seems to fail me! I have perfect confidence in General Knollys and had a most satisfactory conversation with him on Sunday. He has since seen all the papers about Bertie's marriage and says he thinks it perfectly clear that in spite of all the difficulties it is the only right thing to do, and he said: "How magnanimous the conduct of the Crown Prince and Crown Princess has been."[2]

I saw the good Grand-Duke of Weimar yesterday, who was so kind, and made me think of happy, former days; and

---

[1] The King of Portugal married in October 1862 Marie Pie, daughter of King Victor Emanuel of Italy.
[2] Meaning in encouraging the marriage which, because of the Danish question, could not be popular in Prussia and other parts of Germany.

on Monday, Sir C. Locock[1] who is very well and much less deaf. I hope you will take care that Mrs. Hobbs is quite the head nurse else it won't go on! That every one will tell you, who has ever had a nursery.

From the Queen

I shall try and answer your last letters—which I have done so badly lately, but my memory is now so extremely bad that I forget every thing, unless I put it down. It is a great trouble, but it is getting like the poor late King of P.[2] I forget names, places and anything the very minute after I have been told—and a sort of blank comes over me, quite bewildering me. We had Dr. Stanley here for four nights and I talked a great deal with him, and think him quite charming and the most unclerical and yet religious clergyman I ever talked to. Such a large, tender, refined mind. His sermons preached before Bertie, he has printed and I think beautiful—and you can see how they were intended for Bertie.[3]

The Pagets have been here since the 17th and I have talked over every single point with Wally, who is charming, so sensible and full of tact—and also with Mr. Paget and upon that vexed S. Holstein question. To save time I will tell Wally to write all to you. There will be a slight modification in the plan about Bertie. Instead of his returning with me[4]—and then going out again (which might look odd just before his birthday) he would join you at once—and only come back at the end of November or beginning of December. I think, dear, there would be no difficulty about the Osborne for you and Bertie—quite the contrary. I don't think, dear, you should stay the whole time with us

---

[1] The physician-accoucheur to the Queen who was going to Berlin for the Crown Princess's lying-in.
[2] Prussia.
[3] These were publicly circulated in 1863: "Sermons preached before the Prince of Wales during his tour in the East in the Spring of 1862, with Notices of some of the localities visited."
[4] When the Queen came back from Germany.

at Reinhardtsbrunn, because I shall go once between to Coburg and if it is cold I may have to go to Gotha into Uncle Ernest's house. Respecting the children, you will tell me what you settle and wish.

All you say about your politics is very, very sad! How it would indeed grieve dearest Papa—indeed most likely it does, though he sees everything with "larger eyes" as Tennyson says!

From the Crown Princess

NEUES PALAIS, JULY 19, 1862

Fritz is taking a very tiring journey; fêtes, receptions and speeches everywhere. Till now all seems to have gone off very well. It is very difficult for him as the King required of him before he went not to say anything "oppositional" or to allow any criticism of the Government in his presence. It is perfectly impossible to tell what the King calls "opposition" as he takes offence at the most harmless expressions. The King leans very much towards that wretch Bismarck Schönhausen[1] and will probably take him as prime minister. What will be the consequence heaven alone knows, he is a most unprincipled and unrespectable character—a brouillon and an adventurer—quite unreliable and the worst enemy the poor Queen has. Count Bernstorff[2] does all he can to make the King take him—as he (B.) wants to go back to London and have his pay raised. I think it is abominable of him.

Bismarck has been in London and has done all he could to irritate the King against England and Lord Palmerston and Lord Russell and even against poor Lord Augustus,[3] which is too bad, but Bismarck is such a wicked man that he does not care how many fibs he tells to serve his own purposes, and this is the man who is to govern this country.

---

[1] The family came from Schönhausen in Brandenburg.
[2] He was Prussian Ambassador in London (1854–61), Foreign Minister, 1861–2, and returned to London in 1862.
[3] Lord Augustus Loftus (1817–1904), diplomatist. Minister at Berlin, 1860–2.

I assure you it makes my hair stand on end! I only hope some means may be found to avert such a calamity.

Fritz returns on Monday evening. Sir Charles Locock has arrived. It is really a load off my mind, and I cannot thank you enough for having made him come. I have lost all confidence in the German treatment and I really thought if I did not have Sir Charles or an English doctor I should not get through the business at all.

From the Queen

BALMORAL, JULY 25, 1862

I have sent for and begun to read Butler's "Analogy of Religion",[1] a very celebrated book—quoted I believe by Parker[2] also—which Countess Blücher sent me an extract from—and which seems very admirable, though the style is rather involved. But I think you would like it and would be interested by it. Then I have got a book (two small volumes) by old Sir B. Brodie[3] on Psychology which I think likewise interesting, and which might interest you. These are the only things besides religious books which I can fix my attention upon now. Bertie is going to Birk Hall[4] on Monday, and I think it is better now he should. Too long here is not a good thing.

From the Queen

BALMORAL, JULY 29, 1862

Bertie is gone to Birk Hall; yesterday he went. The Biddulphs are there and General Knollys comes on

---

[1] This was written by Joseph Butler, the eighteenth-century Bishop of Durham.
[2] Parker is probably Theodore Parker, the American Unitarian minister, who was widely read.
[3] Sir Benjamin Brodie (1783–1862), surgeon to the Royal Family. He published anonymously in 1854 *Psychological Inquiries* and a second series in 1862 under his own name.
[4] The eighteenth-century manor-house on the Balmoral estate. Later, as a married man, the Prince was lent Abergeldie Castle, which was leased from the owner by the Queen.

Thursday. Poor Bertie!—he is very affectionate and dutiful but he is very trying. The idleness is the same—and there is a great roughness of manner to his brothers and sisters which must be got the better of. Still he is most anxious to do what is right, that is every thing. But his idleness and "désœuvrement", his listlessness and want of attention are great, and cause me much anxiety.

From the Crown Princess

I have read Sir B. Brodie's book on psychology—a little while ago and think it excellent. It is a subject which interests me particularly, and I have gained a great deal of useful information from his nice little book. I have also been reading a book of Dr. Darwin's—which has a great name[1]—besides Parker's and George Combe's other works —and Motley's "Rise of the Dutch Republic", which is splendid and from the beautiful and excellent "Œuvres de ma cher Tocqueville" his life, his speeches and his journey in America, which are beyond measure interesting. I have besides been reading some of "Aeschyllus" and "Euripides" in German as I had not yet read those grand and magnificent works—but of course all these things I could not recommend to you as in your present frame of mind you would most likely not care about them. I have not read so much as I had intended as the newspapers and pamphlets which one must read take up one's time. The Revue des deux Mondes is full of interesting articles—as also the Grenzboten of which Mr. Freitag is the editor, and the Prussian Year-Books.

Samwer was here yesterday—he persists in saying that he knows "from a lady who was educated with the young Princess—that the mark on her neck is from scrofula". Really one does not know what to say to prove the contrary to people who are so difficult to convince!

---

[1] Presumably *Origin of Species.*

From the Queen

I have not thanked you for your dear letter of the 29th. in which you speak of all the books you read. How many interesting, difficult books you read. It would and will please beloved Papa.

Sir B. Brodie's book I like very much indeed; I have not finished the first volume yet. Have you ever read any of Y. Paul's works? His "Silence" contains beautiful things. Dear Papa admired them—much. I find Combe's works so very material! He writes (unintentionally I believe) as if we could live for ever in this world, only minding our bodies for the general good! If the whole world would agree never to transgress any of these laws it might perhaps answer—but as this never will be the case it is a too low view of morality. Life must be risked for higher duties!

Now goodbye and God bless and protect you now and always!—My thoughts and the thoughts of many, many loving and devoted ones are with you now! And beloved Papa's prayers and blessings—far more efficacious than ours!

From the Queen

BALMORAL, AUGUST 8, 1862

You keep us waiting very impatiently, but I take it quietly—hoping that you are not too uncomfortable. We had all hoped it might be on dear Affie's birthday, which would have been very nice. We are very thankful for dear Louise's safety and hope she will go on well. A girl must be a disappointment but as the Duc de Malakhoff said, in announcing the birth of his daughter (which delighted beloved Papa) "Comme les garçons suivent toujours les jolies filles", the boy it is hoped will follow.

Mr. Helps has been here since the 5th and he has read to me his proposed preface to beloved Papa's Speeches, and the character which he has written most beautifully; I talked a great deal with him about beloved Papa and made him alter several of the points—and add some—and now I think it is perfect. And what a character it is!

From the Queen

BALMORAL, AUGUST 12, 1862

We went over to Birk Hall yesterday. Bertie gets on very well with General Knollys who understands him, and our difficulties. I feel more and more nervous as the time approaches, for my seeing the young Princess, and Bertie is himself terribly nervous. We must make it as easy as we can for him.

Baby is most amusing and her sayings are charming. Lenchen shall send you an account of them. One is about Lot's wife;—"Is it the salt I eat with my chicken"? and she insisted on Mrs. Bruce writing to Dr. Stanley to explain it!

From the Crown Princess

NEUES PALAIS, AUGUST 12, 1862

I send you a copy of a most interesting autograph which belongs to Fritz—which I am sure will strike you. It shows what a good and judicious mother the Empress Maria Theresa was—and the advice she gives her son is quite excellent. He was the last Elector of Cologne, and grew to such an enormous size that he lost his balance and fell from his horse while carrying the sceptre at the Coronation of the Emperor.[1]

May I beg for the copy back again when you have done with it?

---

[1] He was Maria Theresa's youngest son. "A good-natured, neither here nor there kind of youth" was his description by the eighteenth-century traveller, Henry Swinburne.

From the Queen

By my telegram and my letters to dear Fritz and the Countess you will know how thankful and rejoiced we are at the birth of your dear little boy,[1] and that all went off so well and you were spared all the usual discomfort and suffering you had before—thanks to (for once) good and reasonable management! To beloved Papa, you owe Sir C. Locock's being with you; for you know how anxious he was for your comfort—and how alarmed at the way things went on the last time. God bless you dearest child!

I hope you will get my little work basket—the first piece of work I touched since December 14!! Yesterday was a very trying day—beloved Grandmama's birthday!

The instructions of Maria Theresa are admirable and seem as if meant for Bertie. You shall have them back by messenger. Mrs. Bruce has copied them for me.

The time fast approaches for my journey and makes me very sad, very nervous, very anxious, but I remain firm to my purpose.

From the Queen

BALMORAL, AUGUST 22, 1862

Many, many thanks for all your dear messages. Since I wrote to you, I have been to Alt-na-Guithasach yesterday morning. We went through a sad ceremony. I and my six orphans went up (I—wonderful to say—in my little carriage) to the top of Craig Lowrigan—just opposite Craig Gowan and placed the first stones (at least some stones), in the front of which all our initials will be carved in large letters; and we have placed at the end the initials of you three absent ones, thinking you would like it! It shook and agitated me much. It will be 40 feet at the base—and 35 feet high and the following inscription is to be placed

---

[1] Henry Albert William (1862–1929), Prince Henry of Prussia. Born on 14 August.

on it—in very large letters: "To the beloved memory of Albert the great and good, Prince Consort. Raised by his broken-hearted Widow.

Victoria R

August 21, 1862

He being made perfect in a short time fulfilled a
    long time;
For his soul pleased the Lord,
Therefore hastened he to take him
Away from among the Wicked."[1]

I hope you will like this—dear child! You know you sent me these most true and most comforting lines!

From the Crown Princess

NEUES PALAIS, AUGUST 26, 1862

I had much wished we could have called Baby "Albert" —but as it would make so much confusion we shall be obliged to call him Henry, but you, dear Mama, will call him by the first and he can be called so in England. He is a large child and I hope will find favour in your sight although I know that little babies are not your taste. To me it is a miracle how he is there at all and how I have gone through everything so well when I think in what sorrow and mental agitation and depression those nine months were passed! But God has been very merciful to us and I am very grateful.

As the time draws near for your journey to Brussels I think continually of you and of Bertie and of the poor young Princess who I am sure must feel so shy and frightened and her parents so anxious and nervous. I can well imagine all you must feel. My prayers and wishes that all may go well and be settled for the best are with you always.

---

[1] So written by the Queen, with slight variations from Wisdom, Chapter IV.

From the Crown Princess

I am going out today for my first drive, as the weather is fine and I feel so well. You will have heard that the King's sudden determination to take sea baths at Doberan[1] has upset all our plans, that the christening will be on the 13th of September. Fritz goes to Carlsruhe on the 9th for a day or two. I grudge it very much, but as it will give Louise pleasure I am glad for her sake. I suppose I must direct this to Brussels as you leave England on Monday. I hope when you see Princess Christian and her daughter you will remember me most affectionately to them, and give my most respectful love to dearest Uncle Leopold— whom I trust you will find better. He wrote such a kind letter to Fritz—do tell him how much pleasure it gave us.

I shall be in such a fever to hear how the "rencontre" between you and Prince and Princess Christian and Alix has gone off, I don't think I ever felt so anxious about any thing else before. So much depends on it—not only the happiness of two young beings but the happiness of so many!

Will the sisters see the Princess?

I hope you will be so kind as to send me a word by telegram when the first interview has taken place. But oh how I feel for you—having to go through it all alone without beloved Papa! But it was his wish that the meeting should take place and that thought will be a comfort to you.

From the Crown Princess

We are anxious and alarmed about the state of politics —I fear there is a storm blowing up.

The Chambers have refused to vote the money necessary for the new organisation of the army if the three years service is adhered to; they will only hear of the two years,

[1] Near Rostock.

and this the King said "he never would agree to—even were it to cost him his head". Fritz is in despair; he has seen several deputies yesterday and is gone to Berlin today to a Council held on purpose for him. The King is at Doberan where the Grand-Duchess of Schwerin will pour the poison of Kreuzzeitung politics into his ear. What is to come of all this I don't know. It looks very threatening.

From the Crown Princess

NEUES PALAIS, SEPTEMBER 6, 1862

Words cannot express my feelings of gratitude and relief on reading your dear and anxiously expected letter just received.[1] I had felt so fidgety since your telegram from Brussels and yet I felt sure you must like her, no one can resist that look of goodness from those sweet blue eyes. I loved dear Alexandra before I had seen her a quarter of an hour! Do you recollect beloved Papa's saying to me— "from that photograph I would marry her at once".

Thank God for this mercy—in all your misery he sends you this sweet young being. Oh may she be happy! May a beam of sunshine return with her to the house—where the sun of happiness has ceased to shine since that once beloved spirit fled!

Did I say too much when I told you how charming she was? I think not. Heaven give dear Bertie strength to prove himself worthy of such a treasure; but I feel sure that her gentle influence will develop the germs of good in his heart, and raise and ennoble his whole character.

I was grievously disappointed at dear Affie's not being able to come as I had looked forward for so long to this visit and to his being here for Baby's christening. I shall not have one of my relations there—as from unpleasant circumstances dear Uncle Ernest does not come.

How could Affie be such a goose, to play such a silly trick and stand in his own light? I feel so pained to think that he should have been so thoughtless as to add to your

---

[1] This apparently is lost.

grief by misbehaviour. It is so disheartening as he had been going on so well in every respect, and is such a darling; dear Papa would have been so vexed! I fear that dear boy is not yet as conscientious as he should be, but I hope, dearest Mama, you will not distress yourself too much about this.

I am quite well and go out every day. I want to go to Church tomorrow but the King would not allow it—he is displeased at my driving out so soon, and I live in dread and fear of his forbidding me to come to you on the 15th. My going about sooner than they do here is considered against etiquette as well as very imprudent and the King wrote yesterday to Fritz that he did not like such innovations.

The Queen of Prussia is much against our long journey as she wishes Fritz and me to go to Baden for her birthday and to stay there sometime, but that I do not mean to do. Fritz dislikes the life there very much and Countess Blücher says that she does not think it in any way desirable for me to go there more than I can possibly help—and that it had also been beloved Papa's opinion expressed to herself. This applies to the "season" which is now at its height. In my deep mourning I do not feel inclined to go to such a place either—and your being at Reinhardtsbrunn will be a good excuse for my getting off.

You cannot think how inconvenient it is to us in every way the christening being put off to next week instead of being today.

From the Queen

Your dear letter of the 6th reached me yesterday and I thank you for it warmly. You did not say too much about dear Alix or Alexandra. No, she is a dear, lovely being— whose bright image seems to float—mingled with darling Papa's—before my poor eyes—dimmed with tears! Dearest child! this very prospect of opening happiness of married life for our poor Bertie—while I thank God for it—yet wrings my poor heart, which seems transfixed with agonies of longing! I am alas! not old—and my feelings are strong and warm; my love is ardent.

Alice comes on the 19th here (to Friedrichstal)[1] and stays till the 30th. I fear there is a secret there, which I am truly sorry for so soon; she is very anxious it should not be talked about or taken notice of, for she is (like me) not so very anxious for it and it is so unpleasant to begin so soon and to have all the "ennuies" the very moment one is married! Few are so fond of having children as you are; dear Papa did not like that. So pray take no further notice of it.

I have two most affectionate letters from Bertie. He landed at Ostend yesterday—paid a visit to Prince and Princess Christian—and was to go yesterday evening to Brussels. Today the "Danois" as Leopold B. calls them, go there and I suppose tomorrow or next day the "dénouement" will take place.

How tiresome to plague you about your driving out! It is so foolish. It would be better if those people did their duty and made their country happy than to interfere with what is good for your health. Baden would never do; dear Papa had such a horror of it; I read only the other day in his letters to you what he thought of it.[2] You must not give up your journey for your own sakes and for Bertie's.

From the Crown Princess

NEUES PALAIS, SEPTEMBER 10, 1862

A thousand thanks for your dear and kind letter of the 8th. Since you wrote it your telegram of yesterday evening tells me that all is satisfactorily settled at Brussels! Oh how happy and grateful I am to hear it. God's blessing rest on those two dear young heads and make them a blessing to you and our beloved country. Oh how one's heart yearns

---

[1] A palace at Gotha.
[2] On the other hand the late Mona Wilson in her chapter in *Early Victorian England*, Vol. II, page 306 (Oxford University Press), thought that the cheerful sociability of the Germans at Baden had a mellowing effect on the aggressive manners of the English abroad.

to be able to talk with Papa about it—how pleased he would have been.

Dear Alice told me herself of her prospects. I shall not mention them. Fritz writes to me that he has seen her and Louis—and that he had observed what was the matter with Alice. Louise of Baden is looking well I hear and her child[1] is quite enormous. Fritz writes he never saw anything like it; I fear that cannot be good. Its right arm was broken coming into the world but it was set again immediately and is all right now! It gives me a pang of jealousy—poor William's arm will never be right or like the other.

I think you are quite right when you say people might take more trouble to govern their kingdoms properly and let us alone; we are dictated to in every little trifle and the feelings of absolutism prevail towards us—the same as in great questions, as you already know.

The Grand-Duchess Marie[2] was here yesterday—as odd as usual, saying the most improper things, but meaning to be civil.

Only think how absurd on Saturday and Sunday I shall be considered a woman in childbed again although I go about driving and walking and dine with the company— all because the christening has been put off.

From the Queen

(No date; written from Reinhardtsbrunn when the Crown Princess was there)

I am better now and perhaps may come down to dinner but I think you are quite right to try and get dear Fritz to have some sleep. I don't like this constant night travelling for him. I hope to see him though a little this evening.

Dearest child, you may guess what has made me ill today. The conduct of Affie has dealt a heavy blow to my weak and shattered frame and I feel quite bowed down with it. And

---

[1] Afterwards Queen Victoria of Sweden, wife of King Gustave.
[2] Of Mecklenburg-Strelitz.

to have to bear alone what darling Papa could not bear alone is too much! This it is that unfitted me for every thing today. Bless you for your love and affection and advice last night. But oh! the bitter anguish that followed Affie's conduct is far worse than Bertie's. Dear children, you don't I think know how shaken and suffering poor Mama is! Or what I suffer often at dinner when jokes go on and my heart bleeds! I am unable to enjoy what I could in happy days.

From the Queen

Thousand thanks for your dear affectionate letter of yesterday morning from Nuremberg. I feel much being for the first time without either you, Alice or Aunt Feodora and I am very tired, very nervous. You are a dear, affectionate, clever, warm-hearted child! and your presence here on that dreadful arrival here was a great support and all through Affie's terrible business! May God bless and protect you both and may you long, long be spared sufferings equal to mine. I think, dearest children, (I include dear Fritz) you often thought me stronger than I am, for few, very few know what a shattered being I am! I was often literally quite unable to bear the satisfaction of having you with me, and feared you must think it strange, but my nerves are such that often and often I could not endure talking, and above all not many at meals. Being here is in many, many ways a great satisfaction, for I see so many places beloved Papa spoke of.

Since you left, I have been again to the beloved Rosenau twice[1]—on Monday afternoon with the four youngest

---

[1] The Rosenau was a mock medieval castle in the hills about four miles from Coburg. The Prince Consort was born here, and spent all the spring and summer in his childhood and youth here. When the Queen and Prince stayed at the Rosenau in 1845 she described it as "like a beautiful dream". Recollections of the castle were not without their influence on Balmoral.

children and good Tilla[1] and Bäuerlein,[2] who were enchanted with it, visiting dearest Papa's little garden, and again yesterday to show it Toward.[3] Yesterday I went in the morning to the new farm at the Kallenburg[4] which is quite English—and today to the Festung[5] with Rothbart.[6] This afternoon to the mausoleum[7] which affected me much. The weather like July. I have seen Avensleben[8] and Mlle de Steinau (Aunt Julie's[9] lady for 41 years!) and the beloved Baron every day—and he is so touching in his love for us all.

The Princess had started her holiday with the Crown Prince and the Prince of Wales and was staying in Switzerland with Prince Hohenzollern and his family.

From the Crown Princess

WEINBURG, NEAR RHEINECK CANTON, ST. GALLEN,
OCTOBER 10, 1862

I fear you will be shocked at my not having written before this, but the fact is I have not had a minute's time on the journey to sit down and write. Our expedition to Hohenzollern was most successful: anything so grand, so imposing or beautiful I never saw, as the Burg Hohenzollern! Fancy in the midst of the hills called the Rauhe Alp—a pointed hill rising straight up 3000 feet (as high as the Brocken), with the beautiful castle on the top. The day was very fine but at first the clouds quite covered the Hohenzollern and by degrees they cleared away from the top but remained round the summit leaving only the building free;

---

[1] Miss Hildyard, the Royal governess.
[2] Fraulein Bauer, the German governess to the Royal Family and a distant relative of Baron Stockmar.
[3] The head gardener at Osborne.
[4] A country seat of the Dukes of Saxe-Coburg.
[5] The fortress which overhangs the town of Coburg.
[6] Unidentified.
[7] Designed by the Prince Consort and his brother in the Italian style for their parents, relations and friends. Known as the Erbbergräbniss.
[8] General d'Avensleben, a member of the Coburg court.
[9] Sister of the Duchess of Kent, see page 113.

it had a magic effect, looking like a burg built on the clouds! The mist all dispersed by the middle of the day and we had a glorious view from the top.

The Castle as you know is being built on the old foundations, by the King and the Princes of H. Sigmaringen and H. Hechingen—it is a strong fortification and contains, besides very fine rooms and halls, two churches—a catholic and a protestant one—and the garrison.

Our reception was most gratifying, the people were so kind and seemed much pleased to see us. The costumes you would have been much struck with. I made some little scribbles—which I will send for you to see. We slept at Prince Hohenzollern's hunting-lodge from where one can see the splendid old Hohenzollern—really one must feel proud of such an ancestral castle.[1]

This house is like Corriemulzie[2] on rather a larger scale—several cottages connected together by a little garden—very pretty, and cheerful.

I found all well here except Princess Hohenzollern[3] and Marie.[4] Antoinette[5] is sweeter and lovelier than ever, but she has grown so thin there seems hardly anything of her; I never saw any one so fallen away, it does not suit her as it makes her head look bigger than her shoulders. The Prince looks so happy in the midst of his family surrounded by his four grown up sons.

Bertie is very amiable and good-humoured and seems very happy here.

We are in great anxiety as the news from Berlin are very bad. I cannot help fearing that we may be called back by telegraph and not be able to go on our journey.

---

[1] The principality of Hohenzollern was in the south of Württemberg; it lies north of Lake Constance.
[2] A house near Balmoral belonging to the Earl of Fife.
[3] Josephine, daughter of the Grand Duke of Baden and Stephanie Beauharnais.
[4] Daughter of Prince Hohenzollern, afterwards married to the Count of Flanders and mother of King Albert of the Belgians.
[5] Wife of the hereditary Prince of Hohenzollern and daughter of Maria II of Portugal.

From the Crown Princess

I could not finish yesterday as we went on an expedition up one of the Alps, the "Ebenalp". We left this at half past 7 in the morning and returned at 11 at night. Anything so tiring as climbing up the Alps you cannot imagine—it is more than Lochnager, and I was so tired that I could not sleep all night.

Today we leave the Weinburg and go on to Zurich, after having paid a visit to the Duchess of Parma at her villa close by.[1]

I have just received your letter containing Affie's and Major Cowell's.[2] I wish I could believe what Affie says and that this could be the turning point of his life but I do not think it. I have not been able to show it to Bertie or General Knollys yet.

We find travelling very expensive, the money goes dreadfully fast. I am enjoying myself as much as it is possible with our misfortune constantly in my thoughts and you before my eyes. A change does one such good physically and morally.

The family here are charming—Leopold[3] I like more and more, there is a great deal in him, and he is the model of a husband, and I see Antoinette is so happy and loves him devotedly. He is clever, talented and amiable, and full of feeling; it is impossible not to like him. I really cannot believe that he was not steady—but still I remember what you told me.

The youngest is very good looking but he does not please me so much,[4] Carl[5] is very agreeable though I fear not quite

---

[1] Daughter of the Duc de Berry, and Regent for her son. Her husband was assassinated in 1854, and the duchy was absorbed in the Kingdom of Italy. To the Queen she was "the poor Duchess".
[2] General Sir John Cowell. Governor to Prince Alfred, 1855–65. Too much of a John Bull to be completely popular with the Queen.
[3] The hereditary Prince of Hohenzollern.
[4] Prince Frederick, afterwards a general in the German Army.
[5] Afterwards King of Rumania.

steady. Anton[1] is very serious and good. Marie is a charming clever girl—though at first not so winning as Stephanie[2] was.

From the Queen

SCHLOSS COBURG, OCTOBER 16, 1862

I am very sorry I could not write to you before, but really my time is so taken up here, the distances are so great, I have so many dear friends and acquaintances high and low to see—the dear Baron every day at 4—and am so weak, so agitated, so sad and bewildered that I find hardly time to write! I must write late at night and then I am drowsy and exhausted.

I send you here a copy of a satisfactory letter from Princess Christian. Imagine the King of Denmark sends a message to say he rejoices at the marriage and wishes that it should take place in England as then it would be performed with more ceremony!!! How impertinent. No answer will be given.[3]

From the Crown Princess

LYONS, OCTOBER 20, 1862

We arrived here yesterday evening having left Geneva at 1 p.m. Unfortunately the weather was so bad at the last named place that we did not so much as catch a glimpse of Mont Blanc. At Bern I saw the grandest view in the whole world—the Jungfrau, Finster Aarhorn, Shreckhorn,—quite clear; it is so beautiful that it quite takes away one's breath at first. I cannot describe what a feeling it gave me—that lovely outline and snow white against the blue sky, and the

---

[1] The third son; he died young.

[2] The eldest daughter, who had married King Pedro of Portugal.

[3] King Frederick VII was not perhaps the most responsible of the Danish sovereigns. When he died Queen Victoria described him as "this wretched king". Walburga Lady Paget said that "he ate and drank as only men can do and as animals never do". But he was possibly too harshly treated in not being invited to the wedding, see Sir P. Magnus, *King Edward VII*, John Murray.

other hills in various tints of blue in front; no picture has ever rendered it to my satisfaction. I went to see dear Aunt Julie's grave and picked some flowers for you. It was so sad to be there, and only see her grave, not herself—whom I had always wished so much to see. It is extremely simple—too much so I think—for on the little black slab in Wale, which is all there is, her title or her arms or her crown are not—only

"Julie-Anne"

and underneath, "Mourir est mon gain, et Christ est ma vie". In front there is a railing and some few plants.[1]

Dear Fritz's birthday was not very merry and he was in low spirits. I could not bring my presents with me, and we spent half the day in the railway carriage—so it was rather dreary.

Oh what a favoured country Switzerland is! It was such a pleasant feeling there of liberty—no bad king (as so many are on the Continent) and peace and quiet everywhere. The people so prosperous and happy. The spirit of liberty seems to live in those grand mountains and the beauties of nature to make man sink back into insignificance.

Before I close I must say a little word on business. Bertie got a letter yesterday from Princess Christian saying she wished her daughter to be back in Denmark for her birthday.[2] Considering that she agreed to let you have Alix for at least three weeks, I do not see how she can ask for that without wishing to break through the arrangement of the three weeks. I hope, dear Mama, you will not give way—but say that you had agreed to having her and you would not change your mind. I advise Bertie writing the same thing to Princess C. I quite see what they want. The Princess's relations at Copenhagen have been setting her on —to try by this means to get Bertie to Copenhagen and that must not be; so I hope, dear Mama, that you will show that

---

[1] She was the eldest sister of the Duchess of Kent and had been unhappily married to the Grand-Duke Constantine of Russia. In spite of the inscription on her tomb, her private life was reputedly irregular.
[2] 1 December.

your intention is unalterable. When that is understood no more difficulties will be made I am sure.

From the Queen

Here we are quite weather-bound and blowing so fearfully that it is utterly impossible to get across! We might just have got over if we had gone straight on board on Saturday 18th and sailed Sunday morning—but at dear Uncle's age and especially after his illness I could hardly—particularly as we had announced ourselves—go by, without seeing him, and so we settled to go either Sunday evening or Monday morning. Well that very Sunday (Saturday it poured the whole afternoon) it began blowing most fearfully, and so it has done ever since—and we had after constant telegrams and consultations with General Grey etc. to give up first Monday morning and afternoon; the same yesterday and after a very quiet night the same today as it is worse even today and with such deluges of rain![1] No packets have gone across either way from Ostend the last two days, and poor Arthur is at Ostend on board the *Black Eagle* since Monday morning!!!

Oh! and here I am with all the children all alone without beloved Papa's counsel and advice and love and feel lonely and so wretched, in this terribly dull place—where really I feel as if one would lose one's intellects. The quiet and the repose I seek are not being shut up in a place like this, cut off from every thing, surrounded by canals, nothing but pavé to drive on, no streets to go into, which are so dreadfully jarring and clashing to my poor sad, wretched nerves. Nothing quieting or "Gemütlich" and so terribly Catholic!

This afternoon (a dreadful evening) I walked about here with Augusta and visited the stables and greenhouses in dreadful weather and it made me feel quite sick for, how

---

[1] The Queen was certainly not exaggerating. The storm did great damage in and round London and on all the coasts of Great Britain. The Thames was as rough as the sea. *Annual Register*, 1862.

often I went with adored Papa about in this way, and whenever we were in a strange place—how we used to walk about and look at every thing, which was his greatest delight, and so often out in the rain!

I miss dear, dear Coburg so much! It was full of all precious recollections—in fact I felt it like the home of my childhood (which you know is swept away in England[1]) the dear German language, all which I feel necessary to my very existence. Do you all cherish it, and do so when I am gone—promise me all of you? Tell Bertie how pleased I am to hear he loves our precious Coburg.

From the Crown Princess

ON BOARD THE 'OSBORNE', HARBOUR, MALTA,
OCTOBER 30, 1862

You must excuse if my letter is not only confused, but very badly written also for I am so completely knocked up by this violent sea-sickness which never left me for 24 hours, that the letters seem dancing about on the paper and I feel too wretched to write any thing like sense. Still I will try and begin where I left off last at Palermo.[2] The day after I wrote to you we went to Monreale and, driving through most lovely country, arrived at the top of the hill where we saw the splendid old cathedral in a strictly byzantine style— all gold and mosaic and coloured marble. It was certainly one of the finest things I ever saw, but all enjoyment was spoilt by the dirt which passes all description; any thing so horrible and disgusting as the beggars that swarmed round our carriages, and the dirty priests and dirty streets—I assure you it quite made one's heart heave. We saw the Archbishop's palace and from his window—oh such a view over orange groves, aloes, cactuses, fig trees and cypresses, over the town of Palermo, the hills and the bright blue sea—

---

[1] On coming to the throne the Queen moved, with her mother, to the official homes of the monarchy and the home of her childhood in Kensington Palace was ended. When the Queen married, her mother did not return to Kensington but went to Belgrave Square.

[2] After travelling to Marseilles the Crown Prince and Princess embarked on the royal yacht *Osborne* for Sicily.

in the foreground pretty, picturesque bits of broken and irregular architecture but of the best style.

The harnesses of the donkeys and mules are extremely pretty of red tassels and feathers, the carts too are very curious. They are all two-wheeled and painted lemon colour, with all sorts of pictures of saints all over them in very gaudy colours and rude art. One sees handsome dark boys sitting on one side on a donkey which is laden with panniers—the children and young men seem to dispense with clothing as much as possible. I saw some approaching a state of nature which made one rather shy to look at.

The women who are young are very pretty, but the old ones are horrible to look at. The smells in the street are enough to knock one down. We saw the garden of a Princess Butera,[1] which really is what you might imagine the garden of Eden to have been, roses, oleanders and daturas in immeasurable quantities perfuming the air with their delicious scent, splendid cypresses, wreathed up to the very top by creeping dark blue convolvuluses, heliotropes in large bushes, evergreen oaks, date palms, fan palms and cactuses —oh so beautiful. How I did enjoy it! The vegetation struck me much more than anything else I saw.

We dined at an hotel overlooking the sea, after we had seen the remnant of a Moorish building called the Zisa. Afterwards the Italian Prefect came on board and was very civil—a very agreeable and gentlemanlike man.

The Bourbons have left not a trace behind them either of recollection or sympathy; in all the palaces and churches the King of Italy's picture is to be found. We saw poor Prince Carini's palace—a heap of ruins.[2]

The *Doris* with Sir Leopold McClintock[3] came into Palermo harbour, and we begged her to accompany us which she did. The next morning, Sunday the 26th, we

[1] Wife of Prince Butera, a prominent minister under the Bourbons before they were exiled in 1860; he had been Neapolitan Minister in Paris.
[2] "Poor" because the Crown Princess would have known him as Neapolitan Minister in London.
[3] Francis Leopold McClintock. He commanded the expedition which confirmed the fate of Sir John Franklin in the 1850's. He was in command of the frigate *Doris* in 1862.

Plate 1. A contemporary drawing of the funeral of
Prince Albert

Plate 2. This photograph, taken in April 1857, shows the tutors of the Prince of Wales. *(Left to right)* Col. Phipps, Mr. Gibbs, the Prince of Wales, the Prince Consort, Baron Stockmar, Mr. Becker, and Baron E. Stockmar

Plate 3. The International Exhibition, 1862, engraved by
A. Willmore

Plate 4. The International Exhibition, 1862. The Majolica
Fountain

Plate 5. The International Exhibition, 1862. The United States section

Plate 6. The marriage of Princess Alice to Prince Louis of
Hesse-Darmstadt, July 1, 1862

Plate 7. Princess Alice in her wedding dress, July 1, 1862

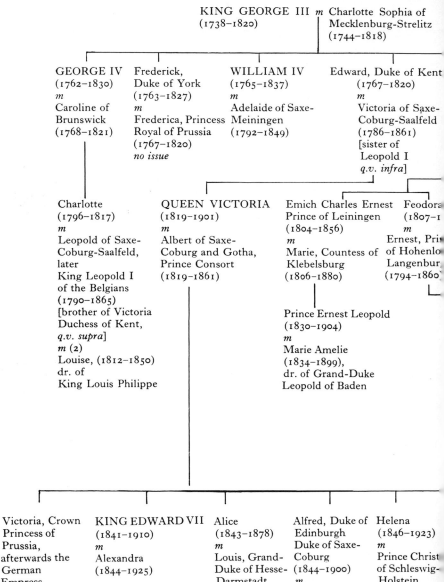

KING GEORGE III *m* Charlotte Sophia of
(1738–1820) | Mecklenburg-Strelitz
(1744–1818)

GEORGE IV
(1762–1830)
m
Caroline of
Brunswick
(1768–1821)

Frederick,
Duke of York
(1763–1827)
m
Frederica, Princess
Royal of Prussia
(1767–1820)
no issue

WILLIAM IV
(1765–1837)
m
Adelaide of Saxe-
Meiningen
(1792–1849)

Edward, Duke of Kent
(1767–1820)
m
Victoria of Saxe-
Coburg-Saalfeld
(1786–1861)
[sister of
Leopold I
q.v. infra]

Charlotte
(1796–1817)
m
Leopold of Saxe-
Coburg-Saalfeld,
later
King Leopold I
of the Belgians
(1790–1865)
[brother of Victoria
Duchess of Kent,
q.v. supra]
m (2)
Louise, (1812–1850)
dr. of
King Louis Philippe

QUEEN VICTORIA
(1819–1901)
m
Albert of Saxe-
Coburg and Gotha,
Prince Consort
(1819–1861)

Emich Charles Ernest
Prince of Leininger
(1804–1856)
m
Marie, Countess of
Klebelsburg
(1806–1880)

Prince Ernest Leopold
(1830–1904)
m
Marie Amelie
(1834–1899),
dr. of Grand-Duke
Leopold of Baden

Feodora
(1807–1
m
Ernest, Prin
of Hohenlo
Langenburg
(1794–1860)

Victoria, Crown
Princess of
Prussia,
afterwards the
German
Empress
Frederick
(1840–1901)
m
Crown Prince of
Prussia
afterwards the
German Emperor
Frederick III
(1831–1888)

KING EDWARD VII
(1841–1910)
m
Alexandra
(1844–1925)

Alice
(1843–1878)
m
Louis, Grand-
Duke of Hesse-
Darmstadt
(1837–1892)

Alfred, Duke of
Edinburgh
Duke of Saxe-
Coburg
(1844–1900)
m
Grand-Duchess
Marie of Russia
(1853–1920),
only dr.
Alexander II

Helena
(1846–1923)
m
Prince Christ
of Schleswig-
Holstein
(1831–1917)

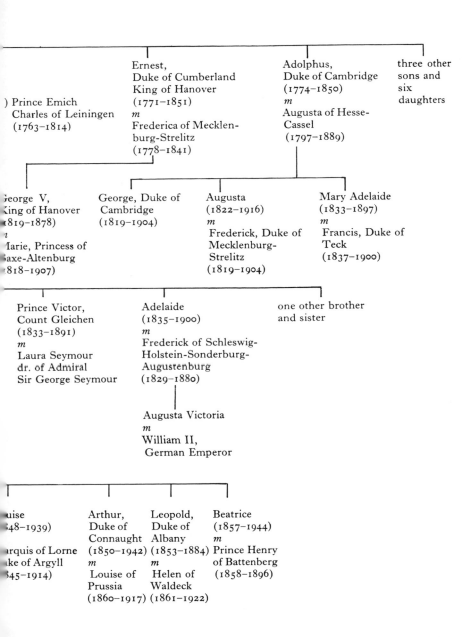

Ernest,
Duke of Cumberland
King of Hanover
(1771–1851)
m
Frederica of Mecklen-
burg-Strelitz
(1778–1841)

Adolphus,
Duke of Cambridge
(1774–1850)
m
Augusta of Hesse-
Cassel
(1797–1889)

three other
sons and
six
daughters

) Prince Emich
Charles of Leiningen
(1763–1814)

George V,
King of Hanover
(1819–1878)
m
Marie, Princess of
Saxe-Altenburg
(1818–1907)

George, Duke of
Cambridge
(1819–1904)

Augusta
(1822–1916)
m
Frederick, Duke of
Mecklenburg-
Strelitz
(1819–1904)

Mary Adelaide
(1833–1897)
m
Francis, Duke of
Teck
(1837–1900)

Prince Victor,
Count Gleichen
(1833–1891)
m
Laura Seymour
dr. of Admiral
Sir George Seymour

Adelaide
(1835–1900)
m
Frederick of Schleswig-
Holstein-Sonderburg-
Augustenburg
(1829–1880)

one other brother
and sister

Augusta Victoria
m
William II,
German Emperor

Louise
(1848–1939)

Arthur,
Duke of
Connaught
(1850–1942)
m
Louise of
Prussia
(1860–1917)

Leopold,
Duke of
Albany
(1853–1884)
m
Helen of
Waldeck
(1861–1922)

Beatrice
(1857–1944)
m
Prince Henry
of Battenberg
(1858–1896)

Marquis of Lorne
Duke of Argyll
(1845–1914)

THE ROYAL FAMILY TREE

Plate 8. The Crown Princess in the uniform of her Regiment
of Hussars, 1861

Plate 9. The Prince of Wales and Prince Leiningen, 1862

Plate 10. Queen Victoria and Prince William

Plate 11. Princess Beatrice in 1862, from the painting
by Lauchert

Plate 12. Lady Augusta Bruce

Plate 13. (Left to right) Princess Helena,
Princess Louise, and Madame Hocédé, 1862

Plate 14. Neues Palais at Potsdam, after a painting by
Christian Wilberg

Plate 15. Prince Alfred, March, 1863

arrived in the Bay of Tunis; the passage had been tolerably good but the wind was blowing up. Captain Bower[1] read the sermon as soon as we had anchored, very impressively and well. The heat was something intense—the thermometer stood at 108 (Fahrenheit) in the sun, which was not shining very brightly but the heat was very pleasant and enjoyable, not oppressive though it was so great. Our Consul-General Mr. Wood[2] and the Prussian Consul came on board and we settled to land and see Mrs. Wood's house and the ruins of Carthage, leaving our visit to the Bey for the next day. My first impression on landing was sand, palms, camels and Bedouin Arabs—a country perfectly sterile and barren, and quite flat—stony, sandy soil, with thick tangles of cactus (or prickly pear), palm trees, and olives, here and there a cypress, it had all the charm of complete novelty for me— and the eastern character about all we saw, made me fancy it was a dream. Those magnificent tall Arabs shrouded in their burnouses all looking like Horace Vernet's pictures alive. Their proud bearing and the wonderfully graceful way the very little clothing they wear, is put on, gives them a really imposing appearance. Most of them had turbans of white stuff, coarse trousers, reaching the knee of grey or brown, and bare chests, legs and arms. Some wore sorts of sandals, and the richer ones had embroidered jackets and waistcoats, and pistols in their belts under their burnouses. On horseback they look so fine and picturesque, I wish you could have seen them! We drove in a carriage with mules to Mr. Wood's pretty Moorish house built by the Bey for him. Mrs. Wood we did not see as she was confined a week ago, but his sister Mrs. Moore—wife of the Consul-General in Syria[3]—an acquaintance of Bertie's, was there. She is a friend of Victoria Wortley's[4]—and has promised me to write an account of our visit to Victoria for you to see.

---

[1] G. H. K. Bower. Commanded the *Osborne*, 1856–64. Wrote *Drops From the Ocean, or Life Under the Pennant*, 1879.
[2] Richard Wood, Consul-General in Tunis from 1855 to 1879. His wife was daughter of Sir William Godfrey.
[3] Niven Moore, Consul in Syria from 1853.
[4] Daughter of Lord Wharncliffe: she married in the following year Sir William Welby-Gregory.

There is little left of ancient Carthage—still the ruins interested me immensely. I picked up some little bits of "verde" and "rosso antico"—also some little fragments of ancient mosaic—near the water cisterns of the city. Going home we visited a Bedouin encampment—a wretched little tent with a camel lying in front of it. The women I saw were lovely but very short and rather stout and, from wearing nothing but a bit of stuff pinned about them with a thing like an old Irish brooch—leaving their arms, necks and legs bare—their figures assume a shape I never saw before. The little brown children are such darlings—I would have liked to have stolen a few. On Monday the 27th we went to pay the Bey[1] a visit; he sent us his state carriage with eight mules and an escort of Turkish cavalry and those splendid bedouins on their Arab horses, with their long carbines. One of the Bey's brothers received us at the Goletta[2] (close to the landing-place) at a palace of the Bey's with the admiral of the port and a quantity of other grandees in Turkish uniforms. After having had some refreshment, we started in the carriages prepared for us, at a tremendous pace, with our picturesque escort, over the horrid roads, nearly smothered with dust. The droves of camels on the road looked so pretty; I counted 63 round a fountain—some lying down, others drinking, with their loads on their backs and their handsome drivers standing in picturesque attitudes. Oh! what subjects for painting. The town of Tunis made a curious impression upon me, nothing but dark faces, magnificent black eyes, white turbans and burnouses, and coloured costumes. The women—some of them wear very short dresses and tight trousers with coloured burnouses and black veils covering their faces above and below, leaving only a slit for their eyes.

We drove to the Bey's town palace which was placed at our disposal and from thence visited the bazaars on foot. It was a very pretty sight—all these oriental dresses, and for the most part handsome men, with such fine frames and

---

[1] Mohamed Es Sadok: he succeeded in 1859.
[2] Or La Golette.

limbs and grave faces—buying and selling and making a tremendous noise—both purchasers and sellers, who sit crosslegged or lie in their stalls smoking their long pipes, or making the articles they are selling. I bought some perfumes and Tunisian stuffs—Mrs. Moore interpreted for me—and the Consuls for the others. I was surprised at the cleanness of the Arabs, though there were crowds in the bazaar there was not the least unpleasant smell, and the hands and faces were very clean. The Mahomedan religion requires seven times washing a day of its observers.

After the bazaar we drove to the Bey's palace out of town—the gentlemen in uniform in a high black gown and hat. The Bey's uncles, cousins and brothers received us at the door—the Bey on the top of staircase. He gave me his arm, and led the way into his immense throne room through two files standing down either side of the room of his suite, who looked well dressed and respectable enough. Four chairs were placed for us and we all sat down.

The Bey is handsome and prepossessing, very quiet, grave and dignified in manner, the conversation though carried on through an interpreter went on quite easily. It turned on you, of course, and our Affie's visit to the late Bey; I asked permission to make the acquaintance of the Princess "Lilla Bembey"—the Bey's wife—he has only one; he asked Fritz's permission whether he might present her, and then led us into his harem, with Mrs. Moore and Hedwig and the Prussian Consul's wife, an American lady. The poor Princess was so delighted to see me that she would not let my hand go for one minute during the half hour that I was with her. She is enormously fat and no longer young but has fine eyes and a very agreeable expression. She was dressed in the most extraordinary way—a short jacket or rather shirt, very narrow of pink and white "moiré antique"—reaching her hips—and then tight, gold trousers and bare feet, bare arms and hands covered with rings, her chin muffled with a veil which hung down in a thin streamer behind and served to hold on an odd little peak or horn at the back of her head. She had her black hair cut short and combed far in to her face. She had her eyes and eye brows painted—also some black marks painted on her forehead, chin and cheeks. She had very good quiet manners although she sat with one leg doubled under her or holding her bare foot in her hand across her other leg. She has a low sweet voice. She was surrounded by slaves—some of the most lovely girls I ever saw, eyes, mouths, noses and hair quite beautiful—but all in the same odd dress as herself—only as they were thin and graceful they looked as if they were acting boys' parts on the stage. The Princess showed me all—the magnificent rooms—all in the style of the Alhambra with marble columns, floors and fountains, only disfigured by common, ugly, vulgar European furniture of a very secondary order. These poor ladies are never allowed to go out or open a window or see any body—except the Bey's brothers. The Princess is very unhappy that she has no children; the Bey has none, so he has adopted the children of a brother of his who is dead—one darling little thing of four years old with lovely black eyes, in a Turkish uniform. They gave me sweetmeats and coffee and asked me all sorts of questions. I gave the Princess a brooch and took my leave. The Bey who is adored by his wife and who does not care for her a bit, was waiting outside the door of the harem for me. The Bey gave Fritz and Bertie orders and swords, and me some scents and four white burnouses. We took leave of him and went back to his town palace, where he returned our visit and smoked and afterwards gave us the pipes as souvenirs. He was most friendly and civil. Prince Napoleon[1] and Princess Clotilde had paid him a visit shortly before, the former left a very bad impression as he had been so rough and rude.

After luncheon which was provided for us at the Bey's palace we returned to the yacht. The wind was blowing hard and I begged much not to start; however afterwards it was settled we should, as there was better hope of the weather.

It was the most shocking passage I ever remember; we

---

[1] Nephew of Napoleon and son of Jerome: his wife Princess Clotilde was daughter of King Victor Emmanuel II.

broke the main shaft of the port paddle, had the rudder across the stern in consequence. The *Doris* had to take us in tow. She pitched and rolled so that we thought the cable would snap every minute, we had a heavy sea and the wind blowing strong against us so that we only made three knots an hour with our one paddle. The weather was too bad to land in Sicily so we had to make straight for Malta—where we have just arrived. For two days and two nights I lay on the deck without changing my clothes or being able to lift up my head or stand. I was sick 21 times, and I feel now more dead than alive. All our poor people were dreadfully ill—Fritz not at all. Nothing can equal the kindness or attentiveness of the doctor, Mr. Hill[1] to every body, but specially to me. I never remember having been so miserable.

We are going on shore soon now—I have seen Lady Le Marchant.[2] Ernest Leiningen's Mama[3] is here; E. and M.[4] are at Naples. I have seen Uncle George's son[5] who is in the 23rd Regiment here. I must end this confused letter here, beloved Mama, begging your pardon for having written so ill, but I feel so giddy and weak and wretched—not having eat or slept, and having been so dreadfully sick!

From the Queen

OSBORNE, OCTOBER 29TH, 1862

I have but a few minutes to thank you for three such dear letters—of the 15th, 20th, and 21st from Marseilles. I told Augusta to give an account of our voyage and the real danger darling Arthur and all my most precious things were in on the *Black Eagle*. I have gone through much—much sorrow since I returned! On the 27th I saw poor, dear Major Cowell, whose noble conduct in remaining with Affie and touching grief about Affie only bring back too vividly all the

---

[1] The surgeon on the royal yacht.
[2] Wife of Sir John Gaspard Le Marchant, Governor of Malta, 1859–64.
[3] Marie (1806–80), daughter of Count de Klebelsberg, who married in 1829 the Queen's half-brother, Charles, Prince of Leiningen. She left her husband for Mr. Spare, who subsequently married her maid.
[4] Ernest and Marie.
[5] See note on page 124.

agonies and miseries of last November. He feels what darling Papa felt!

In Affie's case—there is not a particle of excuse; his conduct was both heartless and dishonourable. But he does feel it though he can't poor boy give utterance ever to any thing. But his great palour, thinness, his subdued tone, and his excessive anxiety by every little act to give me pleasure, to do what I like and wish show me he feels enough. I had wished not to see him and thought for himself it would have been better. But for the world it was necessary. So I saw him on the 28th and he stopped till today. It was very trying. Tomorrow he returns again till the 2nd when he sails.[1]

From the Queen

OSBORNE, NOVEMBER 1, 1862

Two words to tell you I mean myself to declare Bertie's marriage today; it is dreadful for me, but there will only be three lords—Granville and Palmerston and Lord Stanley of A.[2] (as Lord Russell is ill). It will be in darling Papa's room —no one sitting down and all over in a second. Still it is a hard, hard trial when I think of the two former. The last was bad enough—just after dear Grandmama's death (on the 30th of April). But then I had a darling to lean on—I own my despair is almost unbearable.

Poor Affie sails tomorrow for Lisbon and the Mediterranean. He is quieter and subdued—and such an amiable companion.

---

[1] Prince Alfred's behaviour, which vividly recalled to the Queen the Prince of Wales's "scrape" of the previous year, was rendered more obnoxious to the Queen as she was dealing at this time with her ministers over the wish of the Greeks to have Prince Alfred as their King.
[2] Alderley. He was Postmaster-General. According to the Duke of Saxe-Coburg, the news (because of the Danish connexion) came on Germany "like a clap of thunder." *Memoirs*, Vol. IV.

From the Crown Princess

The mail has not yet started which was to take my last letter so I add another short note from here. We took refuge here from the bad weather, and the *Osborne* has been repaired as much as possible in the harbour. I do not feel at all well, so dreadfully giddy—every thing dances before my eyes, the sirocco wind is really most trying, more so than the heat of the atmosphere alone. It blew very hard yesterday but it seems to have moderated quite by this time and I hope we shall get off this evening. I am very glad indeed to see Malta, though I think it the most tiresome place possible: it must be quite dreadful to live here. No trees, no shrubs, no fields—nothing but white rock on which the sun glares enough to put one's eyes out. No shelter any where from the wind and the dust. There are no hedges, the roads are bounded by stone walls; I never saw anything so monotonous or melancholy! The only pretty spot is St. Antonio— where there is a lovely garden though very small. I have not been about much here as I feel too knocked up. There was a large dinner and party the night of our arrival— which was repeated yesterday evening but I could not appear. Sir Gaspard and Lady Le Marchant are very civil and kind—and this palace is a splendid old place though "lugubre" and dilapidated.

Yesterday there was a review of the troops—the first time I ever saw our dear soldiers without beloved Papa; it quite overcame me particularly when the rifles came past.[1] It made me think of Aldershot and former times. Also when your dear health was drunk alone at dinner I had a hard fight to keep down my rising tears.

I have seen Ernest and Edward's mother; she looks very well indeed and much younger than I thought; she seems very clever but has something so bitter and sharp about her —that I can well imagine that it must have clashed with

---

[1] He had been Colonel-in-chief of the Rifle Brigade.

dearest Uncle Charles's quick, lively disposition. Ernest and Marie we hope to see at Naples.

Uncle George's son Mr. Fitzgeorge seems a very nice young man—very like him with a curious mixture of likeness to Bertie and to Alice's Louis, which would strike you directly if you saw him. He seems very shy—poor young man—and never puts himself forward in any way.[1]

We made some purchases here but I have not felt able or inclined to make any sketches. I shall be so glad to be on board again—this air quite upsets one.

Goodbye beloved Mama—Fritz sends you his best love and wishes me to say how happy he is to be on English ground and to see English soldiers.

From the Crown Princess

ON BOARD THE 'OSBORNE', MESSINA,
NOVEMBER 3, 1862

We left Malta on the evening of the 1st. We spent that day in seeing a sham attack upon a gun-boat from all the forts, visiting the splendid church of St. John and seeing different people. The unpleasant air, the number of people and the dreadful rush at Malta quite knocked one up. I saw Ernest L's mother for a very long time that day. She still seems very unhappy, poor thing, and complained a great deal.

We had a good passage to Syracuse which we reached yesterday morning—though it was rather rough. We spent a most delightful day at Syracuse—visited the remains of the ancient town and theatres, caves etc. and saw the catacombs. We lunched in the open air in a most lovely spot—a grove of orange and lemon trees in the stone quarries where the material for building the ancient city came from—at the foot of the Convent of the Capuchin Order. The monks were very civil to us, we showed them the ship afterwards, and gave them some wine and cigars which they seemed to

---

[1] George Fitzgeorge, eldest son of the Duke of Cambridge, by his "marriage" with the actress Louisa Fairbrother. There is a less favourable picture of Mr. Fitzgeorge in Mr. St. Aubyn's biography, *The Royal George*.

like very much. The orange trees in their natural state are too beautiful—nothing strikes me so much here.

We have had a very unpleasant passage this morning and a heavy thunder storm—I and most of the passengers were very sick. We are going to start again in less than an hour for Naples so I must hurry to close these lines begging a last pardon for their being so ill-written.

From the Queen

OSBORNE, NOVEMBER 6, 1862

How very very interesting your long letter from Malta is! I must say you do write beautifully! With so little you say so much.

Good, excellent Lenchen is scribbling away at the copy. I only did not let her see the leaf with "Uncle George's son". Now to tell you that darling Alexandra arrived safely last night by moonlight, with the ships lit up by blue lights—a touching landing. Poor little Leopold (the only Prince in our poor house!) and Lenchen with Lady Augusta and Lady Caroline,[1] General Grey[2] and Lord Charles Fitzroy[3] went down to the pier to receive her, and it was 9 o'clock before they got up.[4]

I waited downstairs, and received her in the hall. She looked lovely and fresh and is very dear, but very shy when others are presented to her. We dined à quatre[5] in the Council room and stayed a short while together. Dear sweet Alexandra looks lovely and clings with such affection to Lenchen—who is obliged to do every thing. It rains and I fear we can't show off the place. I must get a little mouthful of air—for in my weak state I require it.

---

[1] Lady Caroline Barrington, daughter of 2nd Lord Grey and Woman of the Bedchamber.
[2] Son of 2nd Lord Grey, private secretary to the Prince Consort and later to the Queen.
[3] Afterwards 7th Duke of Grafton; Equerry to the Queen.
[4] Prince Leopold was the only member of the Royal Family at the pier. He was much exercised how he should explain who he was and about a bouquet of flowers he was to present. Immediately the Princess landed she gave him a warm embrace.
[5] The Queen, Princess Alexandra, Princess Helena and Prince Christian.

Tell Bertie—he was right to accept the Tunis Order. Tell Bertie I am grieved to find that in spite of all I said and all he promised he never writes to Alix in any thing but English! This I know is mere laziness and it grieves and pains me as the German element is the one I wish to be cherished and kept up in our beloved home—now more than ever; it is doubly necessary in this case, as Alix's parents are inclined to encourage the English and merge the German into Danish and English and this would be a dreadful sorrow to me; the very thing dear Papa and I disliked so much in the connexion is the Danish element. Tell Bertie (who I know wishes to please me) that this pains and distresses me much; he can ask you and Fritz if he is in want of words, etc. I wrote shocking bad German letters to darling Papa before we married.

Get Fritz to explain to Bertie that he must not be indiscreet about the day of the marriage, as he is very capable of that. The last week in February or first in March is what we wish.

Put all notions of Dagmar, or indeed any one, out of Bertie's head for Affie; let him generally reconcile him to marry early but not exactly any particular person. I am in hopes I see some day light there.

One more word. I think decidedly none of you ought to be in colours at the wedding but in grey and silver or lilac and silver, or grey, or lilac and gold and so on but not merely gold and white; it is the first occasion of any of you children appearing in public and as all, when in England, will not wear colours next year I think it ought not to be. But I have said that the "Danois" may do just as they like at the ceremony. "Entre nous soit dit", poor Prince Christian is not bright,—though I think he is sensible about his children etc. but his remarks unfortunately are not to the purpose and a little like "Jules and Jean".[1] He asked Lenchen whether he had not heard a nightingale last night!

---

[1] The youngest sons of Prince Frederick of Schleswig-Holstein: relations of Prince Christian. The two brothers were in the Prussian army.

and called the "Elphin" the "Elphinstones"[1], and thought King Otho[2] was clever!

From the Queen

I write this letter for you and Bertie as I have no time to write to the latter and as I think you have (in a different way) as great an interest in darling Alix as Bertie has. I can't say how I, and we all love her! She is so good, so simple, unaffected, frank, bright and cheerful, yet so quiet and gentle, that her presence soothes me. Then how lovely! She is quite at home, comes in and out of the room to me as the sisters, is most attentive and dear in her manner to me and quite at ease with us all. She and Lenchen adore one another, and seem to suit so well. Louise behaves as well as possible since our return—and keeps quietly, and without grumbling, in her own place. But dear Alix is kind and loving to all of the brothers and sisters. She seems so religious—has such a deep and serious character, and is truly and laudably anxious to improve herself. She will read English with Mrs. Bruce,[3] write with Mr. Ogg[4] also with Mme. Hocédé,[5]—and draws with Mr. Leitch.[6] All this she is most anxious for—as she wishes to be of real use to Bertie. She speaks English very well.

She goes regularly at 10 to bed as her parents wish, and is reasonable and sensible about her health. If she writes (which I think she won't) to Bertie about her maids let him say, I would settle that. Oh! may Bertie be worthy of such a sweet wife! Does he quite deserve it? But he will, if he does all he can to follow in beloved Papa's footsteps and to remember what a husband he was!

---

[1] This is presumably an allusion to Sir Howard Elphinstone (1829–90), tutor to Prince Arthur.
[2] The Bavarian prince who was King of Greece.
[3] Widow of General Bruce.
[4] George Ogg, tutor to the royal children.
[5] Maria Hocédé, governess to the royal children.
[6] W. L. Leitch (1804–83), drawing-master to the Queen for 22 years.

From the Crown Princess

Replying to the Queen's letter of October 22 the Crown Princess
indulges some of her prejudices about the Roman Church.

Here in Italy I saw it in its worst form. I consider it
both demoralizing in the highest degree and blasphemous;
the sad effect it has upon a whole nation is visible here to
an extent one can hardly imagine—accompanied by pov-
erty, misery of every description and dirt and disorder
which are quite shocking.

There is a figure of our Saviour here—and they cut its
hair every year, as they say it grows so fast; another they
pretend sheds tears—in short, I think those who worshipped
a golden calf were more civilised than these soit disant
Christians for whom there is nothing spiritual or sublime in
heaven or earth, but who must drag God down to their own
wretched level! I did not show what you said as you told me
not.[1] Bertie is extremely amiable, accommodating and good
natured and we are as happy as possible together. I think
he enjoys himself very much and really I must say he has
made a great deal of progress: he takes so much more notice
of what he sees and hears, and I am sure travelling in that
respect is very good for him.

The news from home does not please me at all. Bismarck
makes more mischief every day—party spirit is rising on
both sides alarmingly, the King makes the most imprudent
and ill-judged speeches and is more deluded than ever. He
wanted to go to England but was prevented by his ministers
of course. I wish those last named dear people were at the
bottom of the sea with mill-stones round their necks![2] I look
upon our losing Lord Augustus Loftus as a real misfortune.
Many thanks for Lady Augusta's letter giving information

---

[1] i.e. to the Prince of Wales.
[2] On 30 September Bismarck, who had recently been asked by the King
to form a Government, said: "It is not with speeches or with parliament-
ary resolutions that the great questions of the day are decided . . . but
with blood and iron."

about Sir A. Buchanan,[1] all I know about him is—that he cannot speak a word of German, and was a violent Dane at Copenhagen; so that I must say I feel rather apprehensive! There is so much to be found fault with in the present Government at Berlin that it requires but little to make it appear to the English Ministers in the worst light, and a person who does not understand our affairs thoroughly may judge from the mistakes alone and do an immensity of harm. Lord Augustus always tried to interpret what ever was done in the most favourable light.

On the other hand the present Government at B. are so hostile against England that they are prepared to take offence at every thing. Knowing as I do that the safety and peace of Germany and Europe depend on England and Prussia going cordially together, advocating the same principles—constitutional liberty and protestantism, I cannot but be alarmed when I see how every thing that is now done—tends to estrange them! But enough of this sad theme—I hoped we have left it on the other side of the Mediterranean.

Our stay at Naples is delightful. We made a most successful expedition up Mt. Vesuvius, saw a heavenly view and the curious crater, were half smothered with sulphur smoke and tore all we had on to pieces with the sharp lava. It is certainly most curious and interesting but terribly fatiguing both going up and coming down. As one is not safe from Banditti—General La Marmora[2] gave us an escort of Bersaglieri and Gendarmes, they looked very pretty indeed in their picturesque uniform jumping from rock to rock—so active and light.

We have seen Sorento, Castellammare, Portici, St. Elmo, the blue grotto the day we arrived; it was very difficult to get in (General Knollys, Fritz and I lying flat down in a wretched little fishing boat) there was a heavy swell on, and we were drenched through and through. The passage from

---

[1] Sir Andrew Buchanan. He was Ambassador at Berlin, 1862–4.
[2] One of the founders of the Kingdom of Italy. He was in command at Naples at this time: his brother formed the Bersaglieri.

Messina here was not smooth at all and I was very sick again. I am so intensely happy to be on board a ship that I don't care how sick I am. Naples did not strike me as I had expected—the tableau being so vast and the shape of the hills not so fine as at Palermo. I suppose it is my bad taste but I think Sicily infinitely finer. The town is dirty and uninteresting. I am very glad we do not live in it—but out here, where we have Vesuvius and the lovely bay before us. By moonlight it is lovely.

I must wish you joy of dear Bertie's birthday tomorrow —a sad and serious day in all respects. But let me entreat you on his account not to despond about him! He is what he is—but there is much that is good, and with love, patience and forbearance all that will come out, and you will have, I trust and hope, no reason to complain of him.

From the Queen

All you say about Malta is I believe quite what most people think—except Affie who is so fond of it. I admire your courage to go on by sea after being so sick! I am sure I could not. All you say about poor Marie Leiningen Mère interests me. She is so sour and bitter and very unhappy—but I am very glad you saw her. I hope you have seen our dear Marie?[1] That expedition to that blue cave at Capri must have been a great undertaking—and one I should not have joined in, as darling Papa knew well!

I now must come to the one object besides the one which entirely absorbs me and which daily seems to me more and more unbearable. It is our darling Alix! Dearest child, we cannot thank you enough for all you have both done in securing for dear Bertie and us—this jewel. She is one of those sweet creatures who seem to come from the skies to help and bless poor mortals and brighten for a time their path! You couldn't know her, but you guessed what she was, and we love her. She lives in complete intimacy with us

---

[1] Wife of Prince Ernest of Leiningen, the Queen's nephew.

and she is so dear, so gentle, good, simple, unspoilt—so thoroughly honest and straightforward—so affectionate; she has been sitting for an hour with me this evening and I told her all about former happy times, our life, a great deal about dearest Papa, whom she seems to love quite dearly and to long so to see; all about his illness; she showed such feeling, laid her dear head on my shoulder and cried, said how she prayed God to help her to do all she could to help me and comfort me. And I told her—I felt sure when I was gone she would watch over all darling Papa loved—and I can't describe the look of tender pity and affection she gave me! I feel she will be a real blessing to us, and certainly who would have expected it from that quarter? She has plenty of sense and intelligence, and is, though very cheerful and merry, a serious solid character not at all despising enjoyments and amusements but loving her home and quiet—all much more. She is so affectionately attached to me! It is, my dear child, a great blessing and I do thank God for it— that in our misery He has permitted this. I could not expect this, though I hoped a great deal. What a blessing she came now. We could not have known each other so well![1]

13th. I send you the extract of my letter to Uncle L. All this you can tell or show Bertie. Before I leave this subject I wish to mention that there has been and is, I see, on the part of the parents or rather more of those about them, a great wish to bring forward the Danish element and sink the German which is just what the late Emperor of Russia did in his country and what Papa so excessively disapproved.[2] Imagine Princess Christian's asking for that foolish little Danish girl coming with Alix and being on par with her here! Then she brought forward the Danish maid, and from all I see and hear I am sure—and Mrs. Bruce and Augusta are entirely of the same opinion—that it would not be for the dear young couple's happiness—if Alix had a maid with

---

[1] There had been objection—especially from King Leopold—to her entertaining Princess Alexandra in the absence of the Prince of Wales.
[2] In 1850 the Emperor had resisted the separation of Schleswig from Denmark.

whom she could chatter away in a language her husband did not understand. I am sure Fritz will quite agree—and you can both point this out strongly to Bertie. I am sure Papa and I would neither of us have liked such a thing. I said, to show my readiness to meet them where I could, that she might bring a Danish man servant with her—who might look after her letters for home etc. I told Bertie I thought she should have one dresser (like you and Alice have) and two wardrobe maids. I think that my excellent "couturière", who has several times acted as my dresser, Perrett—would do, as the head admirably, and I would readily give her up; then Ellen Roberts as one of the wardrobe maids and a German for the other.

Today is a sad anniversary; beloved Uncle Charles's death; but that sad event is eclipsed by the recollection of the agony and misery of this day last year when beloved Papa first heard of poor Bertie's misfortune! Oh! that face, that heavenly face of woe and sorrow which was so dreadful to witness! Let Bertie not forget it! He was forgiven thank God! or I never could have looked at him again—and I forgave him fully—but I wish him not to forget it.

I have always forgot to tell you of a loss which you will grieve over with us! Dear, old Lord Breadalbane died on Saturday at Lausanne![1] He is a very great loss—personally and publicly for Scotland!

From the Crown Princess

PALAZZO CAFARELLI, ROME, NOVEMBER 12, 1862

Here we are in the ancient city, once the mistress of the world, having left lovely Naples yesterday morning. We drove from there to Pozzuoli, the most heavenly drive I ever took, and to the beautiful bay of Baja where we embarked. I had taken leave of dear Marie L. who left the *Magicienne* and went on board the *Landore*. Ernest accompanied us with the *Doris* to Civita Vecchia—the passage was good and

---

[1] Marquess of Breadalbane, born in 1796. He entertained the Queen and Prince Consort at Taymouth Castle on their first visit to Scotland in 1842.

no one ill.[1] I can't say how sorry I was to leave the dear *Osborne* and the sea—one gets so attached to it—and then it is like a little bit of beloved England with all the kind English faces around one, which do one's heart good. It pours in torrents here—and the town looks very dismal indeed. We went to St. Peters after lunch and certainly, though I had heard an immense deal about it, it quite surpassed all my expectations; any thing so grand and imposing both by its huge dimensions and its beauty it is impossible to imagine. I was struck dumb—with wonder and admiration. We shall see Cardinal Antonelli[2] tonight and most likely pay our visit to the Pope[3] tomorrow. We have brought the doctor off the *Osborne*—Mr. Hill—a most charming and clever man, with us here.

This is the House of the Prussian Legation where the late King spent the winter of '58–'59. We are all very comfortably put up; there is just room to hold us all minus Mr. Meade[4] and Mr. Hill, the former I like extremely he is so good, gentle and amiable and a very good companion for Bertie.

From the Queen

WINDSOR CASTLE, NOVEMBER 15, 1862

These lines are to wish you joy and many, many happy returns of your dear, still so young birthday! Only 22 and already three children! I had only one then! May our Heavenly Father pour every blessing on your beloved head and may you long, long enjoy your present domestic happiness, though that can never be without (as our dear Countess so beautifully terms it) the "cypress branch". Last year, which was almost his last day without feeling ill (though the sleeplessness had begun, from the dreadful 13th) I said

---

[1] The ships referred to were the escorting vessels for the royal yacht.
[2] Cardinal Antonelli (1806–76). The most influential of those responsible for the Government of the Papal States; he was Cardinal Secretary-of-state. A resolute opponent of Italian unity.
[3] Pius IX.
[4] Robert Henry Meade, Groom of the Bedchamber to the Prince of Wales; afterwards in the Colonial Office.

to him, "Of this dear child you can be proud at least." And he answered: "If nothing happens to her—if they do not take too much out of her."

My—no—our gift is you know—the pictures of your two Grandpapas and Grandmama Louise,[1] but I wish you to buy as a gift from me some pretty Roman ornament as a joint gift from us!

God bless and ever protect you, our dear first born! To spend the birthday of one's child as a widow is too, too dreadful.

From the Crown Princess

What inexpressible delight it is to me to hear that you love sweet Alix and that all goes on so well in the house with her! God be thanked that it is so and grant that it may ever go on increasing. She is indeed lovely, her sweet face is always before my eyes! I think she will be happy because, these four weeks I have been spending with Bertie, I have found him so kind and amiable, ready to do anything that could be agreeable to us, and in a very good humour. I find him far from a dull companion: he is very amusing when he likes, and has a very quick repartee. I am quite struck at his knowing so much about pictures; his taste is really very good and I find he understands much more about art than I thought. His is a nature which develops itself slowly, and I think you will find that he will go on improving and that his marriage will do a great deal for him in that way.

I have seen a great deal of this most interesting town already. It is quite different to what I expected—no broad streets and fine open place; one discovers the marvellous beauties by degrees, and often in the corners one would least expect to find them. I have been again to St. Peters, have seen the Vatican and been in perfect ecstasies at the statues and pictures. I assure you there is so much that is

---

[1] The Duke of Kent and Ernest I, Duke of Saxe-Coburg. His wife, Louise, was divorced from him.

beautiful that it almost overpowers one; I cannot take it in all at once but enjoy seeing it bit by bit. How the Raphaels make me think of beloved Papa; my eyes often fill with tears when I look at them—they seem to me to belong all to him—as all that is good, great, right or beautiful must ever be in my mind identified with him.

We have been to Gibson's[1] studio and also to Wolff's;[2] they have some very fine things. Gibson's Venus is quite exquisite. I did not see a coloured one, which I am very sorry for. Fritz and I paid our visit to the Queen Dowager[3] of Naples today after Fritz had seen the King.[4] She is not attractive and was surrounded by pale, delicate-looking children of almost every age. We are to see the Pope on Monday—he is not at all well—and has not been able to receive us before. But it is not known as they keep every thing concerning his health a secret.

The weather has been something too dreadful, raining or rather pouring cats and dogs all day since we arrived, so that the whole town has a most dreary and dismal aspect. Anything like the dirt in the streets you never saw—I think it even worse than Naples. We are devoured by fleas, and swarms of disgusting beggars crowd round us when we are on foot or getting in and out of the carriage. Today I saw a monk blow his nose in an umbrella, which I thought was an instance of civilisation! The shops are very pretty—particularly jewelry and marble things—but so dear that I could hardly buy anything.

We went into the Jesuits Church last night while high Mass was being celebrated in honour of the newly canonised Japanese Saints.[5] The Church was most beautifully illuminated and immensely crowded; the singing sounded like at an opera and the whole thing seemed quite like a per-

---

1 John Gibson (1790–1866). He lived in Rome. His first tinted bust was one of Queen Victoria.
2 Emil Wolff (1802–79), German sculptor of the classical school.
3 Archduchess Therese, widow of King Ferdinand II ("Bomba"). She had nine children.
4 Francis II.
5 No doubt the Catholic missionaries in Japan in the sixteenth and seventeenth centuries.

formance on the stage. I shall have several audiences this evening so have not time for more, dearest Mama.

From the Crown Princess

Full of gratitude for your dear letter of the 12th. I cannot describe how delighted I am with all you say about our beloved Alix. What I have prayed for so often and been so anxious about has indeed come to pass—she is to you as a daughter! Of course I did not know her as you do when I told you about her, but there was no mistaking those sweet blue eyes, with a heaven of purity, innocence and goodness in them.

Bertie told you about our visit to the Pope. He seems a good natured and jocose old gentleman who laughs a great deal but has an amiable expression and is not without dignity.[1] Fritz and I went to hear high Mass performed before him in one of the side chapels of St. Peters. We climbed up to the very top of St. Peters and afterwards went down into the crypt by the Pope's special permission as ladies are never allowed to go down there. The whole of the vault is filled with interesting monuments—the ceiling, which is very low, painted all over—the walls and the floor inlaid with beautiful mosaic. I saw poor "Prince Charlie's" tomb and his father's and uncle's.[2] We went afterwards to the baths of Caracalla, and were lucky enough to pick up some little bits of verde antica. In the evening after sun set we returned to St. Peters, heard the end of the vespers—and saw the cardinals come out, and a whole procession of priests and choristers, bishops, canons, Swiss gardes come out into the nave of the church and kneel there while the relics—a bit of the true cross and such like nonsense—were

---

[1] Later the Pope told Odo Russell, the unaccredited British representative at the Vatican, "he was an old man, but in the whole course of his long life he had never been more favourably impressed by anyone than by her Royal Highness the Crown Princess of Prussia." *The Roman Question*, edited by Noel Blakiston, Chapman and Hall, 1962.
[2] The monument designed by Canova to James III and his two sons. The Crown Princess means brother not uncle.

being displayed on a balcony above the altar. The Church was quite dark and by the light of wax torches here and there, we saw the kneeling figures—in the greatest silence; if one forgot the monstrous idiocy it was all about, the sight was very solemn and impressive worthy of a better cause. The more I see St. Peters the more splendid and grand I think it, it is a treat to me each time I go in—we manage to go there almost once a day. You know we—that is Fritz and I—have seen the King of Naples. He is a wretched object I think, "il fait pitié". He is too frightful, stammers when he speaks and twitches with his eyes. He tried to be as civil and amiable as he could—and has really a very good natured expression, but that is all I can say for him. The old Queen looks very cross indeed. The Count of Trani[1] is the nicest and his wife very pretty and showy-looking though not a real beauty. She must be very like her sister the Empress of Austria—though of course not to be compared to her in beauty. The Count and Countess of Trapani[2] are quiet sort of people and their five children look very delicate.

I have told Hedwig to write and tell you of what we have been seeing and doing—as it is so much that I cannot find time to do it. We are eaten up alive with fleas, the itching drives one nearly mad. Hedwig and I are such figures we are hardly fit to be seen—face, neck and arms covered with bites, and all the rest of one's person is in the same unpleasant condition. Nothing seems to be of any use in preventing this torment. It is really like one of the plagues of Egypt.

From the Queen

WINDSOR CASTLE, NOVEMBER 20, 1862

The middle portion of the mausoleum will be quite ready (excepting the interior decoration) for the consecration

---

[1] Prince Louis, brother and heir to the King. He married Matilda, daughter of the Duke in Bavaria, in 1861.
[2] Francesco di Paola, uncle of the King, and married to a daughter of the Grand-Duke of Tuscany.

and the day after, for what will be too dreadful for me to think of—and mention![1] But I have another great distress! viz. the granite sarcophagus will not be ready for some months, as various accidents occurred to the granite—but I have had a temporary one in stone made, which will be placed a little farther back, with a cast of the splendid, lying statue upon it, and the sacred, precious contents will only be moved from the one to the other, when the permanent one is placed there. As the dreadful anniversary is on a Sunday and every day gained is of importance, I don't think the consecration will be before the 17th. I leave to Alice or Mr. Rulandt—the description of my lying statue, which I hear is most beautiful! Oh! how I wish I were there, relieved from my heavy, pleasureless burthen!

Mr. Thornycroft[2] is making a very pretty bust of dear Alexandra whom we love more and more. Winterhalter[3] is ill and won't come now; but thinks he can in March. As however a picture is much wanted of her, I mean to try and get Lauchert[4] (the next best) to go to Copenhagen to paint her.

All you and General Knollys say of Bertie, and his own letters, are very hopeful. I trust he has been reasonable about smoking? To have lived with both of you, will have done him such good; and then here again he finds a most satisfactory young ménage;—very happy and very sensible.

I think, dear, you need not be alarmed about Sir A. and Lady Buchanan; you will recollect what letters you and E. Stockmar wrote against poor Lord A. Loftus[5]—deprecating his appointment in the highest degree. And dear Papa had to write very strongly to you about it. I therefore hope that in a little while you will find Sir A. Buchanan as agree-

---

[1] The transfer of the coffin to the mausoleum—see page 155.
[2] Thomas Thornycroft (1815–85), sculptor. He did the marble statue of the Queen on her favourite charger, Hammon, for the Great Exhibition.
[3] Franz Xavier Winterhalter (1805–73). Born in Germany and lived in Paris for the last forty years of his life. Royal and society painter.
[4] Richard Lauchert, born at Sigmaringen 1823. Much patronised by European Royal Families.
[5] The Queen uses "poor" because when Berlin was raised to an Embassy in September 1862 Lord Augustus was not appointed ambassador.

able as Lord A. Loftus. Lord Granville is very confident of this. I shall see him and speak to him in the right sense.

Your love for the sea and the yacht in spite of sea-sickness is one I can't understand. For several years past I would go any distance rather than have a sea voyage, and now since our terrible misfortune I can't endure being on board for a moment! It requires good spirits to like it; but of those, you certainly have the most extraordinary supply. Dear child! I think no misfortune would crush you or break those elastic spirits!—For those who have to live it is a great blessing! For me my very misery is now a necessity and I could not exist without it. Like Tennyson says:

> O Sorrow, wilt thou live with me
> No casual mistress, but a wife,
> My bosom-friend and half of life,
> As I confess it needs must be; [1]

This is what I feel; yes, I long for my suffering almost—as it is blinded with him! May you never know such agony.

From the Crown Princess

ROME, NOVEMBER 22, 1862

How can I thank you enough for your dear touching letter[2] which Fritz put into my hands yesterday morning before we got up? You can imagine my feelings on waking. I will not dwell on them, but many, many tears were shed! Your dear letter was a comfort and a joy—and I kiss your dear hands a thousand times for it. Sad indeed were my reflexions when I thought of all the love and kindness which had been spent on me these 22 years, of all the trouble taken and all the anxiety I gave—and how little I have done to repay all this, how useless I am compared with what I ought to be, and how full of faults. I am quite frightened at myself sometimes when I think of all the blessings I enjoy—and the selfish and weak creature I am.

---

[1] *In Memoriam*, LIX.
[2] Of 15 November.

The spirit is willing indeed but the flesh is weak. All the good resolutions seem to come to very little—unfortunately. But with God's help and your and Papa's example, I may be of some use yet in the world—as wife and mother—and to the country to which I now belong—whose welfare I have so deeply at heart.

Nov. 23.

You say you are sorry a Prussian Regiment was offered to Bertie. None was offered—I do not even know whether the King ever had the intention of offering one—as of course a refusal could under no circumstances be risked. Fritz only wished to know how matters stood—as he could have suggested the idea to his father if it had given Bertie pleasure, and I am sure the King would have been delighted to give a proof of his kindly feelings towards England— and affection to you and Bertie. Of course refusing such a distinction would be an offence to him, his army and everybody there, and would not be the least understood. Fritz now knows your reasons against and therefore of course the question will never be mooted again. How sorry I am I cannot say. I thought there could be no possible reason against a purely honorary and formal thing, and I know it would have pleased the Prussian Army and the King. And all that tends in any way to cement the bonds of friendship between the two countries and their royal families must of course appear doubly desirable in my eyes.

I am so sad at dear Bertie's leaving; we have spent such a happy, pleasant time together. He has really been so kind, good-natured and amiable, full of consideration for me, and never has the slightest jar occurred so that the impression left on our minds is a very agreeable one. I assure you he is so much liked by our party that they are all unhappy at his going away tomorrow. We have to thank you, dear Mama, for allowing us to be together on this journey, and oh how important, doubly so now we have no father, it is that we brothers and sisters should hold together in perfect love and confidence. We are so many and so scattered, so often separated that I think it absolutely necessary whenever an opportunity can be found for seeing each other, we should avail ourselves of it. You know how I love dear Bertie, how I share all your anxiety about him and for his welfare! God bless him and his sweet bride and make them be your comfort and your support, which I am sure is their desire and will be their honest endeavour! I must end here, beloved Mama, but not without thanking you for the present you wished me to get here. According to your kind wish and permission I bought myself a necklace which I had very much wished to have, but could not afford treating myself to just now. It cost 10£. I hope you will not think that very outrageous and abusing your goodness. Thank you again and again for it, dearest Mama.

From the Queen

WINDSOR CASTLE, NOVEMBER 28, 1862

I received your dear interesting and beautiful letter of the 19th while our dear, sweet Alix—that bright pure spirit—was still with us! What you say of her is so beautiful that I had it copied for her, to take away with her! It expresses what I have felt! Another great and good man has been taken away—whose loss is an irreparable one to thousands and thousands! Our dear, valued Dr. McLeod whom I felt as a support and tower of strength, whose large, loving heart felt as few do for others and who had such faith, such strength, whom I felt one of my real dear friends, has been taken, and taken even as we were talking of him! He who looked like a Hercules, who poured such balm into my troubled soul—he is gone! but strange to say since beloved Papa left us, it seems as though the good and dear ones who went—were greatly privileged for they go to him! I have a faint hope since I began this it may be his father who I fancy now, since I reflected on it, may be called Norman too. I have just looked in the Royal Calendar and find that father and son have the same name, and by comparing the name with the printed announcement Mrs. Bruce got, we find that it is the father and not the valuable son—for which I am deeply grateful![1] Dear sweet Alix left us yesterday evening and I hardly could bear to let her go! I always tremble lest something should happen to her! She seems to be too charming. She loves us all, and was much affected when she left us. Her father is a good, honest, unassuming man and sensible father and with him there will be no difficulty, but old General Oxholme[2] made all sorts of difficulties which General Grey met very properly. He is very designing and very grand and high and mighty. I hope you have Germanised Bertie as much as possible, for it is most necessary. You speak of time taking away the edge of sorrow. No doubt it does and perhaps ought to those who have still a dearly beloved husband to lean on—and to impart every thing to! Yes, it is easy for them to say that—but not to one, who every, every day meets with fresh cause to pine and long for him who was her guide and support and help. But I never, never shall be able to bear that dreadful, weary, chilling, unnatural life of a widow! It is too dreadful for any one to conceive who is still blessed with a loving husband.

Dear Alice and Louis are very happy—and he quietly, really so; I like him more and more. He is so thoroughly amiable and unpretending and very intelligent. May God bless them. Alice is very well and active, much better than you were. It will be certainly by the 1st of April and perhaps it may be three or four days sooner as the first time, people seldom go quite their full time.

The poor Pope—I am glad you had a satisfactory visit. We are terribly occupied with Greece![3]

---

[1] Reverend Norman Macleod (1812–72), Scottish divine and editor of *Good Words*. The Queen greatly admired his preaching and commenting on his sermon she once wrote, "Everyone came back delighted: and how satisfactory it is to come back with such feelings." The father, somewhat unfeelingly dismissed by the Queen, was born in 1783 and died in 1862. He was Moderator of the Church of Scotland.
[2] Valdemar Tully Oxholme (1805–76), formerly governor to Prince Christian and later Master of the Household.
[3] The selection of a Sovereign for Greece. On 25 November the Queen prepared a long memorandum for the Foreign Secretary.

From the Crown Princess

You will wonder at my not having written to you for such a long time, but I have not been able to find a minute to myself—and usually come home very tired from sight-seeing, and find a great many things to do before dinner time. I told Hedwig to write to you about the sad things that have taken place in this house—and the frightful scene of which we were witness—and which as long as I live I never shall forget. You do not know poor M. de Canitz,[1] so details about him can have no interest for you. He has become perfectly insane, unfortunate man—and is most of the day in a straight waistcoat. His poor wife is not allowed to see him and only looks at him through the key-hole. None of the many Italians and Germans around him knew how to treat him, the only person who could manage him was Dr. Hill who luckily is here. He has been up with poor M. de Canitz four nights. He seems a very clever doctor indeed—and has an immense deal of experience; besides being the only determined man amongst all those about M. de Canitz.

This sad occurrence has of course thrown a great gloom over our party—it is so shocking to think that our host has had to be carried away mad out of his own house. If you wish to hear how it all happened Bertie can tell you for I wrote fully to him about it.

It is a great pleasure to have good Ernest here as a guest; we shall be his on board the *Magicienne* on Tuesday, he takes us to Leghorn and then to Genoa.

As it is Advent Sunday we have been to hear the great mass—in which the Pope officiates and at which all the Cardinals are present in the Sistine Chapel where Raphael's celebrated paintings are. It was a fine pageant though not the least impressive, and a great deal of it positively offensive

---

[1] The Prussian Minister to the Vatican. The royal party was staying in his house.

to one's feelings. The Pope looked very well seated on his throne. I was much interested in seeing it all as I had so often heard of it. This afternoon we were at the English Chapel.

Yesterday we went into a synagogue while service was going on; it was most curious, and I thought interesting. All the Jews with their hats on and white shawls round their shoulders reading the Bible in Hebrew. Then we saw the German Roman Catholic Church, then in the church where one of Raphael's "Sibyls" is—then to the Etruscan Museum in the Vatican. In the afternoon to the Museum of the Lateran—and to the Church of San Pietro Vincoli where Michael Angelo's celebrated Moses is.

Our cicerone is Mr. Pentland—who writes Murray's Handbook for Rome;—dear Papa knew him, and he led Bertie about when he was here last time.[1]

We see Mr. Odo Russell[2] very often. What a clever and agreeable man he is—and how well informed about all that goes on here.

From the Crown Princess

ROME, DECEMBER 1, 1862

I am very sorry our stay at Rome has come to an end, though I cannot get over the disagreeable impressions in this house caused by poor M. de Canitz's misfortune. Yesterday we went about all day from morning till night and I am quite tired. We had Mr. and Lady E. Adeane[3] to dinner —she is really a very nice person, and is in very good looks.

Our visit to the Pope yesterday was a very curious one. I have no time to put down the conversation we had with him. We paid Cardinal Antonelli a visit afterwards, and the King of Naples came to us in the evening. The three

---

[1] Joseph Barclay Pentland (1797–1873). A winter resident in Rome from 1845.
[2] See note on page 136.
[3] Lord Hardwicke's daughter who had married Henry John Adeane in 1860.

before named personages spoke of you and wished to be named to you.

From the Queen

I thank you very much for your last dear letter of 22nd and 23rd. I am so glad my letter arrived in time, and that you bought a necklace you liked, 10£ is very moderate.

We expect Bertie in a few minutes and the favourable account you give of him is very, very gratifying. Here it will be more difficult—for our life is very sad and serious and poor Bertie cannot accustom himself to that! I suffer much when I seem to be—and can for moments be—cheerful! And I feel my loneliness more than ever after that. The affairs of Greece have been a great worry to me—and made me and all feel the want of that beloved hand and head to guide and advise us! Of Affie's going there never was the slightest idea. It never could be, of course.

4th. I don't know when this letter will reach you, but I will write on. Bertie arrived at 8 looking extremely well and really very much improved. It is such a blessing to hear him talk so openly, sensibly and nicely—with such horror of what is bad that I feel God has been merciful in listening to our prayers! If he is good I am satisfied—for I look to the future, and that alone will help us to be happy there as well as here! How dreadful that affair of poor Count Canitz must have been and how well I do understand the fright it must have caused you all! It is too dreadful and most sad for his poor wife. I fear that horrid scene will haunt you for long!

I have been for the first time to poor Buckingham Palace today and went through all our dear rooms! Though dismantled all was standing as in happy, happy, busy times, and I cannot say how overwhelmed I was! Dear Alice (very rightly) persuaded me to go (quite incognito) with her, so not a soul, not a servant knew it! But I saw enough to feel I never can live there again except for two or three days at a time.

I have just heard that I am to send the letters for you to Vienna, which I shall accordingly do. I am very curious to hear how you will find the lovely young Empress. She is wonderfully recovered! I had a letter from dear Ernest L. confiding to me a secret, which has given me immense pleasure (satisfaction I should say for the other word has vanished from my mind and heart for ever). I will keep it —as (after 3 years ago) one must be very cautious; but if there are no appearances like those which they were so stupid as not to understand, I should really hope it might be. But there must be no return—for 3 months, before one can trust. Beloved Papa wished it so ardently, and so do I— for I have such an interest in that property.[1]

Dear old Lord Breadalbane has thought so touchingly of you, William and the King in his Will. He has left an enormous property.

Now goodbye—and God bless you. For fear of any mistake I wish to state again that the consecration will take place on the 17th and the translation on the 18th. Dr. Stanley[2] is coming here for 14th (the Saturday 13th is in fact as much the anniversary this first year as the 14th) and will read a few appropriate selections etc. to us and a very few in the dear room—on the 14th. The same day that that precious earthly robe has been placed in its final resting place, we shall go there together with a select few friends and the Dean[3] will say a few words and we shall go and kneel and pray there! How sad that you cannot be there too, but you will in thought. Tomorrow (by the week) it is a year that the fever was declared.

From the Crown Princess

FLORENCE, DECEMBER 5, 1862

As you know, we left Rome on the 2nd. All our friends were at the railway station—including Mr. Odo Russell, Mr.

---

[1] Their daughter, Albertine, was born at Osborne the following July.
[2] Arthur Stanley, afterwards Dean of Westminster.
[3] Of Windsor.

Pentland, the Duke and Duchess of St. Albans,[1] Mr. and Lady Elizabeth Adeane and most of the English artists.

I do like Gibson so much—he is so simple and unaffected and so original. I was really sorry to leave Rome, as I took such an interest in all that I did and there were so many clever and amusing people there, though I still think it very disagreeable as a town.

We went on board the *Magicienne* directly on arriving at Civita Vecchia, dear Ernest had arranged every thing charmingly—so that we were as comfortable as possible. The beginning of the passage was very good, but in the night it was very rough indeed and everybody was dreadfully sick—even Fritz who had been so well on all other occasions.

It was very cold indeed at Leghorn and so it is here in this extremely pretty place. I think Florence delightful—the buildings so fine, and the situation so good. We have seen the palazzo Pitti where the famous gallery of pictures is, the Gallery "de Uffizi", the Duomo, the Battistero, the Churches of Sta Croce, Sta Annunciata and Sta Maria Novella, the villa of Prince Demidoff, the former husband of Princess Matilde, which is the most marvellous thing I ever saw as regards taste and luxury.[2] It is filled with "objets d'art et de vertu" of every description, beautiful pictures, statues, china, plates, furniture, arms, marbles etc. like a fairy palace, with two chapels—a Greek and a Roman Catholic one—equally costly, green-houses, and grottos and what not. Prince Demidoff has no enjoyment of all this however, as he is always in every imaginable sort of scrape—as soon as he gets out of one he gets into another. Ernest is here with us at Florence. We go to Pisa tomorrow —and from thence in the *Magicienne* to Genoa. We are in a very good and quiet hotel, looking over the Arno. We

---

[1] The 10th Duke, aged 22, and his mother.
[2] Prince Anatole Demidoff (1813–70) married Princess Matilde, daughter of Jerome Bonaparte. Napoleon III had wished to marry her. Her husband had been described as "a peculiarly unpleasant Russian grandee" (F. A. Simpson, *Louis Napoleon and the Recovery of France*, Longmans Green). He was reputedly a flagellant. The marriage was annulled by the Pope.

went to see some lovely water-colour drawings—copies after old pictures by a Mr. Wheelright,[1] marvellously well done. I do not know whether he is an amateur or an artist—but I made out that he was a friend of Mr. Corbould's some time back;[2] do please tell the sisters to ask him whether he remembers Mr. Wheelright in whose room a very good picture of Mr. C's hangs—painted in the year '43.

It is exceedingly cold here—and we are quite frozen after Rome. The mosaic here is lovely—but the prices are exorbitant—and in our present state of finances we have resisted all temptations.

From the Queen

WINDSOR CASTLE, DECEMBER 10, 1862

I know not where to direct—but will take my chance and send this to dear Coburg where you meant to spend that dreadful day, now so fast approaching. It is long since I have heard from you, indeed nearly a fortnight! I trust all is well. Florence I hope you enjoyed and admired, as beloved Papa loved it so much!

From here I have but little new to say, except that every, every day is full of the most trying, dear and sad recollections. And that a sort of fright and anguish comes over me the nearer the time (that is still and will ever be like a most horrible dream) approaches, and the two very trying days of the 17th and 18th. Remember them and also the 23rd as holy days!

The beloved Countess is here since the 6th, and all love and kindness and so dear and charming! Bertie is languid and oppressed and seems very tired.

We are very much occupied (I wish I need not be) with the preparations and arrangements for the marriage. And it will be a tour de force to squeeze every one in. You and Fritz will be lodged in the State Apartments where the

---

[1] Presumably J. Hadwen Wheelwright, who exhibited at the Royal Academy in the 1840's.

[2] E. H. Corbould (1815–1905), water-colour painter; taught the Royal Family. See page 46.

Emperor and Empress were.[1] We must have the marriage and all over by the 12th of March—for then come the sad anniversaries connected with beloved Grandmama, and after that we must be ready for dear Alice—before which the house must be emptied. A first confinement is often a few days too early—therefore after the 23rd we may expect it any day. We wish much you and Fritz could come therefore the end of Feb. and I must ask you to hold a Drawing-room for me—in your capacity of our eldest daughter. I wish you also, dear, to represent me completely in the home, during the three or four days of the visits for the marriage—doing absolutely the honours; for Alice cannot do any thing of that kind then; and Fritz and Louis must kindly help as sons in entertaining the visitors with Bertie and Affie. Prince and Princess Christian with the bride and their four other children (all but the second son) will arrive three nights before the wedding. Uncle Ernest and Aunt Alexandrine will come, and possibly Marie Brabant[2] and Philip.[3] And I was obliged to ask Alix's two Uncles—the Duke of Glücksburg[4] and Prince and Princess Frederick of Hesse[5]—but they only will be here one night. Bertie and Alix will go for their honeymoon to Osborne—and not come to Town for some time. It is necessary they should be quiet at first. All this may be upset as God knows all is so uncertain—but as matters at present are arranged this is the intention.

From the Crown Princess

HOTEL DANIELLI, VENICE, DECEMBER 11, 1862

In this most beautiful, picturesque and poetical of places—I received your dear, sweet but heartrending letter. Oh not a moment passes that my thoughts are not flying home—and passing these sad, sad days with you!

---

[1] Napoleon III and Eugénie.
[2] An Austrian Archduchess married to the Duke of Brabant, King Leopold's heir.
[3] King Leopold's second son, the Count of Flanders.
[4] Duke of Schleswig-Holstein-Sonderburg-Glücksburg, brother of Prince Christian.
[5] Princess Christian's brother, the future Landgrave of Hesse.

I shall spend the 13th with dear Charlotte at Miramar in private—and the dreadful 14th on the railway, travelling from Trieste to Vienna, where we shall arrive in the evening. Oh how I dread that day—the thought of your suffering makes me quite miserable. I am so glad you are pleased with dear Bertie—he has indeed a heart full of good and kind feeling it only requires to be called forth and no one will be able to do that better than dear Alix!

My last letter was from Florence; after leaving it we passed through Pisa under Garibaldi's windows and dined at an hotel close to the one in which the great man is living. . . . We embarked on board the *Magicienne*, for which I have now the greatest affection; it was so nice being on dear Ernest's ship—and he was so very kind and amiable and in most excellent spirits—more lively and merry than I had ever seen him. The night was splendid, the sea as smooth as a millpond—and the moon so bright. We arrived in the beautiful harbour of Genoa by daylight on the 7th (Sunday morning). We had service on deck and heard a sermon with a very minute description of the last judgement from Ernest's parson.

Afterwards Mmde. Rollande[1] came on board and had luncheon with us; I was so glad to see good Rollet again, though it made me sad as all does that reminds one of past happy times never to be recalled.

Also good old Sir Charles Locock came the whole way from Nice to see me, which I was quite touched at. We spent the day at Genoa, in visiting the gardens and churches —and driving about the town talking with M. Brassier de St. Simon our Minister at Turin—the only liberal and sensible Prussian diplomat I know—and consequently persecuted and suspected at home. I was quite distressed to say goodbye to dearest Ernest on the morning of the 8th and leave the ship—the last little bit of England and home. We proceeded to Milan—the cold was biting. Leaving the town of Genoa with its lovely situation looking from rocky heights

---

[1] French governess to the Queen's elder children. Rollet was her nick name.

covered with evergreens and pretty villas, towards the dear blue sea, you pass through an immensely long tunnel and on emerging find yourself in the depth of winter, ice and snow and leafless trees—the contrast was quite melancholy!

As soon as we arrived at Milan we went into the celebrated Duomo—but it was too dark to see it properly—and there were crowds of people.

Prince Umberto the King of Italy's eldest son—came to pay us a visit at the hotel. He is very plain—but not like his father. He stayed some time, seems very sharp and exceedingly determined. Like his papa he seems to have no other thought but soldiers and war, and to be of a rough and hard disposition; he speaks in a gruff, abrupt way—but there seems to be a great deal in him. I was very much interested in seeing him. We went to the top of the Duomo the next morning and saw one of the finest views in the world—the dear Alps—both Tyrolese and Swiss, the Mont Blanc, Mt. Baldo, St. Bernard, St. Gotthard, Simplon etc.—and the whole of the Apennines, but the wind and the cold were so unpleasant that we were half frozen while contemplating this grand panorama. After having seen the Picture Gallery in which is the original of Rafael's "Sposalizio" we left Milan. On the Austrian Frontier we found Count Paar and M. de Binder whom the Emperor had sent to meet us. At Verona General Benedek[1] met us at the station, he and several other Austrian officers dined with us. On the 9th in the morning we went to see all we could of the town—the old Arena, the churches—and last of all "Juliet's" tomb. Verona is most picturesque and pretty. How delighted I am with Venice I cannot say—it is so totally unlike any thing else—and there is a certain sadness about the scene, which just at present is most congenial and soothing to my feelings. The graceful gondolas, and the beautiful old buildings—all is picturesque and striking. I like it beyond measure. We rowed about in the moonlight the other

---

[1] Military Governor of Venetia: in 1866 he was to be disastrously defeated by the Prussians at Sadowa.

evening and the gondolieri were singing; it was so silent, calm and peaceful on the water, we enjoyed it very much indeed.

I knew Marie L.'s secret at Naples, and I am as pleased as you are. Oh! if only all goes right it would be such a good thing and make both her and Ernest so happy; even the prospect seems to make him quite a different creature.

I have seen Prince Alexander of Hesse here—he is quite in love with Alice.[1] I also saw Gustav Weimar at Verona.[2] Of course everyone I see asks after you and begs to be respectfully remembered. What a business all this is about Greece! I wonder what the end of it will be. Of course I never for a moment thought Affie was going there.

THE ELECTRIC AND INTERNATIONAL TELEGRAPH COMPANY

INCORPORATED 1846

GOVERNMENT DISPATCH NO.   DECEMBER 12TH, 1862

Given in at Cornhill at 10.10 a.m. *Received in Cornhill at* 10.23 a.m. *Sent out for delivery at* 10.24 a.m.	*This message has passed through the hands of* G. Warren *Telegraphist*
From C. Princess of Prussia Venedig	,, ,, *Writer* *To* H.M. The Queen Windsor Castle

Venedig the 12th, 9.40 a.m.

Spend 14th travelling from Trieste to Vienna in strict incognito.

[1] Prince Alexander (1823–88), uncle of Prince Louis and father of the Battenberg princes. He served with the Austrian Army, and was in command in northern Italy at this time. See David Duff, *Hessian Tapestry*, Muller, 1967.

[2] Prince Gustav of Saxe-Weimar, nephew of Queen Adelaide. A general in the Austrian Army.

From the Crown Princess

As I shall not be able to write tomorrow—I write today on this first sad and dreadful day! I pray that you may
be supported through this trial as you have been through so
many cruel ones—since your awful misfortune.

How painful it is to me to travel today and tomorrow
you can imagine, but I shall be quieter alone with Fritz in
the railway carriage than I should be staying at a strange
place!

Goodbye and God bless you and comfort you dear
beloved Mama.

From the Queen

WINDSOR CASTLE, DECEMBER 17, 1862

I have to thank you for two letters from Rome dated
30th and 1st and for the one from Florence which I received
before. But I have had none for the sacred and heart-
rending anniversary of the 14th, and only heard of your
spending that day in the railroad and arriving that evening at Vienna—where the Emperor received you!!! Even
now I can hardly believe it! I should have thought that you
would have preferred remaining in the smallest wayside
inn and going to pray to God to support your broken-
hearted mother rather than do that! What I and we all
here have felt I will not now say. (And where are anniversaries of that kind more solemnly kept, even when there
is no great sentiment, than in Germany?) And I will
therefore not speak of the solemn, touching and edifying
way in which we spent that day or of the deep anguish of
my broken heart! One dreary, lonely year has been passed,
which I had hoped never to live to the end of, and now with
a weakened, shattered frame I have to begin the weary
work again.

I send you today Mr. Helps admirable book, which shall
be immediately translated.[1] It has made a great sensation.

[1] See note on page 64.

It blows—and rains occasionally. We are just going to the consecration of the Mausoleum. What will you be doing? And tomorrow will be a dreadful day again—the most trying for me! I trust that at least you will observe that solemn day in quiet.

I hope you will have found the dear children well.

Many thanks to Fritz for his kind letter with the enclosure. If Affie is not to fall again and again into similar sins he must marry early, and this he wishes himself.

> Ever
>
> your loving unhappy
> Mama
> VR.

This is of course a painful letter to read and to receive. In fairness to the Crown Princess it should be said that she had written to her mother in the previous summer saying that one advantage of her visit to Italy would be that she would be spared spending those terrible anniversary days in Berlin. But it is painfully obvious that the minds of the two correspondents were fixed on different things —the Queen was pre-occupied with December 1861 and the consecration and reburial while the Crown Princess was under the spell of Italian scenes. Replying, the Crown Princess said that it was not possible to spend the day as she had wished in "perfect quiet", "*I* thought that this would have awakened your pity rather than your anger, dear Mama." She added: "Fritz will explain to you how it happened."

The reader may here be helped by an account of the arrangements for the interment of the Prince's body. Shortly after 11 p.m. on 14 December 1861 the body of the Prince was laid out on a small bed in the Blue Room in which he had died. This was the same room in which both King George IV and King William IV had died. On the 17th the dressing room was put in mourning to receive the body. The floor was covered with black drugget and the doors and windows were draped with black cloth. The Prince's body was presumably placed in the coffin on the following day in this room. After the funeral the coffin was placed at the entrance to the royal vault (where lay the coffins of George III and his family) and it was made public that this was only a temporary resting place till the mausoleum at Frogmore was ready.[1]

On 14 December 1862 a service was held round the bed in the Blue Room at 9.45 in the morning. The bust of the Prince was on the

[1] See *A Queen at Home*, by Vera Watson, W. H. Allen, 1952.

bed and flowers were round it. There was another service at 12, and again at 9.30 in the evening.

On 17 December 1862 the mausoleum at Frogmore was consecrated. The Queen and all her children in England were present, and the service began with the choir and clergy processing round the building chanting the psalm. The consecration was performed by the Bishop of Oxford. On the following day 18 December the coffin was moved early in the morning from the royal vault to the mausoleum. "Tomorrow will be a dreadful day again—the most trying for me." The Queen and her children attended a service at the mausoleum, and the Dean of Windsor read prayers. Afterwards the Queen and her children knelt down by the temporary sarcophagus, where the coffin had been placed, and each placed a wreath by it.

The Bishop of Oxford described the consecration and "the sight of our Queen and the file of fatherless children" as "one of the most touching scenes I ever saw". He talked to her afterwards and described her as "so gentle, so affectionate, so true, so real—no touch of morbidness". *Life of Samuel Wilberforce*, by R. G. Wilberforce, Vol. III, page 72.

1863

From the Crown Princess

BERLIN, JANUARY 3, 1863

I shall try and do my best about dear Papa's lithograph and the angel[1] but I must entreat you to have patience as I have a good deal to do, and the Queen occupies a great deal of my time. The King has got a severe cold and is far from well. M. de Bismarck and his consorts are "dangerously well" and seem up to anything as indeed they are in the real sense of the word. We live with a sword hanging over our heads, and it will fall when we least expect it and on the innocent ones. I cannot tell you how anxious I feel. Dearest Fritz is overworked again. I see very little of him, and he loses his regular exercise and fresh air which tells upon him directly.

I fear dear Uncle Leopold is not so well again. How much longer will he be spared to us? These attacks seem to recur so often. Langenbeck[2] is going to attend him I hear. I hope he will torment him less than M. Civiale.[3]

My Baron is not at all well; he complains very much and looks far from the thing. I can't imagine what is the matter but he seems to suffer a good deal.

Yesterday we were all at Potsdam in the Friedenskirche as it was the anniversary of the poor King's death. We were nearly frozen in the church.

Prince Charles is ill in bed with erysipelas. Prince Adalbert[4] is also ill; this place is like a hospital, the cold is so bitter and piercing and the changes of temperature so sudden—frost succeeded by rain and wind, then the hot rooms etc. It is really not very wholesome. I have taken to

---

[1] In her letter of 26 December the Queen wrote in connexion with the contents of the Blue Room at Windsor, "Pray paint the pendant angel as soon as you can."
[2] The German doctor attending King Leopold.
[3] A French surgeon.
[4] First cousin to the King, and brother to Princess Charles of Hesse.

my riding again, and take as much exercise as I possibly can and certainly I never felt stronger and better and you would not be so horrified at my figure now as you were at Reinhardtsbrunn.

From the Crown Princess

Your dear letter received yesterday has put me into a state of excitement which you will easily understand. The news is indeed astounding. What will Uncle E. answer? I dare not say more on this subject by post; no one of course shall know anything about it except Fritz who is as much astonished as I am. But we both thank you a thousand times for telling us of this project; may Heaven guide all for the best![1]

About Mary C. and the Grand-Duke of M.S.[2] I am almost sorry that the Queen was written to about it; as she wishes him to marry Addy not because he is the "partie" she prefers before any other for A. but because she feels certain that if she does not marry the Grand-Duke all her relations will push her to take his brother William whom the Queen cannot bear (and not without reason). Moreover the Queen is not favourably disposed towards Mary at present, and she thinks William M. would be the right person for Mary and would be glad to see this come about for the above mentioned reasons. I do not think it is quite fair upon Mary as I cannot help thinking she would rather remain an old maid than take W.M. If he was clever and distinguished one might look over his wildness and think she could be happy with him, but he really is not—his genius all lies

---

[1] A suggestion that the Duke of Coburg should succeed to the Greek throne, which would have meant that Prince Alfred would have had to become the reigning Duke of Coburg.
[2] This passage concerns the matrimonial possibilities for Princess Mary of Cambridge, who was now nearly 30. The Grand-Duke of Mecklenburg-Schwerin, widower, later married the sister of Prince Louis of Hesse, while Prince William married Addy. Commenting on the Crown Princess's letter the Queen says, "I am very sorry for what you say about the prospects for poor Mary."

in the way of spending money and being a dandy. Maroussy and Marietje of the Netherlands have both refused him. Addy does not like him but her father and his mother would persuade her, the Queen thinks, so she had rather A. married the Grand-Duke which is wished for by all the members of the family here.

The Grand-Duke comes here today so I shall hear something more about it. I think Mary would do much better for the Grand-Duke than A. He is a weak and helpless man, completely ruled by his mother, Addy is (though very good) yet rather negative and that would just suit his mother. The position would be just the thing for Mary but I fear there is but little chance. I write all this because I heard the Queen say she was going to write to Countess Blücher about it and I wanted you to know exactly how matters stand.

From the Queen

OSBORNE, JANUARY 7, 1863

I am so worried, agitated and harassed by business and anxiety of all kinds—but especially since Friday by this Greek business, that I can't sleep, or eat any thing and am terribly exhausted. All will I trust go right, and I feel that beloved Papa could not have acted otherwise and, what is more, would have been pleased I think. Dear Uncle E. seems inclined to undertake it and of course Affie will go to Coburg. But there are so many questions and so many things involved that I really know not which way to turn.

I tremble at the state of German and especially your affairs! What on earth will happen? God Almighty knows— I only wish I could help you.

Poor old Whiting died this morning! Another old friend gone![1]

---

[1] John Whiting. One of the very few links between the Queen and her Hanoverian predecessors. He was a favourite servant—page of the backstairs—to both George IV and William IV. He continued in the service of the Queen and escorted the Princess's wet-nurse from the Isle of Wight at the start of her duties.

From the Crown Princess

I shall enjoy the outburst of rage and jealousy here, if Uncle Ernest becomes King of Greece. I am sure Aunt Alexandrine will be in despair, she is so fond of retirement and quiet and dislikes hot climates so. How hard for them both to have no children! It is really a sad misfortune.

You will have heard that poor Princess Charles has the measles and is really very unwell.[1] I am sure it would touch her very much if I might inquire in your name how she is. You know she is so devoted to you, shed so many tears about your misfortune—and of the whole family is the one who has shown me most sympathy on this occasion, and who is the kindest to me. Countess Blücher can tell you the same.

From the Queen

Many, many thanks for your dear letter of the 10th. I telegraphed at once to inquire after Princess Charles. And how is the King really? Affairs look most threatening but I trust that moderation and conciliation will be shown on both sides (I mean Austria and Prussia).[2] You know how strongly beloved Papa felt this.

Now let me say what I am anxious you should do about coming here for Bertie's marriage. We hope if they are not actually frozen up that the marriage may take place between the 5th and 10th of March, the bride arriving three nights before. Well I wish you, as our eldest daughter, to hold a

---

[1] She was the elder sister of the Queen of Prussia, and generally thought to be—like her husband—very worldly.

[2] On the day on which the Queen was writing Bismarck, at the opening session of the Chambers alluded to Prussia's altered position in Germany. The arrangement after the overthrow of Napoleon left Austria paramount in the German Confederation with Prussia on an equality with other German states; this, Bismarck ominously said, "no longer corresponded with the altered circumstances of the time."

Drawing-room for me, at the end of February—either 26th or 28th so I wish you arrive on the 24th. Then I wish you to do the honours in the house for me during those two or three busy (to me dreadful) days, and if possible to remain to be present at the reception held at St. James's in the evening about ten days after the marriage for people to be presented to the young couple. Then I am so thankful to think you may be here before the end of February as then you will see and help us to decide on the memorial for angel Papa, the designs for which are to be submitted to me on my return from here to Windsor on the 11th February and to remain there till the 28th.

Of Uncle E. I can say nothing positive, for he has made conditions which are not admissible. Now (in strict confidence) let me tell you, that failing him, I think the fittest would be Fritz Holstein; of his worth and sense you feel as beloved Papa and I do; he is my nephew by marriage, has children, and has lost his home!! Keep this to yourself, but answer me what you think.

From the Crown Princess

BERLIN, JANUARY 12, 1863

Many thanks for your dear letter. I can well imagine how the Greek business must agitate you! Yesterday while I was with the King he began talking about it and said he had heard about Uncle E. from M. de Bismarck, and as you may imagine the idea gave him the very reverse from pleasure which he expressed very decidedly! About the Ionian Islands he is still angry and the whole subject is one quite useless to discuss with him.[1] The King is much in bed of an evening, there is nothing amiss with him it is only in the morning he feels depressed and low. How should it be otherwise? They won't let him go out (though he has

---

[1] The Duke, though a patriotic German—he had fought against the Danes in the Schleswig-Holstein war—was regarded as too liberal-minded for the King and Bismarck. The Islands were a British protectorate since 1815, and had been offered to Greece in 1862: the King disliked this since he regarded it as an undesirable spread of nationalism.

quite lost his cold) so he has quite lost his appetite. His rooms are never below 70—usually above—it is no wonder his head aches and his nerves are irritable. I think it is chiefly moral and not physical suffering, striving to do his duty in every way, seeing that his mode of doing it does not produce any good results, yet determined not to give way to any other opinion, and persuaded that all those of different opinion wish to limit his power, destroy his army and despoil the crown of its rights. This I think is the real secret of his being attacked.

Sir John Acton[1] has published a book called "Matinées Royales", an infamous libel against Frederick the Great, well known here as such ever since Frederick the Great's own time; and now Sir John publishes it as a composition of Frederick the Great. I cannot tell you what indignation it has caused here in all circles. To have the first of our Kings so blackened at a time when the whole of Europe is laughing at our sad and crippled condition, is bitterly felt—the newspapers have taken it up very warmly and the King and Queen feel much hurt at Sir J. Acton's having brought out the book as he was treated with so much kindness here by every body last year at the coronation.

If the book had not been well known as a fabric (not authentic) less might have been said about it, but even Carlyle in his work pronounces it to be spurious, and it is nothing else than a really shocking libel. I live in dread of this being the cause of another quarrel like the Macdonald affair![2] Baron E. Stockmar is not at all well. I can't think what is the matter with him but he puts me into despair by saying that he must leave me and that he is a confirmed

---

[1] The historian Lord Acton. The book purported to be conversations between Frederick the Great and his heir. Frederick is made to say that the Hohenzollerns "as devout worshippers of Beelzebub" believed his creed to be "the true one". Carlyle called it impudent and forged. The author was in fact a Frenchman, de Bonneville.

[2] In 1860 Captain Macdonald was involved in a dispute over a seat in a railway carriage and was committed to prison at Bonn. High indignation was caused by the incident in England, especially the remark of the public prosecutor that Englishmen abroad were "notorious for their rudeness, impudence and boorish arrogance".

invalid. I fear it is congestion of the spine. This summer he was suffering from one leg and now from both so that he finds standing or walking very painful and looks wretched. I really am quite alarmed.

From the Queen

OSBORNE, JANUARY 17, 1863

Many thanks for your dear letter of the 13th. I can quite understand what the King says about Uncle E. General Grey goes tonight to Brussels to meet him there and hopes for success. It is thought here that E.L.[1] would be better than Fritz H. Failing E.L. then he would do but do you think he would take it? I have written to sound the others in case Uncle should finally refuse. I am quite grieved and distressed about your dear Baron; you could never do without him.

Good old Sir James[2] (who is staying here) will write to you about him. I am much vexed about Sir J. Acton's book; I will see if I can't do something about it.

You of course heard that it was Dr. McLeod's old father and not himself who died. Both had the same name and both were my chaplains. Whiting is also not dead, but dying; he can never leave the house again. He is in Windsor.

From the Crown Princess

BERLIN, JANUARY 17, 1863

I fear I shall not have much time to answer your dear letter as the messenger has only brought my letters this morning.

About my coming to England, dear Mama, there seems no sort of difficulty, any day from the 15th of February I am free here and the sooner you allow me to start on my holiday the happier I shall be—only I must be back here on the 16th of March as there is a great festival here on the 17th which I could not miss under any consideration,

---

[1] Ernest Leiningen, Queen Victoria's nephew.
[2] Clark, the royal doctor.

besides the King's birthday on the 22nd. They will expect me to be back here on the 15th or 16th of March—it is not possible to change that, as it is really necessary I should be at the festival of the 17th on which the foundation stone of the monument of F.W. the IIId will be laid and which day is the 100 anniversary of the institution of the Landwehr. On the 15th of March[1] our Carnival closes, and I should thank my stars to be able to get away for a little while out of this most fatiguing whirl of balls, concerts and daily evening parties which have already begun to my despair.

As you ask me to give you my opinion with regard to Fritz Holstein, I shall venture to do so candidly. You know I have the greatest regard for him and confidence in him, and if this was merely a question of who would make a constitutional, good and respectable king, he would certainly have my voice. But there is this other difficult question: would he accept it? And could one in fairness offer it to him? I think not. To accept it would be to renounce in the eyes of the world all his hopes, claims and prospects as to Schleswig-Holstein, he being the heir apparent, and his father having precluded himself from pursuing those claims, it would be a blow to the whole family and consequently to the whole Schleswig-Holstein cause.[2] There would be nearly the same objection to Fritz's brother because Fritz has no son.

Prince Waldemar Holstein[3] who is an excellent liberal and clever man, might perhaps be a candidate, he is not young and very tall and fat so perhaps he might marry Mary Cambridge—that would be to kill two birds with one stone. Of course this is only a vague idea. He is of the Augustenburg family, we know him very well. He is a great friend of Prince Hohenzollern—also of the Queen.

---

[1] So written by a slip for February.
[2] After the Schleswig-Holstein war Duke Christian renounced his Schleswig estates in return for an annual payment.
[3] Duke Christian's first cousin; he had been born in 1810, and was a Prussian general, but German opinion (which the Crown Princess is here voicing) continued to regard his family as rightful rulers of the Duchies.

From the Crown Princess

Our questions and answers have, in a manner, crossed so that I will not repeat what I said last Saturday. E.L., failing Uncle E., would be an excellent person—but I think he loves his ease and comfort too much to undertake so difficult and doubtful a task. What have you heard from Affie in answer to your letter?

Our matters are getting more and more "embrouillé". The King goes out to the theatre, there seems very little amiss with him. Fritz is looking ill, so pale, so fagged and he sleeps badly—in fact he takes all these political difficulties so much to heart and is so teased on all sides that it tells upon him. I spoke to Wegner about it today and he will give him something strengthening (I suppose sugar water). It is not for a mind to be always harping on one string as it takes away the necessary energy and freshness to meet new difficulties and it can do matters no good as it is not in Fritz's power to change them. This weight is felt by the whole country; we are "under a cloud"; when and how we shall see sunlight again I do not know. I feel more angry and indignant at it all than sad because I think the way people are going on is really tempting providence.

Sir Andrew and Lady Buchanan are liked here—he more than she is, I hope his despatches convey as correct an idea of our affairs to you as Lord A. Loftus's did.

From the Queen

I can only write a very few words—as my time is short. I will however speak at once of your coming. Before the 24th I could not well receive you. A great deal of preparation is going on, and as we shall only return to Windsor on the 11th or 12th of February, I must have some days of as much quiet as I possibly can. You never will believe how unwell and how weak and nervous I am, but any talking or excitement is far too much for me. I must constantly dine alone, and any merriment or discussion are quite unbearable. Poor Bertie is far too noisy for me; he is very fond of disputing and this is what in my best times I never could bear, but now without beloved Papa to lead the conversation and to check the young people, it is quite too much for my very shattered nerves. On the 24th I hope however (weather permitting) to see you arrive. I shall not be able to send you the yacht as she will be wanted so soon after for Alix—but you shall have a packet either at Calais or wherever you like. I can I grieve to say not ask you to bring any of the dear children as we shall not have a hole to spare, and I must put the governesses even into the nursery. I have had to ask all the court attendants of Alix and two of her uncles and this with Alice and Louis, M. Brabant, Uncle E. and Aunt Alexandrine makes a fearful squeeze.

From the Queen

OSBORNE, JANUARY 24, 1863

I did not yesterday thank you for your letter of the 20th with very anxious, sad accounts. The Address and what has followed alarms us all much. Oh! it is a sad and an unnecessary state of things![1] Respecting Uncle E. matters are not satisfactory to my feelings and I feel much worried about it, but can't say more today except that it is not settled either way. I send you here (asking to have it back) a letter from Sir J. Acton. He ought not to have published it but he thinks of nothing but books and writing.

I send dear little William, for whose approaching birthday I offer many, many happy returns and invoke every blessing—in both our names—a hot dish. Charlotte shall have one too and then I wish to have your old one back to

---

[1] The Chamber of Deputies carried, by an overwhelming majority, an address to the King complaining that Ministers were carrying on the Government against the Constitution. The King refused to see the deputation bringing the address but sent a sharp answer to the President of the Chamber.

keep here, for it was not given to you—but only ordered for your use—and I wish to keep it for the use of all grand-children when they are with me.

I agree with you about E.L. Can't you or Fritz say anything (without telling the Queen) to Fritz of Schleswig?

George is very, very anxious about poor Mary. Is there no chance at all?[1]

Now goodbye and God bless you! I feel more and more wretched. Love to dear Fritz who should try not to take things too much to heart, but it is difficult not to do so.

From the Crown Princess

BERLIN, JANUARY 24, 1863

We hear that Uncle Ernest has definitively declined the Greek throne and I suppose it is true. What is to become of it all now? Do you know that now it is settled so, I am glad of it? The more I thought of the idea the more it appeared to me as a thing with two sides and there were many objections. I am most anxious to hear from you what is going to be proposed.

I send you some photographs of the children. Those of dear baby were done yesterday on purpose for you but they are dreadfully unflattering; he is really in beauty now—and these photographs give the impression of the very reverse. There is one of Willy and Charlotte as sailors which is only for fun—as she has on the things that Willy wore at Osborne two years ago. The one as Highlander is not very good—but still perhaps you will like it.

I had no time to write to you yesterday, about the most unpleasant occurrence in our house. The beam under the fire place in my sitting room is completely charred three feet wide and three feet deep, and had the fire not been luckily found out (though it had most likely been smouldering for days) we might have had an awful fire. As it is, the mischief is—though considerable—not difficult to repair.

---

[1] Meaning for her possible marriage with the Grand-Duke of Mecklenburg-Schwerin.

The house is full of stonemasons, carpenters and work-people, the floor of my room taken up and I have only my drawing and bed room "pour tout potage" to see people in and every thing—it is wretchedly uncomfortable. The smell of the fire has got quite impregnated in all our things, and altogether we are in a state of confusion difficult to describe. Something went wrong on the other side of the house with a hot air pipe so that repairs are going on in Fritz's rooms, and in the dining room the doors and wainscots are being painted, so that we are reduced to three rooms between us—and a perpetual noise going on which has given me a racking headache. It will be ten days at least before we can get back into our rooms.

Balls and parties every night, shocking weather by day so that one can hardly get air or exercise—and mental annoyance enough to turn one's brain!

From the Crown Princess

BERLIN, JANUARY 26, 1863

We had not one moment to ourselves yesterday, which was rather hard, it was the investiture which lasted from half past ten to four in the afternoon. Altogether I am getting rather knocked up with parties every night standing about so long in such dreadfully hot rooms and such a crush of people; we are not let off once—the Queen enjoys it you know—but if you were to see Fritz's pale face of a morning you would be convinced that it is not good for every body. The King is really much better, he appeared yesterday.

Many thanks for the copy of Sir J. Acton's letter to Lord Granville also for the original second letter to Lord G. Both confirm what I was perfectly sure of and what I said to every one here—which is that his interest in the thing is purely literary and that he is not actuated by any other motives. I defended him both to the King and Queen and to all the infuriated historians here, and I hope you will tell Lord Granville so. To my mind it is as clear as sunlight that these *Matinées* are not by Frederick the Great—as since I have been here I have had so much opportunity of becoming fully acquainted with his sentiments, character, habits and peculiarities; many of the sentiments are no doubt his though just as many are not—but the way of expressing them, the style and the arguments are most certainly not his. In England he is not sufficiently known for people to be able to distinguish between his real and his popular character but here every child knows all about him and those that knew him are still alive. I know two people who knew him.

I am indeed sorry that this Greek business should give you so much annoyance but oh! what are foreign troubles to internal ones, such as we are at present labouring under! The state of Poland is dreadful, Prussian Poland is still quiet —but every body is very anxious about it.[1]

From the Queen

OSBORNE, JANUARY 28, 1863

We drank darling William's health last night at our sad little dinner, sweet Baby staying up on purpose! God bless him. If you will only bring one person with William, I can put the darling child up in the nursery quite well.

I think it is more than ever likely (between ourselves) that Uncle E. will go to Greece—but retaining (for some time at least) the entire sovereignty of the Duchies, provided his Chambers agree. I received last night a beautiful letter from dear Ernest L. declining (if he should be proposed) in the most modest and sensible way. Poor Aunt Alexandrine is almost frantic, and angry with me, who am utterly innocent about it! It is rather hard.

The photographs are charming; the standing one of darling William in the Highland dress is delightful, and so like Affie and Arthur; the little sailors are charming, but you seem quite wild about that (to me) most distasteful profession. I think it is the worst for morals and every thing

---

[1] Revolution had broken out in the Russian parts of Poland: it had been relentlessly suppressed. A few days after this letter was written, Bismarck agreed to allow Russian troops to pass through Prussian territory in pursuit of the rebels—an unpopular measure with Prussian liberals.

that can be imagined—and the suffering and misery at sea and the dangers!

You don't speak of the Address which alarms us all terribly! What is to happen?

Bertie returns today—and then my bad headaches will begin I fear. But he is very much pleased with his place and takes great interest in it.[1]

From the Queen

I hope dearest William's birthday went off well? I fear Prince W. of H.[2] would not do for Mary, unless he were rich and had a pleasant position. Tell me dear all about him. Poor M. is so much to be pitied.

I am curious to hear what you think of your state in the Chambers? I fear it is very bad!

I am occupying myself in trying to collect and put together the beginning of that private life intended only for the family and our children and children's children etc. in which I hope you will all help me.[3] But my heart breaks in reading over those angelic letters.

From the Crown Princess

BERLIN, JANUARY 31, 1863

I thank you a thousand times for your dear letter and the copy of the Prayers read in the Mausoleum. A heart that has not suffered hardly knows the power and the value of prayer!—

> Who has never eaten his bread with tears,
> Who has not spent sorrowful nights
> Sitting on his bed
> Does not know you—your heavenly powers.

---

[1] Sandringham.
[2] Prince Waldemar.
[3] *The Early Years of the Prince Consort,* which was published for the Queen's family in 1866, was published for the general public in 1867.

It is so true! and Goethe's beautiful words express it so well! Those are the words that Queen Louise wrote down in her prayer book in the dreadful year 1806![1]

I am so happy that I can bring Willy with me; it will be a recollection for his whole life to have been at Bertie's wedding! He thinks and talks of nothing else and is so excited about it that we have to say if he is not quiet we shall leave him at home. He is very much occupied with his Scotch dress—whether Uncle Arthur and Uncle Leopold will put on theirs. I send you two more photographs of the little sailors there are no more, and the plate is destroyed—as it was only done for fun and Fritz does not like Ditta to be perpetually in boys' clothes.

The address is voted in our Chambers and will be accepted—but not in person by the King. I expect nothing of any consequence to occur now till April, as during the early part of the session nothing of importance is on the "tapis". Some expect a "coup d'état". I do not think it likely but I think it far from impossible as with such a man as Bismarck there is no knowing what may happen. The King thinks only of his duty, but unfortunately that term is applied to the very things which are calculated to do most harm. He never would, with open eyes, break the Constitution or do away with it but his ministers have so tampered with it that it is broken already, which the King and M. de Bismarck do not see and call it interpreting the Constitution rightly. There is no knowing where "interpreting" (which consists in giving the very reverse meaning) may not lead to. The difficulty was great and the ministers could hardly help themselves, but if they go on maintaining that they are in the right about the Article 99 of the Constitution they will have the worst of the argument.[2] Two and two will never

---

[1] The disastrous defeat of Jena and the occupation of Berlin by Napoleon. Queen Louise (1776–1816) was the heroic Queen of Prussia and grandmother of the Crown Prince.

[2] Article 99 prescribed that income and expenditure should be authorised by a budget exacted as a law. By another article the power to exact law was given jointly to King and Parliament. But no provision was made for a disagreement between King and Parliament. Bismarck argued that

make five—turn it how you will. Bismarck means to go on governing as best he can for the next year without any great changes; if nothing of importance intervenes it may go on smoothly for a time—but if foreign difficulties arise I really do not know what is to become of it. No cure but a radical one will set us to rights—you can I am sure understand what I mean—and I dare not express myself more plainly. There is no way to get out of such a terrible mess but by beginning afresh and starting on a new and better road and that the King will never do![1]

The feeling of humiliation is the hardest to bear; there is not one good Prussian who does not feel that, I can assure you, at this present moment, and as for the Queen, Fritz and myself, who are so nearly concerned in it all, discouragement and disappointment quite oppress us and nothing remains but silence as passive witnesses of the lamentable mistakes made by those we love and reverence; we cannot defend nor even understand what is being done and duty and affection alike forbid us to blame. It is no pleasant position.

From the Crown Princess

BERLIN, FEBRUARY 3, 1863

I have not heard about darling Affie for such a long time. I read in the German newspapers that he had already passed his examination and become lieutenant. I suppose this is not true or I should have heard something about it from you and the sisters.[2]

Ranke's article in *The Times* is very good and cannot fail I should think to produce the desired effect.[3] Today it is 50 years since the Chancellor Prince Hardenberg called

---

there was a gap in the constitution and that therefore article 99 must be interpreted as justifying the continued levy of taxation even though Parliament might refuse to exact a budget.
[1] The Crown Princess is here referring to the possible abdication of the King.
[2] He was promoted to be lieutenant of the *Racoon* on 24 February 1863.
[3] Emphasising that Frederick the Great's *Matinées* were forgeries. Leopold von Ranke (1795–1886), the German historian.

out the volunteers, and the town is going to celebrate the day by services in the church, processions etc.[1] The King is very angry at it and thinks it a democratic demonstration, has forbidden the Queen, Fritz and myself going to church, as these celebrations are arranged of the Bürgermeister's and magistrate's own accord and not by the King's special order.

The answer to the address was pretty moderate but when it came into the King's hands he changed it and now I fear it will be imprudent.

We go out every night and see a great many people. I wish it were over. I heard Dr. Meyer read a long lecture about the Celts, the Cimbres and Teutons; interesting though it was I could not help smiling now and then he is so absurd. I see him almost every day. I assure you the Queen has a perfect "engouement" for him; one can have too much of a good thing now and then and the dear man has no end to his tongue and such a dislike to soap and water, razors and the like unnecessary articles.[2]

From the Queen

OSBORNE, FEBRUARY 4, 1863

Bertie's marriage is finally to be on Tuesday the 10th; Alix etc. to arrive on the 7th. Oh! if it only was all over! I dread the whole thing awfully and wonder even how you can rejoice so much at witnessing what must I should think be to you, who loved Papa so dearly, so terribly sad a wedding! Dear child! your ecstasy at the whole thing is to me sometimes very incomprehensible! Think what it will be to see Windsor full of people, and both your parents absent; a marriage in state, also without them—that day to which we looked forward with such joy for many years and

---

[1] With the advance of the Russians after Napoleon's retreat from Moscow, King Frederick William III left Potsdam for Breslau and from there a proclamation was issued summoning volunteers to take up arms in defence of king and country.

[2] Presumably this is the Prince Consort's former librarian. The Cimbri are believed to have been the first Teutonic invaders of Italy.

which now is to me far worse than a funeral to witness! Will you be able to rejoice when at every step you will miss that blessed guardian angel, that one calm great being that led all? And poor B.

The Drawing-room will be on the 28th February; all my Court will attend you just as if I was there, and my pages carry your train. But the old practice of the Princesses standing together and then the Princes will again now be followed. It was only on account of beloved Papa's peculiar position as my husband that he stood next to me, else the Queen and all the Princesses stood together, and the King and all the Princes together, a little way off.

I am so glad Lauchert's picture has succeeded. Pray let the print be sent as soon as possible as they want it to be lithographed here at once. You make a mistake about Alix's complexion; it is very clear but not at all fair; she is much darker than our children; she looks brown near them. Do let a photograph of the picture be sent here.

From the Queen

OSBORNE, FEBRUARY 7, 1863

I received your last dear letter on Thursday and thank you much for it, and will answer one by one. First, Affie has not yet passed his examination, but will only do so about the 14th or 15th and then be acting lieutenant. His final examination which will give him his commission will only be in May. He is still in the bay of Naples. He will be back just before the marriage. I believe Major Cowell is satisfied with him; but we must make some arrangement for his studying more on shore and becoming more fit for his future position. Uncle Ernest, who has finally declined (as I believe his States would not consent to his keeping both) and just at the moment when the Greeks particularly wished to have him, says that the country wish Affie to begin to take part in the affairs of the country, and that he will have to make me some suggestions. I feel it is necessary and the old Baron wished it, but how is this to be done to prevent the effect of bad example upon certain subjects?

We have really most extraordinary—quite May—weather; such a winter I never remember; not one cold day, not one night's frost, which was not melted in two hours—and such rain! It is very fortunate for the marriage but very bad for the country.

You will have grieved for poor old Lansdowne! He is the last almost of our old friends and ministers—he was at Kensington when I was born, was one of my first ministers and sat near me at my first Council, was at my first dinner party; saw my bright, happy days and the end of my real life![1]

Poor Lady Theresa Lewis has lost her married daughter Mrs. William Harcourt; she had an internal inflammation which brought on her confinement at eight months;—the child lives but she sunk.[2]

From the Crown Princess

BERLIN, FEBRUARY 10, 1863

The King complains of feeling low again—and I do not wonder with this bad news from Poland! I sadly fear that the Polish insurrections will prevent Fritz from going to England though nothing has been said to him on the subject as yet.

We give a large party tomorrow and another on Friday; I tremble at the thought of it. To prevent the stifling atmosphere—between 80 and 90 Fahrenheit which is in all ball and concert rooms at Berlin—I have had two large panes taken out of every window and flannel put in instead and the panes above made to let down with a string so I hope we shall not be so much smothered.

---

[1] The 3rd Lord Lansdowne familiarly known as the "Nestor of the Whigs". He was 83 when he died and was described by the historian Motley as having "an old-world look about him that seemed to require a pig-tail". Dignitaries of church and state formerly attended royal births. Lansdowne in 1819 held no Government position and presumably attended as an influential leader of the Opposition. He was Lord President of the Council when the Queen came to the throne.

[2] She died on the day her son was born: he was, in the future, the Liberal cabinet-minister "Lulu" Harcourt.

From the Queen

You will have now got my telegraph about Aunt Clementine.[1] Lodge we can not a mouse more; but the Van de Weyers have offered to take any one in at New Lodge.[2] Possibly Fritz and Augusta Strelitz may after all come on their own accord, but I told them I could not invite or lodge them. I hope they won't come.

Dear child, I wish you would say in your affectionate letters that you will do all to help me in checking noise, and joyousness in my presence for I fear you always think that I am not ill, that I can bear it, and I cannot and it makes me wretched and miserable beforehand if I think I shall be excited. I cannot join you at dinner; I must keep very, very quiet.

From the Crown Princess

You will have heard by telegram of the sad anxiety we are in about the darling baby! Thank God at this moment (half past 1) he has dropped off to sleep and though his respiration is still very quick and difficult, yet his skin is a little moist and the oppression is less. Yesterday morning he was really very well though he had a good deal of cough, when suddenly at 3 in the afternoon violent fever came on accompanied with such breathlessness that we sent to Wegner immediately. He gave baby a double dose of the emetic which Charlotte took the other day—he was sick six times from which he remained perfectly exhausted. The fever went down a little and he seemed to open his eyes and take notice again, and towards evening I thought I could leave him. We went to a ball at the King's. Returning from there we found the darling much worse and oh! dear had

---

[1] The Crown Princess had suggested that she should be invited.
[2] Sylvain Van de Weyer was Belgian Minister to London, 1831–67. He lived at New Lodge, Windsor, and he and his children were close friends of the Royal Family.

not God mercifully watched over our darling we should have lost him. I can hardly bear to think of it. I cannot describe to you what I suffered last night, it was the saddest night but one of my life. One felt so helpless watching the dear child, who lay on Mrs. Hobbs's lap, so changed and pale— though in such a burning heat, fetching breath 100 times in one minute; a hot bath, mustard poultice, hot oil etc. were all applied without the possibility of putting him into a perspiration. Wegner was most attentive and kind, but obstinate as ever and not allowing one of my suggestions even a minute's consideration. The Queen kindly came, though it was past 2 in the morning and there we sat together with heavy and anxious hearts. I cannot tell you since our misfortune how dreadfully frightened I am watching a sick person at night and one does not know how deeply and tenderly that little life is entwined round one's heart until it is threatened.

February 14. I have not thanked you yet for your dear letter—my heart was so full of our own troubles. If I come of course you may rely on my studying your wishes in every thing. I certainly never have knowingly done the contrary, and as I shall be for so short a time in England and you will have so many other people to see I hope my presence will in no way disturb or inconvenience you. I shall do my very best to obtrude as little as I possibly can.

I hope the two eldest will be allowed to leave their room at least tomorrow but Wegner is dreadful about that.

From the Queen

WINDSOR CASTLE, FEBRUARY 14, 1863

I cannot say how grieved and distressed I am to think of all your anxiety about poor baby! But Mr. Brown[1] tells me he fears bronchitis less with a child of that age than an older one—but it would be tedious getting well. Please God, therefore the recovery will be steady and you will be able to leave him on the 20th or 22nd. Our winter has been so

---

[1] The doctor at Windsor.

incredibly warm, that I wish the dear children could have been here with me. Perhaps you will entrust William to me for longer change of air; I am sure it would do him good. About Bertie, Affie and Louise at nearly the same age we had also great anxiety about colds.

I do beg and pray that the King will let Fritz come if it is but for two days; it would make Bertie miserable and on account of the Danes I am so anxious he should be there then, independent of the support and pleasure it would be to have him here at that terrible moment for me.

The architect's[1] sketches for the memorials are all up— in St. George's Hall—and will remain till the 28th, and no decision be taken till you arrive. There is only one that would come within the means, and which might be made very handsome. The idea is handsome. One by Scott is very handsome, but too much an imitation of W. Scott's and too like a market cross.

The dear Countess left us yesterday, as her sister is ill; she was to have stopped till the 16th. We miss her sadly. She has quite taken the place of old Stockmar in family affairs and is so admirable.

Have you read Kinglake's book? It is very scurrilous.[2] I go daily to the beloved Mausoleum, and long to be there!

From the Crown Princess

BERLIN, FEBRUARY 17, 1863

The Duke and Duchess E. of Württemberg with their daughter have been here for a few days.[3] The young lady looks clever but is very plain, not so much by her features as by the unwholesome and unkempt look she has—such

---

[1] For the Albert Memorial. Sir Gilbert Scott eventually designed the seated figure of the Prince, and regarded it as his finest work.
[2] The first two volumes of Kinglake's *Invasion of the Crimea*. He was outspoken in his strictures on Napoleon III and—to a somewhat lesser extent—on the English politicians.
[3] The Duke Eugene of Württemberg. He was in the Prussian army. The daughter in question was Wilhelmine, who was 18. His wife was a princess of Schaumburg-Lippe and sister to the unmarried Princess Elizabeth mentioned later in this letter.

untidy hair and a shocking complexion with bad teeth. Her eyes and eyebrows are really very good but that is the only part of her face that is good. She may certainly improve in time but how Uncle Ernest could think of her for Bertie I can't imagine; "du reste" she seems good contoured and amiable. I think she writes poetry. The mother is tiresome and affected and "prête au ridicule". From Princess Elizabeth of Lippe (who is nothing particular) I have heard a good deal about Princess Augusta of Holstein daughter of Prince Frederick of Glücksburg;[1] Princess E. says that the last named young lady (her cousin) is very nice though not pretty. Of her external appearance I only heard that she was fair and had very light eyebrows—and a little like Alix. You know you told me if I ever had an opportunity I was to enquire all about her. I will manage to get a photograph for you.

Fritz Augustenburg is here. We consider him as our special guest whenever he is here and he breakfasts and dines with us. The ice has quite broken between him and me about Alix, he has no feeling of enmity towards her, and I hope that in future they will be very friendly. Of course it is very hard for the poor Augustenbergs.

From the Queen

WINDSOR CASTLE, FEBRUARY 18, 1863

Thank God! that your anxieties for your dear little baby are past! Such little beings rally so rapidly after the danger is past, so unlike grown-up people! But think of my anguish and distress! Our dearest Affie has the same fever that blessed Papa had! Only this morning have I learnt that. On Sunday morning we heard that he was "feverish" (he had had a cold a week before which was not better on the 11th) and his examination had to be delayed. This alarmed me at once very much, and I telegraphed back they should change the air as soon as possible if it was thought necessary; on

---

[1] He was the elder brother of Prince Christian (Queen Alexandra's father). His daughter did not marry till she was 40.

Monday we heard that he was better, but they thought he should leave Naples at once and come home by sea. We heard nothing yesterday and this morning the news which alarmed us all so!—viz. the unmistakable symptoms. May God spare him, but we must go through anxious days and so far off. He is gone to Malta; he sailed last night; of course he cannot be here for the marriage.

I am going to write to dear Fritz to ask him in case poor Affie can't be here, to take his place and "support Bertie".

I am thoroughly worn out since I came here with worries and work. I can well understand your anxiety and suffering. Bertie, Affie and Louise once gave us as great alarm. But those little things have an extraordinary tenacity and vitality—which older people have not! I think you misunderstood me, dearest child, in my observations; I am most anxious to see you much and quietly and have you to myself but I can bear but very little fatigue and excitement and I shall be unable to join in family dinners, when the sad part gets overlooked for the moment and high spirits of youth get the better of everything else. I have much to talk to you about and have had much worry and annoyance lately.

You will have the rooms in the Devil's Tower, which were arranged for Alice and Louis but which they have left now for your former rooms, as the latter are more convenient for her confinement and it was thought safer to have everything ready now, in case she should be taken ill before her time and could not be moved.

Dear William will be in the dear old nursery where he will have every possible comfort and watching.

Oh! if only nothing dreadful happens to turn this very sad wedding into a still sadder ceremony. I pray and trust—but I know now since December 14, '61, that God's ways are not our ways, and it may please Him to take darling Affie! God's Will be done! But my cup of sorrow is so brimfull, one can't think it could be fuller!

From the Crown Princess

After a sad parting like ours it does one good to see people so thoroughly happy as this dear young couple are. As for Bertie he looks blissful. I never saw such a change, his whole face looks beaming and radiant. Dear Osborne is in its greatest beauty and all breathes peace and happiness. Darling Alix looks charming and lovely and they both seem so comfortable and at home together. Love has certainly shed its sunshine on these two dear young hearts and lends its unmistakable brightness to both their countenances.[1]

Before leaving the beloved shore of home—which I always do with the same feeling of pain and sadness—let me thank you again, darling Mama, for all your great kindness to Fritz, Willy and myself. It is your lot to make those around you happy by your kindness. May it be mine too—in the country to which I now belong!

From the Queen

WINDSOR CASTLE, MARCH 14, 1863

Thousand thanks for your dear, little letter from precious, peaceful Osborne. Darling child! you and your beloved Fritz—whom may God long preserve to you—have been of the greatest use and comfort to me in these trying days and I thank you again and again for it. Without you and your loving, tender, sympathising hearts I could not have gone through this fearful ordeal, helpless and alone. You never were more dear and gentle and truly sympathising to me, our darling first born, than this time, and while nothing can make my grief less or my life happy, I do look back with a melancholy satisfaction to our having been together at that time! May we soon and often meet again and may I yet be able to be of use to you all. Precious little William I so

---

[1] The Prince and Princess of Wales were married at Windsor on 9 March: afterwards they left for a week's honeymoon at Osborne, where the Princess had gone prior to embarking for the continent.

dearly love. The good account from Osborne from you and from the young couple is very gratifying though it gives me a pang too—which you will understand. Affie is convalescent and has been out today.

From the Crown Princess

BERLIN, MARCH 16, 1863

This is a sad day on which to write my first letter from here to you—two years since dear, kind Grandmama died. I cannot describe my feeling of depression and sadness at being here again, away from you all and from your quiet peaceful life—back to a scene of continual mistakes and dissensions in which Fritz and myself are not only silent spectators but sufferers! I enjoyed my stay at home so much and have so much to thank you for, beloved Mama.

The sea (which you do not like my love for) was very gracious to us. After having left sweet, blooming Osborne and the dear happy young couple we had a most splendid passage which I enjoyed very much indeed. We were all in very low spirits when we arrived at Antwerp, and are already looking forward to the time when we shall arrive there again on our way to—and not from—beloved England. Oh if you knew how my love daily increases for my dear home—("the home of the brave and the free"); attached as I am to this country and anxious to serve it with might and main, the other will ever remain the land of my heart and I shall ever feel the same pride of being born there, a child and a subject of yours. I was too tired last night to go to see the King and Queen but Fritz went and gave your letters; he said that the humour had been none of the best so I am just as glad I did not go. Willy was very good on the journey excepting calling Princess Frederick of the Netherlands and her daughter with whom we travelled from Hamm—"ugly monkey".[1] We had the pleasure of kind, good Prince Hohenzollern's company from Dusseldorf.

---

[1] Princess Frederick was the sister of the King of Prussia, and her daughter Princess Marie.

From the Queen

Your dear letter written on that sad anniversary, which was the beginning of all our terrible suffering and misery, I received and am thankful for! But dreadful as was my grief then, it was heaven compared to now! And now that "the light of his countenance has departed from amongst us" I wonder how any one can care to come here! That unbounded love for every thing English I own I can't share. Loving and admiring my own country as I do, I have seen so much of the cold, harsh cheerlessness of my countrymen and have seen with such grief the very bad effect it has had on your two elder brothers—in so many ways—that I cannot admire much of it as you do. I know the bad and mischievous sides of it more than you can do.

Today is poor Louise's 15th birthday.[1] These days are so sad now, and yet I wish so much that they should not be so for the children—as Papa was very anxious about that.

The young couple returned yesterday looking well and happy. To look at darling Alix and into those eyes is a satisfaction. And then she is so quiet, so placid, that it is soothing to one, and I am sure that must do Bertie good. He looks bright and happy and certainly totally different to what he used to be. They have been photographed together this morning in their wedding dresses! Later they will be done with me. Tomorrow "tous les Danois" will arrive at 12 and stop till 5. On Friday they (Bertie and Alix) go to town for the Reception.[2]

I had not an opportunity of saying to you any thing the last day about the letter I wrote Fritz respecting Lenchen, and I know General Grey spoke to you about it. I only wish to add that if Abbat should speak to Fritz that I should wish to hear what A. says—when he learns my determination[3]—

---

[1] "Poor" Louise because she was regarded as backward and less intelligent than her sisters.

[2] At St. James's Palace.

[3] The determination was that Princess Helena, whoever she married, would have to stay in England.

upon all points. The accounts of dear Uncle are much improved; Langenbeck has been to a certain extent successful and hopes to be completely so. Pray, dearest, when you write to Bertie and Affie don't write with frantic adoration of the Navy and all English feelings—for our sole object is to smooth that down and to Germanise them! Now, without beloved Papa, it is more than ever. To your sisters that is quite different.

From the Crown Princess

BERLIN, MARCH 21, 1863

I did wrong in allowing my feelings vent in writing to you about England; I thought afterwards it would bore you and my "schwärmerei" would make you impatient. But I have so few to whom I can think aloud, and from whom I need not hide feelings which are so strong and which grow every day, called forth by a multitude of things which are not agreeable and cause one to cling to all that is English. One never knows the value of a thing until one has lost it.

My thoughts are perpetually occupied with Bertie and Alix—God bless them. I offer up earnest prayers every day for their continued happiness! We have a newly married couple here—Maroussy and William; the latter looks just as he always did—I do not see that change in him which I perceive in almost all men old or young directly they marry. He does not seem to belong to her at all. She is charming I think, so good natured and amiable; it is a pity she should be so fat.

I was quite ashamed to telegraph to you about a donkey for the children but really it will not do any longer without one, and Wegner has been advertising without end in the newspapers without any success. In the south of Germany one can only get them in April and May they say, so we were obliged to have recourse to your kindness.

The nurse is of no use whatever to poor Baby and the milk does not seem to agree with him so that we shall wean him as soon as the donkey comes. The cow milk here is shockingly bad. Princess F. of the Netherlands and the old

Grand-Duchess of Schwerin are here as you know. I think them more disagreeable every time I see them, they are living in corporations of pride, prejudice and spite—the first usually and the latter always. Marietje I like.[1] The Queen is very unhappy. Good dear Prince Hohenzollern is here; he was treated "en chien" by the Queen when he first arrived. I told her I thought it was such a pity when one had enemies enough in the world to be on bad terms with one's friends, and it has been patched up again I am happy to say, though the Queen has not come round altogether yet.

Affairs are in such a mess as never was. The King is amiable and kind as ever and seems in happy unconsciousness of the real dangers which surround us whilst nervously apprehensive of imaginary ones; but on the whole he is in the best of spirits, gay compared to all others. Adalbert goes out again—he is most sensible and quite of our opinion as regards politics and internal affairs. Princess Charles who enquires unceasingly after you and takes the most lively interest in every thing that concerns Bertie and Alix is going to Hyères and Paris.

As to Abbat—he has not spoken to Fritz that I know of. I suppose and I hope that in all concerning Lenchen's future you consult the old Baron, who is the fittest person to give advice on so important a subject.

From the Queen

WINDSOR CASTLE, MARCH 21, 1863

Alice is extremely well and drove me out with the large ponies yesterday morning, but I think in twelve days about, it will take place. All the executioners will begin arriving next week—first the nurse and then Sir C. Locock.

The great Reception took place last night and I long to hear how it went off. Dear Alix is not I fear reasonable or careful of her health and I must speak seriously to both else there will be mishaps and an end to good health and possibly to much of their happiness. It is amusing to see how Bertie

---

[1] Princess Frederick's daughter.

keeps her in order (not in an improper way) and takes care of her; so, I hope to be able to get him to understand what is necessary. She will require care, that I am sure of. The whole Danish Family came down here on Thursday to take leave and Bertie stops with Alix in town till Tuesday. Then they come down here for two or three days before going to Sandringham.

From the Crown Princess

BERLIN, MARCH 24, 1863

I have been very busy yesterday and today doing a bust of darling Papa; it is a work which completely engrosses me and about which I feel very nervous as, if it should fail, it will be a great disappointment. It is now 1 and I have been at work since 10 this morning; when one is busy the hours fly with extraordinary quickness. I feel sanguine about the bust and I hope you will like it. How I wish you were here to give advice! Professor Hagen[1] helps me, he never saw dear Papa—so he can hardly judge of the likeness. He is a very clever artist—and finishes all that I cannot do about it. If it succeeds I hope you will order it in marble and let him execute it. You did promise me one of dear Papa you know; and if it was done here I could so often go and look at it whilst in progress and have it done just as I wish, the "console" for it to stand on is already ordered in Rome as you know. I fear you will think me very bold. I shall not be able to send you a cast before two months from this time, but I will have the bust photographed when finished. I go by Theed's[2] and Marochetti's busts. It is too strange how they contradict each other though both are full of valuable truths; Marochetti's is the better work of art but the other is much more like.

I like Maroussy more and more. I see a good deal of her; she has hurt her leg and has to remain on the sofa and I go and sit with her. She is a noble, generous, high-spirited

---

[1] Not identified.
[2] William Theed; he did the statue of the Prince at Balmoral.

creature, frank and warm hearted—and so unaffected and modest withal—very sensible and unprejudiced. William may consider himself a lucky man. I hope Louise[1] will not preach to her, as it would make one so lively—rather impatient I should think. I never saw such jewels as she has got, a set of rubies that are quite marvellous.

I might just as well be in England for all that I see of Fritz. I am always alone, and of an evening those detestable, everlasting parties, where I have the same fight every evening to keep my eyes open which is next to impossible in the suffocating atmosphere at the King's. I always envy the sentry every night as I go in to the Palace—walking up and down outside in the fresh night air!

From the Queen

WINDSOR CASTLE, MARCH 25, 1863

I send you the extract of a letter from dear Uncle Leopold which I beg you to give dear Fritz and tell him that I feel Uncle is quite right and that he must not remain long a passive spectator for that he, your children and his country will suffer—may be irreparably, if he allows his name to be mixed up as even a tacit and unapproving witness in the councils of what is done and said. I speak in beloved Papa's name, as much as in mine and most earnestly, as I can assure you that your and our grandchildren's interests are very near my heart and I feel I owe it beloved Papa to do all I can to be of use to you.

The dear young couple are here and I must again say that I am quite astonished at Bertie's improvement. Dear Alix felt the parting from her parents very much, but she is always calm and sweet and gentle and lovely. Very clever I don't think she is, but she is right-minded and sensible and straightforward. Dagmar is cleverer, and would I am sure be very fit for the position in Russia; she is a very nice girl. Our foolish government is bent on making poor Willie

---

[1] The Crown Prince's sister who was married to Prince William's brother.

King of Greece, and I fear that Princess Christian may consent.[1] Alix and Bertie are much against it.

With respect to my consulting old Stockmar about Lenchen's future, you know from experience how impossible it is any longer to rely on his advice, how seldom he answers any questions and how little Papa could consult him though he always wished to do so. He knows however my views and those of my best friends, to a great extent—and I can only repeat that my letter to Fritz contains all that I can and wish to say on the subject and is a final decision.

From the Crown Princess

The photographs of Alix and Bertie are too lovely. I did not give any to the Queen as Alix and the marriage etc. is still a sore subject with her and she never speaks about it. She is altogether in a very bad humour indeed, poor thing, and angry with me too—so I often get snubbed. She has an idea now that I can't speak French and that I ought to take French lessons as I had such an English accent, and it was so necessary for princesses to speak good French. I certainly have not a Weimar accent[2] but I did not know that my French was any the worse for that—and I have plenty else to do besides learning French grammar when I am past 22. Prince Hohenzollern is still in great disgrace with her. Hélas!

I showed the extract from Uncle Leopold's letter to Fritz. But the question of the abdication is not on the "tapis" at present! If this question should ever be mooted again you can tell Uncle L., that F. would only accept on condition that he is left sole and undisputed master of the position; this is his firm resolution. As for the rest Fritz can do nothing whatever; till nothing more flagrant is done, he cannot take up a more oppositional part. The King perfectly happy and

---

[1] Prince and Princess Christian's second son. He accepted the throne of Greece in the following June and became King as George I.
[2] Alluding to the Queen being a princess of Saxe-Weimar.

satisfied with the state of things and we others—perfectly miserable!

I send you the photographs of my bust, but I must beg you not to judge too hastily, as it looks unfinished in clay. I think on the whole you will like it but I cannot take the whole credit to myself as Professor Hagen did a great deal to the chief part of the work, but not having ever seen dear Papa of course he could not judge what it should be like and did not do a stroke without my direction. If you like it will you give it to Fritz and me for both our birthdays and Christmas in marble and order it here? It would be so delightful.

My letter must be a short one today, dear Mama, as I have a great deal to do today (notwithstanding the Queen's saying she wished I would occupy myself a little more).

P.S. I forgot to say, dear Mama, how grateful I am for the donkeys; they arrived quite safe. Baby takes to the milk with great appetite and it seems to agree with him very well indeed. Charlotte takes it also.

Talking of donkeys reminds me—I wanted to say that Count Bernstorff in his despatches always finds fault with every thing done at our Court—and said that the reception on the 17th was badly managed. I only say this in confidence, but it makes me angry with him as he invariably writes in the most "dénigrant" style of every thing in England; and especially of what happens at Court. It is nothing new to me as whenever he came to see Fritz (when we were on a visit to you formerly) he used always to be making unpleasant observations about everything—besides his very silly political opinions. However I merely say this to you.[1]

---

[1] Bernstorff was Prussian Minister in London. He is alluding to the reception for the Prince and Princess of Wales. "The affair was very select," grumbled the Second Secretary of the American Legation in London.

From the Crown Princess

The Queen wished me to write to you about her going to England; she hopes you will allow her to decide a little later. I know she has a great wish to go, but she feels it rather awkward being invited without the King—as of course she would have to ask his permission. Could you not ask him too? He would not accept, it I think, but I am sure it would give him great pleasure, besides if he did come it would be only to bring the Queen or fetch her away, and they understand quite well that you cannot do anything to entertain them. Would you let me know soon please as I believe the Queen is going away on the 7th?

As to politics, Samwer can tell you, if you care to hear, in what a wretched state they are, and how unhappy and uncomfortable everybody except the King and the Government feel. I cannot see the issue out of this miserable condition, but of all alternatives an abdication is the most unlikely I think.

From the Queen

WINDSOR CASTLE, APRIL 1, 1863

Many, many thanks for your dear and affectionate letter of the 28th. What you say about the Queen and your French amused us so much; poor dear soul, her worries and annoyances make her quite cross.

Your bust pleases us all very much. I like your eyes better than Theed's but the nose, mouth and chin I like best in Theed's; your nose is too thick. But I like it extremely, and wish only I could show you all I mean. I have made a few marks on the bad impression as I think you would like to know exactly what I think, dearest child.

From the Queen

WINDSOR CASTLE, APRIL 4, 1863

Regarding the Queen's coming she has also written to me that she could not decide it yet, but hoped to do so. I fear

I could not ask the King; in the first place he is so disliked and abused here just now that to invite him would be almost to expose him to insult; and in the second place I can't invite sovereigns and princes whom I can't do anything for, or entertain in any way. The Queen would come to see me, and to be with her poor, unhappy friend. If the King wished to bring her or fetch her away—in the face of all this—that of course is another thing, but I really don't see how I can invite him. What do you think can be done?

I have very satisfactory accounts from Sandringham of the young couple; Bertie is said to be so improved. They lived in the rooms you had here, only with one additional room (their bedroom being the one William had). In London they had the Bourbon Rooms downstairs.[1]

Alice is well. I can't deny that it is very trying and nervous work to watch, and when one sees one's own dear child in such a condition, one has a strong wish to give the husband a good ducking and all sorts of things, for one feels so indignant at all one's poor child is put to.

From the Crown Princess

BERLIN, APRIL 4, 1863

I am sorry you did not quite approve of the bust from the photograph; but really you cannot judge from that as it was not quite finished. The nose is no thicker than Mr. Theed's; it measures exactly the same in breadth and the mouth is the very same as his with the only difference of the moustache being cut off straight instead of being a little turned in, which throws a different shadow on the lip of course. Theed's measurements have all been so carefully kept to, except in the eyes which never pleased me on his, and the cheeks which seemed a trifle too round. Forgive this long explanation.

We took the sacrament on Thursday here in our little chapel with the King and Queen, the whole family, the

---

[1] In Buckingham Palace. More generally called the Belgian Rooms on the ground floor.

suites, and our servants. It was very solemn and impressive, and I thought much of you and dear Papa and of Alix and Bertie!

It is a serious and disheartening thing to look back a year in one's life and think how far short of one's mark one has always remained, how little one has kept to one's best resolutions, knowing what is right and wishing to do it how often one's feelings have betrayed one into doing what one afterwards repents! How often one has thought of oneself instead of others, of one's own pleasure and convenience before duty, how severely one has judged the shortcomings of others and forgotten that one has committed worse errors oneself! All this I feel so much with regard to myself and think if I were to die today how little, how very little I should have done of what I ought to have done or even of what I meant to have done. How I should like to repair every mistake, make up for each lost minute and unsay each harsh word! I am sure heaven and hell are in our own conscience for no pain can be greater to a heart capable of warm love than the remembrance of wrong great or small, done for the most part unintentionally, in a moment when we are not keeping watch over ourselves!

What is all this business about that Dr. Colenso and what are they going to do with him? I follow it all attentively in the reviews and the newspapers. The last letter of the Bishop of Oxford forcibly reminds me of the middle ages; controversy on points of doctrine has always made people mad, and there is no nonsense too great for clergymen of all sorts—especially bishops—to talk on this subject; they invite scepticism instead of annihilating it, by insulting people's common sense and feeling of justice.[1]

---

[1] J. W. Colenso, a Cornishman and Cambridge graduate, was at this time Bishop of Natal. In 1862 he published a book on the Pentateuch attempting to disprove the literal accuracy of the Old Testament. The Bishop of Cape Town deposed him from his bishopric and excommunicated him. It was found that the Bishop of Cape Town had exceeded his powers. But the English bishops, supporting him, appointed a new Bishop of Natal. For some 14 years there were two bishops discharging their diocesan duties. The Bishop of Oxford (Samuel Wilberforce) was

From the Crown Princess

BERLIN, APRIL 7, 1863

About Willy of Holstein and the throne of Greece I said nothing because I really did not know what to say. I cannot imagine that it can ever answer.[1]

I have not had an opportunity of speaking to the Queen yet about her visit to England, and as she is so irritable and cross at present I fear I shall not be able to do so before she leaves this evening.

Of our unfortunate affairs I can say nothing: they go on gradually getting worse but as one cannot be sure that M. de Bismarck does not stop and read our letters before they leave this—it is best to keep details for the messenger.

From the Queen

WINDSOR CASTLE, APRIL 8, 1863

Thank God! All goes on most prosperously. Sir C. Locock gave you an account of the labour, and confinement. In fact she was only ill from $\frac{1}{4}$ past 9 and the child was born at $\frac{1}{4}$ to 5 as naturally as possible, and during the last hour and a half chloroform was freely given, especially quite at the last. But I thought it the most dreadful thing to witness—possible. Quite awful! I had far rather have gone through it myself! It is far more dreadful to be born into this world than into the next! Easter Sunday is a beautiful day for it. Of course I shall take great interest in our dear little grand-daughter, born at poor, sad, old Windsor in the very bed in which you all were born, and poor, dear Alice had the same night shift on which I had on when you all were born! I wish you could have worn it too. But I don't admire babies a bit the more or think them more attractive. She is very like Alice, has a long nose and beautiful, long fingers like Alice. Alice sleeps like a top; is very hungry;

---

one of Colenso's leading critics, and drafted the letter, agreed by the English bishops, appealing to Colenso to resign.

[1] Apart from possible objections because of the Danish connexion, he was only 17. He was brother to the Princess of Wales.

she has had to be kept up very much, far more than I was with the elder ones. She had beef tea the same day, fish the next—chicken yesterday and boiled mutton. She is very calm and quiet, but not as strong as I was. She reminded me so much during the labour and even now lying in bed of dearest Papa when he was ill. I was dreadfully shaken and agitated by it all. I was with her the greater part of the time and never got to bed till $\frac{1}{4}$ to 6. To see good Louis, who behaved beautifully, hold her in his arms was so dreadful! It seemed a strange dream and as if it must be me and dearest Papa—instead of Alice and Louis! And then for me to direct every thing which beloved Papa always did and would have done! I had so wished for one other and had thought it very likely that Alice and I would have followed each other very closely!! Then to see Mrs. Lilley[1] and Sir C. Locock both there seemed the same thing over again! I like Dr. Farre[2] extremely; he is so quiet, and a very agreeable clever man to talk to, speaks German and is the same sort of doctor as poor Dr. Baly and Dr. Jenner.[3] You would be charmed with him I am sure.

All what you say about one's feelings at the end of a year is what I used to feel with such bitterness and sorrow. I feel now that my immense sorrow, my anguish and my constant crosses—with the anxious wish to do my duty and the constant thought of blessed Papa and hereafter—make me feel more than I ever did before that I have made great progress!

I have not been able to follow the Colenso dispute, but I saw and heard enough to feel just as you and dear Papa would. And that letter of the Bishop of Oxford's made me most indignant. I send you also a most wonderful telegram I received from Louis of Portugal. Ask Fritz what he says to it! To telegraph such a thing!![4]

You must have misunderstood me, about your dear

---

[1] The Queen's monthly nurse.

[2] Arthur Farre, a celebrated obstetrician.

[3] The royal doctors. Dr. Baly had been killed in a railway accident in 1861.

[4] Announcing that his wife was expecting a child.

bust; I like it excessively; I only thought the nose seemed a little thick, but I have no doubt that when more finished the photograph will come out much more clearly. Pray let me have some more photographs of it. I must now end this voluminous letter.

How is my darling William—Charlotte and little Albert Henry? We have got a pretty, nice little Irish nurse born the same day as you and who has three children—one born the same day as William. She had hardly any clothes and we are dressing her and had to wash her! She is just the right nurse—very dark and thin and plenty of milk.

From the Crown Princess

BERLIN, APRIL 11, 1863

Lady Buchanan is still most strange about her unhappy daughters. She told the Queen Dowager the other day that she had nothing whatever to do with them and to another lady she said "Jamais je ne penserais a usurper la titre de leur mère." She will not allow them to drive to church in the same carriage with her, and told Sir Andrew that either he must drive with her or walk there with his daughters. Accordingly last Sunday they went on foot with their Papa—and instead of being allowed to sit in the same pew with Sir A. (where Lord Augustus always sat with his children) they sat far back in another part of the church! I like them so much; they are nice, quiet, well-brought up girls not pretty but ladylike—and very unpretending. It is really half cracked of Lady B.; she is such a nice, good-natured person in all other respects.

Dr. Colenso occupies me very much. I admire him, and I hope our Church will not disgrace itself in the eyes of all Europe by doing him any harm. All Germany is intently watching for what is going to happen, and I hope that we shall prove to the world that we carry our principles of liberty of opinion and of personal independence into our Church! Sooner or later dogmas so preposterous as the Protestant Church still holds, will be abandoned by all classes—as they are now already in Germany—by all the thinking and intelligent men. Science and learning are slowly preparing the ground for a new reformation. In the searching light of truth all errors will appear so absurd that people will be ashamed to hold to them. We are farther advanced in Germany than in England. The times are past when the Church ruled with force and terror. If she does not now stand on the ground of only requiring people to conform outwardly to all her rules and allow [them] to think and believe what they please and as their reason and love of truth will let them, she will force all fervent Christians who love their religion, unmixed with confused and mythological theories of dark ages, to leave her pales. Since the times of Luther our Protestant Church all over the world has made no progress. The glorious building of which he so courageously laid the first stone has never been continued but has been left a ruin; we have gone on with rapid strides improving every thing. Steam and electricity have put a new face on the world, and we have left our Church as it was in uncivilised times of cruelty and ignorance. We have let in the light of truth on all else; our pure religion, the first of all working principles we have been satisfied to leave surrounded with institutions which were good in their time but which now are not in accordance with the state of civilisation (no more than absolutism is). Is it a wonder then there should be so many dissenters? All this is less felt in England, as the national character is perhaps not so "thinking"—at any rate not so speculative, and because our lower and middle classes here are much more educated. English people feel the same respect and love for their church as they do for their laws and constitution, therefore the great current of popular feeling will be with the bishops and clergy against Dr. Colenso—if they are wise enough to let him alone. I am sure I bore you with all this and perhaps after all you do not think as I do—but I hope if you have a moment's time you will read Colenso's book.

From the Queen

We have all been dreadfully shocked by the sudden loss of our excellent, valued, distinguished friend Sir C. Lewis,[1] who died quite unexpectedly on Monday. No one knew he was unwell even, till the fatal news was given me by Lord Palmerston yesterday. He is a dreadful loss to me and the country! He is again one of those very trusty, tried, upright, honest, clean, fearless men who were invaluable to us; and now to me, bereft of my sole adviser, support, protector and guide, the loss of such a man is indeed too, too dreadful! Beloved Papa had such a regard for him— liked his original turn of mind so much.

I had told him I hoped so to show him our dear old Coburg when I next went, and now he too is gone! How mysterious that all our best, most valuable men are taken, and the others left! It shows us that there is much and important work to do elsewhere, for why must else useful and valuable intellect be taken away from this poor world, where it is so much wanted? God's will be done! I feel that I can depend on nothing any more, and that all those I most want may be taken!

What you tell me of Lady Buchanan and her poor step-daughters is really too bad. She ought really to be told "de ménager les dehors".

I am so glad that the asses' milk has answered so well. How are the little foals?

I don't think I told you that Victoria Wortley is going to be married to a Mr. Welby—a rich man—whom she seems to think perfection.[2]

---

[1] Sir George Cornewall Lewis was a statesman and writer. He was Chancellor of the Exchequer in Palmerston's Government in 1855. Writing to his widow the Queen said "we delighted in his society: we admired his great honesty and fearless straightforwardness. . . . Since my terrible misfortune I clung particularly to characters like his, which are so rare." Greville described him as "cold-blooded as a fish".

[2] Victoria Wortley had been Maid of Honour to the Queen: her husband, later Sir William Welby-Gregory was a Lincolnshire landowner and member of Parliament.

Samwer is arrived, but I have not yet seen him.

I went to see poor old Whiting today; a sad, sad sight; he can't speak above a whisper, sits in a chair with a shepherd's plaid shawl pinned round him, a handkerchief tied round his head, unshaven—with a quilt over his poor legs, which are frightfully swollen and full of sores![1] He was so pleased to see me and I said I would go again, but to see the wreck of an old servant, who was with us in all our happy years, going away also is very melancholy.

From the Crown Princess

BERLIN, APRIL 18, 1863

Dr. Colenso is certainly not a clever man or he would have found out all his scruples long ago when he was 18 or 19 instead of at past 40, and would not have felt so much compunction at giving up old ideas after he found they were mistaken. But I think the pious and almost childlike simplicity and humility of his language very touching, and I admire him for his honesty and his courage; his arguments are nothing very wonderful and his discoveries not new— but a good and a disinterested man is always rare, and be he wise or dull I think inspires one with respect and interest. There is a Frenchman who is very clever and who belongs to the protestant party in France called Edmond Schérer,[2] who wrote an excellent résumé of Colenso's book in the *Revue des deux Mondes*—which is well worth your reading, dear Mama, as it is so clear and well put. I read all his articles in the *Revue* and they always strike me as very remarkable. I wonder whether the General[3] reads them?

I am of course rather shy of recommending these— particularly to ladies—as they attack many popular prejudices and consequently would offend many devout and well-meaning people. Oh how I miss dear Papa! There is no one to whom I can "say my say" (as the phrase goes)

---

[1] Whiting died on 21 April.
[2] He was at this time editor of *Le Temps*.   [3] Grey.

on those subjects now. I am afraid of boring you, as your mind and still more your aching heart is taken up with so many other things and I feel so interested about it all that I could write volumes about it.

What a pleasure it was to write to dear Papa and tell him all one thought—was it but ever so silly or confused one was sure of his listening kindly and attentively and bending his great intellect down to one's own humble level, take an interest in what one was engrossed with, taking the trouble to set one to rights! How anxiously did I expect an answer each Saturday sure that he would enter on every subject and then feasting on his words—each one a jewel, wise and true!

Poor Sir Cornewall Lewis, I was so distressed; I was sure you would feel the loss of so valuable a servant and so kind a friend. Poor Lady Theresa! her daughter and her husband. I saw King Lear here the other night and was so struck again by the passage

> The worst is not
> So long as we can say 'This is the worst'.

From the Queen

Many, many thanks for your dear letter of the 14th and for your good wishes for our dear little darling Baby! She is the only thing I feel keeps me alive, for she alone wants me really. She, perhaps as well as poor Lenchen, are the only two who still love me the most of any thing—for all the others have other objects; the married daughters care (of course) much more for their husbands and children —and the wretched, broken-hearted mother, who was the dearest object of two beings[1] for so many years, is now daily learning to feel that she is only No. 3 or 4 in the real tender love of others. And dear child, all this is right and natural, but to me most agonising. . . . You, dear child, can't imagine what I have here described but it is that, which is

---

[1] Her husband and mother.

so dreadful—the belonging to no one, any more. I know how you all love me, but I see and feel with my terribly sensitive feelings that constantly I am *de trop* to the married children and that every thing I love I must give up! This is a long episode but I could not help saying it for I think no one reflects on that when they speak of all I have left and for which I am (God knows!) truly grateful.

It would indeed be a very great satisfaction to me if darling little William could be sent to England and to Osborne, and I would be quite ready to bring him back with me to Germany. You know what a feeling I have for him; he was such a favourite of beloved Papa's and such an object of interest to him! He would live in the nursery and be watched over with the tenderest care. Pray do carry out that plan; I shall quite love Wegner for recommending it. I shall be here probably from the 5th or 6th of June till quite the end of the month, and then I must be at Osborne for dear Marie.[1] She and Ernest arrived at Cowes on Thursday, all well, and Ernest is coming here tonight. Bertie and Alix will be here this afternoon for 10 days.

Alice's child is to be called Victoria Alberta Elisabeth Matilde Marie, and will be called Victoria—the first of our grand-children that will be called after either of us. This I know was not your fault—but it grieved me.

From the Crown Princess

BERLIN, APRIL 21, 1863

The charming photographs[2] quite delighted me. They created quite a sensation here yesterday morning. Those of beloved Papa are lovely—his dear, sweet face so handsome and young without the expression of care it so often wore in later years. And you dear Mama, with such a funny bonnet and gown! Affie too adorable. I kissed the photograph over and over again; he was the handsomest darling

---

[1] Princess Marie of Leiningen was expecting a child.
[2] This refers to some old daguerreotypes which the Queen had sent to the Princess.

I ever saw! Alice—still with such fat cheeks—and myself such a perfect monster.

They are so amusing and yet they made me oh! so melancholy. I thank you so much for them.

How well I remember when those of you with us five eldest were taken in the French-house in the kitchen-garden at Windsor by Mr. Kilburn—at the same time as Aunt Victoire and her two boys were done.

Wegner began to have his doubts about Willie's going to England as they are going to put the poor child in a machine on account of his not being able to hold his head straight, but I explained to him that it was one reason the more why he should want change of air and better food and sea-bathing—as this machine is sure to exhaust him a little. I protested against this proceeding as Caesar Hawkins[1] did also; Langenbeck is also against it, as he says it is of no use but thinks the turn of the head is serious and the only thing he thinks doubtful about Willie. He wishes to cut the right side of the neck and then the machine to be worn for a short time (which would of course be necessary) but wearing without an operation before, Langenbeck thinks uselessly tormenting the poor child. Wegner was very obstinate about it but I hope Langenbeck (who is very sensible) may bring him round.

Of course, dear Mama, if we send him we should be obliged to beg that no one should see him with this machine on—not the servants or brothers and sisters and that it should not be talked about as it would be very painful to us. He would only wear it for a short time in the day. All this torments me much.

From the Queen

WINDSOR CASTLE, APRIL 22, 1863

Your dear, affectionate letter of the 18th touched me much. All what you say is so dear, warm hearted and affectionate that it overcame me very much when I read

---

[1] Serjeant-surgeon in Ordinary to the Queen.

it! Poor, dear child! for you with your clever mind and love of all that beloved Papa loved, the loss of that intercourse is quite dreadful! How I feel that, words cannot say, but it is not the least of all my bitter sufferings to feel what you children have lost! I always feel when I write to you what stupid, uninteresting letters mine are—for Papa's were and are so beautiful. You possess a mine of wealth in those letters. Never mind writing to me all you think. It does not bore me, though I feel more and more disinclined to take any interest in any thing; I am so uninterested because of tiredness and of total exhaustion. I am so dreadfully overworked, that I really can only compare myself to a hunted hare! I am dead beat, and then come headaches, and such forgetfulness and bewilderment, with such yearnings and wild longings for Papa—and accumulations of work which are so annoying and distressing, and I can never get to do what I wish and what would to a certain extent be a comfort. I hope at Balmoral to be a little quieter.

I will make a point of reading E. Schérer's article. You know I care so much more for all those things now, and for any thing learned and scientific; first because I require clever heads (loss of that is most dreadful in our daily life) and because I know he liked it, and it seems to bring me nearer to darling Papa here as surely it will hereafter, if I use my head and intellects and strive to improve them. So don't mind writing fully to me on all interesting subjects, it will be of real use to me, though I can't answer you as well.

Only imagine my fright yesterday when Brown[1] told me he thought General Grey was threatened with fever—and Albert Grey[2] has really got one—though he is better and it is not typhoid. The dear General is much better today but still feverish and I feel much "dépourvu" without him! We are much occupied with the christening. It is to be at one on Monday in the Green Drawing-room as (to

---

[1] The Windsor doctor.
[2] General Grey's son.

the Dean's distress, and my infinite disgust and feeling of shame) by the Act of Uniformity no clergyman not of the Church of England can perform any service in any consecrated place!!! Well, the Court Chaplain, Bender from Darmstadt, and Mr. Walbaum[1] will perform the Service; I shall hold the dear little baby and only our people here, and two of the Ministers, Lord Sydney, Lord St. Germans,[2] "Laddle"[3] etc. will come for it.

Bertie and Alix are here since Saturday. I do so wonder how she can be happy. He has let himself down to his bad manners again. She is dear and good but I think looks far from strong and will never be able to bear the London season unless she has but few late nights. She is but 18 and has gone through so much.

From the Queen

WINDSOR CASTLE, APRIL 25, 1863

Your dear letter of the 21st reached me the day before yesterday. I am horrified at the idea of cutting poor dear little William's neck and putting him into a machine and have asked Sir James's and W. Jenner's opinion—but you may rely on my mentioning the subject to no one, and no one seeing the dear child with that dreadful machine. I can't bear to think of his being put to such torture. Poor dear child!

I am quite proud of the poor Windsor asses. I am so glad you liked the old photographs. Those were happy times—all of you children, not such a dreadful amount of work and all our dear ones alive and well round us!

Dear Alix is not strong and I do feel very anxious for the future. B. is not improved since I last saw him and his ways and manners are very unpleasant! Poor Dear Alix! I feel so for her. I fear she will never stand London.

Are you not delighted about the memorial and how

---

[1] Pastor of the German Chapel at St. James's.
[2] Lord Steward of the Household.
[3] Sarah, Lady Lyttelton, formerly governess to the elder royal children.

beautiful are Lord Palmerston's and Mr. Disraeli's speeches.[1]

From the Crown Princess

After referring to the christening of Princess Alice's baby, the Crown Princess writes:

How well I recollect how nervous, weak and sad I felt on Willie's christening day and how it went to my heart to see him half covered up to hide his arm which dangled without use or power by his side, and how everybody except the English gentlemen said what a small delicate child he was, and asked me so many questions! He has been a constant source of anxiety ever since he has been in the world. I cannot tell you what I suffered when I saw him in that machine the day before yesterday—it was all I could do to prevent myself from crying. To see one's child treated like one deformed—it is really very hard. Of course all that is necessary for his good one must submit to. Doctors are so odd sometimes; they don't mean to be unfeeling I am sure, but they appear so. Wegner said it did not matter if Willie walked about with this thing on; it need not be made a secret of, and the man who made the instrument would be sure to talk about it in the town. Of course we were horrified and forbid any body seeing him with it on. He is to wear it for an hour every day and, towards the end of May, Langenbeck will decide whether or not to cut the neck. I must say I do see the necessity for doing something effectual which I did not when I was in England as I had no idea to what an extent the tension of the muscles on the right side of the neck had come. The machine consists of a belt round the waist to which is affixed an iron bar or rod which passes up the back to which

---

[1] Parliament decided to grant £50,000 in addition to the £60,000 collected by subscription. Disraeli pleaded for a monument rather than "a work of utility"—a monument which should signify "the sublime life and transcendent career" as recognised "by a grateful and admiring people".

a thing looking very like the bridle of a horse is attached. The head is strapped into this and then turned as required with a screw which moves the iron. When the head is firm in the leather straps it is made to turn towards the left so as to stretch the muscles of the right side of the neck; the object is to prevent his head from being drawn down to the right side which it undoubtedly is and which prevents him from turning it about freely and would most certainly in time make him look completely crooked. Langenbeck thinks the result to be obtained from this machine is very uncertain but still prefers at all events making a trial of it before he decides to cut. I have explained it as well as I could but no doubt Dr. Jenner will be able to make it more comprehensible to you. I have great confidence in Langenbeck—and we mean to adopt whatever course he advises as what he has hitherto proposed has always proved judicious—except leaving off the galvanism which I own I think a mistake. William is very good about it as it does not hurt him but I fear in a few times more it will and then we shall have a great piece of work to make him wear it—as he flies into such violent passions when he does not wish to do a thing. It seems so cruel to torment the poor child, still it would be no kindness to save him inconvenience now at the expense of causing him much greater hereafter. My fear still is that it will make his glands swell; but Wegner says no.

You must excuse my writing you all these details, which may bore you.

The poor asses have caught cold, and cough very much but they are not ill otherwise—this climate is so abominable that they feel the change. I am wicked enough to wish it affected all the two-legged donkeys in the kingdom—it's the way Ernest Leiningen used to wish the easterly winds to affect the old admirals.

From the Queen

Your dear letter of the 25th arrived just after the christening, which was a trying, touching ceremony. Thinking of the little baby and holding it (so long that I thought I should drop it) helped me, and it was not so dreadful as a wedding and fortunately different to ours—though the Lutheran Service is almost the same. The Font out of which all of you were christened was used, and little Victoria behaved as well as possible. It is not my fault that we were not at the christening of our first-born grand-child—but I was prevented by old Stockmar and every one, and cried my eyes out about it, that I can tell you. If you should like once to come here to be confined while I am alive, you are quite welcome to it, and the baby could be christened here in the same way.

I send you today Guizot's translation of adored Papa's speeches etc. The short preface, I am sure you will admire; and the translation is by Guizot's daughter and I think extremely well done.

I am much struck by Prince Alexander of Hesse.[1] I think him very clever and agreeable. He was talking to us yesterday evening of the Peace of Villa Franca[2] and I thought old times were returned, and Papa must be listening to it or that I must tell it him all again! How it would have interested him for he was so unhappy about all that. Do you not remember his sitting down at Osborne with Max and Fritz and listening to the former's accounts of the Italian War? Oh! and now there is this Polish complication and he is not here to help us! But don't fear—I have got "the eyes of Argus", in spite of my broken heart, and I have, since he left me, the courage of a lioness if I see danger, and I shall never mind giving my people my decided opinion and more than that! Yes, while life lingers

---

[1] He was uncle to Prince Louis and father of the Battenberg princes.
[2] The treaty of Villafranca in 1859 when Napoleon III unexpectedly came to terms with the Austrians. Prince Alexander was a general in the Austrian Army and had fought at Solferino.

in this shattered frame, my duty shall be done fearlessly! That's all I am still fit for—and to try and be of use to others!

From the Queen

OSBORNE, MAY 2, 1863

I received your long letter about dear William of the 28th—the morning we left for Osborne. By Sir James's and Dr. Jenner's letters you will see how strongly they deprecate any thing of the sort. I shall show your letter to Dr. Jenner today. None of the children will know anything about it, but I doubt the wisdom of making a secret of what will ooze out. Poor dear child—it is most sad to think of all he suffered—or indeed rather more you suffered—from the time of his birth about him! Good Alice feels much for you, the wonderful contrast between herself and you—and this wonderfully flourishing, fat baby— without a mark or spot! Victoria is a most flourishing personage, and though I am in general no amateur of babies I shall miss the quiet interest of this little being and her beloved parents sadly!

I have seen Mr. Scott.[1] The statue he proposes should be sitting, 14 feet high—and gilt!

From the Crown Princess

NEUES PALAIS, POTSDAM, MAY 2, 1863

Many thanks for your dear letter received yesterday; it gave me great pleasure particularly what you say about Poland—for which I am really grateful. I am so uneasy and alarmed about it all that it is a great comfort to hear what you say.[2]

---

[1] George Gilbert Scott (1811–78), the celebrated architect. He designed the Albert Memorial in 1864.

[2] In England there was widespread sympathy for the Poles, and alarm at the opportunity, which the rising gave for the "murdering habits of the Russian soldiery". The words are Russell's, the Foreign Secretary. Although the Queen was sympathetic to the Poles, she realized that

The King and the Government here are perfectly aware of what they already owe to England in this complication, and that it rests with England alone to save them from a perilous war and all Europe from dreadful calamities. But I am afraid there is some perverseness in them, in as far as they may not be as ready as they ought, to do what is necessary in order to enable England to help them out of their difficulties. They are now under the baneful effects of their own previous faults. But what you tell me encourages us to hope that your Government will exercise forbearance, that they will like the Government of the older and most experienced constitutional country, make allowances for the errors of a Government which has only recently entered upon constitutional life (under peculiar circumstances and is now labouring under peculiar difficulties) that they will not take the present unfortunate state of things for a permanent one—and look to the future. Lord Palmerston as the first statesman is sure not to overlook the frightful consequences which a war now and under these circumstances would have for the whole world! I fervently hope that the present danger may be turned away by you—I pray that we may not "be rewarded after our iniquities".

The people at large here are far from sharing the views of the Government on Polish affairs and this will be made clear to the whole world by the approaching debates in the second chamber.

From the Crown Princess

NEUES PALAIS, MAY 5, 1863

I have arranged a little garden here for the children and ourselves which gives me a great deal of pleasure, as we have now a corner where we can sit unobserved and where the children can play and run about without being stared

---

England could not intervene and that it was therefore damaging and pointless to taunt the Russians or their Prussian allies. (See *Queen Victoria's Letters*, Second Series, Vol. I, pages 82–4.)

at like so many wild beasts. We are going to have a little summer house too like the tool shed near the Swiss Cottage at Osborne. All this is a great step—an amusement and an interest. We are both so fond of the Neues Palais and like living here so much; it seems quite like Liberty Hall after Berlin. After all independence is the greatest enjoyment in life and the one most difficult to get as it is the most universally coveted.

From the Queen

OSBORNE, MAY 6, 1863

The Queen speaks of coming, but seemed to have misunderstood the time. She speaks of "towards the end of June" when you know I always said that I hoped to receive her in June but not after the 1st of July—for then I must come here and the best rooms will be occupied by poor dear Marie whose confinement will be between the 9th and 16th of July. And she has no other house to go to and no relative to have with her but me—the more so, as Ernest is so nervous that he declares he shall run out of the house the moment it begins! I have written to set this all right. But I hope the Queen won't stay longer with me than 10 days or a fortnight—for I have so much to do, that I should be quite worn out with a longer visit.

We have had Dr. L. Playfair[1] here for two days which reminds us so much of blessed, former days. And today we expect Sir C. Lyell[2] whom Louis was so anxious to see, having read his book. Clever, scientific people are now a positive necessity for me.

I trust all will go well as regards our conduct about Poland. God knows every one is miserable here about your Government—and forbearance has to be preached! Dear Uncle L. is very wise about all this; he tells me he has

[1] Lyon Playfair. He played a considerable part in helping the Prince Consort with the Exhibition and was at this time Professor of Chemistry at Edinburgh.
[2] Charles Lyell, the geologist. The book no doubt was *The Antiquity of Man* which was published this year and went into three editions.

— 208 —

written to you, so pray write fully and openly to him, for it will give him great pleasure and interest him so much. He is so anxious to be of use.

I dare say being confined in your own home[1] where you have been before is more convenient, but as for its doing Fritz and the children harm if one were born in England or anywhere but in Prussia I can't believe or agree in; for a child's being born in another country has nothing whatever to do with its nationality or sentiment and feeling. Moreover, after Charlotte's birth you told me, you were sure Fritz would never object to it, should you wish it. I trust however that any such prospect, wherever it may be, is out of the question for some years. I fear there is none with Alix and though to be sure, unintellectual children which one might fear with B.'s children, would be a great misfortune, it would be very sad if they had none, and I sometimes fear they won't. Are you aware that Alix has the smallest head ever seen? I dread that—with his small empty brain—very much for future children. The doctor says that Alix's head goes in, in the most extraordinary way just beyond the forehead: I wonder what phrenologists would say.

I want now to trouble you with another commission. Winterhalter is most provoking, saying he won't come to England, that he has Russians and Poles to paint, that he is very ill and that he will paint me in Germany. This he cannot, for I go to Germany to be out and to see old friends and be quiet and not to be painted. He may give way, but I doubt it. At any rate I won't let myself depend upon him and I should like to get Graefle[2] to come over to paint me in October or rather more November and to paint Louise too and possibly Alix and Bertie. Would you communicate this for me, dear, and tell me where he is now etc.? I think after Winterhalter his likenesses are far the best.

---

[1] The Crown Prince had written to the Queen explaining why it would be difficult for the Crown Princess to come to England for a confinement.
[2] A. Graefle. His pleasant though sentimental painting of the Queen sitting by the bust of the Prince was finished in 1864.

NEUES PALAIS, MAY 11, 1863

You are so kind, to ask what I should like for our little bit of a garden and I ventured to telegraph that a few roses would be a great addition as they are both scarce and dear here. I have made several improvements—such as having a swing, a see-saw and a giant strides put up for little and big children, also arranged a crocket [*sic*] ground.[1] It sounds very grand but the place is very small. We have pitched Fritz's tent in one corner and I sit and write and work there and listen to the nightingales which sing here in legions.

Mr. Toward[2] must have thought me a "l . . . l lunatic" (as Lord Dundreary[3] says) to telegraph to him about milk pans but, after much trouble, I have been able to arrange a bit of a dairy in a small [word missing]. The milk was so bad that the tea and coffee were undrinkable and I eat dry bread for breakfast as the butter tasted like anything but butter, though the people assured us it was the best that could be had. A gardener here has got 6 cows and his wife who is a nice, handy, good-natured person keeps a dairy and has excellent milk and butter which she sells. We have bought two cows for ourselves, and we are going to let them out in the fields—and this person will manage the dairy for us.

They have deep earthenware dishes instead of milk pans; the consequence is that they have hardly any cream as it only rises in dishes that are moderately flat. You one day said you would send Mr. Toward here; I wish you could do so in the first days of June. I shall be all alone here and I could show him everything and ask his advice about a hundred things. If he could be here for two or three days,

---

[1] The game was just becoming popular and was noticed by *Punch* this year. It was introduced in the 1850's and it is believed that Lord Lonsdale had the first ground.

[2] The head-gardener at Osborne.

[3] The character in *Our American Cousin* by Tom Taylor, which was first produced in New York in 1858.

he could see all. We hear Uncle Ferdinand of Portugal is coming. How glad I should be to make his acquaintance!

We give a ball in powder tomorrow as this old Palais will have been up 100 years.[1] It will be a pretty sight in those fine old rooms. I wish that, with the dress, we could bring back the old King; he would be astonished to see the mess his country is in and the blockheads which his great nephew has got for ministers. He would say again as he said once—"I am tired of reigning over slaves." We want a Frederick the Great now![2] When will there be another? All is going "de mal en pis"—that wretched B. will not stop his mad career until he has plunged his King into ruin and his country into the most dangerous difficulties! It is pleasant to be a silent spectator when things are going to the "Cuckoo" as one says in German—so long as we do not go there too which is what I am fully expecting.

From the Queen

OSBORNE, MAY 13, 1863

Toward begged me to tell you that he could not take up the roses yet but should do so later. Only think that they wrote in the telegraph: "Thorne robes" and I couldn't imagine for some time till the correction came what was meant.

Affie passed a very good examination yesterday. But he gives me cause for sorrow and anxiety still (I mean morally) of which more next time.

From the Crown Princess

NEUES PALAIS, MAY 16, 1863

You have no idea in what a mess we are now! There is a regular pitched battle going on between the Chambers and the Government, the latter being as usual in the wrong. Many believe in a revolution; I cannot say that I share this

---

[1] It was begun in 1763 and finished in 1770.
[2] The King was, of course, Frederick the Great's great, great nephew.

opinion. The King is very violent against the House of Commons and determined to uphold Bismarck who is the author of all this mischief. People are much excited but the time is not come when Fritz can do any good by coming forward with his opinion—his only course is to avoid any thing that is doubtful and only to speak when there can be no question about his position, it would only "embrouillé" things doubly were he to take a premature step.

From the Queen

BALMORAL, MAY 19, 1863

I just received your dear letter of the 16th for which many thanks. Here we are! I can't say that I find it soothing or benefiting! It is cold and I am too weak to walk but very little, and feel chilled and this place is so sad, so lonely! I am sadly cut off too, for excepting Augusta I have no one to open myself to; dear Alice I miss dreadfully. I miss Dr. Jenner very much too as I talk so much to him; Mr. Brown is here for I would not take Dr. J. away from his practice.

The Drawing-room was a fearful one—lasting till 6, but Alice was less tired than Alix. Poor dear, she looks so sallow and is losing her "fraîcheur". Alas! she is deaf and everyone observes it, which is a sad misfortune. Strong she is not, and they overtire her too much.[1]

---

[1] The Drawing-Room was held on 16 May and the numbers attending were prodigious. An American observer wrote "The Princess looked very well, tho' somewhat tremulous. But compared with the Princess Alice, her shoulders are thin and her figure fragile. There is no doubt about her having been overpraised for her beauty . . . she has a pretty, amiable, kindly face, large expressive blue eyes, regular classical features, and a finely shaped head, indicative of talents and natural ability. But her complexion is not good, and as de Bille, the Danish Minister, said to me she wants some of the roast beef and ale of England to give her flesh and more development. . . . Nearly three thousand ladies paid their respects or were presented and it was long after 5 o'clock before the ceremony was over. So trying was it at one time that the doors had to be closed to give the Princess some rest. Mr. Adams [the American Minister] says the poor girl was absolutely exhausted: I may say that it was barbarous to impose so much upon her and none but the English people would have done it." *Journal of Benjamin Moran*, Vol. II, page 1163.

Alfred is well but not strong; he is quite wild about salmon fishing. In confidence I may tell you that we do all we can to keep him from Marlborough House as he is far too much "épris" with Alix to be allowed to be much there without possibly ruining the happiness of all three and Affie has not the strength of mind (or rather more of principle and character) to resist the temptation, and it is like playing with fire. Beloved Papa always said the feelings of admiration and even love are not sinful—nor can you prevent the impulses of one's nature, but it is your duty to avoid the temptation in every way. You may imagine how anxious this makes us. It makes Affie however anxious to marry and I hope he will be able to fix his affections securely even if he can't marry for two years.

From the Crown Princess

NEUES PALAIS, MAY 19, 1863

I received yesterday your dear letter from Windsor on your way to dear, lovely Balmoral! When shall I see that blessed spot again, those lovely blue hills, the sparkling Dee, and breathe the pure fresh air scented with heather? My thoughts carry me back there so often—to the times when we were so happy! I have never seen that dear place without darling Papa and I cannot imagine it at all without him. When I think of his pretty room with the green paper, the prints of Rafael on the wall and the pink vases with white roses on the chimney piece, I seem to see him writing at his table and his things lying on the sofa or hanging over the back of the screen before the fire ready for him to put on.

I went yesterday into our old rooms at Babelsberg in which I had not been since we left them as I had disliked living there so much![1] I thought of darling Papa so much, and sat down on the sofa where I sat and talked with him

---

[1] Babelsberg was at Potsdam, and had been built by the King in the 1830's. It was described by Queen Victoria as "gothic bijou". The Crown Prince and Princess lived there during the first summer of their marriage.

when he came early in the summer of '58, and I told him how I felt;[1] he said you would not believe what was the matter with me, and then he allowed me to read a letter you wrote him the only letter of yours to him I ever saw and he was so kind and so gentle and I was oh! how happy to see him! When he went away I was in despair and crying, and he said "It is not so bad as it was the first time—or is it?" But parting from him was always awful. I assure you it used to make me feel quite ill, and so wretched I felt I could have wished to put an end to myself.

I showed Sir A. and Lady Buchanan all over Potsdam yesterday; the day was very hot indeed, the sun scorching and the air suffocating, the mosquito-gnats devouring one alive. They were really much struck by the beauty of the palace which was looking bright with lilacs, laburnums, thorns pink and white, snow balls and horse chestnuts red and white in full bloom.

I am quite tired of telling you how bad our state of things is in—but I must alas! again repeat it in sad earnest.

If the Government does anything unconstitutional Fritz will protest. He will give a written declaration that he does not pass any opinion on the present course of affairs or criticise any measures, that he does not give any sort of advice as to what ought to be done (as he would thereby be rendering himself responsible for things of which he has not the guidance) but that he will not be a party to any unconstitutional step; the King might think it necessary and advisable but it was in his (Fritz's) eyes dangerous and he could not on his conscience acquiesce to it, he hoped the King would find his measures succeed, restore peace, quiet and satisfaction to his people. I think Fritz cannot do better than this and I certainly do not think he is justified in any way to do or to say anything more!

Wegner has received Mr. Paget's[2] opinion about the

---

[1] Referring to her pregnancy.
[2] George Paget—the distinguished doctor and subsequently Regius Professor of Physics at Cambridge. This is probably George Paget and not his brother James, who was the royal doctor. George Paget was a leading authority on forms of paralysis.

treatment of Willie's arm but neither he or Langenbeck agree with what he says. I think they are going to write an answer.

I have seen Anna's[1] poor little baby—it is a fine child but quite blind. It is most sad to see. One eye is very prominent and all blue without any white, and the other is very deep set with only one little blue spot and all the rest white, Graefe[2] gives some hope that this last one may be couched later.

Poor Anna is quite heartbroken about it. I think her looking much changed, old and worn-looking; it worries her to death. E. Stockmar is gone, he means to stay away many months. I have not a single person at this critical time to give me advice or support and am left solely to my own resources. It is really dreadful but worse for Fritz than for me. I have nobody to give me any information when Stockmar is not there—there are so few people whose judgement one can quite trust to.

From the Queen

BALMORAL, MAY 22, 1863

I have little to tell you from our sad and lonely life. If you or Alice or Aunt Feodora were here it would be more bearable; I wish you could come here this autumn, it would do you both good. I telegraphed as I did, because I heard from Sir A.B. that suspension and alteration of certain Articles of the Constitution were in contemplation, and that he meant to ask to see Fritz; if any thing of that kind happens, F. must not remain passive.[3]

---

[1] Wife of the Prince Frederick William of Hesse and daughter of Prince Charles of Prussia.
[2] Albrecht Graefe. Generally regarded as the founder of modern ophthalmic surgery.
[3] This is important because what Sir Andrew Buchanan had heard was correct. On 1 June an alteration was made in the Constitution which made it possible for the Government to ban the publication of periodicals and newspapers.

From the Crown Princess

Poor Willie is so tormented with all these machines and things, that it makes him cross and difficult to manage. Poor child really he is sadly tried. He is so very funny sometimes. He has a sergeant who comes in the morning to make him do exercises, in order that he should be made to hold himself more upright and use his left arm. When he does not wish to do his exercises he begins to say his prayers and bits of poetry, and the other day he asked the man, before Sophie Dobeneck who was shocked, "Do you put a nightgown on when you undress yourself and go to bed?".

The King is all right again now since he has got rid of the stone which caused him so much pain—nephritic stones. I suppose nephritic means the kidneys but I am not sure.

Affairs are in a fine mess—whatever is going to be done I do not know. For Fritz and myself it is very hard—we are the bane of the Kreuzzeitung party and unpopular with the mass of liberals because Fritz does not come forward. They consider his present line of conduct, weakness and fear, but it is neither one or other. He is doing his duty in every way and should not on any account forsake the line he has taken.

From the Queen

On the evening of this sad day,[1] I must write to thank you with all my heart for your dear, loving, warm-hearted letter and lovely drawings of Henry. You write to me as you, and all those who really feel, ought and perhaps only can. You are your father's own child in mind and genius. Little faults you have, but they are much less than they were and who have not their faults? But you have a noble, loving, tender, devoted heart, and a very clever head, and such power of expression! Often and often do I long for the assistance of that head! You must come here this autumn.

---

[1] Her birthday.

I must bring you back, and carry you off and Fritz must come and fetch you. It would be a real comfort to me.

The table was as last year in the sitting room, and the dear children loving and affectionate; then I gave Affie the Garter and the others trifles. After that Dr. McLeod performed the service beautifully, then I drove with Louise, Leopold and Tilla,[1] and then this afternoon I went with the six children up to the fine large Cairn for beloved Papa, a pretty walk! I feel poorly and exhausted having been very unwell all day yesterday with violent headache, sickness and great prostration. I struggle hard to keep up enough to do my work but I am nearly unable often to keep up. I have not had a letter from Fritz.

From the Queen

BALMORAL, MAY 26, 1863

I this morning received your affectionate letter of the 23rd by which I am sorry to see what the poor King's indisposition was. I only wish it would make him more reasonable.

In your dear long letter of the 19th you tell me what Fritz intended to do in case of any violation of the Constitution which I think would be quite right; only don't delay it the moment there should be anything like a violation or else it would ruin Fritz's position. The more you are both away the better. I must repeat it—let me bring you back, and let Fritz come and fetch you! You can say I want you. But I fear I could not put up the children this time. Dear Aunt Feodora will also be here, and she often cannot go out with me, and you could do what you liked and it would do you all good.

How well you describe that beloved room of Papa's (where Lenchen is now sitting and writing). There I always breakfast, see the ministers and sit of an evening till Lenchen and Affie leave me, and then before I go to my poor dressing-room.

I have been reading three such admirable sermons by

---

[1] Miss Hildyard, the governess.

Dr. Stanley and an admirable letter of his to the Bishop of London (caused by this shameful persecution of Colenso) which I send you as I am sure you will be struck and pleased with them.[1] There is also an admirable preface of Dean Milman's[2] to a new edition of his History of the Jews which I will send you, as soon as I can get another copy. I am much occupied with all this searching after truth.

What a dreadful account you give of that poor little child of Anna of Hesse! It is a visitation on her, poor thing, for the sins of its father and grand-father I am sure!![3]

From the Crown Princess

SALZWEDEL, MAY 26, 1863

I have not time to give you a detailed account of our journey but I will try and give you a sketch of it. We left Potsdam after church on your birthday and left the railway at Genthin from whence we drove through towns and villages to Tangermünde—a most picturesque old town on the banks of the Elbe. The country is of course quite flat and not particularly interesting but the Elbe winds its silver way peacefully through the pleasant, green fields—gay with daisies, buttercups, clover and sorrel. The meadows look quite English so rich and fertile—the land looks everywhere well cultivated, the people healthy, well-dressed and contented. Everywhere triumphal arches, flags, flowers etc.— the whole neighbourhood turned out in holiday attire, and every one most civil and kind which I really wonder at, considering the present state of things.

We spent the night of the 24th in an inn at Stendal where we drunk your health, with some sadness but with

---

[1] Stanley stood aloof from the parties in the Church. He regretted the publication of Colenso's book but "could not join in the indiscriminate outcry against an evidently honest and single-minded religious man".

[2] Milman, the Dean of St. Paul's, had published his history of the Jews 30 years earlier when it had met with censure and opposition. In the preface, to which the Queen refers, he wrote that all the marvellous discoveries of science were "utterly irrelevant to the truth of Christianity".

[3] By grandfather the Queen means Prince Charles of Prussia.

many good wishes. Yesterday was a very fatiguing day—
receptions and dinner in the morning and posting from
3 o'clock till 10 at night when we arrived at Tilsen—a pretty
place with a quaint, curious old house belonging to a Mr.
and Mme de Kneesebeck where we are going to stay a few
days and from where we came this morning to look at this
town and give a dinner to the authorities.

From the Queen

BALMORAL, MAY 28, 1863

Pray thank dear Fritz so much for his dear, kind letter
received yesterday and tell him how I wish and hope he and
you will come here this autumn for a fortnight or three
weeks. At Coburg, it would not do well; I can't lodge you
and I fear we should see but little of each other between the
Rosenau and Coburg. Therefore pray come here instead. It
would be very good if Fritz were away from home a good
deal now. Another thing I wish you to help me in. You
know I have been trying (though I have had no time for
some weeks or months to go on regularly with it) to put
down an exact account of our happy life, as a picture of it,
as well as all I can remember beloved Papa said. Well I
began with the life at Windsor beginning in October and
going on (which I think I showed you) and I have got down
to the description of Christmas and the end of the year.
Well you describe so beautifully that it would be a very
great help to me, if you would describe New Year's day as
it used to be, not any one particular one but a picture of the
New Year's day beginning with you children standing in
our room waiting for us with drawings and wishes; Grandmama at breakfast, then you children performing something or a tableau, and your playing and reciting and in the
evening generally a concert or performance with orchestra—
then our wedding day the same. I send you here, as a guide
a rough sketch of the last day of the year, asking you to let
me have it back, as I have not copied it yet. Pray now, do
write those two days down—and later my birthday perhaps,
in short try and help me a little bit, and put down any

picture of darling Papa's manner—as I am very anxious to get everything I can together for my book (which will belong to you all after my death) and for the private life. General Grey is working at that. I saw poor Mrs. Farquharson on Tuesday, grown so old and grey—and she was much affected poor thing. It was my first visit since '61 to Invercauld and to find that house also with a hatchment was most sad! Sitting below with her and the poor girls and taking tea—it seemed all a dreadful dream![1]

From the Crown Princess

NEUES PALAIS, MAY 30, 1863

I fear, dear Mama, that it is quite impossible for me to go to Balmoral this year for many, many reasons—at any rate I could not promise now that I could come. This time is so critical for us that I do not think it my duty to leave Fritz. Stockmar is not here—and among his other gentlemen he has no one who could afford him the slightest assistance. I should not think it right to leave him.

I shall be separated from the children for a whole month now and should I be allowed to spend November and December elsewhere than in town at Berlin I should have to leave them again; this is a minor consideration to be sure —as if I could be of use to you I should not consider my own wishes and convenience. It sounds too delightful to think of seeing dear Balmoral again which I have wished and of which I have dreamt and thought so long, besides it would be such a pleasure to be with you, dear Mama, as the last time I was in England I saw so little of you and kept away, knowing that Alice was more agreeable and useful to you—but now I should be able to do all the little services for you of which I feel so jealous. But I am afraid, dear Mama, it cannot be—at any rate it is impossible to decide at present.

We have returned much pleased and satisfied with our

---

[1] Mrs. Farquharson, born a Dundas, had produced nine sons and four daughters. Her husband had died the previous November.

little tour and with the unfeigned kindness and civility we met with everywhere on the road but the news of the state of feeling in the country on the whole and in the rest of Germany is very bad indeed, and the belief that, after so many disappointments, nothing good can ever come out of this dynasty, is pretty generally expressed in many intelligent circles.

People are angry with Fritz for not coming forward but we must bear that and much else that the blind folly of the Government have brought upon us. Fritz is doing what is right and what will in the end have its reward. The King has sent him an order to go to Poland, the thing of all others to be avoided, which has put me into a state of uneasiness and alarm. His presence in a moment such as this may cause unpleasant demonstrations, besides those wicked, horrid Poles think nothing of shooting people. How the King could think of exposing his son—if not to absolute danger—to every sort of disagreeable.

From the Queen

BALMORAL, JUNE 1, 1863

I am glad you have been travelling about and will do so again as it must do much good. But affairs are in an awful state. God only knows how it will end. Only do prevent Fritz's getting at all identified with such terrible misconduct. Lord Palmerston says that the poor King's conduct is like Charles Ist and Charles the Xth!!

What you tell me in your preceding letter about William's sayings are too delightful. You must find out whether it is true about Princess Christian? She has never once seen Wally since she returned from England, which is very wrong and very rude—for to Wally she owes all. I dislike her so very much; I think her insincere. Did you hear that Sir A. Paget was nearly drowned by the upsetting of a boat the other day?[1]

---

[1] This episode is dramatically described in *Embassies of Other Days* by Walburga Lady Paget—especially when the future Lord Lytton, in

I trust that if matters don't get worse you and dear Fritz will be able to come here in the autumn. But I must scold you, dearest child, for a little jealous remark about poor Alice which is not right! In the first place you know how much there was to do when you were at Windsor and how much you yourself wished to see, but you remember too, how invaluable you and dear Fritz were to me at that (to me) time of dreadful recollections and how impossible it would be for me (as I told you both over and over again with many, many thanks) to have ever gone through it without you. Alice's position is a totally different one to yours—she was much more with me than you had ever been, for you married at 17—she only at 19—and beloved Papa was then my blessed companion and support. Then Alice's husband has nothing to do at home now; they are not rich, and their best work is to be a support and comfort to me. If Alice could not be with me much hereafter—why, then Lenchen must be, because, dearest child, your position is too great and high a one ever to be able to be here long at a time or to devote yourself solely to me. Therefore why speak jealously of those who can do so. No darling, you must not do that.[1]

I do not encourage Coburg apart from 2 or 3 days because I know I could not see you quietly and easily there, and I do want to see you and hear your clever conversation, which is so useful and so agreeable to me but you will find me get duller, and more and more listless. The state of your affairs makes me terribly anxious. Fritz should not go to Poland; he really (I think) should refuse.

---

order to see what was happening, waded into the water up to his chin with the *Revue de Deux Mondes* in one hand and a tortoiseshell paper knife in the other.

[1] Replying to the Queen about Princess Alice the Crown Princess wrote on 8 June ". . . I forgot to say that in your last letter you complain of my having made a jealous remark about dear Alice. I am sorry that I should again have so ill expressed myself as to be so completely misunderstood and that you should put such bad motives under my zeal to serve you. I am not the least jealous of her. I know the difference of her position and mine quite well, and would not change mine, difficult as it is, for any other in the world. . . ."

I asked General Grey to write to you a little about politics.

From the Crown Princess

I shall be most happy to help you to write down any thing you like relating to former happy, blessed times; I have not time at present to write any thing down but as soon as I find a leisure moment I shall.

I have been writing so much for Fritz—drafts and letters and copies—besides my correspondence with the Queen and Stockmar owing to our sad state of things that I have but little time to myself, besides which the day after tomorrow I shall be off on my journey where I shall have little opportunity of writing. Fritz left last night, before he went he wrote a long letter to the King saying he had no intention of meddling in things which did not concern him, of criticising the King's Government or of making himself in any way responsible by giving advice as to what should be done, but that he could not see the danger the King was in without warning him, and begging and imploring him never to give his consent to any unconstitutional measure his Ministers might propose as the only way to get out of present difficulties, as such measures would endanger the peace of the country and the dynasty and nothing good could possibly be obtained by them. It will be Fritz's painful duty—if not withstanding his warning they are adopted—to protest, and declare that he declines the responsibility of being accessory to such acts and will have nothing whatever to do with them. I hope it will not come to this—indeed I hardly think it will. The King is going to Carlsbad soon for sometime and afterwards to some other watering place.

I fear there is not much chance for Mary with the Grand-Duke of Schwerin, he does not seem to think of marrying again and, if he did, people say he would marry a Princess Reuss! I wish Uncle George would marry—he could marry Addy who [is] such an excellent girl and much admired here; she has plenty of her own—one million dollars from her mother; she would have a hundred thousand from the King if she married—and the same from her father most likely.[1] How I wish you could set that going! But I don't think Uncle G. ever would marry; he is so like an old man for his years.

From the Crown Princess

(Not addressed but written from Danzig.)

JUNE 5, 1863

Only two words from here. We are in a sad state of perplexity and alarm and quite alone—without assistance or advice. The King has taken unconstitutional measures—not "au pied de la lettre", but certainly against the sense and spirit of the Constitution; and people are indignant.

We arrived here yesterday and the town refused to prepare a reception for us; there were no decorations on the houses, no flags and scarcely any one in the streets. Fritz wrote as you know to the King begging and imploring of him not to do anything so dangerous or pernicious as sophistically interpreting the letter of the Constitution so as to annul its sense. The King answered Fritz a sad letter full of hard and most unjust reproaches—ordering him to speak in the sense the King desires.

I travelled all night in a state of great anxiety, brought this letter of the King's with me—to which Fritz answered a beautiful letter of which I shall send you a copy as soon as I can. As we have not a single soul about us who can help us I must make all the copies as well as the drafts and send them to the Queen and to Stockmar.

We are in a dreadful position, the country loudly clamouring for Fritz to come forward and he receiving the most peremptory commands from the King and no thanks for the tact and self-denial Fritz has been showing the last whole year—only reproaches for having opposed the King. We cannot conceal from ourselves that the times are most

---

[1] Her father was the King's brother Prince Albert: her mother was the daughter of the King of Holland. They were divorced.

serious! This second letter will infuriate the King. I should not be astonished if he put Fritz under arrest. But what can we do? We both cannot sleep for excitement and worry. Fritz is quite ill from it. What would darling Papa say?

I have not time for more, dear Mama, pity us and think of your much tormented

Affectionate and dutiful daughter
Victoria

I am prepared for a catastrophe!

From the Queen

WINDSOR CASTLE, JUNE 8, 1863

I have two letters to thank you for—of the 1st from the Neue Palais and of the 5th this morning from Danzig which fills me with anxiety. The speech dear Fritz made has not made a good impression here, but I think the translation may have given a wrong idea of what was intended![1] Oh! dearest child! how distressed I feel for you both! And darling Papa, not being here to help us and advise us! If I only could be of any use I would do anything to save you sorrow and anxiety! But let Fritz be firm! He must not shrink from separating himself from all his father's unhappy acts! People who are most devoted to you like General Grey are loudest in entreating Fritz should protest. I know Papa would have said the same. He cannot satisfy his father by half measures and he may compromise his and his children's position if he does not clearly show to the country that he not only does not belong to that party, but highly disapproves what has been done! Oh! why is all this worry and trouble going on? Why do people torment themselves and bring on such misfortunes? I am sure that things would

---

[1] On 1 June an emergency measure had been passed permitting a ban on the publication and distribution of periodicals and newspapers. In his speech on the 5th the Crown Prince said that he had been astonished by the press rescript. He explained that he had been absent and had had no part in it. He went on to adjure them to have confidence in the excellent intentions of the King, and it was no doubt this addition which was not liked in England. See Count Corti, *The English Empress*, page 104.

never have come to this pass at Berlin if beloved Papa had not been taken from us.

I have just been speaking to General Grey and he feels so strongly and anxiously upon the subject that we are determined to send off a messenger with this letter, and General Grey writes also to you. He says and I am sure beloved Papa would have said the same; the Crown Prince should respectfully refuse to travel about and absent himself from the country and come here. This house—your old home—sad and shaken as it is—is open for you. Come here with the children and you can be with us or in town, or in the country or wherever you like—only don't stay in Prussia. I speak in beloved Papa's name, I hear his voice, and his blessed words: "You should come here." Mr. Rulandt also, entirely shares this opinion; Fritz may be fatally compromised if you do not do this.

I have heard today from the Queen, that she will come here on the 18th. Could you come here with her?

I am very poorly; I feel so much worse, and all this anxiety about you beloved children does not make me better —God knows.

Bertie and Alix left Frogmore today—both looking as ill as possible. We are all seriously alarmed about her—for though Bertie writes and says he is so anxious to take care of her, he goes on going out every night till she will become a skeleton, and hopes there cannot be!! I am quite unhappy about it. Oh! how different poor, foolish Bertie is to adored Papa whose gentle, loving, wise, motherly care of me when he was not 21 exceeded everything.

I fear I cannot do anything about Uncle George; he is too old (of his age) and out of health to think of it.

From the Crown Princess

SCHLOBITTEN, JUNE 8, 1863

I can only write very few words, as I have but little time, and my head is so full of what is going on, that I find it difficult to collect my ideas.

I told you, on the 5th, that Fritz had written twice to the

King, once, warning him of the consequences that would ensue, if the Constitution was falsely interpreted in order to take away the liberty of the press. The King did it all the same, and answered Fritz a very angry letter.

Fritz then sent his protest to Bismarck on the 4th, saying he wished to have an answer immediately.

Bismarck has *not answered.*

Fritz wrote on the 5th to the King, as I told you. On the same day Mr. de Winter, the Oberbürgermeister of Danzig, a great friend of ours, a worthy and excellent man, as clever as liberal-minded, told Fritz he would make him a speech at the Rathaus, and begged Fritz to answer him.

I did all I could to induce Fritz to do so, knowing how necessary it was that he should once express his sentiments openly and disclaim having any part in the last measures of the Government. He did so accordingly in very mild and measured terms—you will have no doubt seen it in the newspapers. To this the King answered Fritz a furious letter, treating him quite like a little child; telling him instantly to retract in the newspapers the words he had spoken at Danzig, charging him with disobedience, etc., and telling him that if he said one other word of the kind he would instantly recall him and take his place in the Army and the Council from him.

Fritz and I sat up till one last night, writing the answer, which Captain von Luccadon[1] has taken to Berlin this morning, and in which Fritz says that he is almost broken-hearted at causing his father so much pain, but that he could not retract the words spoken to Winter at Danzig; that he had always hoped the King's Government would not act in a way which should force him to put himself in direct opposition to the King; but now it had come to that, and he (Fritz) would stand by his opinions. He felt that under such circumstances it would be impossible for him to retain any office military or civil, and he laid both at the feet of the King. As he felt that his presence must be disagreeable to the King, he begged him to name a place, or allow us to

---

[1] The Crown Prince's equerry.

select one, where he could live in perfect retirement and not mix in politics.

What the upshot of this will be, heaven knows. Fritz has done his duty and has nothing to reproach himself with. But he is in a state of perfect misery, and in consequence not at all well. I hope you will make his conduct known to your Ministers and to all our friends in England. We feel dreadfully alone, having not a soul from whom to ask advice. But Fritz's course of duty is so plain and straightforward, that it requires no explaining or advising.

How unhappy I am to see him so worried, I cannot say; but I shall stand by him as is my duty, and advise him to do his in the face of all the Kings and Emperors of the whole world.

A year of silence and self-denial has brought Fritz no other fruits than that of being considered weak and helpless. The Conservatives fancy he is in Duncker's[1] hands, and that he dictates his every step. The Liberals think he is not sincerely one of them, and those few who do think it, fancy he has not the courage to avow it. He has now given them an opportunity of judging of his way of thinking, and consequently will now again be passive and silent till better days come. The way in which the Government behave, and the way in which they have treated Fritz, rouse my every feeling of independence. Thank God, I was born in England, where people are not slaves, and too good to allow themselves to be treated as such.

I hope our nation here will soon prove that we come of the same forefathers, and strive for their own lawful independence, to which they have been too long callous.[2]

---

[1] A German Liberal politician and historical scholar of much note.
[2] *The Letters of Queen Victoria*, Second Series, Vol. I, page 86.

From the Crown Princess

The messenger has just arrived, bringing your dear letter, and the one from General Grey; allow me to answer them both together.

We are well-nigh worn out with mental fatigue, anxiety, excitement of the most painful kind. I was ill all yesterday, and feel still very confused!

I send you all the papers that you may see what Fritz has done, said and written!

He has done all he could. He has, for the first time in his life, taken up a position decidedly in opposition to his father. His speech in Danzig was intended to convey in a clear and unambiguous way to the hearers, that he had nothing to do with the unconstitutional acts of the Government—that he was not even aware of their being in contemplation! The effect produced on those fifty or sixty who heard it was exactly the one desired, but I know there are many who will not agree. Many of the Liberals pick holes in it, but as many I have heard praise it unconditionally. The Conservatives are in a state of indignation and alarm, the King very angry! We are in this critical position without a secretary, without a single person to give advice, to write for us, or to help us; whatever we do one way or the other is abused.

After having read all these papers, you will understand that Fritz can do no more than what he has done! My last letter will explain much of what has happened. We are surrounded with spies, who watch all we do, and most likely report all to Berlin, in a sense to checkmate everything we do.

The Liberal papers are forbidden, so we do not even know what is going on. Fritz's speech was much praised by newspapers in Frankfort-on-the-Main. As for coming to you, dear Mama, you are too kind to say so; at present we can decide nothing, as we have received no answer from the King; our fate is not settled. If it becomes necessary for us

---

[1] This is mis-dated; it was clearly written on 11 June.

to leave the country, I can hardly say how grateful we shall be to be once again with you, in that blessed country of peace and happiness!

Now goodbye, my dearest Mama, I kiss your hands. I am sure you will think of me in all this trouble. I do not mind any difficulties so long as they end well for Fritz; indeed I enjoy a pitched battle (when it comes to it) exceedingly. Fritz feels his courage rise in every emergency; only the thought of his father makes him feel powerless. "Think if it was your father," he says to me, "would you like to disobey him and make him unhappy?"

I find that I cannot send you all the papers I intended, as they are either with Stockmar, Fritz of Baden, or Prince Hohenzollern, but we send you here all we have by us. Luccadon has just returned. The King does not accept Fritz's resignation, and wishes us to continue our privacy, forbidding Fritz, however, to say another word openly. We shall therefore carry out our plan of travelling here till the 1st of July, when we shall go to the Isle of Rügen. In August I hope to see you, dear Mama, for a day or two; in September are the Manœuvres and a Statistical Congress, which Fritz is to open: therefore I fear Scotland will be quite impossible. Oh dear! what a sad wretched time we have of it, and no help, no support, surrounded with people determined to put an insurmountable barrier to all we wish to do in a liberal sense, and tormenting the very life out of one! Please send back the enclosed as soon as you can. As soon as the rest of the papers are returned us, Fritz will send them you.

M. de Bismarck has not even answered Fritz's letter, and the King has forbidden him to give it to the rest of the Ministers![1]

---

[1] *The Letters of Queen Victoria*, Second Series, Vol. I, page 92.

From the Queen

I cannot tell you with what unmixed satisfaction I received your dear letter of the 8th from Schlobitten, in which you mention the line Fritz has taken. You are the best and wisest adviser he could have, and the worthy child of your beloved father who will look down approvingly on you. May God bless and protect you and guide you in your arduous and difficult task! All your friends and all the Ministers to whom I mentioned it are much rejoiced and relieved to hear it, as there is but one feeling of anxiety lest dear Fritz's position should be seriously compromised. But what a terribly painful trial for so good and excellent a son as Fritz is.[1]

From the Crown Princess

RASTENBURG, JUNE 14, 1863

Since I last wrote nothing has occurred in politics and I know of nothing. We are so far north that we only get the news of what is going on very late. All this excitement has made me quite ill. I am off my appetite and sleep, have a sore throat and an aching head and a whitlow on my thumb! Our tour here in Lithuania is very interesting.

We left Königsberg on the 12th, had a rough passage of six hours across the bay to Memel, in a little nutshell of a steamer kept by a Scotchman. At Memel a troop of forty young men and women—Lithuanian peasants—came out to meet us on horseback and escorted our carriage at a tearing pace. All the women ride—and all the young girls astride—in their picturesque dresses and their baskets on their arms and large switches in their hands; it looked very

---

[1] Yet it could be argued that the sway of the Crown Princess over her husband's mind was dangerous. Urging him to maintain his liberal views, soon after her father's death, she told him that he owed this "to your future, to the country and to your children". Though a fine man he was easily influenced.

strange and very pretty. They sung their wild extraordinary songs which sound like wailing and screaming but not like music. Hardly any of them understand German except those who had served as soldiers.

I forgot to tell you that I saw more than a hundred Polish peasants at Danzig sitting, lying and standing about the streets in white coats lined with sheepskin and curious large straw hats, and sorts of sandals with coloured strings; they looked very picturesque but very dirty. Yesterday we were in the magnificent forest of Ibenforst the wildest and finest forest I ever saw—filled with wild flowers quite unknown to me—wild callas and rosemary and sorts of little "cyclamens". Fritz did not get a single shot at an elk which was very unlucky; there are about 200 there but very difficult to get at. I saw one—the most extraordinary monster I ever beheld—and perfectly frightful, something like a deformed horse—so large, dark and clumsy but marvellously swift.

It was very interesting sport however. First we were up to our ankles in marshy ground, broiled by the sun and devoured by every manner of stinging insect, then came the most frightful thunderstorm I ever remember—clap on clap of thunder, deluges of rain wetting us to the skin in a minute.

From the Queen

WINDSOR CASTLE, JUNE 17, 1863

Your dear long letter of the 11th I received on Monday and return you all the enclosures with many thanks. I admire Fritz's letters very much, but I cannot say as much of the others. I cannot however conceal from you that your P.S. with the news that you after all continue your journey, grieves and disappoints me and all your friends. I send you the copy of a letter from Lord Clarendon which will show you what he thinks of Fritz's position. All your friends think the same and so do many liberals in Germany. I also add an extract of a letter from Sir A. Buchanan and a draft from Lord Russell which I thought you ought both to see. My anxiety for you is very, very great! So much depends on Fritz's position not being compromised. I feel, however, deeply and fully, believe me, what he, who is so excellent a son, must suffer! It is terrible.

I do not wish to add to your sorrows and annoyances by saying any thing to distress you, dear child, but I must ask you whether you and Fritz know of Abbat's and his sister's intention of coming to England this year? I can't think you did, or you would at once have tried to stop it, knowing after what I told and wrote to you both, that I could not see him. The worry, anxiety and distress this has caused me, have made me quite ill. I hoped all was set at rest for this year and you may imagine my extreme astonishment when I heard this. I trust it may yet be stopped.[1]

From the Crown Princess

STEINORT, JUNE 19, 1863

How delighted I was to receive your dear kind letter of the 13th. It was indeed a relief and a comfort to see that you understood Fritz's conduct as it was meant. I cannot take any praise to myself though. M. de Winter, good excellent man, is the person to whose advice Fritz owes most of what he did.[2]

From the Crown Princess

NEUES PALAIS, JUNE 25, 1863

Coronation Day

In answer to what you write about Abbat's journey to England I have only to say that it in no way concerns me. I certainly knew of his intention to go; moreover I was

[1] The explanation for this is that Abbat (Prince Albrecht, nephew of the King) was a possible bridegroom for Princess Helena.
[2] On the other hand in *Embassies of Other Days* Walburga, Lady Paget, describes how her sister Valerie, who was the Crown Princess's lady-in-waiting, came to stay with her immediately after the Crown Prince's speech and "related, with great glee, how she and the Crown Princess had composed a speech and talked airily about the consequences".

asked what I thought of it: I declined giving any advice on the subject, naming as a reason, that I had promised you not to interfere in this business; consequently I had of course no right and no reason to prevent his journey to England.

He has not the remotest idea of taking steps with regard to Lenchen at present, therefore I really cannot see why one should treat him as if he had, and discussions on that subject would therefore not only be premature but very strange. He knows that Henry of Hesse,[1] the two young Danish Princes[2] and the Prince of Orange[3] have been in England lately and sees no cause why he should not go there too. I think you must be under some great misapprehension if you suppose that he has any further idea at present than merely going to look about him, and I really should be much embarrassed to find a good reason to give him for not going, as the fact of my dissuading him would presuppose the very step having taken place, or being at any rate intended which I understood you wish to prevent—certainly for two years to come and then altogether if the conditions you have named are impossible.

I shall however tell Abbat that you decline seeing him.

From the Queen

FROGMORE, JUNE 24, 1863
In the garden

I write here, where I love to sit. Now there is poor little Leopold (who was quite well and strong) since yesterday on his back from that internal bleeding. We can account for it in no way but from his riding which the poor child had just begun to enjoy and which now must be stopped (except at a foot's pace) for another year! It is very sad and I miss darling Papa again here so awfully. Oh! how this alarmed and distressed him! I feel all these terrible anxieties are sent, and must be borne with patience! But oh! the illness of a

---

[1] Brother of Prince Louis.
[2] Brothers of the Princess of Wales.
[3] The somewhat disreputable heir to the Dutch throne.

good child is so far less trying and distressing than the sinfulness of one's sons—like your two elder brothers. Oh! then one feels that death in purity is so far preferable to life in sin and degradation!

I always tremble lest Affie (who is much improved and so clever, industrious and amiable) should again fall into sin from weakness! He must (and is very anxious himself for it) marry early. There is no other safety for him, and indeed when one sees that silly ——[1] running after and catching the Prince of Orange—one feels none of our sons can ever remain in London unmarried.

Dearest child, I will not repeat what I said in my last letter except that we are all most anxious—once that this unfortunate journey has been continued (which I and our friends consider a mistake)—that Fritz should not return to Berlin, but go away after Putbus for a time, and remain quite away for some time, which will prevent any personal opposition and which will not compromise Fritz's position further. If he does not do this I see the greatest possible danger for the future. In this the Queen quite agrees. Her dear visit is a real comfort and satisfaction to me;[2] it seems like a bit of blessed old times! She is so clever, so good, so noble-minded, so free from all pettiness, so adores adored Papa, misses him so dreadfully, feels so deeply for me and pities me so truly. She sees how crushed, and worked and fagged I am and has such forbearance—and won't allow me to change my life in any way. We are both so unhappy, that we understand each other so well. We have spoken openly on all delicate and difficult subjects and I can only say what darling Papa said: viz. that he always found her so sensible, so clever, so understanding, so affectionate and so unselfish, that he had, and so have I, the greatest esteem, and respect and admiration as well as affection for her. Oh! and he pitied her so—and so do I! And she is so very kind and indulgent about the King who is so harsh to her! Oh! her fate is a terrible one. She breakfasts with me in my room and we

---

[1] Impossible to decipher.
[2] Prince Alfred went to Dover to meet the Queen of Prussia on 18 June.

— *235* —

lunch and dine together in the oak room. She thinks Alix very pretty and nice, but she says Alix must try and get Bertie to occupy himself; unfortunately she never does any thing but write! She never reads—and I fear Bertie and she will soon be nothing but two puppets running about for show all day and night! It is regretted by every one.

From the Queen

I received your dear letter of the 25th this morning from the Neue Palais and thank you for it. It has crossed mine and mine to Fritz which will I hope have settled everything satisfactorily about Abbat. As regards your journey I have given my opinion and E. Stockmar shared it—but it is very gratifying to hear you were so well received every where.

The dear Queen's presence is a satisfaction and a support to me! Oh! how I admire and love her! She is so noble-minded. She is much pleased with Alix but I fear she will never be what she would be had she a clever, sensible and well-informed husband, instead of a very weak and terribly frivolous one! Oh! what will become of the poor country when I die! I foresee, if B. succeeds, nothing but misery— for he never reflects or listens for a moment and he [would][1] do anything he was asked and spend his life in one whirl of amusements as he does now! It makes me very sad and angry.

From the Crown Princess

NEUES PALAIS, JUNE 27, 1863

Fritz has sent me the letter you wrote him. We under-stand every thing you say quite well. Abbat and his sister do so too and I am heartily glad that the matter is so far smoothly arranged. May I now venture to beg as a favour to me that you will let Addy see the sisters she will not name

---

[1] One of the rare occasions when the Queen leaves out a word by mistake.

her brother. But she is not only my cousin but my friend and we have always got on so well together; from the first day I arrived she has always been most kind to me. She always speaks of you with the greatest respect and affection and would feel it very much I think if she was not allowed to see the sisters.

Last night I sat till 12 in the beautiful moon-light—so still and peaceful—enjoying the perfect calm and the perfume of the roses. How my thoughts wandered to you and to beloved Papa and oh! how many tears flowed for him and for you.

My imagination paints the thousand dangers of life, of our several positions, so vividly and my courage sinks when I think that he—our only support, guide and adviser—has left us his children to fight their battles alone! No not alone for there is a gracious Providence that directs the trembling steps of those who earnestly strive to do their duty. How weak the flesh is (though the spirit is willing) no one knows better than I who have an ever burning desire to be and to do what I should and who fall so lamentably short of it!

From the Crown Princess

NEUES PALAIS, JUNE 29, 1863

As soon as I had written my last letter I went to inform Alexandrine by your desire that you would not see her brother. I do not think I ever had a more disagreeable errand to perform; it pained me to give so much offence to people whom I like so much and it was really very difficult to explain. Altogether it made me quite unhappy. The day after I received your telegram telling me not to say anything until I had read your letter to Fritz. It was too late— but I returned to Addy and imparted the contents of your letter to Fritz so it is all in order now I hope. I think you are quite right if you do not wish Lenchen to marry yet—not to let her see young princes. But I think in that case there should be no exceptions made; and I would not offend any one before I was certain that I meant to refuse him at all events. You will be better able in your own mind to judge of Abbat's merits or demerits etc. when you have seen him. Forgive my saying all this, beloved Mama, and think it no want of respect. You have always allowed me to say what I thought and condescended to listen in patience to the expression of my humble opinion.

It is a great and real source of satisfaction to me to think that the Queen's visit should be a comfort to you and to her. The more our two families hold together the better for both of them, for our countries and for Europe—of that I am firmly convinced. And now darling, precious Papa is gone we must do all we can to keep up the link which I often thought had loosened within the last year—which I saw with no little alarm. Be quite easy about Fritz; he will do all he should, he will let himself be guided by Stockmar and you will see that all will go right, but it wants a little time and as we are all scattered it causes a good deal of correspondence.

From the Queen

WINDSOR CASTLE, JULY 1, 1863

Our letters have crossed but I am glad all has been satisfactorily settled about Abbat and his sister. Lenchen has seen no one, and will see no one. You know I could not avoid Alix's two brothers at the marriage or Heinrich at the christening—but those are excluded from the candidature even. As regards Abbat—it is really wasting time, dear child, to repeat what you know are the objections as well as the necessities for me regarding Lenchen. What you, dear child, wished it for, would never do—viz. to be your assistant in Prussia. Papa over and over again objected to that. God knows what events may bring about but I must have Lenchen with me for the greater part of the year when she is married, and this she knows and wishes.

The Queen sees and understands my terrible difficulties better than any one, but I see that she also leans to Abbat. All this is hard upon me, without a protector and others ought to be particularly careful.

I have terrible governess troubles. You know I told you

of Mme Hocédé[1] in February–March. Well, I found (without now blaming any one else) that she was not truthful or to be relied upon—and so, painful as it was to part from any one who had lived with us in former, happy times—I have been obliged to tell her that (which is in fact true) I no longer want three governesses and therefore her services would be no longer required and she would have a pension. Please say nothing but this to anyone. I find out however that she has done Louise a terrible deal of harm, made her deceitful and has disobeyed orders, and now—when specially told to mention nothing to any of the children, has told "qu'elle était renvoyé". It is terrible to feel all this now when I am all alone. Oh! many things would not and could not have happened in adored Papa's time—at least he would have stopped them quite at the beginning. Is it not hard that I should have all this anguish and misery now?

From the Queen

WINDSOR CASTLE, JULY 3, 1863

I can only write a few hurried lines after dinner, and it is so terribly hot I can hardly sit still or hold my pen. We start for Osborne at 10 tomorrow. I feel leaving Windsor very much. The last happy and sad days of my blessed married life were spent here and I feel bound to it by the most sacred ties which, while I am on earth, must ever draw me towards this spot.

The beloved Queen left us at $\frac{1}{2}$ past 3 and her visit has been a real comfort and support to me. On all subjects I have talked most openly to her—and she knows and understands all my feelings, views and terrible difficulties. I have never admired and loved her more than this time; how noble-minded, how wise, how fair, how good, how right-minded, how clever!

---

[1] She was French governess to the royal children.

From the Crown Princess

I am so glad to be here again in this charming place of which it is not the least attraction that it is so far from Berlin. Dearest Fritz joined me at Stettin. We had a good passage of seven hours though it was a little rough.

We are living in the pretty schloss of Prince Putbus.[1] I see the pretty garden and fine trees of the park out of my window and a little bit of the beloved blue sea beyond, which I consider England all the world through!

I have had hard battles to fight even here. People wished to persuade Fritz to go to Carlsbad now to pay the King a visit saying it would please the King and in some way atone for the pain Fritz had given him of late. They made all this as plausible as they could, but I think that this plan if carried out would be productive of every sort of harm, certainly unnecessary and most likely dangerous. I have done all I could to prevent Fritz going there and I think he has given up as he was much averse to the idea. He left me yesterday morning and returns tomorrow. Our existence is not a pleasant one now. We live in a perpetual state of anxiety and excitement as to what will come next, under these circumstances the old phrase is really the best advice "hope for the best and prepare for the worst".

The articles in *The Times* have caused a tremendous sensation, people suppose I have got them put in and both our friends (to whom Duncker belongs) and our foes consider me as "la génie du mal".[2] I must say I care very little

---

[1] On the Isle of Rügen. It belonged to Prince William of Putbus, married to the brilliant Princess Wanda with whom the Crown Princess was friendly.

[2] *The Times*, under Delane, had been consistently anti-Prussian and Delane had described their articles as "that most cruel of all afflictions—good advice". They were in full cry at this time against Bismarck and the King for flouting the constitution and liberal opinion. The King, it will be remembered, was taking the waters in Austria, and a day or two after the Crown Princess wrote, an article was published from the paper's Berlin correspondent, which was designed to draw attention to the differences in the Royal Family. "The King has been accompanied on

for what the newspapers say as I have always held they had a right to say what they liked, and to pick up their information wherever they could, but it will take long before that point of view finds its way into the head of a Prussian.

Even Duncker says Fritz must be prepared to give the King an explanation of how such articles got into *The Times* —and that every one in Germany was shocked at it (which I don't believe). Stockmar, Mr. Morier[1] and I are supposed to be the conspirators, the two first are accustomed to hatred and ill usage from the Kreuzzeitung campaign—and I can laugh at all the venomous inventions they put about of me. Fritz is frightened every time an article in *The Times* appears about him and fancies they do him an injury. I must say I do not think so, but I regret the belief which is universal here, that the only thing I live and long and care for is the "praise of the English Press". You cannot think how painful it is to be continually surrounded by people who consider your very existence a misfortune and your

---

his bathing trip by Herr von Bismarck and Councillor Sitellman—the chief of the Government Press.

"The King in Austria, the Queen in England [Queen Augusta was at Windsor] and the Crown Prince travelling about in a distant province —thus the most influential members of the dynasty have separated for the present intent upon different objects."

The article ended with the information that the rifle match of the Brandenburg Volunteers "has been prohibited as a thing too liberal and advanced to be permitted in the Prussia of today".

But much more serious was a leading article in *The Times* a few days earlier in which it said that the Crown Prince was to be congratulated on "having a consort who not only shares his liberal views, but is also able to render him so much assistance in a momentous and critical juncture". The article gave a perfectly correct account of the Crown Prince's letter to his father, of the Crown Princess's share in it and, for good measure, referred to the King of Prussia as a self-willed sovereign with a mischievous cabinet.

All this explains the foundations of the hostility between Bismarck and the Crown Princess. "She has succumbed to the concerted influences of the Anglo-Coburg combination," he wrote at the time. The King of Prussia wrote in the margin of one of the Crown Prince's letters, which he showed to Bismarck. "Be kind to the young man, Absolom."

[1] Robert Morier, at this time second secretary at the Berlin Embassy. An apostle of liberalism and much disliked by the German right-wing. He was excellent company though described by Walburga, Lady Paget, as "a fat old elephant".

sentiments evidence of lunacy! A great many of the Conservatives are really my very great friends—clever, good and excellent people whose opinions and abilities I greatly respect, but that cannot make me change my conviction, and I can talk my tongue off before I can make them see even an atom of sense in what I think.

One has the unfortunate feeling of—by doing what one considers conscientiously one's duty—losing one's friends and augmenting the number of one's foes, which of course increases all the difficulties one has to fight with ten-fold, and is besides very harassing to one's feelings. I will not repeat all that I have already said about how sad and hard it is to think how much distress we are causing the King! His home is not a happy one, and I had always looked forward with pleasure to the time when his children's love and affection should make his old age a happy one free from care and trouble! I have no darling Papa left, and I feel as a daughter for the King whose kindness and whose endearing and amiable qualities make him creep into one's heart. Fritz adores his father, and till now in his eyes obedience and subordination were the first duty. Now I see myself in duty bound as a good wife—and as a really devoted and enthusiastic Prussian (which I feel every day more that I am) of using all the influence I possess in making Fritz place his opinions and his political conscience above his filial feelings.

Do not think it is easy, dear Mama; it costs me many and many a hard struggle. I know what a responsibility I take upon myself in taking advantage of my husband's reliance on my judgement and in giving any advice as positively as I can.

Until I find the person whose judgement I can feel greater confidence in than in my own, I shall go on with might and main trying to assist Fritz in pursuing the only road I consider right and safe.

It is very disagreeable to me to be thought meddling and intriguing. Mixing in politics is not a ladies' profession. I should like to conciliate all parties and particularly to live in peace with all those by whom we are surrounded, whose affection I know I could gain if I sought it by having no opinion of my own. But I should not be a free-born English-woman and your child if I did not set all those things aside as minor considerations. I am very ambitious for the country, for Fritz and the children and so I am determined to brave all the rest!

My conviction of what is right and what is necessary is so strong and clear and rises in proportion to the difficulties which appear that it is comparatively easy.

I have not a bright prospect before me; when I think of the poor Queen with all her great good and noble qualities, far better and greater than any I possess, and think of the position she now has—disliked by almost the whole aristo-cracy and without a particle of influence at home! The Queen's position is only easier in one single respect which is that it does not cost her anything to offend to Kreuz-zeitung aristocracy—she is at quits with them: from the time of her marriage they have behaved ill to her: they have hated her and done all they can to do her harm; they have been her open enemies so she can have no regrets. But towards me many of them—indeed I may say the majority (though they looked upon me with jealousy as a stranger and as an Englishwoman, and though they thought it was a pity their future King had married one so plain and so unornamental for society) were civil to me, although they continually say I dislike Germany, I cannot get accustomed to live out of England, I wish to change everything and make everything English, they cannot help seeing that I am full of good will towards them and that "je ne demande pas rein" than to be friends with them. On this journey they have been full of kindness, cordiality and civility, which I must say I wonder at—as they could have "bouded"[1] me with impunity.

In all other respects my position is ten thousand times easier than the Queen's. I have a husband who loads me with undeserved kindness, indulgence and confidence, with whom I live in unity and happiness and whom I daily learn

---

[1] Half-English, half-French meaning "cold-shouldered me".

to respect, admire and love! All this the poor Queen has not —and she is much to be pitied, besides she has a much more violent and excitable temper and bad health.[1]

From the Crown Princess

PUTBUS, JULY 6, 1863

This is a fine house with a lovely garden and we feel very happy and comfortable and try to forget those horrid politics which make one's life a burden and everything a torment.

We shall go to Coburg when you come, dear Mama, for a few days to Uncle Ernest, but he says we cannot bring the children, and then I hear you wish to see Alice and Louis— when we shall betake ourselves off again. I am sorry you will not see Henry he is grown a fine little fellow and is such a sweet tempered child.

I fear I have not much to tell you that would interest you or amuse you, and I have read nothing but the newspapers lately. I am almost frightened every day when I take one up for fear there should be something about us in it. Where are Bertie and Alix? Is not Alix going to have some sea bathing, surely it would be so good for her health? Are there no hopes as yet?

From the Queen

OSBORNE, JULY 8, 1863

Your long, interesting and enthusiastic letter of the 3rd reached me on Monday. Your position is indeed a very difficult one, but I trust that by quiet firmness Fritz will be able to keep in the right position without too much irritating his father, but also, even if that should be, Fritz must not

---

[1] Queen Augusta was a great Francophile and this helped to explain her unpopularity in a land where the Napoleonic occupation was vividly remembered. She was often snappy and patronising to her daughter-in-law. A characteristic example was her remark *a propos* Bismarck "If you are childish enough to have some illusions, I am sorry for you. Time will soon teach you differently." Count Corti, *The English Empress*, page 124.

Plate 16. (Left to right) Princess Helena, the Duchess of Coburg, and Princess Louise, September, 1862

Plate 17. The Prince of Wales and Princess Alexandra of
Denmark, January, 1863

Plate 18. Photograph taken at Windsor, March, 1863, on the occasion of the marriage of the Prince of Wales. *(Left to right seated)* Prince Christian, Princess Christian, Princess Alice (Princess Louis of Hesse), Prince Louis of Hesse, Princess Helena, the Crown Princess of Prussia, Princess Dagmar. *(Left to right standing)* Prince Frederick of Schleswig-Holstein, the Crown Prince of Prussia, Princess Alexandra, the Prince of Wales, Princess Louise, and Prince William of Schleswig-Holstein

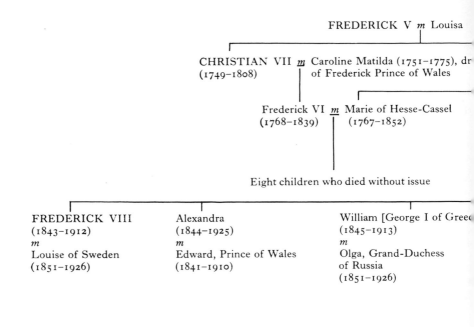

FREDERICK V *m* Louisa

CHRISTIAN VII *m* Caroline Matilda (1751–1775), dr
(1749–1808)   of Frederick Prince of Wales

Frederick VI *m* Marie of Hesse-Cassel
(1768–1839)   (1767–1852)

Eight children who died without issue

FREDERICK VIII   Alexandra   William [George I of Gree
(1843–1912)   (1844–1925)   (1845–1913)
m   *m*   *m*
Louise of Sweden   Edward, Prince of Wales   Olga, Grand-Duchess
(1851–1926)   (1841–1910)   of Russia
                                                    (1851–1926)

THE HOUSE OF DENMARK

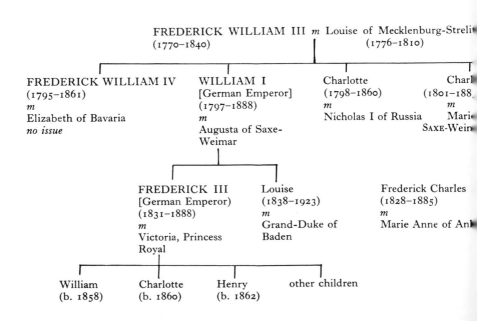

FREDERICK WILLIAM III *m* Louise of Mecklenburg-Streli
(1770–1840)   (1776–1810)

FREDERICK WILLIAM IV   WILLIAM I   Charlotte   Charl
(1795–1861)   [German Emperor]   (1798–1860)   (1801–188
m   (1797–1888)   *m*   *m*
Elizabeth of Bavaria   *m*   Nicholas I of Russia   Mari
no issue   Augusta of Saxe-   SAXE-Wein
                         Weimar

FREDERICK III   Louise   Frederick Charles
[German Emperor) (1838–1923)   (1828–1885)
(1831–1888)   *m*   *m*
m   Grand-Duke of   Marie Anne of Anl
Victoria, Princess Baden
Royal

William   Charlotte   Henry   other children
(b. 1858)   (b. 1860)   (b. 1862)

(1724–1751), dr. of George II of Great Britain

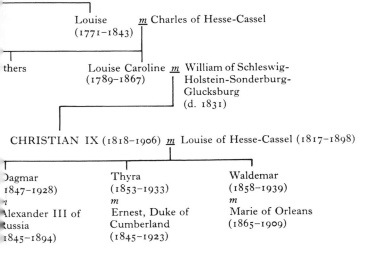

Louise   *m* Charles of Hesse-Cassel
(1771–1843)

thers   Louise Caroline *m* William of Schleswig-
          (1789–1867)   Holstein-Sonderburg-
                       Glucksburg
                       (d. 1831)

CHRISTIAN IX (1818–1906) *m* Louise of Hesse-Cassel (1817–1898)

)agmar	Thyra	Waldemar
1847–1928)	(1853–1933)	(1858–1939)
t	*m*	*m*
Alexander III of	Ernest, Duke of	Marie of Orleans
Russia	Cumberland	(1865–1909)
1845–1894)	(1845–1923)	

Note: 1. Frederick VII (d. 1863) was descended from Frederick V by his second marriage.
      2. King Christian IX's right to the throne was not strictly hereditary but the result
          of a family compact endorsed by the Danish Parliament.

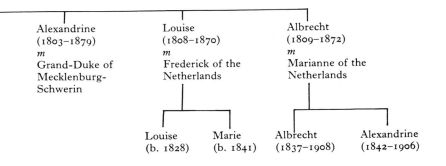

Alexandrine	Louise	Albrecht
(1803–1879)	(1808–1870)	(1809–1872)
m	*m*	*m*
Grand-Duke of	Frederick of the	Marianne of the
Mecklenburg-	Netherlands	Netherlands
Schwerin		

Louise	Marie	Albrecht	Alexandrine
(b. 1828)	(b. 1841)	(1837–1908)	(1842–1906)

THE ROYAL HOUSE OF HOHENZOLLERN

Plate 19. The Crown Princess of Prussia, January, 1863

Plate 20. The Crown Prince of Prussia with Prince William,
October, 1863, at Balmoral

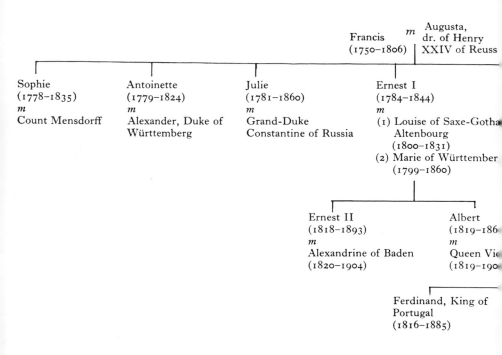

Francis *m* Augusta, dr. of Henry
(1750–1806) | XXIV of Reuss

Sophie
(1778–1835)
m
Count Mensdorff

Antoinette
(1779–1824)
m
Alexander, Duke of
Württemberg

Julie
(1781–1860)
m
Grand-Duke
Constantine of Russia

Ernest I
(1784–1844)
m
(1) Louise of Saxe-Gotha
Altenbourg
(1800–1831)
(2) Marie of Württember
(1799–1860)

Ernest II
(1818–1893)
m
Alexandrine of Baden
(1820–1904)

Albert
(1819–186
m
Queen Vi
(1819–190

Ferdinand, King of
Portugal
(1816–1885)

THE HOUSE OF SAXE-COBURG AND GOTHA

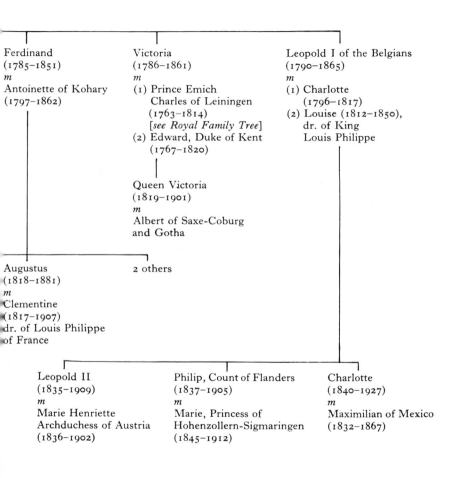

Ferdinand
(1785–1851)
m
Antoinette of Kohary
(1797–1862)

Victoria
(1786–1861)
m
(1) Prince Emich
    Charles of Leiningen
    (1763–1814)
    [*see Royal Family Tree*]
(2) Edward, Duke of Kent
    (1767–1820)

Queen Victoria
(1819–1901)
m
Albert of Saxe-Coburg
and Gotha

Leopold I of the Belgians
(1790–1865)
m
(1) Charlotte
    (1796–1817)
(2) Louise (1812–1850),
    dr. of King
    Louis Philippe

Augustus
(1818–1881)
m
Clementine
(1817–1907)
dr. of Louis Philippe
of France

2 others

Leopold II
(1835–1909)
m
Marie Henriette
Archduchess of Austria
(1836–1902)

Philip, Count of Flanders
(1837–1905)
m
Marie, Princess of
Hohenzollern-Sigmaringen
(1845–1912)

Charlotte
(1840–1927)
m
Maximilian of Mexico
(1832–1867)

Plate 21. The Mausoleum at Frogmore

Plate 22. Queen Victoria with Princess Victoria of Hesse,
Balmoral, October, 1863

Plate 23. Memorial to Stockmar at Frogmore designed by the Crown Princess

Plate 24. Prince William and Princess Charlotte of Prussia,
November, 1863

Plate 25. The Crown Princess in her garden at Potsdam with (left) Countess Brühl and the Baroness de Dobeneck, July, 1864

Plate 26. The Crown Prince and Princess, Potsdam, 1864

Plate 27. Prince Arthur and Prince Leopold with Major
Elphinstone, 1864

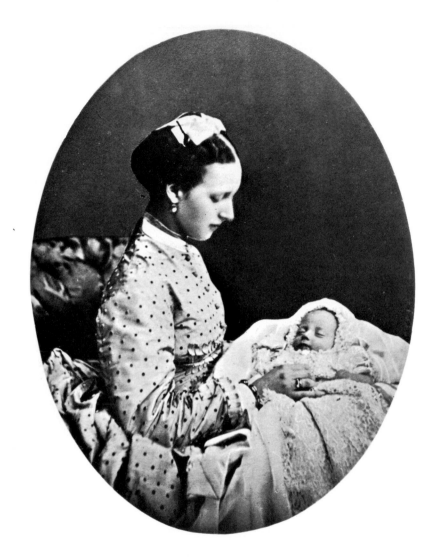

Plate 28. The Princess of Wales with Prince Albert Victor

swerve. The best way however to avoid this (and this is the opinion of all your friends) is by going away for a time which would prevent the necessity of any open opposition. Upon this you never answer. Fritz should try and avoid the Manœuvres, come to us in Scotland and then you could later go on any other journey, leaving the children with me, that you liked.

If the King's home is not happy, the beloved Queen's is far unhappier for she suffers so dreadfully from seeing and knowing the danger and being unable any longer to help her husband, who is so unkind to her! And yet she spoke so beautifully and kindly of him, and altogether so gently and mildly about all things—so wisely and sensibly about married life—taking quite an altered and right view of these things. I talked over every thing with her, and her fairness, kindness and wisdom made me think constantly of darling Papa and how he loved and admired her. She spoke with such true love and affection of you both.

Oh! how bowed down I am by these news of the beloved old Baron. This blow is again a dreadful one. Our oldest, dearest, wisest, kindest and most intimate friend! And though he latterly could not actively assist us, and though he often of late would not listen to reason when it disagreed with his own decided opinion (as in the case of Bertie's marriage) he ever was so kind and affectionate and so wise when one saw him. And one of my principal reasons for going to Coburg again this year was to see him! He possessed all our inmost thoughts; he adored Papa and he—him—and if dear Stockmar goes, the one cheering thought to me is that they are together again!

From the Crown Princess

PUTBUS, JULY 8, 1863

We are in a terrible state of anxiety about the beloved Baron! Should it please God that the life which is so valuable—which has been spent in doing services which none can repay, should now come to a close, my grief would be most bitter and deep.

I did not enter in my last letter upon what you said about Mme Hocédé. I am glad to think that you have made up your mind to part with her though I am sure it must be most painful to you.

When I was last at Windsor I saw and heard what made me wish you would not entrust the sisters to her much longer, but it was no business of mine and I did not wish to meddle in other people's concerns, make you uneasy, burn my fingers or make mischief in any way—so I said nothing and kept my reflections to myself. French women are seldom to be trusted entirely even the best of them: its not in their nature to be upright and straightforward.

From the Queen

OSBORNE, JULY 11, 1863

How dreadful is this new and totally irreparable loss! Our dearest, beloved, wisest friend! I knew he was ill, as I wrote to you, but never never did I dream of a sudden blow like this which would deprive us of this invaluable friend! I fully believe that if the dearest old Baron had continued his visits to England adored Papa and he would both be alive—for Stockmar's support and advice lightened Papa's burthen so much, and being here kept up the dearest Baron's spirits and nerves! And now that loving father, as he ever was to us both (Papa and me) and God knows to you too, is gone and I am more and more desolate! What we owe to him words can never, never express! How he helped and assisted us in all our early days, in your education, in your marriage! How different the house was— even when all was bright and happy—when the beloved Baron was there!

Bertie and Alix are at Frogmore since the 8th (having much over fatigued themselves in London, as every one has observed) and stay there till the 18th, when they come here for a fortnight, and I hope she may then bathe, and get a little fatter and stronger. There are no hopes and I sometimes have my fears and misgivings about it altogether. After that, they go by Halifax and Edinburgh to Abergeldie.

I send you dear Alix's letter I received this morning to show you that, though very affectionate and dear, she does not write well. I fear the learning has been much neglected and she cannot either write or I fear speak French well.

Bertie feels the dear Baron's loss—deeply.

From the Queen

Respecting Mme Hocédé, dear child, you ought to have told me at once all you heard and saw and it was quite your duty to do so! Don't you think if Papa or I had heard or seen any thing about your ladies, governesses, nurses, etc. that we should have told you directly what we thought? Dear child, that was neither right or kind—the more so, because I talked to you about all the trouble and anxiety I had had. No, you must promise never to do such a thing again—but always to warn me if you hear anything or above all see anything. I am in the most forlorn, dreadful position without beloved Papa, and our dear married daughters must stand by and help me. Only in one case you must not mix and that is in talking with your brothers and sisters (before you had asked me) of their future possible marriages. But that is only before having ascertained what I wished; but anything concerning the entourage it is quite a duty to me to tell me and I rely on your doing it in future.

From the Crown Princess

PUTBUS, JULY 15, 1863

I am most anxious about our coming to England, there is nothing in the world we should like so much—and we wish to avoid spending September, October, November and the greater part of December in Berlin, but how this can be managed we do not yet know.

As for Fritz's staying away from the Manœuvres—that is quite impossible; he takes a command and could not be absent of course. During that time I shall be at Potsdam with the children. Perhaps you will then let Affie come and pay me the long promised visit? After that we must go to Baden for the Queen's birthday. What we shall then do I am unable to say as it must depend on so many things.

Samwer is here—we wished to have somebody to talk to upon affairs as there is no one here. Count Schwerin[1] we saw a few days ago; he seemed quite satisfied with all that Fritz had done. It is very difficult for us just now, and the newspapers are continually printing articles about us which do not improve matters.

From the Queen

OSBORNE, JULY 18, 1863

I have but little to say. I am sitting in the Upper Alcove —expecting to see dear Papa every minute!! I suppose dear you have plenty of the beloved Baron's photographs and also some of his precious hair? If not I can send you some of both.

Leopold is not quite right yet, and is kept under very strict treatment but is in perfect good health otherwise. Arthur passed an examination very well, upon the whole, the other day, was present at the consecration of the chapel and distributed the prizes at Wellington College on the 16th (which will interest Fritz) and came here the same day.[2]

I received a letter from Addy (very kindly written) yesterday and I shall see them on Thursday next to luncheon. The three sisters will be on an expedition that day, and the following week or so Addy will come alone to see them. I will send Bertie and Alix over to return the visit. Only think how dreadful—that last Monday one of our housemaids, a very good person, threw herself from the

---

[1] Count Maximilian von Schwerin-Putzar, one of the leaders of Prussian liberalism.
[2] The school was founded in 1853 for the sons of army officers in memory of the Duke of Wellington. E. W. Benson, afterwards Archbishop of Canterbury, was headmaster and strengthened the religious side of the original foundation. The chapel was dedicated to the Holy Ghost.

roof at Windsor on to the North Terrace, and was killed on the spot. It was temporary insanity! But what a mercy we were not there. How shocking too is the Duke of Hamilton's death! He had I fear been drinking too much in a café at Paris!! Poor thing, I feel so much for her![1]

From the Crown Princess

We have been having disagreeables of every kind and have really spent some most unpleasant hours. I am sorry that it is impossible to tell you what about; I hope when we meet that I can explain it all to you.[2]

As to what you say about my not having said any thing about Mme Hocédé at Windsor, my simple reason for not doing so was this—that it is very dangerous to make remarks about people which may injure them before you feel quite sure. You told me you knew of her having given Lenchen books to read and then telling her not to mention it to you or Miss Hildyard, and yet you meant to keep her.[3] If she had been with me and I had heard that, I do not think I should have kept her as it would have completely shaken my confidence. I consequently saw that I could do no good by saying anything on the subject.

---

[1] The Duke died at the Maison Dorée, on the Boulevard des Italiens. His wife was Princess Marie of Baden, the daughter of a former Grand Duke of Baden and Stephanie Beauharnais. The Duke had a conspicuously dignified manner and was called by Brougham "very duke of very duke".

[2] This probably concerns the right of the Crown Prince to attend cabinet councils about which the Crown Prince sent a memorandum to his father. In commenting on this Bismarck wrote: "The question of discretion is that which presents most difficulty, especially in regard to our foreign relations, and must continue to do so until his Royal Highness, and her Royal Highness the Crown Princess, have fully realised that in ruling Houses the nearest of kin may yet be aliens, and of necessity, and as in duty bound, represent other interests than the Prussian. It is hard that a frontier line should also be the line of demarcation between the interests of mother and daughter, of brother and sister: but to forget the fact is always perilous to the state."

[3] This of course means the type of book then regarded as unsuitable reading for young ladies.

Besides, dear Mama, you had Alice in the house who knew all this a great deal better than I, as I had only been a few days in the house, consequently could only have an impression from what I heard, but could not with certainty come forward with any thing.

I was afraid of making mischief. I do not think she did Lenchen any good and I think both Lady Caroline and Miss Hildyard felt uneasy about her.

From the Crown Princess

A thousand thanks for your dear letter received the day before yesterday. We are almost daily expecting to hear of poor Uncle Fritz Louis's death.[1] He has had repeated strokes the last few days—but I believe he may last a long while yet. His sons were sent for, and he recognised them immediately. He is in such a sad state that it would be a real mercy if he were taken poor man. I saw him the day I left Potsdam, and was quite shocked to see him in such a condition.

Marquis Wielopolski[2] is here; he does not live five minutes off but he has not paid us a visit yet.

How beautiful is Meyer's speech at the beloved Baron's grave—it touched me so much. All he says is so true—and shows such appreciation of the dear Baron and such tact and good feeling.[3]

---

[1] He was the great-nephew of Frederick the Great and step-son of Ernest Augustus, the Duke of Cumberland.

[2] The Polish statesman. He was at the time in the service of the Russians in Poland, and strongly anti-Prussian.

[3] "Even indispensable people pass away. This man's death is felt by distant Kings and Queens in this solemn and consecrated hour, as if they had been the only ones who possessed, who loved and who have now lost the departed." Meyer was the clergyman at Coburg and known as Superintendent Meyer.

From the Queen

I will answer about Mme Hocédé and the book on Wednesday. It is not quite as it appeared and that was the least of the annoyances. I see your delicacy about it—but beg you to have none in future.

Oh! dear child, thank God! darling Marie is safe with her magnificent baby but it was an awful labour—48 hours in pain and 18 in constant labour! And at last at two in the morning of Friday (I was in and out the whole day for it began at $\frac{1}{2}$ past 8 on Thursday morning and only laid down on a sofa downstairs at 12) after she had had three hot hip baths in all her agony, borne without a murmur or more than a little, gentle, piteous moan and full of love and gratitude to all around her, that no real progress was made and soon after Dr. Farre said she must not be allowed to go on or she would be exhausted and the child would die and so instruments must be used!! Poor Ernest was in despair and crying—and so I sat by her and they put her completely under chloroform and she was like as if she slept, I stroking her face all the time and while Dr. Farre most skilfully and cleverly delivered her without her knowing or feeling any thing, and only woke when she heard the child cry and immediately said she wished to have a prayer read to her for she was so thankful, and wishing only she could give her life for me and restore beloved Papa to me!! This quite overcame me! She is an angel of gentleness, resignation and unselfishness and I love her as a daughter. Poor Ernest would hardly be persuaded she was not injured and at first would not look at the child—feeling so anxious for her.

From the Crown Princess

A thousand thanks for your dear, kind letter by messenger and for the charming frock you have been so kind as to send for Ditta. I kiss your dear hands for it. Her grandparents here have not taken the slightest notice of her birthday—the King has not an idea what day it is on, and neither the King or the Queen ever give her anything, so you see your gifts are a double pleasure, dear Mama.

Our charming stay here is coming to an end at last for which I am so sorry. I do so enjoy it; it is such a sweet place so calm and quiet—the lovely blue sea and the charming scenery with the plants and foliage and lovely woods. I went out seal stalking all alone with Fritz and a Jager; it was so nice, we got into a little boat and tried to get to some rocks about half a mile from the shore unseen by the seals but the wind was unfavourable and they found us out, and dived into the water. Fritz got a shot at one but it only just grazed the creature's head and it disappeared with a great plunge sending the spray up far around. We saw four close together; they are very difficult to get at as they are so very shy. This is a sort of second Osborne; I only wish it belonged to us; it would be a perfect Eldorado; the air is so delightful only a little too cold; we have hardly had one very warm day since we have been here. Prince and Princess Putbus are such amiable, agreeable people—and have got three of the loveliest little girls I ever saw; they are like little "amours". I just wish you could see them—Willy does nothing but kiss them. One could quite fancy oneself in England here—the garden and the Park are so fresh and green and well-kept and there are so many pretty flowers. I really love the Isle of Rügen, this time I like it even better than the last.

From the Queen

OSBORNE, JULY 27, 1863

I wrote in such a scramble that I did not say my say. The principal object of my writing today is to tell you (though I know you have difficulties) that dear Aunt Feodora is not alas! coming to me for Scotland, as she had intended to do, as she dreads the length of the journey and will meet me D.V. on my return. I therefore write again to say how really necessary and useful it would be if you could come, and that I could take in all the children there as dear Aunt doesn't come—if you brought but one lady and Fritz but one gentleman. It would do you all so much good. I suppose we shall get there by the 13th of September and stop till the 20th or 21st of October. Pray do try. I could give 3 rooms (those where Arthur used to be) for your children. It would be a little squeezing but could well be managed, or I could make another arrangement even, and give them the three rooms Lenchen and Louise used to have.

The visit of Abbat and Addy took place on Saturday for luncheon. He was unembarrassed and is unchanged—as tall and thin, but more talkative. Addy is very good natured—not pretty nor interesting and very like Emily Villiers.[1] She was very nervous. Bertie and Alix and Leopold were here—the others on an expedition. Bertie and Alix are gone to see them today and on Saturday Addy is coming over alone.

From the Queen

OSBORNE, AUGUST 5, 1863

I have to thank you for two dear letters of the 30th and the 1st. As I shall write on Friday by an extra messenger, I will only today answer yours of yesterday respecting the correspondence.[2] The correspondence was seen by no one but General Grey (who knows every thing) to whom Mr. Rulandt translated it; it never left the house nor indeed did any of the ministers ever see it. Only one of your letters written before you sent me the correspondence was read

---

[1] Daughter of Lord Clarendon, and afterwards married to the first Lord Ampthill.
[2] This letter is seemingly missing. The Queen when writing "yours of yesterday" means "yours received yesterday". Evidently the Crown Princess had written to ask whether the correspondence between the Crown Prince and his father, which the Crown Princess had sent to the Queen on 11 June had been seen by unauthorised people—a fact which might explain the articles based on it in *The Times*. Writing to Bismarck at this time the King of Prussia sent him a newspaper article "with an *accurate* reproduction of my correspondence with my son—too accurate to be inventions". See the *Correspondence of William I and Bismarck*, J. A. Ford, 1903.

to Lord Russell, and Sir George Grey[1]—but it never left our hands. You know that it was no secret what Fritz did and said and that his views were necessary to be known. But no one saw the correspondence. I think the King should look nearer home for such things—as dear Uncle Leopold says. Remember Niebuhr's papers—also a letter of beloved Papa's to the present King![2]

Why doesn't Fritz answer my letter? I expected some notice of my affectionate and confidential communication, and it is really not pleasant to have no answer! You will receive a long letter from General Grey—which I hope you will acknowledge.

From the Queen

OSBORNE, AUGUST 8, 1863

I will first answer through you dear Fritz's letter—thanking him for it. I am surprised that he should express himself about Affie's marrying early as he does, knowing Papa's feelings on the subject and the position (this he cannot entirely judge) of a Prince here. All that I have done in this business is with Affie's consent and knowledge —he himself wishing to marry as early as Bertie, and after due and mature reflection and consultation with our best and wisest friends. I know I can however rely on both of you holding the same language to Affie and not trying to deter him from what will be his salvation?

I think your idea of our joining in a monument to our beloved Baron's memory a very right and proper one; I will mention it to dear Uncle, and you will I hope make the design. There is a very fine article or sketch of his dear,

---

[1] Respectively Foreign Secretary and Home Secretary.
[2] Marcus Niebuhr, cabinet-secretary to Frederick William IV. A letter from the King to the Prince Consort was copied in the post, and sent to Napoleon III. Although the source of the information given to *The Times* has never been explained it is possible that it came through the English Government. Grey, the Queen's private secretary, showed the letter to the Foreign Secretary and the Home Secretary. (See *The Empress Frederick* by Richard Barkeley, Macmillan, 1955.)

great life by Professor Hellner[1] in one of the German newspapers, which I have no doubt you have seen. His life must hereafter be carefully written.[2]

I still hope and trust you will all be able to come to me for three or four weeks to Balmoral—between the 13th of September and 20th of October. I wonder you could go to see the poor seals shot at! Papa could not bear their being shot, he was so fond of them!

Dear Affie is well, and much improved. Every day he gets more and more like adored Papa in his ways! I would propose your taking him back with you from Coburg—and he might stay three days with you.

From the Crown Princess

NEUES PALAIS, AUGUST 8, 1863

Many thanks for your dear letter which I received by messenger yesterday. Fritz answered you as soon as he could; he had too much to do before.

Your answer about that vexed correspondence was just what I expected. When shall we ever hear the last of it? The King might indeed as you say look a little nearer home. We feel sad, uncomfortable and oppressed here—our position is a most disagreeable and forlorn one, and it requires all one's determination and courage to keep up to the mark.

I add a few words to my letter of this morning to say that the King has telegraphed to Fritz to go immediately to Gastein![3] You can imagine how we are both taken aback by this! Fritz will have much that is painful, difficult and embarrassing to go through, and that I cannot be with him at such a trying time is a real sorrow to me. He dreads the meeting with his father, and I dread M. de Bismarck and consorts'[4] machination.

---

[1] Unidentified.
[2] The "Young" Baron published his father's memoirs in 1872. The Queen was shocked by it.
[3] The King was on holiday at Bad Gastein.
[4] Consort is used in the sense of colleague.

Fritz was looking so well at Putbus now all this agitation will make him look as ill as he did at Königsberg and Danzig.

The ministers are of course determined to put an effectual stop to Fritz's opposition, and to dispute the fact even[1]—if they can obtain any thing by it. I think the King counts upon Fritz's "repentance" for the past and obedience for the future—and not a stone will be left unturned to persuade Fritz to come over to the other camp I am sure. But he will not let himself be bullied into forgetting his duty and he will adhere to his principles and opinions; but I dread for his tender and sensitive heart all the scenes and discussions that are sure to take place! I wish I could be there to smooth the way, to comfort and encourage him. Pity me, dear Mama, as we are really in a most unpleasant position; it does seem such a shame to torment one so good as Fritz—so unselfish and forbearing. I wish I could give these charming people about the King a piece of my mind that they could not misunderstand. I shall not have a moment's peace until Fritz returns.

From the Crown Princess

NEUES PALAIS, AUGUST 10, 1863

I feel so uneasy about Fritz's visit to Gastein; it torments me so, as I am sure he will be so teased. I begged and prayed of him to take it all coolly and not to mind it but scenes with his father are what he dreads of all things; he is such a good son; his first thought is always how to give his Papa satisfaction.

Professor Max Müller[2] from Oxford paid us a visit, and today the Moriers come.

---

[1] i.e. to deny that he was in opposition.
[2] At this time he was emerging as the outstanding authority on philology. He was also Taylorian professor of modern languages at Oxford. Though born at Dessau he was a naturalised Englishman.

From the Queen

Fritz's call to Gastein must indeed be a great anxiety and distress to you. I long to hear the result and feel deeply and anxiously for you!

The heat is quite dreadful! Like in '58, when we went to Babelsberg. But for me now—to whom travelling is misery, and no interest and who am so weak, so shaken and exhausted it is quite terrible. I am sitting out without a bonnet or any shawl or "mantille" and can't hardly write! Leaving dear Marie was a great trial. I can't say how I love her! She is so good, and so gentle and so attached to me!

Dearest Uncle is quite recovered, and wonderfully well. How grieved I am the King has refused the Emperor of Austria's invitation![1]

I am going to see Princess P. of Oldenburg and her daughter this evening. I will tell you all when I have seen her.[2]

From the Queen

THE ROSENAU, AUGUST 16, 1863

We were pleased with Princess C. of O.,[3] Affie decidedly so. But she is not "a beauty"; clever, sweet, gentle and full of character, with lovely eyes and eyebrows and a fine

---

[1] The German Confederation formed after Napoleon, with its Diet meeting at Frankfort, was in conception sensible but in reality a muddle. Austria in 1863 was anxious to make the Confederation work, and the Emperor visited the King at Gastein to tell him that he was going to invite members of the Confederation to confer on the constitutional reform of their body. Considering Prussia's powerful position in Germany the King felt that he should have been consulted beforehand about the nature of the reforms. He therefore refused to attend.

By this meeting Austria intended to strengthen the Confederation, but the meeting only underlined Prussia's ability to defy Austria. See Agatha Ramm, op. cit.

[2] Princess Peter of Oldenburg and her daughter Catherine who was 17.

[3] Princess Catherine of Oldenburg.

forehead;—she is pretty but not handsome or showy-looking. Very good teeth and skin.

From the Queen

I cannot let this blessed and ever dear day pass without saying how thankful I am for the few days we spent together, for all your love, affection and sympathy and how I pray God may support, strengthen and comfort you! How I pray to be able to be of use to you beloved children, how much I feel the sacred trust beloved and adored Papa has left to me, to watch over you all, and to try—while life still exists in this poor shattered frame—to work for you all! Yes, and that I will as much as lies in my power. I talked long and satisfactorily with Lord Clarendon last night, walking up and down in the moon-light.[1]

From the Crown Princess

Sad and wretched I was when I left you last night and thought that the meeting I had looked forward to for so long was already passed, and melancholy was the long journey here! Parting from you, beloved Mama, gives me an indescribable pang and makes my heart feel sore and heavy! I contrast the little silent group in the moon-light round the door of the pretty Rosenau with the many partings from home in former days when you and dear Papa stood together and almost all the dear brothers and sisters! It was harder to bear then perhaps but it did not fill one with that deep and indescribable nostalgia which it now does.

---

[1] Lord Clarendon, the statesman, was not in office at this time. He was staying at Wiesbaden, and being well-versed in foreign affairs he could advise the Queen on the difficulties facing the Crown Princess. He also attended the meeting of the Diet at Frankfort as an observer. Commenting on his reports from Germany the Foreign Secretary remarked that a hundred spies could not ascertain as much as one English gentleman in whom Princes and Ministers believed that they could trust.

I feel much more confident in a tolerable issue of this vexed question at point—now I know you will not let yourself be taken in too much in favour of the Emperor and of Austria.[1] God grant that whatever you may say may produce the desired effect and I was almost going to say as the prayer book has "turn the hearts of the disobedient to the wisdom of the just". I hope you will not think this very profane!

From the Queen

THE ROSENAU, AUGUST 27, 1863

Many, many thanks for your dear beautiful letter received this morning. How true every word is! Yes, dear child, I do deserve pity for my lot is a terrible one! I long for peace and quiet, and to be able to rest and dwell only on my adored angel; and that necessary quiet is never allowed me! Worried and worn and worked and constantly struggling against the attempts to force me to do more, when I feel worn out by what I have to do—by the awful responsibility! It must indeed be a sad sight to see me standing alone, with a few orphans, when we were ever together! God bless and protect you in your trying and painful position! I have no answer from the King! You may be quite easy as to my interview with the Emperor.

From the Queen

ROSENAU, SEPTEMBER 1, 1863

I am so done up, so worn, so worried and the poor King's visit so agitated and worried me yesterday that I passed a bad night and am very trembly today. However I send a messenger with this and a memorandum I dictated to Augusta before I went to bed, for you and Fritz to see, and which you can keep if you like or perhaps take a copy of it and send it me back. You see your visit to Scotland is

---

[1] The Crown Prince had wished his father to attend the Conference, but later changed his mind. The Queen was to see the Emperor.

allowed without a moment's hesitation![1] I send you also a dear, charming letter from Alix which I am sure will please you.[2] Since you left, Affie's prospects have changed inasmuch that his first opinion was communicated to Princess Wied (and this could not be avoided as the Princess expected it).[3] Well it seemed now very important to see the Princess of Altenburg[4] (of whom the Queen of P. has had a very favourable report from Prince Hohenzollern and who is now no longer living with her mother) so I telegraphed to the Queen of Hanover to Hummelshain saying Affie would pay her and the Duchess of A. a visit today and just as he was starting I heard from her that she unfortunately would be gone, but the Duchess would be delighted to see him. So he is gone. But oh! I am so tired, so worried so really driven wild with work!

Uncle Ernest is expected back tomorrow, for which Alice stays else she would have gone yesterday. The Emperor is expected on Thursday.

You know, dear, that if you find Balmoral an inconvenience you must not come, but I fear I may not be able to receive you next year or at least not with the children. Alice wishes me to tell you how stoutly she has defended and does defend Prussia against the many attacks which alas! are made against her! And that poor Princess Charles[5] is quite wretched at all she hears against it, being so very Prussian in her feelings—very naturally. You may be quite sure that I shall say what you were anxious about to the Emperor. But I am quite worn out; it is really too, too much for any poor woman's head and body—bowed down by grief besides. God bless and protect you all in these very sad and serious times.

---

[1] The King was accompanied on his visit by Bismarck. He told the Queen that Austria was deliberately planning to ruin Prussia. He urged that England and Prussia should combine to oppose this. "Bismarck makes this impossible" was on the tip of the Queen's tongue but she restrained herself. Count Corti, *The English Empress*, Cassell, 1957.

[2] No doubt announcing that she was expecting a child.

[3] The daughter was Princess Elizabeth of Wied.

[4] Princess Marie of Saxe-Altenburg.

[5] Her mother-in-law, a Prussian princess.

From the Crown Princess

NEUES PALAIS, SEPTEMBER 1, 1863

The King arrives today also the Archduke Leopold my particular friend.

All is like a desert here; all gentlemen have disappeared —the whole garrison has left. Fritz leaves today and all his gentlemen with him; we are left to the care of a very funny old gentleman of the bedchamber who wears a "ratelier" and is very tiresome besides. I did not speak to Affie much about his marriage—I merely said to him that now he knew the Princesses he must seriously reflect in his own mind and balance all the advantages and disadvantages before he settled any thing, and at any rate should look for an opportunity to make better acquaintance with the one that pleases him most before he fixes his choice.

I could not give him any other advice as I really cannot say which is the most desirable. Addy seemed to please him rather—but perhaps you think her too old to be put on the list.[1]

Here is a letter from Princess Christian to me. I shall not say all I think of it as it would not be very flattering to her. You will judge for yourself whether you think it need be answered or not, I think certainly not.

From the Queen

ROSENAU, SEPTEMBER 5, 1863

Princess Christian's letter is not a nice one, and the writer I most particularly dislike. Oh! dearest, it is a wonder to me that Alix is what she is—when I think of the whole family! I wrote immediately most tenderly to her—for her letter is indeed charming. But all that all our dearest friends said against the marriage is quite—and indeed but too—true—excepting Alix herself. That she should be so well, is I think very odd. But they say it is not a sign of strength.

---

[1] She was two years older than Prince Alfred.

Affie returned quite charmed with Princess Marie of Altenburg and with his whole visit there. He is most anxious for this match in every way, says she is far the nicest of the three,[1] is very pretty, very tall, slight, with beautiful, large, thoughtful, grey eyes—fine marked features and fine very dark hair! Major Cowell was delighted with her also, said she was very ladylike, quiet, and sedate, though cheerful and animated when she spoke, had evidently read a good deal and spoke English extremely well. In short he said: "I have not seen any one at all like her for a long time." I now only wait to make some further inquiries as to her health etc. and then I will let Agnes (the Duchess of Altenburg) know that her charming cousin had made a very favourable impression on Affie and that he wished much to see more of her next year. Should the account of her health not be favourable (which I hope there is no fear of) then, if the account of Princess C. of Oldenburg's health is good, I should wish him to make her further acquaintance as I think he would be sure to like her.

I must now tell you about the Emperor of Austria's visit. It was very, very trying for me in every way, for it was an official visit. I drove to the Schloss early and waited there. Uncle went to the station to fetch the Emperor and then brought him over to me. Alice and Lenchen were with me, and I went half way to meet him;—he was in uniform, very quiet, simple and unaffected, not talkative, but very dignified. The luncheon was in that tapestry room—an awful, large, long family-table all the relations and Edward L.[2] Oh! how dreadful these visits are now, and I feel as I did in former times as a child—unprotected and unsupported. Very soon after luncheon he went away. I had but little opportunity for conversation, but I took care to say what you wished, and repeatedly to observe upon the necessity of Prussia's being put upon a footing of equality. He assured me that this was his wish, and that there was no other wish in Germany—that I might assure you (I asked what I

---

[1] The Princesses of Oldenburg and Wied were the two others.
[2] Leiningen.

should say) of the very friendly disposition of Austria. He said (and did Uncle Ernest) that the plan would be submitted to the King and if he would not accept it, they hoped he would state his objections which would then be considered. He regretted the King's non-appearance and lays the whole blame at the door of Bismarck and not of the King. How I pray that the King may be persuaded to make some onward step, for I am sure it is all in his hands.

Don't forget the design for the dear Baron's grave; I was there today and in our mausoleum and placed wreaths on our dear Papa's,[1] poor Mama M.'s[2] and Papa's own dear mother's[3] sarcophaguses. I am thankful to have done it.

From the Queen

KRANICHSTEIN,[4] SEPTEMBER 8, 1863

Just before leaving this pretty old Schloss in a splendid Park, I write to tell you of our having arrived here safely at $\frac{1}{4}$ past 8 this morning after a prosperous journey last night; it was very dark when we left the dear Rosenau. Dear Alice and Louis have established themselves very nicely here.

I now come to what Alice has written to you, and which will, I fear, dear child, be a great disappointment but every attempt to get any one to come to Balmoral where it is now for me, so sad, so lonely—had failed:—1st, dear Aunt Feodora who only gave it up in July; 2nd, you, alas!—though I urged you again and again, and though now you know the King would allow it; 3rd, the Leiningens—who had to return to Amorbach; 4th, Uncle Ernest and Aunt Alexandrine, who also cannot go away now; 5th, Fritz and Louise of Baden who had at first intended to accept and who now decline on account of Fritz's taking sea baths; and 6th, dear Countess Blücher who can't come till the winter! The thought of my utter loneliness with no lady even—except Augusta—who is of any real recourse, for Lady Churchill good and excellent as she is, is not that—to one

---

[1] Duke Ernest I.   [2] His second wife, Marie.   [3] His divorced wife.
[4] The summer home of Princess Alice, a few miles to the north-east of Darmstadt.

like me—unable to take part in any thing, or to take exercise etc. I cried bitterly yesterday morning at the thought of what it would be, and then in my distress I telegraphed off to Louis and Alice to ask whether they could come, and on my arrival here, they affectionately and kindly said they would come immediately—their only great regret being they could not now come to you, though they hope to do so later in the winter. I am grieved to think they should by their devotion to me cause you, dear child, a disappointment, but as you could not come—you will, I know, at once see that I, in my forlorn position, have a prior claim to you!

The baby is splendid—and looks like six months! and is so very good.

I had a long talk with Mr. Samwer yesterday and he is most alarmed at the state of affairs in Prussia. The great thing, and indeed the most important, is that dear Fritz should be very firm, and let no threats or orders from his father make him attend the Councils. It would be most fatal if he did that. Do tell him so from me. I need not tell you how constantly and anxiously I think of you and your great troubles and difficulties. It adds much to my many sorrows and anxieties!

From the Crown Princess

BERLIN, SEPTEMBER 8, 1863

Your dear, kind and long letter was a real satisfaction to me. How kind and good of you to say what I begged to the Emperor of Austria—I am sure it will have done some good. I had a good opportunity of speaking to the King yesterday—he was touched and grateful that you should have spoken in the sense you did. He is exceedingly desirous that an understanding should be come to; he will state all his objections and wishes, when the time comes, he says. Austria has really not behaved well towards us—the feeling of resentment here is as general with all parties as it is strong.

If you would only ask my Baron to write you his view of the question—also Samwer you would hear a very different story from what the enthusiasts for Austria say and believe. Fritz goes to the first sitting of the Statistical Congress today.

I came here yesterday for the great parade which took place with an obligato accompaniment of bitter cold wind and rain. Afterwards there was a large dinner and a stupid ballet. I stay here tonight in order to see Sanny and her husband who come through tomorrow. I saw Prince Peter[1] and his very hideous son yesterday; they beg to be remembered to you—also Prince and Princess F. of the Netherlands and Mariechen. I seldom saw so many ugly people together as yesterday!

What you say about darling Affie's visit to Altenburg gives me great pleasure. I heard yesterday from someone who knows the Princess and her daughter very well indeed, that the daughter was very good and charming, and heard some very pretty little traits of her character; of her personal appearance I heard from the same source that she was very pleasing—but sickly-looking, had bad teeth and very large bones, and large hands and feet! What I heard made me decidedly incline to think that she was the most desirable of the three—but I would earnestly advise you to enquire about her health seriously—if she is delicate perhaps sensible treatment may do her good if it is not constitutional, but they are not a healthy family; this I say not to raise an objection but merely to name a consideration which dare not be overlooked. Goodness is the first thing, the first condition of happiness, the rarest thing to be found —in the long run the only one that never loses its value, and conquers more difficulties than the sharpest wits. I get more convinced of it every day, and that it is only that which makes domestic life a Paradise! For Affie's wife and your daughter-in-law—I wish a "sympathetique" person whose presence alone brings comfort and happiness to those around. I do not think, with all her delightful qualities, E. Wied would ever be that—there is that quiet self-possession and "équilibre" wanting in her composition which

---

[1] Prince Peter of Oldenburg, father of Princess Catherine.

is indispensably necessary to make all go smooth in so large a family of which the members are so young as ours! We are all possessed of high spirits, a very good thing they are sometimes and much needed in the present times—so an element of quiet sense and steadiness without being a "bonnet de nuit" would be very valuable. There are other families where a little bit of life and energy infused does wonders—and for such a one Elizabeth Wied would be perfect, particularly if her mama-in-law had strong nerves and enjoyed noise.

Has not Fritz sent you the paper yet? I have not had an opportunity of asking him as I only catch glimpses of his blessed face now and then, when relapsing from the glow of military ardour into which we are all plunged at present; he comes to talk a bit of politics or mention any casual subject on hand.

We like the Archduke Leopold so much: he is not gifted but so good tempered and great fun sometimes.

The Empress of Austria speaks very low as she is rather shy, and the other day she spoke to a gentleman who was very deaf and said "Are you married?"; the man answered "Sometimes"; the Empress said "Have you children?" and the luckless man bawled out "At times".

From the Crown Princess

NEUES PALAIS, SEPTEMBER 12, 1863

I have but little time to answer your dear letter from Kranichstein. As you suppose, dear Mama, it was a great disappointment to me that Alice does not come—particularly so as I thought we were still expected in Scotland and still was counting on the possibility of overcoming the difficulties in the way of realising the plan and complying with your wish! Today I have heard that the Queen does not wish us to go to Baden, so I should have been able to say yes to your invitation; and now we consider it as settled that we do not go. There is not room for two "ménages" and four children with nurses etc.

The people of the Statistical Congress have just been here! At the opening, Mr. Farr (one of the English members) held a very nice speech in memory of dear Papa.[1] I could only speak to very few as it was so badly arranged.

From the Queen

I am glad that you see you can trust me! I know you always had a very poor idea of old Mama's wits, and never cared for my opinion, which was natural perhaps when our blessed oracle was with us, but now that I do nothing without thinking of him and without remembering his words and his wishes, you may have some confidence in my opinion and conduct. I do indeed hope that the King will try and agree as much as he can! I have never been enthusiastic about the Austrian plan as I felt sure there must be another side to the question so I had Morier and Samwer to talk to me, and I soon saw how matters stand. But Uncle E. is useful, I think.

With regard to the Princess of Altenburg, I have taken means to ascertain all about her and her health, and am anxiously awaiting the result. Affie says only one tooth is not good, and that she has not large feet and hands. He is very desirous for it, and I think a Princess of a Saxon House particularly desirable—so thoroughly and truly German, which is a necessity!

I grieve truly to think of the disappointment to you, dear child, if Alice is not coming to you but you are too good a daughter not to feel I had a prior claim, as you would not come yourself.

Your proposal respecting the beloved Baron's tomb, I entirely agree in and will act in all as you suggest. It sounds beautiful.[2]

---

[1] William Farr, a prominent statistician who had been employed in the Registrar-General's office.
[2] The memorial was designed by the Crown Princess and is inscribed "dedicated by his friends in the reigning families of Belgium, Coburg, England and Prussia".

From the Crown Princess

I have been out at the Manœuvres today, the weather being abominable, but I enjoyed it all the same riding about on a nice horse, and seeing the soldiers and what is going on is always pleasant. I shall get quite browned at last!

By messenger I shall most likely have things of importance to send, and if not by the one of this week then by the following. Pity us when you think of our position. I assure you it takes away every feeling of ease and security I have; it is perpetually on my mind day and night.

From the Queen

BALMORAL, SEPTEMBER 17, 1863

Your dear letter of the 12th received the morning of the day we started for Scotland distressed me very much for I had urged and pressed you so earnestly to come, for so long —and you not only said you thought you could not but you let me know through Alexandrine you could not. You gave Affie and every one the impression you did not wish to come and even when I wrote to you the King would allow it— but I would not ask you to do it if you did not wish it—you passed this over in silence. And I naturally felt there was no longer any idea of it. Left without any one to cheer my loneliness here, when I am now so very peculiarly forlorn here, that with no one but the children who are always with me, I felt I should sink under it. I therefore in my despair telegraphed off to Louis and Alice and they at once consented to come, and arrived here yesterday afternoon— baby and all. I feel however peculiarly distressed as I know that affairs are now such that what I always thought would be the best is most ardently wished, and that Fritz should be got away from Berlin as soon as possible, and that you should keep away as long as possible. I always felt this and it is very annoying that you should only have found this out at the eleventh hour—but I think I can manage to squeeze you in, for you shall never find your parents' door closed against you, dear children, no, never. There are two means of doing it, first to put you two up here, bringing only one lady and gentleman and very few servants, you especially only one maid and Fritz only one valet. The children and other dressers etc. joining us towards the end of October at Windsor. Or if you came only at the beginning of October when Bertie and Alix leave Abergeldie you could go there where you would have plenty of room; if you brought your own cook, the children could all come too—for I can't well divide my establishment, and though if you and Fritz were only there you could always come up for luncheon and dinner—for little children that would be impossible. I can't tell you how all this worries and distresses me and how anxious I am to do anything to be of use to you in your sadly trying position. Let me hear by telegraph what you think you could do. Only come away from Berlin.

God bless you and let me hear soon.

From the Crown Princess

NEUES PALAIS, SEPTEMBER 19, 1863

Whether we can come or not we cannot say as yet; you will be quite tired of the same answer but it is the truth. Fritz is away and, without speaking together about it all, I cannot settle anything.

My visit to Dolzig was charming—I enjoyed it so much. Pity I was unwell all the time. Ada's house is so nice, and her children such dear pretty little things. I had not been with Feo and her for so long; we were very happy together. Fritz Holstein is such an excellent and kind friend. I wish you could see more of him. I am sure you would become as fond of him as I am. I find a special pleasure in talking to him—his views on politics are characterised by their great justice and moderation—and by his thorough knowledge of our Prussian condition; people, so sensible and quiet with such sound judgement are very rare—and he is so modest! A little pedantic—but what does that matter! It is far better than being confused and inaccurate.

Dear Feo I brought back here with me; she returns on

Monday to Dolzig from where her husband fetches her. Ada and Feo are both in such beauty that I could not help continuing looking at them and thinking what fine handsome young women they had grown and how proud dear Aunt Feodora must be of them—just as good amiable and unaffected as they used to be as children!

I have seen Sir Andrew and Lady Buchanan—the former told me you had seen him—and given him a message to Fritz. What I intended to have sent you I cannot, as Fritz wishes me to wait for a little while. I can explain all later—at present the less is said about what he does and thinks the better.

From the Queen

BALMORAL, SEPTEMBER 22, 1863

I this morning received your letter by messenger, for which many thanks. Your continued indecision about coming signifies less now as I can let you have Abergeldie from the 2nd, Bertie and Alix leaving on the 1st. I have also to thank you for your letter of the 15th. I can't comprehend Fritz's conduct; I fear it will do him great harm.

I am so glad you have seen your dear cousins and especially Feo, for I was afraid that from George's peculiarity there might be an estrangement between you which would grieve me greatly. Fritz of H. I have the greatest regard for and hope to see more of hereafter—but this wretched Schleswig-Holstein business makes it difficult at present— even if I had an opportunity.

We have not a fine season here—colder than for the last three years and much rain and wind—all which to one in my weakened state and low spirits is not congenial. Besides, being here now at this season is dreadful! All the interest for sport and expeditions gone, so that all about sport is kept from me, for I wince under it. Oh! you, with your extraordinary spirits, never could know what suffering like mine is.

Bertie and Alix seem going on extremely well; he is much improved and she has done a great deal for him, and is indeed a dear, noble excellent being whom one must love and respect. There is no doubt, I am sure about her condition, for, though she has not suffered from sickness and has been particularly well here—she has increased very much in size—her waist being quite broad and her clothes having all to be let out.

Dear Alice and Louis are a great comfort to me—so good and kind and so quiet; he is so improved, really so excellent, with much decision and firmness of character. I do love him dearly. Oh! if the boys (our sons) had his golden heart—especially Affie—who is a slippery youth, for I never feel sure (alas!) of what he says. However I hope everything from his marriage and indeed from his engagement. The accounts I have received from Countess Blücher as to Princess M. of Altenburg's health are quite satisfactory, and I shall very shortly write to the Duchess of Altenburg (to whom I owe an answer) telling her of the favourable impression which her charming cousin made upon Affie and asking whether he might, next spring, make further and nearer acquaintance with her. Affie is very anxious I should do that at once!

From the Crown Princess

I hope you will not be vexed that I did not answer your dear letter sooner but I did not like to write until I could tell you something decided! We now hope soon to see you, dear Mama—to leave this as soon as we can with the children, leave them in London or Windsor if you will be so good as to make it possible for them; we two could then come on to Balmoral with a Gentleman and Lady and stay as long as you stay and meet the children again when we return to Windsor. What then our further plans would be we should be able to settle there, and from thence, by the King's permission, to stay away for the winter, or if that is not allowed at least a part of the winter.

Could we have a ship as the children make so much "embarras" on a packet? I could send my wardrobe-maid with the children. Will all this suit? Please answer by telegraph. I am really in despair that we should give so much trouble but we could really not help it.

From the Crown Princess

NEUES PALAIS, SEPTEMBER 26, 1863

I hope the change will do the children good and that our dear little Henry will win your good graces which I fear he does not possess at present, but as he is teething he is not always amiably disposed—particularly to ladies; there are days when he will not look at me; when I offer to take him he screams the place down, but sometimes he is very well disposed and he is really a great darling and, as far as I can judge, the cleverest of the three.

Ditta still looks very thin. I hope she will not be shy with you but she is afraid of strangers particularly ladies and it is difficult to make friends with her; Willy talks of all his uncles and aunts in turn! Alfred is "a dear angel": Louis is "a fine man—quite my taste", "I love dear Grandmama, will she give me something good? Can I ride with her?" He chatters all day long like a little magpie.

I must end in hurry as the house is turned upside down and out of window—and the agony of packing affects the nerves and the temper of my good people a little.

From the Queen

BALMORAL, SEPTEMBER 29, 1863

You must not expect merriment and joy—all that is hushed! The sport is never spoken of, and all is quiet and silent but warm, loving hearts you will find and the joy of the dear, devoted people to see you again is indeed touching. Many old women prayed "to be spared to see the Princess Royal once again", and when yesterday I spoke to Brown of your being out of the habit of climbing and we wondered whether you could get up Loch-na-gar—he answered "We should be happy to carry her to the top!" Such attachment and the touching sympathy they show me, the deep sorrow which takes away, as they say, the very look of the place as it used to be—is indeed most gratifying and soothing and makes me love them all, more even than before in happier, bright times. There is nothing like the Highlanders—no, nothing.

Alice is so delighted to meet you here—and to show you her really precious little baby. How I rejoice to see your darlings, our especial favourite little William and the other dear little ones. Little A. Henry will be quite a new acquaintance, never mind their being shy at first. They will soon get to know poor old Grandmama.

From the Crown Princess

GORDON CASTLE, OCTOBER 26, 1863

You said you wished to hear from me sometime or other —so I hasten to write although I fear it will bore you to see my writing so soon after our leaving. I was so sad leaving dear Abergeldie—and all the good, kind people. We parted from dear Louis and Alice and the sweet baby at Aberdeen —the German party being reclassed into its component parts of Prussia and 'esse—each going their own road. That dear baby it is such a love, so pretty and so good. At Aberdeen we looked at the monument.[1] I can really not see any thing about it to find fault with; it is very fine, very dignified and noble and I like the "emplacement" too. There is only one little thing that strikes me—but as it is but a trifling detail I dare say but very few would remark it; viz. the footstool. It is too like a board on which dear Papa's feet are; it should have had a rim or feet or something in short to make it a better-looking object—particularly as it is the part nearest the spectator when one stands in front of the statue.

This is a very fine place but not Highland like, quite English in its appearance. The Duke and Duchess[2] are very

---

[1] The bronze statue by Marochetti. This was uncovered in the presence of the Queen, the Crown Princess and other members of the Royal Family on 13 October.
[2] Of Richmond.

civil and amiable, luckily there is no large party staying here—only two or three inoffensive gentlemen, who are not alarming.

From the Crown Princess

KILLIN, OCTOBER 29, 1863

We have just arrived here. We might really have swam the whole way as it never ceased pouring since we left Blair Atholl and we saw no scenery at all. We saw Blair in the finest moon-light—the moon rose full behind Beny-Glow[1] as we walked up to the house. Fritz and I went up—not to pay a visit but to enquire at the door after the poor Duke— as we thought it would be more civil than merely sending to ask.[2] We met the Duchess, who had been down to the inn during our absence, near the house. She asked us to come in and said the Duke was up and would be disappointed if he did not see us for a minute, so we went into his room. He is certainly a most sad and affecting sight—so altered and so thin. We only stayed a minute or two. It was so sad saying goodbye to him; we shall never see him again. Blair made such a melancholy impression upon me. I thought of all the changes that had taken place since you and dear Papa had lived there. I recognised the house and some of the rooms directly, I remembered where your room was and which way the windows looked. We looked through the rooms by the light of one candle.[3] The rooms in the Bridge of Tiltinn were so cold that one could see one's breath in them and I woke with a horrid stiff neck which has been very painful sitting about the whole day in the carriage. How splendid Taymouth is; we went all over the house and admired it so much—but it is sad too without its kind old master! How sad it is to think that we have seen Balmoral without darling Papa, Abergeldie without dear Grandmama, In-vercauld without Mr. Farquharson, Blair with its dying

[1] Beinn a' Ghlo.
[2] The 6th Duke of Atholl; he was dying from cancer of the neck. The Duchess had been Mistress of the Robes.
[3] The Royal Family stayed here in 1844.

master, and Taymouth without Lord Breadalbane! All the furniture is going to be divided and everything taken away. We saw a blotting book—with half of a letter of dear Papa's blotted on one of the pages![1]

The Duchess of Manchester travelled part of the way with us from Gordon Castle to Blair—she had been paying a visit to the Duke and Duchess of Sutherland. It is such a bore the weather should be so bad as we have really seen nothing of the view. We enjoy our tour very much in spite of the weather—and of the melancholy impressions of yesterday and today.

Here is a letter from Countess Hohenthal, Valerie's aunt, about the Princess of Altenburg with a photograph: both are for you to keep if you like; the former will please you I think. From the photograph you will see that I am right about the hands. Pretty she is not but nice looking I should think.

From the Crown Princess

INVERARAY, OCTOBER 30, 1863

Many thanks for your dear letter just received. I gave your message to the kind Duke and Duchess of Argyll, who seemed much pleased and very grateful.[2] We have another wretched day; rain, snow, hail, wind and mist the whole way from Killin. The glimpses we could catch of the landscape were very fine—and of the true Highland character. The inn at Killin was dreadfully cold so that my rheumatism has not decreased. I thought of you so much at every luncheon and dinner in all the inns when the mutton appeared; you would not have liked it I am sure; I thought it delicious in every form. What a beautiful place this is! Such a lovely view from the windows—if one had but a ray of sunshine to light it up.

Fritz wishes me to say he admires all he sees very much

---

[1] Presumably this was a curious souvenir of the Queen's and Prince's visit to Taymouth in 1842.
[2] The 8th Duke, a Liberal politician of note. His wife was the daughter of the Queen's friend, the Duchess of Sutherland.

indeed and is quite in love with the dear Highlands. How I enter into all you say about them, they and their inhabitants certainly have a peculiar charm.

From the Crown Princess

INVERARAY, OCTOBER 31, 1863

I have received a letter from Bertie today, saying we had promised to spend his birthday with him at Sandringham, and as he had seen us so little this year he hoped we should come on the 4th of November and stay a fortnight.

The latter we cannot do as we do not know how soon the King may not recall us, but I understand you to wish us to spend the 9th with Bertie at Sandringham. Would you approve of our going there from Edinburgh and arriving at Windsor on the 10th or 11th? We think it would be better than first going the whole way to Windsor and then leaving again so soon. Would you please telegraph if you approve of this plan? Meanwhile I have written to Bertie to say what we think of doing unless you should object. To our despair we see another ill advised speech of the King's at Magdeburg in the papers! worse than ever! The weather continues dreadful; but we enjoy our stay here very much indeed—the Duke and Duchess are such delightful people.

From the Queen

WINDSOR CASTLE, NOVEMBER 4, 1863

I had hoped to have thanked you yesterday in person for your four affectionate letters from Blair-Killin and two from Inveraray and am sorry that I must answer by letter instead. Still I think that you have done right in going straight to Sandringham. Your tour in spite of the weather must have been a very interesting one in that most beloved of countries, the dear Highlands. But sad indeed is the heavy cloud of mourning and woe which overhangs so many houses there!

As Dr. Brown-Séequard[1] leaves England on Friday and

---

[1] He was at this time physician to the National Hospital for the paralysed

gives up practice altogether, I settled with Dr. Jenner he was to bring him down here tomorrow and as you are not here, it may be a satisfaction to you if I see him himself— which I shall do and take care a full report is written of what he says. I love William so dearly (he was so precious to beloved Papa) that I would do any thing for the darling child. Both he and Charlotte are very affectionate to me but I don't spoil them and insist on obedience. Little Henry is also very flourishing.

From the Crown Princess

SANDRINGHAM, KING'S LYNN, NOVEMBER 5, 1863

We arrived here yesterday before luncheon—very tired with our night's journey as we had not been able to sleep. You will have heard that we had an accident leaving Inveraray which, though of no consequence whatever, might have been very disagreeable. The horses began to run away, Mr. Fisher[1] put on the drag and we happily went into a ditch, crash up against a bank so that the carriage could not turn over though it was all on one side. The springs were broken, the pole snapped right off, the traces broken and one of the splash boards was broken right off; if it had gone down the other side of the road we should have all broken our necks as the bank went steep down in to the loch. The Duke of Argyll was so kind as to send us his carriage, which we took on to Balloch. We had a splendid day for that most beautiful drive over the hills past Loch Long and along Loch Lomond. I never saw any thing finer; the colours and the lights were so lovely—it far surpassed my expectation.

At Edinburgh we found dear Affie and William[2] very well and happy. They went with us to Roslin Chapel and

---

and epileptic in Queen Square. He subsequently practised in America and France. At the end of his life he invented a liquid which converted old men into young men but which was unsuccessful when applied to himself.

[1] Mr. Fisher of Braemar, who was acting as courier.
[2] Prince William of Hesse, younger brother of Prince Louis.

also to the picture galleries. In the evening Major Cowell was kind enough to arrange a soirée which Affie gave so that I could see some of the notabilities—"professorial dignitaries" as Affie calls them—of the university whose acquaintance I was most anxious to make as I had read and heard so much about them. It was a most interesting and agreeable evening. I only regretted it was so short as we had to leave at half past 10. Old Sir David Brewster is a wonderful man. He is 82 and has a baby not a year old![1]

At Peterborough we stayed two hours, so we went to look at the beautiful Cathedral and paid the old Bishop a visit—who sends you his respects. His room is full of all the prints you sent him.[2]

This seems a charming place so quiet and country-like, and a delightful house furnished with great taste and comfort. Bertie and Alix seem to like it very much and to be very happy and comfortable. Dear Alix seems very thin but looking well; she shows her condition very little though her figure is much changed already—she seems perfectly well, has not an ailment of any kind or sort to complain of and has a very fresh colour. When I think of what I was the first time I cannot help thinking that she is wonderfully lucky.

From the Crown Princess

SANDRINGHAM, KING'S LYNN, NOVEMBER 6, 1863

Your dear letter made me very happy, you are very kind to take so much interest in our dear little Willy—but he wants it, poor child, as he is so much more helpless than other children and is debarred from so much that others can do!

Is it not dreadfully provoking that the King has sent for

---

[1] He was the Principal of Edinburgh University. Actually the baby was born in 1861.

[2] George Davys, Bishop of Peterborough since 1839. He had educated the Queen. The Queen pressed his appointment on Lord Melbourne who was nervous that he would side with the Conservatives. These fears proved unfounded, though in his day Peterborough was facetiously known as the Dead See.

Fritz to be present at the opening of the Chambers which takes place on the 9th? He will have to leave tomorrow. Of course I hope and trust he will return in a few days but should he not be allowed to do so he has promised to send for me immediately. But is it not a sad pity—that long, tiresome, fatiguing journey for a mere ceremony and just before Bertie's birthday? I don't think it is very considerate to give one such short notice and send for one from the other end of the world in that way. I cannot say how sorry I am for many reasons.

From the Crown Princess

SANDRINGHAM, KING'S LYNN, NOVEMBER 7, 1863

The Dean has written to me to say the people of Windsor kindly wish I should lay a foundation-stone of a Church, at which I am of course greatly flattered.[1] They name my birthday as the day. I did not wish to answer the Dean until I know what you wished, as perhaps you might not like it to take place on my birthday. I myself should like it very much, but of course you must decide as to what you think would be the best. If you think it would do perhaps you would be so kind as to let the Dean know.

From the Queen

WINDSOR CASTLE, DECEMBER 16, 1863

It grieved me much to part from you, dearest child, and to see you so wretched at going and to think of all that awaits you! How I wish that you could remain at Carlsruhe for a time and not return to Berlin till the atmosphere is cleared![2] We all feel this so strongly! The sweet little children, whom I love so much, are much missed.

---

[1] Windsor New Church in Francis Road.
[2] Meaning that they should stay with the Crown Prince's brother-in-law—the Grand-Duke of Baden.

From the Queen

OSBORNE, DECEMBER 19, 1863

I have been late today, and cannot therefore answer your dear and affectionate letter from Brussels as I ought. Many, many thanks for it. I saw your grief at leaving, and can well understand how trying the return will be—but you must take courage and be as calm and passive at this critical moment as you can.

You say how you wish to console and comfort and assist me. Dearest child—the only, only way is by trying to soothe, and weep as it were with me, not by trying to divert me from the one beloved object. For my constant, hard and unassisted work irritates, excites and exhausts my poor, shaken nerves—and it is only by great quiet and great sympathy that I can find repose and relief. My nerves are much worse of late again and all the excitement, worry and anxiety about S. Holstein has done me a very great deal of harm. My deafness which continues is almost entirely from the nerves, and I feel the absolute necessity for that repose —which I can never get.

I must end again clasping you and the precious children in my arms and saying how anxious I am on all and every occasion to be of use and help to you all.

From the Crown Princess

CARLSRUHE, DECEMBER 21, 1863

Your dear letters of which I have just received the last gave me the greatest pleasure—many, many thanks for them. I could not write before this as my time has been so much taken up!

From all I hear we have more reason to dread the return to Berlin than I even imagined! All seems to be going as wrong there as it can be—politically and otherwise; ours will be a life of the greatest difficulty, but that is not what I fear—I enjoy difficulties when they can be met openly and fairly dealt with—but a continual flow of little annoyances and persecutions quite overthrow even the best of intentions to be firm, prudent and courageous. Dear Fritz of Baden is a great comfort and support. I am only sorry that we cannot see more of him. Louise seems very well—the boy much improved and the little girl very fine; I do not think her plain at all—on the contrary she has pretty eyes and eyebrows, fine hair and a good skin. I think her much better looking than her brother.

Schleswig-Holstein you can imagine is in every one's mouth and I may add in every good German's heart at this moment, but it is in the most "embrouillé" and complicated condition one can possibly imagine—no wonder the English cannot understand it.

From the Queen

OSBORNE, DECEMBER 23, 1863

I am at a loss to understand why you have not (who always write so much) found time to write me a line from Carlsruhe or telegraphed your departure or your arrival at Berlin. It seems most strange to us all! I trust all the darling children are well and your toe better?

I send you the wreath I took out of the mausoleum (and which was at adored Papa's feet) on Thursday as I think you will like to have it.[1]

Lauchert's picture of Baby has arrived and is lovely and so like, but I am not satisfied with the colour of the background, and fear I must send it back as the sky is a leaden, lilacy blue—with no white clouds. Will you see Lauchert and tell him of this and that it will not match with the fine turquoise-blue skies darling Papa made Winterhalter paint into our family picture and the one of the three children? It is not the case in Charlotte's as I suppose you prevented it, but it is in Alix's and it looks as if a heavy thunderstorm were impending. I enclose the copy of my letter to the King, for you, Fritz and the Queen to see.[2]

---

[1] Wreaths were no doubt laid in the mausoleum for the service on the second anniversary of the Prince Consort's death.

[2] This is presumably the letter which the Queen wrote on 14 December

From the Crown Princess

BERLIN, DECEMBER 25, 1863

We arrived here quite worn out on the morning of the day before yesterday.

The night had been spent on the railway with good Fritz Augustenburg and Samwer and other gentlemen we wanted to meet. Our distribution of presents at the King's was a sad and dull affair—the whole family was there, and though the humour was just tolerable yet it was stiff and uncomfortable in the extreme.

I had a grand skirmish with Wegner this morning about the arm; he and Langenbeck will not hear of Willie's being electrified every day; they consider it decidedly damaging and say it would do more harm than good. All my arguments were not of the slightest use; at last with a great deal of difficulty we made a compromise. Wegner promised that he would try electricity every day for a fortnight and made me promise that if he thought it injured Willie's health I would have it stopped and only done once every two days. This is the only way in which I could make him do it at all. Of the dry cupping Wegner and Langenbeck think nothing at all—but they have no objections to its being tried.

About the electricity. I have no one to bear me out about the electricity as Wegner is most positive and said he could name two cases of grown-up people, men—patients of his, who could not stand electricity being applied every day and who only experienced the benefits of it when they rested two or three days between, and that with a child he could not allow it every day.

What am I to do? I feel so convinced that electricity is the only thing and that it does the child no harm—but I cannot have it done in spite of Langenbeck and Wegner both!

---

and was brought to Germany by the Crown Princess. In it she said how she rejoiced that the King had agreed to "exempt Fritz from the ministerial sessions". Of Schleswig-Holstein she said that she hoped that "in conjunction with you and my other allies" I may succeed in averting war. *Further Letters of Queen Victoria*, edited by Hector Bolitho.

Please tell dear Aunt Feodora and also Dr. Jenner; he is in correspondence with Wegner on the subject and might do some good if he gave it as his opinion, founded on actual experience, that electricity carefully applied did not injure people's health, even if used daily.

The application of veratrine salve both Langenbeck and Wegner decidedly forbid.[1] You see having Willie in England, which you had so kindly offered, would have been no sort of use as they would have upset the whole treatment here.

Thank you very much for the copy of your letter to the King. He is alas! very ill disposed; he was kind to Fritz and to me—but much colder to me than he ever was before, which I am very sorry for.

Yesterday we invited all our enemies to dinner: Bismarck (who can be very agreeable if he likes), Manteuffel[2] (idem), Roon[3] who is always as heavy as possible. Besides we had some good-natured twaddlers (to wit) Count Redern[4] and old Wrangel[5] all asking after you, with much interest.

From the Queen

OSBORNE, DECEMBER 26, 1863

I am glad your visit at Carlsruhe passed off so well, and hope that you will find matters less trying and difficult than you expect. Only do not urge war—whatever your feelings and excitement may be for a just cause to a certain extent, it is not woman's mission on earth to urge violent measures and to join in a general outcry which is to a great extent exaggerated! I hope however it will be avoided yet.

---

[1] A vegetable alkaloid, and presumably recommended by Dr. Brown-Séequard.
[2] Prime Minister, 1850–8.
[3] Minister of War; organiser of the victories against Austria in 1866 and France in 1871.
[4] Chamberlain of the Court.
[5] The Prussian field-marshal familiarly known as "Papa" Wrangel. He had fought at the Battle of Leipzig and was to command the Prussian forces against Denmark in the following year.

We have received all the touching, beautiful and heart-rending accounts of poor dear Lord Elgin's illness and death. It was all owing to the exertion of going over that pass and the very dangerous swing bridge.[1] He sent the most touching messages to every body—to poor Katherine: "Write to K. that I am gone to join dear Robert"; to his poor daughter Elma: "Tell her that her dear Mother's last words were 'I am so happy'." And to me: "That I have ever tried to serve her faithfully, and that my summons was too sudden for me to address her." His sufferings were fearful and he prayed to die, thought of every one but himself, settled where he was to be buried, made poor dear Mary choose the spot—himself approved the design for his tomb. Her conduct is described as beautiful and perfectly heroic. Poor dear, how I do feel for her! My heart seems to yearn towards all who have passed through that fearful scene! And we were playfellows!

Upon reflection—though I regret the rather leaden background to Baby's picture—it had better be left. At some future time, if he paints any thing for me again, he must not give such a background. It is a lovely picture.

From the Queen

OSBORNE, DECEMBER 30, 1863

May every blessing be showered upon you both and the beloved children (who I trust think of Grandmama sometimes) during this and many years, is my earnest prayer. May God in His mercy avert the calamity of war—much as many seem to wish and, what is worse, to encourage it, little thinking of the awful blood-shed which will be the consequence!

Many thanks for your letter of the 26th received on Monday and for the two lovely paper-weights. The Cross is extremely pretty too but it arrived (as is generally the case

---

[1] He was Viceroy of India, and was making a journey over the Himalayas to Peshawar. Katherine Bruce was the widow of his brother. Elma was his daughter by his first wife. His second wife was the daughter of the statesman Lord Durham.

with what comes from Berlin) all broken; it can however I think be put together.

Christmas was as sad as possible. How you can be as merry and happy as formerly—and how you can say "Thank God those dreadful days are past"—is to me incredible. How have these days passed? They have left your old home desolate and wretched and broken your mother's heart and health, and hastened her end![1] Is this "thank God! that they are passed"? My good, dear child, you have wonderful spirits—and you like ever to shake off all that is sad!

---

[1] In her letter on Christmas Day the Crown Princess described how she and Countess Blücher sat together "stunned" on the day news came of the Prince's death. Perhaps it was an unwise (though understandable) comment to add "Thank God that dreadful time is passed." The Queen perhaps supposed that she was referring to the anniversary days which were just over.

1864

From the Crown Princess

BERLIN, JANUARY 1, 1864

For us here in Germany the time is one when hopes and fears agitate one and the excitement and depression which follows the quick succession of events make themselves keenly felt. The more German one feels—the more jealous and ambitious for one's country's honour and welfare the more one has to suffer here! The aims and sentiments of the Germans as a people are high, I only pray that their courage and determination together with their perseverance may prove that they are worthy of so good a cause!

Fritz is not looking at all well; it strikes everybody how pale and different he is looking to when he arrived, and no wonder—he has almost more worry than any one here.

Of politics I can say nothing, only this much which will give you pleasure which is that the King is much kinder to Fritz and that the Queen is much pleased with him.

My thoughts and wishes are with Fritz Augustenburg who has embarked on a difficult course though it was the right one. But I feel much for poor King Christian; with his kind feelings and good heart he must find the position he is in doubly disagreeable. I hope dearest Alix does not fret too much about it all. King Christian has himself to thank for the fix he is in. Why did he accept—and allow himself to be put in a place not rightfully his own? He might now be living in peace and quiet![1]

---

[1] The Princess of Wales's father became King of Denmark as Christian IX, on 15 November 1863. On the following day he was proclaimed ruler of the United Danish Kingdom, i.e. including Schleswig-Holstein. On the same day Frederick Augustenburg announced that in virtue of his agnatic rights (i.e. by male descent) he was assuming the Government of Schleswig-Holstein as Frederick VIII.

From the Queen

I write to say I cannot write, but thank you much for your dear letter of the 29th. Bertie and Alix have just left; she is very unhappy about her poor father and cries much. I hope and trust that Peace will be maintained and violent counsels will not succeed. I must end in a great hurry. All are well except me.

From the Queen

OSBORNE, JANUARY 6, 1864

May God grant that this year may be one of peace and that the many, violent passions—the many, conflicting rights and wrongs may be adjusted with impartiality and justice. Oh! could there be but more Christian feelings and less of passion in this world!

I was much interested in making on Sunday the acquaintance of Baron Bernhardi the author of Toll's *Denkwürdigkeiten* which interested adored Papa so. He is a clever and extremely well-informed man though I should think rather steeped in Prussian conceit.[1]

We have intense cold, and one has to be terribly wrapped up in going out. I dislike it now, for the large fires one has to make, scorch one and I am not able to walk enough to get the air I wish. My deafness and general ailings continue and while I am so anxious this cannot be otherwise. Poor dear Alix worries herself much about her parents and country—and I hope it will do her no harm.

From the Crown Princess

BERLIN, JANUARY 9, 1864

This morning's news was the greatest surprise I ever remember, I could hardly believe my eyes when I read

---

[1] Baron T. von Bernhardi, an historian of distinction, had come to London, to advance the Augustenburg cause. Toll was a commander in Russia during the Napoleonic campaign.

Bertie's telegram![1] Let me wish you joy, dearest Mama, of this little English grandson. May he grow up to be dear Papa's own grandson in all that is good and great and may he ever be a comfort and a delight to you! I am so grateful to God that in midst of your sorrow He should send you this joy. May this dear little child be a harbinger of peace and comfort and be a new tie and a new interest to you for this world which is to you so sad and desolate.

May God bless this darling little babe and its sweet, gentle mother! Dear Bertie, how much I think of him; God give him strength too for his new duties.

How astonished you must have been! I hope the event was not premature but if not she must have made a great mistake in her reckoning.

I suppose they will have had nothing ready for the poor baby—no nurses and doctors and layette and I am most curious to hear how they have arranged it all and how dear Alix bore it. She certainly has had the easiest and most prosperous pregnancy that I ever heard of!

I am very glad you saw M. de Bernhardi; conceited he is, but that your imagination should combine that naturally with a Prussian is very amusing!

The cold continues great and we enjoy the skating very much indeed. We have large parties on the ice. The children cannot go out in this weather in consequence of which they are looking pale. I am taking Italian lessons—you say I am mad about Italy. I hope I shall be able to rave in Italian before long.

From the Queen

FROGMORE, JANUARY 11, 1864

I am writing from this dear house at dearest Grandmama's table, and can give you perfectly good accounts of both mother and child, but by Lady Macclesfield's letter

---

[1] The premature birth of the Prince of Wales's eldest child—the future Duke of Clarence. Just before the baby was born the Princess was being pushed in a sledge on the ice. The baby was christened Albert and the Victorian wags called him "All but on the ice".

you will have heard that the baby is a 7 months child, and that the whole was over in an hour—Brown[1] only being there and he only for 20 minutes!!! No one but Lady Macclesfield[2] to do every thing which the nurses do! There is no reason whatever for this event, but I should fear general weakness, and perhaps not lying down quite enough and the child being so very low. She is going on quite well and is well kept up. The dear little baby is kept in cotton-wool and has to be kept very warm, but is quite healthy and very thriving. It has a very pretty, well-shaped, round head, with very good features, a nice forehead, a very marked nose, beautiful little ears and pretty little hands. Good Mrs. Clark has charge of it and I repent much having recommended Mrs. Innocent for Alix, as she is very trouble-some, cross, grand and a great nuisance. The doctors have had to threaten her she shall be sent away, if she gives more trouble. Alix doesn't like her. But I hope it will go on well. I feel anxious to get back to Osborne and be quiet but still I feel I can be of use here which is a great satisfaction to me. Alix does not sleep well as she sleeps too much in the day; she looked very lovely and dear in her bed this morning but dislikes the whole business extremely and is utterly disgusted with it all. And she has (till today) had the dis-advantage of not having two beds as she was confined of course in her own bed. Of course there were no clothes and things had to be got in a great hurry. The baby is in two of the three rooms where dear old Späth[3] lived, and its cradle, one of our children's and the one in which little

---

[1] The Windsor doctor who had attended the Queen and her family since 1838. He died in 1868.

[2] Mary Frances (1821–1912), wife of 9th Earl of Macclesfield, and Lady of the Bedchamber to the Princess of Wales. Lord Stanley of Alderley (familiarly known as Ben Backbite) wrote to his wife when he heard that Lady Macclesfield had been appointed as Lady of the Bedchamber: "That precise little stick Lady Macclesfield is to be appointed—in short the Queen wishes the new court to be as dull and stupid as her own." *The Stanleys of Alderley*, edited by Nancy Mitford, Chapman and Hall, 1939.

[3] The Duchess of Kent's lady-in-waiting: she came to England with the Duchess.

Victoria was, just under adored Papa's print in armour which seems to be there as a patron saint!

From the Crown Princess

Do you not think that dear Alix did a little too much? She stood and walked for ever, and with her long back and long waist one ought to rest doubly; she did not seem to feel fatigue or to know what pain was when moving about! And what an easy confinement. Really she can hardly know what it all really is. Is she rather low and does she require to be kept up much?

The cold is intense, and though I enjoy our skating matches very much yet I do not feel well and am off my sleep and appetite. This climate does not agree with me in the winter; there is something irritating and exciting in the air without being bracing. The carnival begins on Monday which I am in terror of; it is too tiresome and fatiguing and this cold weather makes the contrast with the crammed ballrooms, steaming with gas and all manners of exhalations, with the biting air in the open doorways when one gets in and out of the carriage really dangerous. It is impossible not to catch a desperate cold!

Were any of the ministers at Frogmore when the darling baby made its appearance?[1] Has Baby got any hair? Has it got nails? There I am with my questions again in spite of my determination to ask no more! But I am so much interested in my little nephew!

From the Queen

I will only write a few words today to say that all is going on well at Frogmore whither I am going directly;

---

[1] The child was born at 9 p.m. and the Home Secretary, whose attendance in those days was customary, did not arrive till 11. The Lord President (Lord Granville) was present because he happened to be shooting at Windsor.

Alix, sweet child, her nights are not good; she can't get to sleep till so late; I fear Bertie's late habits have caused this. I yesterday planted a small evergreen oak at Frogmore in remembrance of the dear little child and it will be a striking tree if it lives as Dr. Cureton[1] planted the acorn on the dreadful 23rd December '61 and sent me the little plant last year, and it has grown very much and now I planted it out in honour of the dear little grandchild, who will be called Albert Victor; but don't mention this to any one till you hear from Bertie, or to him—either. Dear Augusta (Stanley—I can't bear to call her so) spent some hours with us on Monday, quite her own self and not at all like a married woman.[2]

From the Crown Princess

BERLIN, JANUARY 15, 1864

Our spirits are low and depressed by the dismal state of things everywhere; the future seems hid in a dark cloud; this country seems to me like a ship tossing about on the waves, a reckless, inexperienced and short-sighted man (B) at the helm and storms gathering around—ourselves and our children at his mercy! Captain the ship has none, and that the crew do not mutiny often astonishes me.

From the Queen

OSBORNE, JANUARY 16, 1864

The baby has a good deal of hair; it has all its nails. Imagine the dear Dean asking me at dinner yesterday before Lenchen and Louise, the Countess, Mrs. Wellesley[3] and Sir G. Grey, "whether a 7 months child was smaller than

---

[1] The Syriac scholar; a canon of Westminster.
[2] To the great indignation of the Queen, Lady Augusta Bruce had married Arthur Stanley the previous November. Announcing this to the King of the Belgians the Queen said that Lady Augusta had "most unnecessarily decided to marry", and that this was her greatest sorrow since the Prince's death.
[3] The Dean's wife, Magdalen, daughter of 6th Lord Rokeby.

other children?" Is it not too naïve? ——[1] was horrified. This dear baby will indeed be an object of great interest to me if I can be of real use to it, but B. is so odd that he often listens to the greatest nonsense of stupid, inferior people and is inclined to follow their advice rather than that of wise and sensible people. Still I hope this will improve.

From the Crown Princess

BERLIN, JANUARY 20, 1864

We are all in a sad state of anxiety and excitement as you can imagine. Fritz Carl and Abbat join the army and leave tonight. Fritz intends to leave very soon—you can think how unhappy it makes me. His baggage and suite are being got together and I am very sad! God knows what will come of it all. The Queen is much against his going but I do not say a word to prevent him as first it would not be listened to and secondly it is best for him to do what would be justly expected of him! In the midst of these serious things the fêtes and parties are going on and one feels so unfit for all merriment![2]

From the Queen

OSBORNE, JANUARY 20, 1864

Well can I understand your feelings of anxiety for the present and future. One must however not lose courage, and feel that there is an all-powerful God—who "ordereth all things". If it were not for that I could often not go on at all!

---

[1] Indecipherable but probably a familiar name for Countess Blücher.
[2] The Danish authorities had evacuated Holstein and by the beginning of January it was occupied by Saxon and Hanoverian troops. On the 18 January the Danish Government rejected Bismarck's demand that the Danish Constitution should be revoked and on that day Prussian and Austrian troops began to move against Schleswig.

From the Queen

Oh! well can I understand your anxiety and sorrow, and truly do I grieve for you and for many in these sad and confused times. Peace I still hope will be preserved, for I have too great a horror of war and too great a conviction that one now would be fatal to the best interests of Germany in its results—to bear to think it could take place! Poor dear Fritz, I only hope and pray his precious health may not suffer. But I think he could not avoid going: it would not have done if he had remained behind.

From the Crown Princess

Your dear letter from Windsor reached me yesterday on that ever dear day which was sadly spent this time, I feeling very unwell and not being able to go out, and the prospect of Fritz's departure throwing a gloom over us both!

Here all are in a state of suspense; few really believe in the certainty of war. I must say I think things wear too serious an aspect to expect anything else! I am quite resigned to Fritz's going and think it quite right he should do so, but it gives me a great pang notwithstanding and I dread the separation much!

Fritz is looking thin; anxiety and a good deal of work he has to do now are the cause. When he is gone I shall be left so alone on a "terrain" which is neither easy nor pleasant, do you not think you could send Countess Blücher, dear Mama? You know I have no other friend here and it would be such a comfort.

Alice who was at Gotha half let me hope she would come here, but now says the political conditions did not permit it! This I own I cannot understand. We did not care what was said here when we went to pay her a visit and to Baden—although Prussia and the Bund[1] were "à

---

[1] The German Confederation: Hesse-Darmstadt, with other South German states, was increasingly apprehensive of Prussia's power.

couteaux tirés"—and I think the public opinion of Darmstadt would have forgiven them for visiting their sister when they were only 8 hours off! And I must say I was hurt!

From the Queen

With regard to this sad S. Holstein question, I can really speak with more thorough impartiality than anyone (and that the dear Crown Prince can bear witness to); my heart and sympathies are all German. I condemn the Treaty of '52 completely, but once signed we cannot upset it without first trying (not by war) to maintain it, and this adored Papa would have felt and did feel, for all his efforts were directed only to the carrying out by the Danes of the promises made to Germany in '51 and '52. Where I do, however, blame Germany is in their wanting the two great Powers to break their engagements, and in not being contented with all the rights of the Duchies being obtained. They have mixed up the two questions, and gone so violently mad upon the subject, that they lose sight of the far greater evils which may be produced by provoking war. And depend upon it that the want of forbearance now towards the King of Denmark—now that he means to do all he can, at the risk almost of his Crown—will and must have a very bad effect in Europe and injure the just cause of Germany. That England is detested I know, alas! too well; but I must bear it, as many other trials and sorrows, with patience; and continue to do all I can to prevent further irritation and in future to avoid further complications. I am glad darling Papa is spared this worry and annoyance, for he could have done even less than I can.[1]

---

[1] *Letters of Queen Victoria*, Second Series, Vol. I, page 153. The original of this letter, of which this is a part, cannot be traced. The Queen would have written "Fritz" in line 3.

From the Crown Princess

I write today instead of tomorrow as Fritz leaves tomorrow evening, and the last few hours I can spend with him I wish to keep undisturbed.

This parting is a very bitter one. I do not know for how long it is and he will be exposed to such dangers! However there is not a word to be said against his going so I say nothing and hope for the best. His life is very precious but if I were in his place I should feel that I could not but expose it, with so many others, in a good cause.

The staying behind here will be dreadful. I dread the being without news or hearing false news so much! It is very kind of you to let Countess Blücher come, thank you so much for it, dear Mama, it will be the greatest of comforts to me having her in the house.

Fritz takes no doctor with him, only his two gentlemen M. de Schweinitz and M. de Luccadon; of this I am glad. The former will be of great use to him and many people would have been an encumberance and of no service. Wetterling, one footman, a cook and our butler go besides Mehler and some grooms—Fritz's six best horses. So you see it is a very small suite, one fourgon will be all the baggage.

I am sure these details will bore you—but still I thought you might wish to know.

Austrian troops pass through here every day. I went to see some today—they were making a great noise, hurraying, kissing their hands to the ladies in the streets; it was very funny indeed, as they looked out of the windows of the train.

From the Queen

I begin my letter by saying thank God, there will be no war! The feeling for peace in the country is very strong— but I rejoice to think that what would have been madness, and might have led to most serious consequences is not to be; what it would have been for you and me—words cannot describe![1] However it is of the utmost importance for the future good understanding of the two countries that Prussia should be moderate, and now surely—as she has no threats to expect—she can show that it is merely for Germany and for the Duchies that she has taken up the sword and not for conquest and for the entire destruction of Denmark. The warlike feeling here might be roused again were that to be the case, but that I am sure can neither be the King's or Fritz's wish.

From the Queen

OSBORNE, JANUARY 30, 1864

I am thinking much of you in these sad and trying times, and my prayers will be offered up for our beloved Fritz. I still disbelieve in war; you were not so much against it—so will perhaps think it more likely to occur.[2]

As for Alice's visit I think it may still be possible; but if they or she came, avoid politics—just as I do with dear Aunt and you did with Alix. Politics must never divide relations—at least not the female part. We ought to have nothing to say to them, but ought to pour balm on the wounds and be peace-makers. Oh! would to God I had not to be plagued with politics. It is so ungrateful a task.

As you are so alone and in such anxiety and without Fritz and you ask me, I will let the dear Countess go (if she can travel without injuring her health, for she suffers severely from the cold) but I was most surprised at her being asked, without my being mentioned, if she could come. You know she is my guest, and since this summer had settled to stay with me, a good way into February. I was,

---

[1] The Queen is referring here to war between England and Prussia. If the French would have supported England in order to thwart the Prussian and Austrian attack on Denmark the case would have been altered. The Foreign Secretary (Lord Russell) said that there was "no question of our going to war single-handed".

[2] The Queen means here a Dano-German war.

I must say rather hurt at this want of "égard". When you ask me and say how sad and alone you are, I am ready to give her up, painful as it is—but, dear child, this must not (except in case of great illness or a long absence of Fritz's) happen again.

I have good accounts of Alix and Baby—but he is backward.

I have got a permanent successor to Mr. Rulandt—a Herr Sahl,[1] a friend of Becker's; he brought him here and I like him very much; he is quiet, gentleman-like and "gemutlich"—also from Darmstadt. Dr. Becker is going to Berlin so you will see his kind face.

From the Queen

OSBORNE, FEBRUARY 3, 1864

I cannot tell you how my thoughts are with you! I had hoped that this dreadful war might be prevented but you all (God forgive you for it) would have it! However all I pray is—it may remain a local one and that it may lead to a peaceable and satisfactory solution of this vexed and dreadful question. May God preserve dear Fritz! I dread this bad climate for him! Many thanks for your dear letter of the 29th (the anniversary of dear Grandpapa's death)[2] and for all the interesting details of dear Fritz's campaigning. Though I blame the haste and violence of the Germans my feelings and sympathies in the war can only be with them! So it was in Italy—with beloved Papa and me.

Poor Alix is in a terrible state of distress and Bertie frantic, thinking every one wishes to crush Denmark! This is not true.

---

[1] Though Rulandt and Sahl are sometimes called librarians they were in fact German secretaries to the Queen. Sahl makes some delightful appearances in Lady Longford's biography of Queen Victoria.
[2] The Duke of Coburg.

From the Crown Princess

The state of suspense and anxiety I am in is very great and the loneliness therefore doubly trying.

Fritz writes to me every day and so do his gentlemen, so that I hear what has happened! But all day long we are worried with false reports—telegrams with tidings that are in no way officially confirmed. Darling Fritz says he is well and his gentlemen write that he is in good spirits! I expect news of a battle before the end of the week—how the thought makes me tremble! I hope the whole campaign will be short and successful; I cannot think it will last longer than a fortnight if the frost remains. The day before yesterday the last detachment of our dear troops left. I went out on the balcony to see them and was too thinly dressed so I have got a fresh cold which makes me feel very miserable.

I go to no balls in Fritz's absence. I have not the spirits, when I think that he may that very moment be exposed to danger but Marianne dances till 2 o'clock in the morning wherever and whenever she can.[1] Feeling so unwell makes one take a gloomy view of things!

I am happy to say that dear Willie is looking better, he sleeps and lives down in my room while his papa is away and is very proud of it. Langenbeck was here the other day and was much pleased with the arm and said it would get all right except the length. I fear he is a little too sanguine.

I have had no news from my Fritz yesterday or today— I do not even know where he is. The turn the campaign has taken—astonished us all very much as we thought the taking of the Dannevirke would be a dreadful business and no one dreamt of the Danes abandoning their position![2]

I hope and pray that the war may end with honour to

---

[1] Her husband, Prince Fritz Carl, was in the fighting.
[2] Their fortified position in Schleswig which they abandoned because if they had remained they could have been destroyed by a turning movement. The Dannevirke held for 5 days: Napoleon once said that it would be impregnable for two years.

our dear troops and attain all the result which Germany expects. You say, dear Mama, that you are glad you have not the blood of so many innocents on your conscience. We have nobody to thank for it but Lord Palmerston and the Emperor Nicholas; if they had not meddled with what did not concern them in the year '48, these sad consequences would not have ensued. I was much pleased at Lord Derby's speech—all he said to Lord Russell about his policy was so true.[1] It is impossible to blame an English person for not understanding the Schleswig-Holstein question after the mess the two great powers of Germany have made of it; it remains nevertheless to us Germans plain and simple as daylight and one for which we would gladly bring any sacrifice!

From the Queen

OSBORNE, FEBRUARY 6, 1864

I received your dear letter of the 3rd this morning and am thankful to hear you have good accounts of our dear Fritz. I am sure you will be surprised at the moderation of the speeches (indeed the justice of some) in Parliament—and all against war. I am thankful for it—and also for not having the blood of the many innocent ones, who have fallen already, on my conscience. For all this—it may be that by this—more shedding of blood may be averted. How it will end, God knows! The Danes cannot hold out long! I am really so sorry for the poor King for he would have done all so willingly that was wished, but he could not, from the violence and obstinacy of the Danes. You are not only quite right not to go to balls etc. but it would have been quite improper if you had done so while Fritz is with the Army. Altogether going out and about without one's husband I disapprove—and never did!

---

[1] Particularly no doubt Lord Derby's hope that the Government was not in any way committed to a conflict with Germany. Lord Derby asked how England could expect "to play the part of mediator" when she had "alienated France, offended Russia and more or less quarrelled with every Power in Europe".

From the Queen

OSBORNE, FEBRUARY 10, 1864

I have no letter, no drawing—nothing from you[1]—but don't expect it at this anxious moment. Please God! this dreadful and really bloody war will soon be over! Many thanks for your letter of the 6th. I am thankful dear Fritz bears all so well, for I tremble to hear of illness from the cold. Pray let me hear as much as you can—for we only hear through the papers and by telegram. Poor old Gröben[2] has lost a son—I fear. Who else whom I should know, has been wounded or killed? It is very satisfactory, and also very useful for the Emperor Napoleon to see how very well and rapidly the Allies have conducted the campaign but I trust that they will not sully their victories, by doing more than they have publicly declared they would do! That would be very serious.

From the Queen

OSBORNE, FEBRUARY 13, 1864

I return the letters with many thanks.[3] Till now Fritz has seen hardly any thing—but I thank God! he has not been exposed! Many thanks for your affectionate letter of the 8th which I received on the 10th. What you say about the real cause of the war I cannot deny, it is but too true. But what I suffer now, alone without adored Papa, without help, or support, or love and protection, living in dread of some false move which may aggravate affairs, words cannot say. My rest disturbed, torn to pieces with anxiety and sorrow, and overwhelmed by the one great abiding sorrow.

---

[1] The Queen's wedding-day.

[2] A Prussian cavalry officer who had been sent by King Frederick William IV with an offer of mediation during the Crimean War.

[3] The Crown Prince's letters from the Front. In one of these letters the Crown Prince wrote to his wife "In spite of all the serious and shattering experiences we have had in our young married life, never has even a little cloud disturbed our family happiness, and we can speak calmly and joyfully of our six years honeymoon." Count Corti, *The English Empress*, page 123.

And then, our worst fears about B.'s marriage realised—so that there is division in the family!! Oh! it is too much for human mortal to bear, and I hope it may all soon be over for me!

Oh! if Bertie's wife was only a good German and not a Dane! Not, as regards the influence of the politics but as regards the peace and harmony in the family! It is terrible to have the poor boy on the wrong side, and aggravates my sufferings greatly.

Is Rotkehlchen[1] with the Army?

From the Queen

WINDSOR CASTLE, FEBRUARY 24, 1864

I can only write very hastily for I had to write much already and am so unwell from worry and anxiety. I am quite shattered. I trust that this horrible war with all its fearful sufferings on both sides will soon cease. Anyone who urges its continuation now that the pledge has been obtained is sinful indeed![2] The bravery and endurance on all sides is very great. I am thankful Fritz is safe.

I cannot tell you how grieved and how surprised I am at the news conveyed in your letter received today.[3] I thought you both knew how highly important the doctors (Sir C. Locock, Dr. Jenner and Sir James) thought it that you should have two years complete rest before these—for you—particularly trying events again began, and again in the very worst season for mother and child! I will say no more except that I pray God fervently to protect you and the child! I little needed this additional anxiety in my present sorrow and worry! May God order all for the best!

I went to see poor Lady Elgin yesterday and found her a perfect shadow but so touching and looking so young and pretty. We understand each other.

---

[1] Red-breast, Prince Fritz Carl.

[2] The Queen means by this that the occupation of Schleswig, then virtually complete, satisfied the terms of the original ultimatum by Prussia and Austria that Schleswig would be occupied as a pledge for the fulfilment of Denmark's obligations.

[3] The Crown Princess had written "I have hopes again".

From the Crown Princess

I am so sorry to hear you are so worried at this time, though it is but natural and you share that disadvantage with many! The times are serious no doubt; and the small evils of daily life are not those that make themselves the least felt—particularly when one is sad and has not spirits to meet them. I am sorry that the news I gave you should distress you as to most it is not a cause of sorrow but of gratitude. I have had a good rest, my health is strong and good—though I cannot stand this climate and the fatigues of the season in the winter, and I hardly know any one who can.

No one was stronger and looked younger than you, dear Mama—and I was born in '40 and Affie in '44[1]—whereas I have been married six years and have only 3. I am very glad they come no faster but I think no one can say that my health has been injured or that I have had them too fast. Children are much easier to bring up when they are near of an age and I look upon it as a great mercy from God, whenever another is sent. We are not so poor that we need look forward with anxiety to their future. It will not be in the worst time of the year; September is not hot at Potsdam, and afterwards we can try and go for a month or two to a warmer place before we return here. Of course I should have liked it better if it had been all ready in June—but over these things we have no control.

I hope dear Alix's baby is well. I am very busy arranging my christening present, it is to be a large, German bible with a fine ornamental binding. I am having Raphael's little picture of St. George and the Dragon copied in water colours for the title page. I hope it will all succeed. The plate is not good enough here to be given to an English prince and would only be sending coals to Newcastle. Jewelry he can make no use of—so I thought a handsome bible would be the best.

---

[1] Four children in four years.

Prince Charles is gone off to the seat of war. Heaven knows what sudden burst of patriotism or military ardour has come over him to risk his precious and careful life for his country!

I read the English papers with no very pleasant feeling. I think *The Times* gets worse and worse; the nonsense and the untruths it contains—out of mere spite and hatred to Prussia—are beyond belief! It reminds one of the Kreuz-zeitung during the Crimean War that was always talking of the defeats of the English army just as *The Times* says we have been defeated! However never mind—abusing, lying and railing is the privilege of newspapers and as they are useful in a thousand other ways, one must just not mind their provoking ill-nature and ignorance, and luckily here we have broad shoulders.

From the Queen

WINDSOR CASTLE, MARCH 2, 1864

I return the letters with many thanks.[1] How can a clever, sensible person like you think that I should talk of what is in those letters to Bertie, with whom you know I can't say a word on the subject and purposely avoid speaking to him upon what only cause family discord! Really I could be very angry at such an insinuation. Nobody but Aunt, Lenchen, Dr. Holzmann[2] and General Grey (who is quite for S. Holstein) see them.

As regards yourself, my dear child, I can only say what I said before—that you ought to have had two good years rest before you began again; my example cannot be quoted; first of all I began full three years later than you did, never suffered as you did and do—bodily—but it did my nerves terrible harm;—dear Papa knew this and was most anxious

---

[1] These are the Crown Prince's letters from the front.
[2] Sir Maurice Holzmann (1835–1909). At this time he was acting as German secretary in the Prince of Wales's household. He was afterwards secretary to the Princess of Wales. "The strongest man in Marlborough House . . . a Continental Liberal." Philip Magnus, *King Edward VII*, John Murray, 1964.

that our daughters should not run the same risks. No one recognises more than I do, the blessing of having children, but the anxieties and trouble—not to say sorrows—are quite as great as the blessings and you little know what awaits you. Sons especially are far more sorrow and anxiety than joy—especially if there is no father!

The bible will be a beautiful present, and far the fittest. Poor little child, I trust it will have a good chance to become good! My gift will be very beautiful, I think, but I will let you have a photograph of it.

The newspapers are very bad, and the feeling against Prussia very strong. I saw Mr. Oliphant[1] on Sunday (whom you never told me you had seen). He is such an agreeable clever man. I had seen him formerly. Augusta and the little Dean were here on Monday—looking as unsuited as possible. He runs after her like a little boy and looks at her whenever he speaks!! Both were rather embarrassed. He read to us after dinner part of a lecture of his on Isaiah— which is very interesting.

From the Crown Princess

BERLIN, MARCH 2, 1864

I have good news from Fritz—but he says nothing about his return and thinks the place he is now "stopping" at awfully dull. I send him little treats now and then such as novels—the English papers which are (I only mention in passing and not to use a very correct expression) enough to make a saint swear—champagne, a cake, and cigars.

From the Crown Princess

BERLIN, MARCH 7, 1864

I have only time to write a few lines before Count Fürstenstein leaves.[2] We thought it right at this moment

---

[1] This brilliant man had just finished his diplomatic career. He went to Poland to look at the insurrection in 1863 and then to see the Schleswig-Holstein fighting of which he doubtless gave the Queen an account.
[2] Gentleman-in-Waiting to the Crown Prince.

when politics divide to do all we could to show that these differences have not affected family ties, and to prove our respect to you, and the interest we take in dear Bertie and Alix and the darling baby. You were so kind as to send two Gentlemen to Willie's christening—and Bertie has sent Gentlemen on several occasions so we thought it only right that as I am godmother my chamberlain should go.

From the Queen

WINDSOR CASTLE, MARCH 9, 1864

After warm and mild weather, it is snowing hard today. Many thanks for your dear letter of the 5th. I am very poorly; very weak and exhausted and know not how I shall go through tomorrow! The very house—room, all will be over-whelming and I know not how I shall bear up.[1] My weakness, nervousness and trembling has so greatly increased. All this I know you can hardly understand, my good, dear child, for you think I have greater strength and courage than I have and can go through all that—as a queen; but oh! thorny and agonising is that unenviable Crown. How can people wish for them!

I just hear that Count Fürstenstein is arrived and I will leave this letter open till I have seen him. Uncle George is to represent the poor King of Denmark. There will be a large breakfast like at Beatrice's christening, but at which of course I don't appear. Bertie gives a great dinner in the evening at Marlborough House. I return quietly in the evening with Leopold, Baby, Augusta, and Mrs. Bruce to be quiet. Dear Uncle remains for a few days in London and the sisters till Friday morning.

I hope and trust dear Fritz will be prudent. I hope you tell him how often I ask after him and say I pray daily for his safety.

---

[1] The christening was held in the private chapel at Buckingham Palace.

From the Queen

I desired a full account to be written to you of the christening. I never felt more thoroughly shaken than I was all through. The poor baby roared all through the ceremony—which none of you did. Alix looked very ill—thin and unhappy. She is sadly gone off; the fraicheur is gone. Count Fürstenstein will, I doubt not, tell you all about the party in the evening at Marlborough House; and also of Bernstorff's tactlessness.[1] I went to Marlborough House on my way back to Windsor. Every one tells me my poor, sad dress was much liked, and thought "bien convenable". How sad and shocking is the sudden death of the poor King of Bavaria![2] I wrote instantly to the poor Queen. What a moment for the poor young King! I feel much for both mother and son.

What do you say to the shameful bigotry at Oxford and the poor Archbishop's awfully unchristian letter? The Dean[3] is shocked but really it is monstrous to see how Christians can wish for others to be eternally damned! The good little Dean[4] will be so horrified.[5]

---

[1] It was generally believed that at the luncheon after the christening the Prussian Ambassador, Count Bernstorff, declined to drink the health of the King of Denmark. At the toast of the Queen of England he said, "Ah that's a toast anyone can join in." Probably the first part of the story, though widely circulated and bringing Bernstorff a snub from the Prince of Wales, was untrue but he may well have said something unwise on drinking the Queen's health. "His tendency to impertinence is incurable" was Lord Clarendon's comment on hearing the story. See *Journal of Benjamin Moran* and *Dearest Duchess*.

[2] King Maximilian II. He had been born in 1811 and succeeded to the throne in 1848 when his father abdicated on becoming entangled with Lola Montez. He was a scholar, liberal-minded and unsympathetic to the church. His people grew violently antagonistic to Prussia during the war, but he lacked the inclination to put himself at their head as a third force within the German Confederation. He married the daughter of the King of Prussia's uncle and it was through her that his son, Ludwig II, was supposed to have inherited insanity.

[3] Of Windsor.

[4] Of Westminster.

[5] This concerns a doctrinal case arising out of *Essays and Reviews*,

I wish to ask your advice about something. Winter-halter is coming over, to paint Alix and Bertie (in May). Now what do you advise?—Should I have a half length of her with the baby on her lap—and Bertie at the back, for Osborne, or a full length of each for here? Both, neither of us can afford. I think I will let him paint a full length of me with Beatrice, for here.

From the Crown Princess

BERLIN, MARCH 12, 1864

The poor King of Bavaria's death is very shocking—so sudden, and that poor boy to have become King who was so backward for his age—and always kept like a school boy. They say he is as amiable as his mother and has her pretty face; Adalbert often talks to me about him! Poor Mariechen,[1] it is too sad for her left all alone—and not of an independent disposition or able to shift for herself.

I always forgot that I never told you how much we saw of Mr. Oliphant when he was here. We like him so much —clever and agreeable, with a remarkable talent of under-standing foreign countries and their conditions.

Fritz Strelitz is here—unfortunately he protects a very worthless lady who has already rendered many others unhappy. This connection began last summer—a Countess Hahnstep, mother to Countess Lehndorff.

---

which had been published in 1860. Two of the contributors were sus-pended by the Church authorities for a year ab officio et ab beneficio. Appealing to the judicial committee of the Privy Council the two clergy-men had this sentence reversed. One of them in *Essays and Reviews* had advocated German methods of biblical criticism and had questioned the accuracy of the book of Exodus: the other had proclaimed complete doctrinal freedom for the clergy. A petition against the Privy Council judgement was organised by the Archdeacon of Taunton and was signed by over 11,000 clergymen and presented at Oxford.
[1] The widowed Queen.

From the Queen

As you wished so much to see what your friend Mr. Odo Russell wrote, some day, I send you this long despatch but ask to have it back by return of messenger and you must not mention to anyone that you have seen it.[1]

From the Queen

I have to thank you for your nice letter of the 12th. I thought you would have telegraphed to me on this sad, sad anniversary![2] All came back so vividly to my mind! This morning, a brilliant day, I have been with the children, Lady Fanny,[3] Augusta and her little Dean and Katherine, to the dear mausoleum, first to place flowers below and then to gaze on the statue, of which a cast has been placed on the pedestal. Her dear names and the following inscription has been placed beneath it: "Thy Children shall rise up and call Thee blessed", from Proverbs—and the following beautiful lines written on purpose by Tennyson beneath that.

I can't write it by heart so I enclose a copy of it, which you can show Countess Blücher and the Queen.[4]

Count Fürstenstein is to tell you every thing. Pray show the Queen all the accounts which I cannot give her myself. He dined with us on Monday night and will be able to tell you also what a stupid mess and shameful con-

---

[1] Mr. Russell, afterwards Lord Ampthill, was at this time at Rome in a diplomatic if unrecognised post. The despatch is almost certainly one of 15 January 1864 which describes an interview of Russell with the celebrated Pius IX. He paid many compliments to the English Royal Family—"no Sovereign in the world inspired him with more admiration, sympathy and respect than did the Queen". Russell's despatch is extremely entertaining. See Noel Blakiston, *The Roman Question*.

[2] Her mother's death.

[3] Presumably Lady Frances Baillie—sister of Lady Augusta.

[4] Long as the heart beats life within her breast,
    Thy child will bless thee, guardian mother mild,
And far away thy memory will be bless'd
    By children of the children of thy child.

cern there has been about poor Bernstorff, which I myself believed when I wrote to you.

From the Crown Princess

Many thanks for your dear letter received on Monday. I studied the accounts of the christening in the newspapers —it seems to have gone off so well. I have not heard whether my present was approved of, I hope it was. What did Count Bernstorff do that you allude to in your letter? No one has told me anything about it—and I find nothing to lead me to guess what "maladresse" he has been guilty of in the newspapers.

He is a worthy, but blunder-headed individual, stiff and heavy and by always being so ready to take offence—he ends by giving it when I do believe he does not intend it. He has been a long time in England but he never will learn to enter into the spirit of its institutions or to understand the feeling there. He might have profited immensely by his stay there but I always find him just as "borné" and as old fashioned in his ideas as ever.

Dear Fritz writes that he is very well but that his Gentlemen have got awful colds; he will not be back for the King's birthday and I fear not for Easter. If so I shall not take the Sacrament on Good Friday but wait until he comes home, that we may take it together.

From the Queen

WINDSOR CASTLE, MARCH 19, 1864

Many thanks for your dear letter of the 16th in which however you neither take notion of that dear, sad anniversary, nor of Louise's birthday which was yesterday—nor did you telegraph for either! I am so grieved I wrote about Bernstorff's indiscretion when it was a stupid, wicked invention. I hope very shortly to be able to tell you of a doctor who could attend you without costing so much.[1] Sir

---

[1] Meaning as on previous occasions when a doctor came out from England.

James and Dr. Jenner are both taking great pains about it. There are several excellent ones—and not fashionable. Sir C. Locock is much concerned at your prospects. He is ready to come also if you wish it. He is not at all deaf just now.

From the Crown Princess

BERLIN, MARCH 19, 1864

I have got another cold which again began with a feverish attack but has now gone to my head. I cannot think how one catches such frequent colds here. Every one is ill now, and yet I use cold shower-baths etc. This is a very nasty and treacherous climate in the winter.

Today it is eight weeks since I saw Fritz; it seems a year! The siege of Düppel or Dyppal[1] has begun in earnest it seems; I fear the losses will be great, and I tremble whenever the telegrams arrive.

You ask me what I told you about Countess Lehndorff;[2] it was at her house I was staying in East Prussia last summer—in that lovely place which I enjoyed so much.

Count Fürstenstein's mother was a Countess Hardenberg—a lady in waiting of Queen Louise whom people say the Queen was rather jealous of. She married M. Le Comus, who was created Count Fürstenstein and was at the Court of King Jerome. The mother is still alive—but childish.

From the Queen

WINDSOR CASTLE, MARCH 23, 1864

Many, many thanks for your dear letter of the 19th. I send you today some photographs which I think you will like. But my good child seldom now says anything about what I send her. Pray do answer me about the picture or

---

[1] Düppel was the strongly fortified position guarding the approach to the peninsula of Alsen, and possibly most easily captured by a flanking movement through Jutland which the Austrians were reluctant to authorise.

[2] Count Lehndorff was a member of the King's court.

pictures Winterhalter is to paint of Alix and Bertie. Perhaps full lengths for her would be the best. And then I shall have one done of myself with Beatrice and perhaps a grand-child.

Alice I am sorry for also, but she has no son, and will have waited a month longer than you did between William and Charlotte. You should try and get a little change again before you are laid up till the end of autumn, in May and June for 3 or 4 weeks. We always got change before I was doomed to be shut up, and travelling would do you no harm—quite the contrary.

Louise has difficulties to contend with, no doubt—but also great advantages over her sister. She is so handsome (she is so very much admired) and is so graceful and her manners so perfect in society, so quiet and lady-like, and then she has such great taste for art.[1] Poor dear Lenchen, though most useful and active and clever and amiable, does not improve in looks and has great difficulties with her figure and her want of calm, quiet, graceful manners. Nature certainly divides her gifts strangely. She is however in perfect good health, free for 2 months and a half from neuralgia and colds and able to go out in all weathers.

You never told me how you liked the lines under Grandmama's statue. I must end, dearest child—and send you a small box of primroses.

Don't forget to ask dearest Fritz for some of those photographs of himself and of the late King of Denmark and Countess Danner. Can't you let me have one of you (a full length one—"carte de visite") in your dress at Bertie's wedding? I have got all the others but you.Mr. Thomas has got his picture—and it is as good as poor Mr. Frith's is bad.[2]

---

[1] In her letter of March 19 the Crown Princess alluding to Princess Louise's birthday said "God bless the dear child—who is so affectionate and has so many difficulties to contend with. I hope and trust she will get over them all in time and still become a most useful member of the human family."

[2] G. H. Thomas was a favourite painter of the Queen: Frith had been asked to paint the Crown Princess's wedding and, in view of the Queen's

From the Crown Princess

As it is Passion Week—and on account of the war, the celebration of the birthday was a very quiet one. I breakfasted with the King and Queen, and then stood about till half past 11 (ready to drop) while the King was receiving the congratulations of the Queen Dowager, the Grand-Duchess of M. Schwerin, of the family and other princes staying at Berlin. At 5 I gave a large family dinner, and in the evening we were at Princess Charles's—where the only amusement was making charpie.[1]

There are so many sick and wounded here in the hospitals—but I do not think it would quite do for me to go and see them as I fear some poor creatures are much disfigured, and in this condition it is not advisable, though I am very sorry for it.

From the Queen

WINDSOR CASTLE, MARCH 26, 1864

What do you say to the monstrous conduct of our clergy? Is it not too disgraceful and humiliating? It is quite monstrous. Pray write to me about it that I may show it to the "little Dean". He is in despair.

Little A.V. is not like Bertie really. His large eyes and large nose may give that appearance, but he has a tiny pretty little mouth and a well shaped head and a great look of dear Alix. He is suffering much with his vaccination. He is a very pretty, but rather a fidgety baby. What is Anna's dress made of?[2] I am going to send her a Hunting Stewart velvet and a handsome bracelet with my picture.

We are doing all we can about a doctor for you—I hope soon to tell you. How I wish our dear Fritz was safe back.

---

remark, perhaps wisely refused. The Queen is here referring to their pictures of the Prince of Wales's wedding.
[1] Surgical-dressings.
[2] Prince Louis of Hesse's sister who was being married.

But I should think Düppel will very soon be taken. Garibaldi's coming here is not at all pleasant; but he is said to be coming here for his wound.[1] Dear Uncle Leopold is all kindness and affection and helps me in many ways as he used to do when I was a helpless child! Oh! to feel so utterly desolate as I do, is dreadful! We took the Sacrament yesterday—for the first time again in that place where I took it for the last time with beloved Papa and you and Alice. Alix had not yet taken it with me. And Uncle also took it.[2]

From the Crown Princess

BERLIN, MARCH 26, 1864

Many thanks for your dear letter of yesterday, for the box of sweet, lovely primroses—the first sign of spring I have seen yet—and for the photographs of dear Grandmama's mausoleum. I am afraid I did not quite like the lines under dear Grandmama's statue. I thought them not quite simple enough—not one of Tennyson's happiest efforts, but that is a matter of taste and I suppose you all like them very much.

I am so sorry that I answered your questions so irregularly but I assure you it is all I can do to recollect all I have to write to Fritz and to execute all his commissions and give his messages right and left. My head is altogether confused some times and the less important things quite slip out of my memory in spite of notes taken on the backs of covers and in books. First then I think there can be no doubt that Alix and Bertie should be full lengths by Winterhalter— then perhaps a little sketch of her without a background (like Lady Constance Grosvenor, Lady Gainsborough and Lady Ely) for Osborne.

---

[1] He arrived on 3 April and—no doubt to the Queen's annoyance— spent much of his time in the Isle of Wight with the Liberal M.P., Mr. Seely.

[2] As was usual at that time the Easter Communion was taken on Good Friday (25 March). The improvement in the appearance of the King of the Belgians was remarked. He had started to wear a new wig in exchange for one which looked like a night-cap.

My great wish is to have some change of air this spring before I settle down at Potsdam, but I see no possibility as yet—the weather is too cold now, and travelling without Fritz I do not like.

What you say about Louise and Lenchen is so true. I am sure I should think the very same in your place. Lenchen cannot help her looks though, poor child, and I think you will see she will grow into them and, though she may never be as pretty as Louise which I do not think she will, still she may be much admired. Grace of manner is also a gift—and happy those on whom it is bestowed as it has more charm than real beauty.

Fritz has got a long beard I hear which must alter him very much. The description of the state the unfortunate soldiers are in—because they cannot wash or change their clothes—is dreadful. They are nearly eaten up by insects!

From the Queen

WINDSOR CASTLE, MARCH 30, 1864

Many thanks for your dear letter of the 26th. I grieve to think of this long, long separation for you; now think what my fate is! No letter or message—all silence.

Mr. Paton[1] has been ill ever since you left and never been in the house since! But he is going on slowly and yesterday he sent me a most exquisite little picture representing the Blue Room by moon-light, and me kneeling (as I do every night) by the bed side. It is beautifully done.

The arrangements for the memorial are making great progress, and I hope shortly it will be begun in right earnest. I was today at a Flower Show at the Horticultural Gardens, where a great deal is to be done. It was for hyacinths—the finest and newest imaginable, and for splendid early, forced roses. It had snowed in the morning heavily and was far too slushy to walk in the garden. I am sorry and surprised you do not like the lines under dear Grand-

---

[1] Presumably Waller Paton—the Scottish landscape painter. He was first commissioned by the Queen to do a drawing of Holyrood.

mama's statue. I admire them much especially that line "Thy Child will bless thee, Guardian-Mother mild."

Dear Alix was very much upset by the—at last sudden—death of her old "Amama".[1] The dear child is looking terribly thin; her face is like a knife and she is as flat as a board. I fear greatly she will never get her looks back again as they were before she married. This unfortunate little baby, small as it is, has taken that all away. It is very plump, though less in its face than elsewhere but, though it is nearly three months old now, it is not bigger than Alice's was, at a fortnight!! But Bertie imagines it is bigger than it is, so we don't say this to them. You never answer me about these dreadful religious disputes here?

I grieve to think of the suffering of the unfortunate soldiers on both sides.

I am glad to hear that Sir C. Locock has undertaken to attend you.

From the Crown Princess

BERLIN, MARCH 30, 1864

Many affectionate thanks for your dear letter containing so much pleasant news about Alix's dear baby, which I can never hear enough about, and so many questions which I hope to answer to your satisfaction—though I am writing against time! First then, Count Fürstenstein did tell me about the row about poor Bernstorff. I thought it intensely silly.

You wish to know what I think about the behaviour of the English clergy and the letter of the Archbishop, I regret with you that so much disharmony should be stirred up again and create angry feelings, but I think they are logically perfectly consistent and from their point of view quite in the right. I am so sorry for poor Alix having lost her grandmother. She was not a benevolent or a virtuous

---

[1] Grandmother on her mother's side. Louise Charlotte—a Danish princess—married to the Landgrave of Hesse-Cassel.

lady but still her family were fond of her—and I have no doubt she was a kind relation.

Anna's wedding dress is pretty but does not the least look bridal. It is of plain white "moiré"—not silver-trimmed with three tassel flounces of silver blonde, and one row of silver blonde round the train which is of the same material as the dress—no tulle or ribbons, no flowers or lace, nothing light, or young, or wedding-like—but I suppose it is the fashion at these German Courts and as it is a handsome gown, she will no doubt look well in it—as she is usually so very ill-dressed.

Fritz writes daily. I wish the operations could be performed a little quicker and some termination could be come to; perhaps in another week or two—at least I hope so—and then to have my dear Fritz back. Garibaldi's visit in England is very strange. As you know I have a secret weakness for that individual; I feel much interested in what he is about.

From the Queen

WINDSOR CASTLE, APRIL 2, 1864

I received your dear letter yesterday and the Countess's the day before. I am truly glad that you can have Sir C. Locock again as he understands you so well, and Lady Caroline shall also go and Mrs. Innocent, so you will I hope have every comfort—and then not be in a hurry again, for I can assure you all the doctors wish a longer rest.

There is a very good letter in yesterday's *Times* about that horrid and unchristian doctrine of eternal punishment which you ought to read.

Here the feeling about Denmark has cooled down very much. Alix and Bertie and little A.V. are gone to Sandringham, for a good month and trust it will do good to poor dear Alix and fatten her a little for she is wretchedly thin. On Tuesday Alice's darling baby will be a year old. She must be a great darling.

From the Crown Princess

BERLIN, APRIL 2, 1864

I have by dint of begging and tormenting, obtained the
King's permission to have some more rooms in the Neue
Palais; we shall leave our old ones to the children. I am
very glad of this as we were too closely packed last year,
but it was very difficult to get the King to allow it as he is
particularly averse to innovations of any kind. I had hoped
we should be able to leave this the 1st of next month but
if the weather remains as bad as it is now—of course we
cannot. I long for a little liberty and quiet, and shut up and
alone in a house in the town without a garden for so long
a time is very sad—I assure you—particularly when one
feels neither very well nor in good spirits, and is more or
less in perpetual anxiety.

The Queen had meant to go away to Baden soon but I
think she has given it up now which I regret for many
reasons.

How all the others can go about every night to parties
and to the theatre while their husbands, sons and
brothers are, to say the least, exposed to danger I cannot
understand. I am the only one who does not do it unless the
Queen expressly orders it which she does now and then—to
my despair.

I wonder whether anybody in England is prejudiced or
unjust enough to believe the infamous lies which the
Danes and particularly *The Times* Correspondent at the
Danish Headquarters (the famous Signor Galenga)[1] write
about the Prussian troops. I am sure if I had never admired
them before I should now be filled with respect for them;
the way in which both officers and men have done their
duty in every way and borne untold hardships, fatigues and
privations, never losing their courage or even their good

---

[1] A remarkable man—Italian by birth and upbringing—who, in middle
life, became a special correspondent for *The Times*. In the first instance
The Times office remonstrated with him for being pro-German: he was
ordered to Copenhagen and thereafter his despatches were much more
sympathetic to the Danes. His correct name was Antonio Gallenga.

humour for a minute, is quite heroic. I could tell you so much about it; they are really such a fine set—so kind-hearted and so enduring, considering how young they are, how short their time of service. I think it very wonderful; it speaks well for the serjeants and the officers, who in so short a time can transform boys—many under 20—into such good soldiers.

I fear the wounds have been very dreadful and the sufferings very great. Fritz writes to me that when I have an opportunity I am to send you his best love and duty! How funny he must look with his beard. I own I am very anxious and curious to see what it is like and hope he will not cut it off before his return.

From the Queen

WINDSOR CASTLE, APRIL 6, 1864

I am so glad to hear you are to have more room at the Neue Palais and are going there soon. But I still urge change of air in June, and so does Dr. Jenner. Nothing is so important, and you will get none at all this summer and really that would be very bad for you.

This horrid war will I hope soon cease; the conference is to meet on the 12th and I trust an armistice will be very shortly agreed upon. I can well imagine that Signor Gallenga writing untruths. But it is very wrong.

From the Queen

BUCKINGHAM PALACE, APRIL 9, 1864

I am come here to receive the Corps Diplomatique (a great effort for which I am very unfit—for my cold oppresses and weakens me sadly) and am writing from beloved Papa's dressing-room—his dear dressing-table! I could not bear the silent room near me out of which he always came looking so beautiful to take me to Drawing-rooms and levées—too, too dreadful![1]

---

[1] In a leading article on 1 April 1864 The Times alluding to the Queen's

This bombardment of Sonderburg is very sad and unfortunate and raises such bad feelings against the Prussians. It is sad and I think so much unnecessary loss of life ought to be prevented! It is not right.[1]

Max and Charlotte have had much annoyance about this wretched Mexico which I so fear will end badly for them. It really grieves me deeply.[2]

From the Queen

I can only write a line, as Augusta has told you how ill I have been with neuralgia and what I have suffered since Saturday! I never was in greater agonies, continuously. I am much better again but much shaken and not well yet. I send you some more photographs; give some of them to the Queen. I send you also some sermons, which are the finest and most original I think I ever read; Augusta knew Mr. Robertson, and the Dean of Westminster and Tennyson recommended them to me.[3] I have not read many yet— but they are all most striking and original. Pray tell me how you like them.

---

appearance at Buckingham Palace and to her supposed prejudices over Schleswig-Holstein said:

"The most secluded people can not shut out the reality: and they who live ever so much in the past will still find the living intrude. Indeed they are apt to give way to feelings on the questions of the day all the more because they have indulged too much in recollections and regrets, and on the shadows of a bygone time."

[1] Sonderburg was regarded as an adjunct to the Danish stronghold of Düppel, but it was generally felt that the civilian inhabitants should have been given twenty-four hours warning of the bombardment. Several women and children were killed.

[2] The Archduke Maximilian had sailed for Mexico where he had been acclaimed as Emperor under the influence of Napoleon III—"the souspréfect" as he was scornfully described by Lord Clarendon. His brother, the Emperor of Austria and, as this passage shows, the Queen correctly regarded the enterprise as foolhardy.

[3] The Queen is evidently referring to F. W. Robertson who had an immense following—especially among working-people—when he was in charge of Trinity Chapel at Brighton. Four series of his sermons were published in the late 1850's.

Do tell your Baron to write to me a little account of the state of politics at Berlin, and pray send me what you get from Fritz—for I know nothing but from newspapers.

From the Crown Princess

If the bombardment of Sonderburg has raised ill-feeling towards us in England—the most absurd, unjust, rude and violent attacks in *The Times* and in Parliament upon us can only increase the irritation or rather more contempt which is expressed in no measured terms here, and generally felt for England's position in the Danish Question.[1] But even the French see this and defend us against the really childishly indignant attacks upon us in the "Presse" of the 10th.

I can see nothing inhuman or improper in any way in the bombardment of Sonderburg; it was necessary—and we hope it has been useful. What would Lord Russell say if we were every instant to make inquiries about what is going on in Japan, where Admiral Cuper was not so intensely scrupulous as to bombardments?[2]

I quite agree with Mr. Bernal Osborne who calls—in his most excellent speech in *The Times* of the 9th—the perpetual unnecessary questions which are asked of us here and at Vienna—"hysteric fussiness".[3] The continual meddling and interfering of England in other people's affairs has

---

[1] In those more civilised days there was a distinction between a war with a limited objective and one of unlimited aggression. The bombardment of the civilians in Sonderburg produced a violent reaction in Parliament.

[2] Admiral Sir Augustus Kuper. It is fair to add that his bombardment of Kagosima was the subject of critical debate in the House of Commons. Before the bombardment he told the Japanese ministers "You must remember that we are one of the first nations of the world, who, instead of meeting civilised people as you think yourselves, in reality encounter barbarians." *Essays of Lord Salisbury*, 1905, page 180.

[3] A brilliant and independent-minded Member. He argued that the prestige of England had been damaged by the Foreign Minister (Russell) leading the Danes to believe that if they resisted Prussia, help would be forthcoming from England.

become so ridiculous abroad that it almost ceases to annoy. But to an English heart it is no pleasant sight to see the dignity of one's country so compromised and let down, its influence so completely lost.

The highly pathetic, philanthropic and virtuous tone in which all the attacks against Prussia are made has something intensely ludicrous about it. The English would not like, if they were engaged in a war, to be dictated to in a pompous style how they were to conduct it. Indeed I am sure they would not stand such interference. Why should we then be supposed to submit to it?

From the Queen

Dear Uncle Leopold is in town since Wednesday to see people and alas! leaves on Tuesday altogether. I forbear answering your letter the tone of which was not quite the thing to your own Mama. I am no defender of those shameful attacks in the papers, or of course of bragging, but I wish I could think the conduct of the Prussian Army quite free from blame!

I trust dearest Fritz keeps well. I pray daily for him and wish he was safe back with you. Dear little William's letter is charming, and your present to Baby—beautiful. But poor, good Leopold ought not to have been quite forgotten. He suffers so often, and leads so sad and solitary a life. A pretty classical German book would give him such pleasure and if you would ask the Queen to send him her print, he would be delighted.[1]

I saw Sir E. Landseer for the first time on Wednesday and he cried dreadfully.[2]

---

[1] Princess Beatrice's birthday was on 14 April and Prince Leopold's on 7 April.
[2] The first meeting since the Prince's death: Landseer at this time was afflicted by nervous depression.

From the Crown Princess

What a tremendous fuss is being made about Garibaldi. It is a little exaggerated I must say—particularly on the part of the haute Valée who treat him like a sovereign. In spite of my sympathy for him I think it is going a little too far. Here people are frantic about it which I think very silly.[1]

From the Queen

I am free from pain, but sadly shaken and nervous, and hardly able to bear any thing and this makes me still worse. We are going shortly to Osborne where I hope to have some more quiet. You will now I hope see Fritz again soon, for this great success of the Prussian Army and the terrible loss of these poor wretched Danes will I trust and think put a stop to further bloodshed. Fritz Carl I fear would have no feeling for this![2]

I am glad to say Garibaldi is going away on Friday. People have been too foolish and absurd and I am quite ashamed of it. The "Garibaldiana" in the *Saturday Review* is excellent. Pray do tell Stockmar to write to me as I begged. If I never know any thing I can never be of any use—though I well know that my opinion is of no avail with you; you are always so much wiser than Mama. I know what Papa wished and felt, and that ought to have weight with all his children.

Alix is said to be much better, and the baby growing and improving daily. Affie will be with you on the 1st; he goes to Altenburg for three days; how I long for that to be

---

[1] Garibaldi was in England from 3 April to 27 April, and greatly fêted. The Crown Princess means that the inhabitants of the north of Italy, then in the possession of Austria, were treating Garibaldi like a sovereign and that the Germans were frantic at the way he was being lionised in England.

[2] On 18 April Prince Fritz Carl stormed Düppel, and the whole of Schleswig fell into Prussian hands.

settled; it will be such a blessing to have a real German daughter-in-law. Alix's parentage has greatly added to my sorrows and troubles and puts a great bar between our intimacy. You will I know also do all you can to encourage Affie; his wife would be such a support and assistance to me.

From the Crown Princess

You can imagine our joy and gratitude that Düppel is taken, it was a brilliant, and signal victory. The town has been illuminated here for two nights—it is all decorated with flags, crowds in the streets, the King and Queen were much cheered and appeared on the balcony of their Palais. The guns fired till the houses shook!

Of all this I heard and saw nothing as I have been in bed again, my "grippe" having become much worse again. I am still very wretched—coughing violently and can hardly look out of my eyes.

I send you a copy of a letter from Fritz which I have just read; it is for you to keep; it describes the whole affair. Alice and Aunt Feodora may like to see it, also Bernstorff. Could you be so kind as to manage it?

We have been separated now all but three months, a quarter of a year! and the whole time I have had one succession of detestable colds or rather it has been the same one—which has never completely gone on account of the bad weather and my being obliged to go to the King's in a low gown in those hot rooms before I was half well enough. But if one is not actually in bed or unable to move, the Queen takes a refusal so very ill and is so very cross that I have often gone out when I felt it would have been more prudent to stay at home merely to keep her in good humour.

I am sorry you were displeased with what I said in my last letter but I can only repeat that no one can cast any sort of blame on the Prussian Army; those who believe that there is any fault to find with it—are totally misinformed. It has behaved most bravely and nobly, and the spirit of generosity and chivalry towards the enemy which pervades all its ranks is undisputed by all impartial judges! Impartial I am not—as I am heart and soul with it—but if you ask anyone, any stranger who has had the opportunity of seeing our troops in the field you will hear the same thing.

From the Queen

OSBORNE, APRIL 23, 1864

Many, many thanks for your dear letter of the 20th and for the most interesting enclosure from dear Fritz, which I shall communicate just as you wish. Dearest child, believe me, it is only because I do feel so much for the honour of the Prussian Army that I was so distressed to think that things had (perhaps) been done which must do them harm here. Every one knows how kind they are to the prisoners etc. and how admirable their discipline is. And I believe the truth about Sonderburg is all being known now. Only I do pray for an armistice now; those wretched Danes have suffered very much, and it is sad to think of poor Alix's poor countrymen being killed in such numbers. After all how could they resist such an overwhelming power?

From the Queen

OSBORNE, APRIL 27, 1864

I thank you much for your little note of the 23rd written in great haste. Garibaldi—thank God!—is gone. It has been a very absurd and humiliating exhibition and was becoming very dangerous by the connection with Mazzini[1] and all the worst refugees etc. The whole crowned by the incredible folly and imprudence of your thoughtless eldest brother going to see him without my knowledge! It has shocked me much and his people are much to blame. For no foreigner can be presented to the Royal Family who has

---

[1] Giuseppe Mazzini (1805–72), the Italian patriot. He would not have endeared himself to the Queen by his remark, "Monarchy will never number me among its servants or followers."

not been received by the Sovereign and none be presented to him or her except by his own Minister!

Alfred is accompanied by Major Cowell, who is in his old position and by his Equerry, lately (by Major Cowell's urgent wish) appointed and a most fortunate choice. Mr. Haig[1] (of the Engineers) is clever, well informed and quite excellent, so that Affie has a true and safe friend and companion in him; you must like him. I refrain from entering into what I deeply grieve to see you take no interest in.[2] I can therefore only ask you to say nothing whatever to Alfred about Altenburg or else you might do irreparable mischief. The course pursued with him is precisely the same as Papa pursued with Bertie—step by step—only that here the young Princess (whom I have enquired quite as much about as you did about Alix) is nearly 19 (and she[3] was not 17) and cannot be left in uncertainty to be snatched away by others.

Miss Lyttelton,[4] whom we all liked so much, is going to be married (I am sorry to say) to Lord Frederick Cavendish, second son to the Duke of Devonshire—a very good match—and I am going to take Florence Seymour[5] in her place.

Elma Bruce[6] is also going to marry Mr. Thurlow,[7] Lord Elgin's excellent and devoted secretary—but that is not to be for six months.

---

[1] Lt. Colonel Arthur Haig. He is the writer of an extremely amusing letter to Henry Ponsonby animadverting on the Coburg court. See *Henry Ponsonby* by Arthur Ponsonby, pages 349–50. He was with Prince Alfred for many years.
[2] Prince Alfred's marriage.
[3] i.e. Princess Alexandra when the Crown Princess first met her.
[4] Lucy, grand-daughter of Lady Lyttelton, governess to the royal children. Maid of Honour to the Queen.
[5] Daughter of 5th Lord Hertford.
[6] Lord Elgin's daughter.
[7] A diplomat: afterwards 5th Lord Thurlow.

From the Crown Princess

BERLIN, APRIL 30, 1864

I write to you full of joy today as dear Affie has just arrived. I went with Willie to the railway station to fetch him at half past 7. The dear boy is looking well and handsome as ever, and is so sweet and amiable! How proud you must be of him! I do not know how to thank you for having sent me this ray of sunshine in my loneliness! I have had so few pleasurable emotions lately—that I think this one will cure me of all my miseries.

Many thanks for your dear letter by messenger, dear Mama. I do not know why you should think I would interfere in Affie's concerns against your wishes; I never gave you any cause to believe so and in my last letter I said I hoped for your sake the visit would be satisfactory as you wished it so much. How can I take a livelier interest in a cause I know so little about? You never told me about all your enquiries or the answers you received; you only once alluded to the subject "en passant" at Windsor. I trust and hope all is for the best, and no one can wish more ardently than I that Affie should make a marriage to ensure him true and lasting happiness and that his wife should be a comfort to you in every way.

From the Queen

OSBORNE, May 4, 1864

Many, many thanks for your dear letter of the 30th.

I am so touched and gratified at the King's giving Affie the Black Eagle now. Do thank him—as well as for his letter and say that I will write next time. Affie's sudden predilection for the Princess of H.[1] has startled me! That would I fear be a doubtful thing. As for the other, dear child, I did show you some accounts at Balmoral and you sent me some yourself. I feel terribly nervous and anxious about the whole affair—and altogether feel very poorly—

---

[1] Hanover.

can't get rest or quiet and the state of affairs and our shameful press makes me so anxious.

From the Crown Princess

Darling Affie is just gone and the house is sad and lonely again. I cannot say how I felt parting with him this time. The visit had been such a pleasure and so enjoyable. He is such a charming companion, so amiable and affectionate; it is pleasant only to look at him he is so handsome and so often reminds one of dearest Papa in a thousand ways. Dear boy he is so endearing, one cannot help making a pet of him. I hope all his affairs will turn out satisfactorily. The "forbidden subject" was only approached on the vaguest terms so that you have no reason to dread the "harm and mischief"—I can do him.

The King was most kind to him; it quite touched me; he seems to have a real affection for him. I have not seen him in such a good humour and so kindly disposed for a long time; he had always a smile on his face when he looked at dear Affie and so had the Queen, who was also much pleased with him.

The Armistice[1] does not seem to be coming off—the King and every one seem very anxious for it here; if it is only proposed in terms such as we can accept, which of course the continuation of the Danish blockade is not. Till then Fritz will not be able to return as he has virtually the command of every thing out there and Wrangel only the name. But I must return to dear Affie the subject uppermost in my heart today.

I think him so much improved, so much more open, his conversation more serious—and not so anxious to run after

---

[1] The London Conference which was convened to discuss the whole political consequences of the Schleswig-Holstein question opened on 25 April. Lord Russell presided and the neutral European countries as well as the belligerent powers were all represented. The neutrals at once proposed an armistice but Germany and Austria insisted that Denmark must first lift the blockade of the North German ports.

amusement. He was quite content to spend his evenings alone with me; we talked together of home, of you, dearest Mama, of darling Papa and he showed so much feeling and good sense I thought.

From the Queen

I write one line to say that I am quite bursting with indignation at a shameful and utterly disgraceful observation in *The Times* today about the King's most kind decoration of Alfred! It is monstrous! But it is shared by no right thinking person! Pray say this to the King and all. It is the pure vulgarity of the Press. I took it, as you know, as a valuable token of the King's wish to be on good terms with England. Oh! what I suffer—no one knows.

ENCLOSURE: Cutting from *The Times* – May 6, 1864

A VERY QUESTIONABLE HONOUR. On Sunday the King of Prussia conferred the Order of the Black Eagle on his Royal Highness Prince Alfred.

From the Queen

OSBORNE, MAY 6, 1864

I received your dear, affectionate letter of the 4th today, and thank you very much for it. I wish Affie could have stayed longer with you in your loneliness but he could not now; in the autumn I have no doubt he can run up from Bonn to see you. He is very much improved, and most amiable, clever, and companionable and really quite happy to lead a very quiet life. Character and principle are the things he is still, I think, wanting in—but they are improved and, with such solid tastes as he has, I think all that must and will come. His wonderful likeness to adored Papa in so many things is very comforting and soothing to me. I can't say I feel happy about his prospects as this little Princess of H. seems to have filled his head—but I have told him (all by cypher) to be in no hurry and not to do anything to make in the end the match with Princess Marie impossible—for, from all we have heard (which the Queen kindly obtained for me) I think she would be far preferable to one from that family, which I think really objectionable on the score of health and blood. What have you ever heard of them? The best way will be not to "brusquer" anything with Affie and give him further opportunity of seeing Princess Marie while we can inquire fully about the other. I am so glad the King seemed pleased with Affie.

Oh! this dreadful Dano-German question ! What I have suffered from it and do suffer words cannot describe. I see all, understand all and can do very little! Those Danes are so obstinate! I can't say more today but I can assure you my troubles and trials without adored Papa are fearful! Think, if you are sad and forlorn and lonely but have the blessed prospect of seeing your dear husband again, what it must be for me to have none on earth but to have, after 22 years of blessed intimacy and happiness, to live alone, without that one who protected, advised, helped, loved, cherished and lived for me!! And I am so helpless, so clinging, dislike to do anything alone so much more than you do. It is very hard and sad that you should be alone and that dear Fritz isn't yet able to return but I trust very soon now. I am not at all surprised at the article you send me and yet Johnny is by no means the violent one. The old one is the one![1]

7th. I dare not say what I feel, for it is too distressing to see such blindness and to be unable to make people see the true and real interests of the country, though I feel sure that this will come in time. But meantime it is a terrible trial for all.

---

[1] Palmerston.

From the Crown Princess

I am so glad you were pleased that Affie received the Black Eagle. I feel certain you would have been gratified by the reception the King and Queen gave him; they were so very kind. At this moment when the English press is teaching the German how to abuse—and the latter is an apt scholar—it was quite a relief to see the kindly feeling shown to Affie.

How well I understand how much you must be worried at present. What with politics and one thing and another there is really "du fil à tordre". It was quite a surprise to see that Affie seemed struck with the elder Princess of Hanover—which he certainly did. Whether or not she would do for him I cannot presume to give an opinion upon. She is said to be grown a fine girl and to be very good natured—but I have never heard more. I should not think the impression could be very deep—the visit having lasted so short a time; but he certainly seemed pleased with her.[1]

From the Queen

Thank God! that the Armistice is settled—for no doubt it will be renewed, and please God some settlement may be come to—but how God only knows. This terrible question— and people are so foolishly mad and excited—that it is dreadful to bear, for they run away with an idea of the great oppressing the weak, and talk a heap of nonsense it is difficult to believe or hear without indignation and impatience. The worst and saddest is the bitterness it produces. Oh! if darling Papa were only here to help us! And yet he could almost do less than I do—as a German himself.

---

[1] She later married Baron von Pawel-Rammingen.

11th, BUCKINGHAM PALACE

I am here for today's reception writing at my own table —and every little trifle that has lain on these tables for years—is still here and I think all is right. Only the silence and my shattered frame and aching heart tell me—all is gone and altered and I am alone, unprotected, and writhing under every harsh word and unjust remark. Affie's affairs have worried me very much though I believe more than need have done. But Hanover is out of the question on the score of health alone—and good Sir James has positively declared this. Three generations of blindness and double relationships which, if you will reflect on, you will see there are—viz. the late Queen[1] was first cousin to the late King of H. and the present Queen is her great niece—and Fritz of Strelitz (also blind) is first cousin to George of H. I have told Affie positively it cannot be. Therefore if he don't in the end (I mean after seeing her again in the autumn) like Princess Marie of A.—he must look for somebody else! Mr. Cowell describes her as charming.

Meyerbeer's death grieved me much; I do so admire his music and so did darling Papa!

From the Crown Princess

NEUES PALAIS, MAY 11, 1864

I can only write a short letter today, as I expect to be off tonight to Hamburg, unless Fritz telegraphs to the contrary! I own my joy of yesterday is a little cooled down since the news of this morning of the ill luck the Austrians have met with at sea, because I fear that will make the Danes more obstinate and the peace more difficult to arrange; and an armistice of four weeks with everything beginning again afterwards is not a cheerful prospect. Your telegram first gave me the news, and I thank you so much for sending it. I have heard nothing from here yet, and I believe the official announcement of the armistice has not reached the Army yet. Many, many thanks for two dear letters. I cannot

---

[1] A princess of Mecklenburg-Strelitz and niece to George III's wife.

say how mortified or rather disgusted I am at the odious *Times*, which is really disgracing itself by its monstrous language and very great stupidity. I assure you I can hardly read it. The family here look upon me with a certain look of virtuous indignation and raise their eyes to the skies when they mention England, as if I could help it. The Grand-Duchess of Mecklenburg-Schwerin said yesterday to Princess Charles she never ceased regretting that there was an Englishwoman in the family, "et par-dessus le marché si anglaise". It is not very pleasant for me just now. Another newspaper (not the Kreuzzeitung) says it hopes the infamous conduct of England towards Prussia, as declared in the English Press, will open the eyes of all for ever and prevent the danger arising of English and Coburg influence returning.

People spread at Berlin that I was unhappy at the success of our troops. They comment on every single thing I say, do, and put on, to my disadvantage. I cannot do the simplest thing without its being found to be in imitation of something English, and therefore anti-Prussian; even the Oratorio did not please on that account, magnificent as it was, and was apostrophised as a copy of English concerts!

I feel as if I could smash the idiots; it is so spiteful and untrue. I am sure I would almost quarrel with my real and best friends in dear England rather than forget that I belong to this country, the interest of which I have so deeply at heart—more deeply, I venture to say, than a great many born and bred here. But you see there are and will be narrow-minded donkeys everywhere, and the best way, after all, is not to mind what they say—their nonsense is not worth troubling about. I never was popular here, but since the war you can well imagine that my position has not improved owing to the English Press.

I cannot help thinking and hoping that all this will pass off.

The Garibaldi fever with which everybody was so taken in England shocked people most of all here, but I own I often enjoyed the horror and indignation exhibited at the very mention of his name. It was a piece of folly, all that reception, etc., and it was a mercy that it all went off without more disagreeables. "Du sublime au ridicule il n'y a qu'un pas", and certainly that "pas" was made by most people in London.

From the Queen

How I do rejoice to think you are now with dear Fritz! How I pity you for all you have to go through but I assure you my difficulties are quite as great. But I am full of hope that things will be satisfactorily settled in time. There is a real comprehension of the true state of things now on the part of the Government—that I can assure you.

Sir Augustus Paget and Wally I saw yesterday. They are very Danish and he I think is not anxious to return![1]

Really idiots and donkeys there are every where, but you are quite right, don't mind it—be patient and all will yet come right again. The present excited state will all pass away.

I think it no use to inquire about the Princess of Hanover as I can't allow it, on account of the blindness as I wrote to you.

From the Crown Princess

I should have answered your dear letter yesterday had I but been able to find a single spare minute. Indeed I did think of you when we met—we both did, and we always do whenever anything reminds us of the pain of separation and of the joy of being with those we love! Much more is felt on this subject than ever uttered! My darling is looking very well; his beard changes him a good deal so that I did not recognise his head out of the window of the railway carriage, but he looks so handsome I wish you could see him before he will have to cut it off. They all look very brown

---

[1] To Copenhagen where he was Minister.

and very different from what we are accustomed to in times of peace. We have given up returning to the North and are going on today to Lübeck.

We have seen dear Fritz Augustenburg these last two days—he came on purpose; I think his patience, fortitude and disinterestedness beyond all praise, he is so thoroughly good and noble-minded, so free from all that is little. He looks very care-worn and much thinner, his hair too is sprinkled with gray. May he be rewarded as he deserves! May he come into his own again and enjoy it for his people— for us! For Germany and Europe it seems to be the only solution which will ensure peace. God grant it may come to pass—I hardly ever so earnestly wished for any thing, as I do for this, and feel so firmly convinced that it will be for the good of all—and if it does not happen—this unhappy question will never terminate.

I was on board the Adleir yesterday.[1] No trace remained of the horrible scars of the last days—two days ago the ship was so covered with blood and in such a state that it would have been impossible to have gone on board her. A great many of the poor Austrian sailors she brought here are dead —the others in a dreadful state here in the hospital. Of course I did not go in with Fritz to see them. I saw our wounded officers who are about again.

This is a charming town. Parts remind me of Geneva, parts of Frankfort-on-Main—but the country around and the villas are quite English-looking. I wish I could tell you all the details about the war I hear, they are so interesting! The English Press has misrepresented almost every thing grossly! The feeling against England is very trying to me as you can imagine—altogether the different emotions politics produce!

---

[1] On 12 May two Austrian frigates had a sharp sea-fight off Heligoland with three Danish ships-of-war. The Austrians disengaged but their courage was acclaimed throughout Germany and Austria.

From the Queen

BALMORAL, MAY 19, 1864

I quite agree in what you say as to what should be the right settlement for the good of all; it is what I have been trying to impress on every one with a perfect spirit of impartiality but with a strong sense of what was really justice! And it is understood now—and please God! there is every appearance of a pacific and satisfactory settlement. The Government here quite see it in the right light. Those poor wounded sailors I pity much.

Winterhalter has arrived but refuses to paint full lengths of Bertie and Alix—so they are to be the size of yours and Fritz's by Lauchert.

From the Crown Princess

NEUES PALAIS, MAY 20, 1864

I send you two photographs of Fritz with his beard which is now cut off—I am sorry to say. I think they are very good. You know he has received the command of the 2nd Corps d'armée; of course I am very proud of this mark of confidence in him and reward for his unceasing exertions during the war, but also it will involve his being very often separated from me as the troops are scattered all over the province of Pomerania, besides its giving him a great deal to do and making us much less masters of our time. Many, many thanks, beloved Mama, for two dear letters I have received from you which were so kind and gave me so much pleasure. The trip to Lübeck I enjoyed particularly; it is such an interesting and picturesque town and the country around so pretty. We saw the poet Geibel, who took a charming drive and walk with us. You admire his things too very much, if I remember right.

Here we found all well—our position trying and difficult as ever, full of thorns and annoyances—but Fritz universally praised. He is so modest about it himself—but every one knows that what successes we have had are to be attributed to him and not to Fritz Carl.

From the Crown Princess

I could not write yesterday as I intended. We were at Berlin for a parade, a large dinner and the theatre, after which we returned here; it poured all day and was little above freezing point—most wretched.

On your birthday we gave a great gala dinner the King proposed your health, God Save the Queen was played and so the day was celebrated in due form for the first time again—as the two last years we did nothing thinking you yourself would not wish it and being altogether too melancholy for any outward sign of rejoicing.

I really do begin to think politics are taking a more favourable turn, and do not despair of things ending pretty well now! What a blessing! Furious as every one is here about England—the King never misses an opportunity of saying how much he owes you—and how grateful he is to you for your endeavours to keep peace etc. which he feels certain would not have been preserved but for you. I hope and trust a peace will be made on a basis which will for ever prevent the recurrence of hostilities on the subject of the Duchies and which will bring them and their Duke to their lawful rights. One thing I own torments me much; it is the feeling of animosity between our two countries; it is so dangerous and productive of such harm! It is kept up too by such foolish trifles, which might be so well avoided. Prussia has gained no popularity for itself since some time on account of the King's illiberal Government, but the feeling against us now in England is most unjust. Now dear Papa is no longer here I live in continual dread that the bonds which united our two countries for their mutual good are being so loosened that they may be in time quite severed! A great deal depends on who is minister (that is ambassador) here. Sir A. Buchanan, who is an excellent man whom I honour and like personally, is quite unfit for the place and has made himself a very bad position here. He knows no German and understands nothing whatever of German affairs nor of the position Prussia holds in the different questions which arise. He does not listen to those who do know and is consequently continually misinformed, and misrepresents things totally as I saw out of the blue book.[1] He is very unpopular here and has no sort of influence. He picks up his information from bad sources such as other silly diplomatists who understand nothing at all (the Brasilian for instance). Then he depends on Mr. Lowther[2] entirely, who is without exception the stupidest man I think I ever saw—besides being violent and "tactless". He has made so many messes! Sir Andrew is a high tory and dislikes every thing liberal, the consequence of which is that he totally misunderstands the positions of our political parties; our Conservative Party in England cannot be compared with the Kreuzzeitung; it is quite a different thing. Strange to say in spite of all the ill-treatment he has received at its hands Sir A. has a secret liking for Bismarck.

Good excellent Morier whom I cannot praise enough, who has been a true friend to us and whose great talent makes him most valuable is not in favour with the Buchanans, and there is a feud between the Lowthers and Moriers. Mrs. L. is jealous that in society Mrs. M. is so much liked, and the poor Moriers see that Lowther is so stupid that he can never rise higher and that he is consequently a bar to Morier's progress; the latter is not in a brilliant position. Sir A. is a violent Dane and angry with Morier for not being the same. M. is most disinterested, as he is quite aware that his impartial views will not raise him in Lord Russell's favour or in the favour of the Foreign Office; he has an enemy too in Mr. Hammond.[3] Morier is going to England for a leave of five months and it does not seem quite certain whether he will return! What a loss it would be to

---

[1] This contained the Foreign Office's despatches on Schleswig-Holstein from the middle of January 1864 to the end of March.

[2] Mr. William Lowther, brother of the 3rd Lord Lonsdale; a minor diplomat and subsequently a Conservative Member of Parliament. He was father of the Speaker. His wife was a daughter of Lord Wensleydale.

[3] Edmund Hammond, Permanent Under-Secretary at the Foreign Office.

Fritz and to me I cannot say. I do not know what we shall do! Would it not be possible to send Sir A.B. to St. Petersburg, which is just the same in point of rank, and give us Lord Napier?[1] And send Lowther with Sir A. as they are so hand and glove together—and promote Morier into Lowther's place here? That would be a capital arrangement. I know very well that Lord Napier has his drawbacks but he understands a great deal more about Germany and would not be above taking advice from the right sources. Neither Sir A. nor Lady B. will ever get on here —the position they have made for themselves is quite "manqué".

People say here—"We have a Danish Minister in de Quade, and a Danish Ambassador in Sir A. Buchanan: a pity the Ambassador is not as moderate as the Minister."

I know the above named arrangement would delight the King as he only yesterday said how he wished we had a less Danish Ambassador from England and that Morier was the only sensible member of the whole Embassy.

I am quite aware that it is no business of mine to meddle in these things, but I thought it right to tell you how matters stand and it wants an intelligent hand to smooth down all the irritations which Lord Russell's (if I may say) impertinent interpellations have produced here.

After the peace it would be such a good opportunity and would be turning over a new leaf. I hope you will turn it over in your mind, dear Mama, and consider it; perhaps it can be managed somehow or other. I am so very anxious for it, and it makes a great difference to us two, in particular, who is your representative here.

---

[1] The 9th Lord Napier. At this time he was British Ambassador in St. Petersburg and was moved to Berlin in September 1864. Lord Lytton described him as "the only man of genius in the diplomatic service".

From the Queen

I have to thank you for two dear affectionate letters—the one of the 26th and the other of the 29th received today. I am very glad you tell me all you do about Sir A. Buchanan and I have all along felt just what you say; I always feared his Danish views. I will do what I can without compromising any one to get a change both in him and in Mr. Lowther who is a very stupid man. As regards the estrangement between our two countries since our terrible misfortune, (though of course beloved Papa's wisdom, and knowledge and influence can never, never be replaced and the loss of them are constantly felt and everywhere)—yet that need in no way occur, if only I am properly informed through you and Stockmar of the true state of things. But I am grieved and distressed to say that the feeling against Prussia has become most violent in England and quite ungovernable, and, as I heard from some one, the people are carried away by imaginary fancies and by the belief that Prussia wants to have the Duchies for herself and that she has (and this we can't entirely get contradicted) broken through the stipulations of the Armistice by her exactions in Jutland. I don't share these ideas, and invariably say that I know it to be false but the feeling is there, and at present no reason is listened to. I hope that my opinions and my actions will not be quoted in opposition to my Government —for that beloved Papa never permitted and in the present instance the Government are perfectly impartial and only anxious to come to a settlement which can once for all be accepted by Denmark and Germany. But their position is most difficult on account of the violent feeling here, and that explains the despatches—which I much regret. Lord Russell, I can assure you is any thing but Danish and if he alone could have acted from the first, things might have been different. As it is, the great object now is not to fight and quarrel about comparatively smaller questions, for else God Almighty knows what may not happen! You will have seen the infamous attack or more properly insinuations of

Lord Ellenborough against me in the House of Lords.[1] Feeling so anxious I have written to the King very openly and send here a copy for dear Fritz and you. If I have been able to preach moderation and impartiality—and if I condemn one-sided violence, and if in the end my efforts should be successful I shall not grudge the suffering and misery I have gone—and do go—through. But my task must not be made impossible by too great demands on the side of Germany and by separating me ostensibly from my Government. That would paralyse every effort for good on my part.

I am shocked and grieved to hear of caricatures and poems etc. Let Fritz not open them, but throw them at once in the fire and they will soon cease.[2]

---

[1] A former Governor-General of India and a stalwart Conservative. It was agreed at the London Conference that hostilities between the Danes and Germans should be suspended on 12 May for one month, and that during that period the Germans should exact nothing from the inhabitants of the territory which they had over-run, and pay for all provisions. It was strongly and widely believed in England that exactions were none the less taking place. The Earl of Ellenborough voiced this feeling in the House of Lords a few days after the suspension of hostilities and attributed the conduct of Germany to England's diminished influence, and protested against the principle that the wealth and power of this country were never to be employed in the defence of right against might. He suggested that our policy had been in some measure controlled by the natural prejudices of a great personage. He added for good measure that the first two Georges had been supposed to be influenced by German feelings, but George III always supported a truly British policy, and such a course ought to be followed now.

The reactions of the Queen were instantaneous. She thanked Lord Russell for what he had said in rebutting Ellenborough's attack which she called "ungentlemanly". To Lord Derby, the leader of the Conservative Party, she wrote to express her regret that he had not said a few words in contradiction of "the malignant and unmanly attacks" against her. In her letter to Lord Derby she emphasised that her "sole anxiety had been to preserve this country from war". To Lord Russell she referred to her sufferings at watching her own country hurried on by the Press and by many public men into violent excitement against "our natural ally" and that she had striven to prevent further mischief and to calm "excited passions on all sides". *Queen Victoria's Letters*, Second Series, Vol. I, page 197 ff.

[2] In her letter the Crown Princess told her mother that her husband was receiving anonymous letters from England—"insulting" and containing "the most horrid caricature of the King".

From the Crown Princess

Fritz Holstein was here today; he goes to Dolzig tonight and meets Uhden[1] at Berlin. He was looking still much harassed but better I thought than at Hamburg; his is a most thorny position. He fills it as admirably as I am sure he will in future a happier and better one. The Duchess of Augustenburg[2] and her daughters are at Berlin. I went yesterday to see them—found them very anxious poor things of course. The poor old Duchess is in a sad state, she cannot move without assistance and shakes and trembles in a dreadful way.

Tomorrow the Grand-Duchess Helena[3] arrives and brings Elizabeth Wied with her. I am anxious to see the latter as they say she is so much improved. We do not look forward with any delight to the Russian imperial visit which is to be on the 9th. The imperial family are so Danish that Costi was quite rude to us when he was here a week or two ago.[4] Fritz is alas! going away again for "inspections"—it is really too bad! The King is going to Carlsbad and Gastein after the Russian visit. How are Bertie and Alix and the baby? We have not been in correspondence for so long that I only know what the newspapers say of them, I hope they are all well.

---

[1] K. A. A. von Uhden, a jurist and reactionary. A member of the Prussian Ministry.

[2] Louise-Sophie, born Countess Daneskoid-Samsoe. When she had to flee from Augustenburg during the first Danish war she insisted on travelling with her pet pigeons and doves. She was also encumbered by numerous rose-trees. *My Memories of Six Reigns* by Princess Marie-Louise, Evans, 1956.

[3] Sister of the King of Württemberg and widow of the Grand Duke Michael, a younger brother of Czar Alexander I.

[4] The Czar's brother, the Grand-Duke Constantine.

From the Queen

I hope you will find the house at Stettin do for you. Dear Papa was so anxious Fritz should have a command out of Berlin.

No final agreement is yet come to—but I pray it may. Every hour's delay adds to the irritation here, and God forbid the difficulties should come from the German side. I shudder to think what would be the result. The boundary line seems now to be the only point at issue. There must be a compromise on both sides, about this. For God's sake—not to let things break off upon this! It would be dreadful![1]

The marriage at Claremont seems to have gone off extremely well—and the sight to have been very pretty and the warmest and best feeling shown towards the whole family. That shows how feelings change! For the first two or three years and more I could only see Aunt Victoire by stealth and with difficulty, and every year it gets better and now they are so popular and go everywhere.[2]

From the Crown Princess

NEUES PALAIS, JUNE 4, 1864

I am very happy to find that my observations concerning Sir A. Buchanan were not unacceptable to you. Fritz and I feel truly grateful to you for all you have done and are continually doing, amidst all the difficulties you have to contend with, to prevent any serious misunderstanding

---

[1] At the Conference on 28 May the Germans proposed that Schleswig-Holstein should form an independent state under Prince Frederick of Augustenburg. The British then proposed that Schleswig should be divided along an east-west line from the Dannevirke to the mouth of the Schlei—the south of the line going to Germany and the north to Denmark. At the meeting on 1 June the Danes wished the line pushed farther south while the Germans wished it pushed farther north.
[2] The marriage of Louis Philippe's grandson, the Comte de Paris. Aunt Victoire is the Queen's first cousin who married Louis Philippe's son, and the Queen is alluding to the feeling against the King and his family when they first came to England as exiles.

between our two countries. As for worry and anxiety I assure you "nous pouvons en offrir autant" as we are in a perpetual state of suspense having such a man as B. at the head of the Government. It is very sad to think that your courageous moderation should expose you on the one hand to unwarrantable and, to say the very least, unjust attacks like those of Lord Ellenborough, and on the other hand to the foolish and dangerous praise of those who, while fully appreciating all you do, extol it in contradistinction to the conduct of your Government, which is most mischievous. I, for one, can say that on every occasion I have combated and contradicted this distinction between yourself and your ministers, knowing that it can only do harm to yourself and consequently to the good cause—besides being so very contrary to the constitutional principles I always advocate here. I was sorry to see that one of the first articles in that sense on the continent was in a Coburg paper published under the inspiration of Uncle Ernest, an article which was reproduced by most of our German papers because it had a look of a sort of authority.

What you say in your letter to the King is very true.[1] There is danger in the prolongation of Dano-German complications and I think it would be prudent on the part of Prussia to avoid irritating the neutral Powers by insisting on things which are not absolutely indispensable. I believe we might afford to treat the Danes generously on subordinate points, like the contributions, the expenses of the war, but we can never forget that we have some great objects to gain; there are some main points, the partition of Schleswig and the question of succession upon which we could never suffer ourselves to be overridden by what may be agreeable to Denmark. If we did so—where would be the

---

[1] The Queen wrote to the King from Balmoral on 28 May. Her letter included the sentence—"Your Government has repeatedly declared that it had no ambitious objects of its own in view, which I have always believed, but alas! not my people." She went on "If you are uncompromising as to the line of frontier to be fixed . . . you will strengthen the prevalent belief . . . I tremble for the consequences that might ensue. . . ."

use of all our sacrifices? We should lose the fruits of our victory and cover ourselves with ridicule and dishonour. This is felt very strongly—and I share the feeling with all my heart. Moreover if the line of partition is not now determined in such a manner as to correspond with the wishes of Germany and of the Duchies and with the real boundary of the nationalities and languages, no settlement can prevent a renewal of the war in a comparatively short time, and the blood which will then be shed will have to be answered for by those who now render a definitive and satisfactory arrangement impossible.

The Duchies seeing their cause deserted by the great Powers, would most likely rise up and fight for their own rights. Fancy what that would be!

I regret that our Government here should not think it worth its while to contradict the lies of the Danes, and inform the world of the real state of things and the details. They have an intense and just contempt for the language of the English Press and the absurd nonsense which is believed in England against us which is the while creating such a feeling of hatred against us. I think a great deal of the hue and cry might be prevented if the facts on our side were more openly and often stated. We will try and see what can be done in this way.

I saw Elizabeth Wied at the Grand Duchess Helena's yesterday and was much pleased with her. She is so much improved, grown now quiet and soft in her manners, and much prettier in appearance; she made a very agreeable impression upon me which she used not at all. Graceful and elegant her figure and her walk never will be, but she is a very pretty person now and the Grand Duchess praises her so much! Have you quite given up all thought of her for Affie? The Princess of Hanover is struck off the list—and the choice limited to Princess Marie of Altenburg. Should you not have one person still "en réserve" and reconsider Elizabeth? Clever she is—that is to say learned—good and excellent she is too, and all the qualities which made me object to her so much—or rather which made her so unsympathetic to me—seem to be wearing off, and would do so still more perhaps. It is no business of mine. I merely say what struck me yesterday.

From the Queen

Many, many thanks for your dear letter by messenger in which you take so sensible and right a view of my position; I thank you much for it. I am very much heated and though I slept the greater part of the night have so much to do and so many people to see that I must ask you to excuse these hasty lines. I saw Winterhalter's two of Bertie and Alix which are very fine, but he is so poorly himself that he can do nothing else.

I quite agree with you about Elizabeth Wied and wish you would write openly to Affie about her. He is still (I am sorry to say) leaning to Hanover. However I think reason will put it out of his head.

From the Crown Princess

NEUES PALAIS, JUNE 11, 1864

Your dear letter arrived yesterday by messenger in the midst of all this bustle and confusion after which I feel completely exhausted. The night before last the Emperor and Empress arrived about 11.[1] We were all at the railway station—that is to say all the gentlemen of the family and myself, the other Princesses were at the Schloss. Yesterday the Emperor was at the great parade at Berlin; I stayed here to do the honours to the Empress and drive with her to the Queen Dowager. The Empress I found kind and amiable to me; she looks delicate is not good looking but pleasing—not a bit like the Darmstadt family.[2]

The Emperor is not good looking now but I suppose he must have been; he was stiff and made a far less pleasing impression on me than his wife at which I was surprised as I had expected the reverse. There was a dinner and a tea—

---

[1] Alexander II and Marie of Prussia.
[2] Alexander II. The Emperor was sister to the Grand-Duke of Hesse, and aunt to the Battenberg princes.

a great deal of dressing and undressing, standing about and waiting and driving from one place to another in a broiling heat so that I am quite knocked up.

If you like I will write to Affie about E. Wied. I can only tell him what I think and advise him to reconsider this other chance for himself, without trying to influence him one way or another, which is impossible as I do not know Princess Marie of A.

From the Crown Princess

NEUES PALAIS, JUNE 14, 1864

I was much vexed with Wegner this morning. I think William looking pale and not as robust as he should considering he does not grow fast and has nothing to complain of, so I wished to send him to Ostend or Norderney for change of air and sea bathing, as alas! England is quite out of the question on account of the political complications. Wegner said other sea bathing except in the Baltic (which you know is hardly salt and has no tides and no sands and is like a river) was dangerous for children; it excited their nerves and he would not allow it. I said he had bathed at Osborne and it had done him worlds of good. Wegner said he would never have allowed him to bathe there if he had been present and had thought it most imprudent and that nobody did such a thing. I told him of the thousands of children in England but he would not listen to it. He said William was pale by nature and would never look fresh like the two others (which is not true, because in Scotland he looked just as well as they did) and sea baths in the North Sea would be a remedy to resort to when he was much older, and such artificial measures could do him no good now. I urged the air alone would be bracing; he said the air of Ostend was no better than the air here, and if I wanted to send him any where I was to send him to some of the places near Stettin, on the sea coast and there he could bathe. I myself think that of little or no use as the air on the Baltic can hardly be called sea air, and those places are on the same level and same soil as here and the vegetation is the same, so it does not in my opinion answer all the purposes of a complete change of air and will not have the bracing effect I feel convinced the child needs. Some children want bracing—others do not; his constitution particularly does and I am sure that sea bathing in the Channel is the right thing, but what am I to do when my doctor so positively disagrees and says he will not have it and gives no better reasons in support of his opinion than those which I have stated—which seem to me all nonsense. It does annoy me so much! I wish you would tell Dr. Jenner and Sir James; they can write to me about it—not to Wegner—one might as well try to persuade a stone to make him listen to anybody who differs from him.

The English newspapers make me furious!

From the Queen

WINDSOR CASTLE, JUNE 18, 1864, WATERLOO DAY

Let me now thank you for your dear letter of the 14th. I cannot see how (if matters do not get worse) the present political difficulties can prevent a little child of five from coming for its health to its grand-mother for sea bathing!! Did I not send Affie to Berlin to see you? This seems to me far overdone. I can't think if he were sent to Osborne with his governess and a gentleman how that could interfere with political affairs. I can't think the King would even object to that. And I should be too glad to have dear William. But however that may be—Wegner is too absurd and stupid to object to his bathing except in the North Sea.[1] Endless children are sent to England for sea-bathing from Russia and elsewhere. I will desire Dr. Jenner and Sir James to give you their opinion. Really you must try to get another doctor.

In my last letter I forgot to tell you that poor Susan Vane's dreadful husband died quite suddenly last Saturday —I believe in a struggle with his four keepers when he burst a vein in his throat.[1] She is left penniless and her

---

[1] The Queen means here the Baltic.
[2] Lord Adolphus Vane-Tempest, son of 3rd Lord Londonderry.

child is supposed to be an idiot.[1] Is this not retribution? He tried to kill her last week and also the child—so that I believe it is to her a real release too!

I now must ask you or dear Fritz (to whom always my tenderest love) to try and help me in getting the point mentioned in this letter satisfactorily answered. It is naturally of much importance.

From the Crown Princess

NEUES PALAIS, JUNE 18, 1864

Things seem to look very black in politics—people here seem to look on the possibility of a war with England with much more probability and the Government are prepared for it. Yesterday Sir A.B. told Bismarck, England would go to war with us if we did not comply with what was wished. Mr. de B. said he quite expected it. I do not however in *The Times* or *Saturday Review* see any signs of the feeling in England turning more particularly that way now than before.

If England goes to war with us she can only stop our harbours and burn our sea towns—she surely will not send an army to land? Having the whole of Germany as an opponent is not a light thing. In case of a war with England, here we should try for an alliance with the Emperor Napoleon, which he would be the more likely to accept as it would give him the long wished-for opportunity of isolating England and even perhaps attacking her. He would then try to finish us off single handed afterwards. The prevailing opinion is here that the Conferences will not end in securing a peace and that the war will break out again—whether with or without England against us no one seems to know.

Fritz Augustenburg's chances are not so good now as the Grand-Duke of Oldenburg has treacherously put forward claims—which though much laughed at in Germany are an obstacle to Fritz's recognition and increase the confusion and

---

[1] Afterwards a major in the Durham Light Infantry.

delay.[1] We are very anxious about the whole state of things and think they look very unsatisfactory.

From the Crown Princess

PUTBUS, JUNE 22, 1864

I still live in the greatest dread of a war with England; it would be too awful and I fear public opinion is much that way now in London. Here people still think that it may come to pass but quite see what would be the dreadful consequences on both sides. I shall stay here till the 3rd most likely, when I shall meet Fritz at Stettin.

From the Queen

WINDSOR CASTLE, JUNE 22, 1864

I received your dear despairing letter of the 18th on Monday and thank you much for it, and for the hint in it about Sir A.B., which without mentioning you I took advantage of and it has been very useful! Always, dear child, write to me anything you hear and are anxious about, just as you did to dear Papa—for it is very useful, and do ask the good Baron also to write. In spite of things looking very black, I see a "silver lining to the cloud" and out of all this horrid strife and bitterness—good may come.[2] The

---

[1] The Grand-Dukes of Oldenburg, belonging to the house of Holstein-Gottorp, certainly had a claim, as had the Russian ruling-house through a marriage in the eighteenth century. The Russians had renounced their claim in favour of the Grand-Duke of Oldenburg, who in turn abandoned his claim in 1852 when, by the London Protocol, the question seemed settled in favour of Prince Christian. At the London Conference in 1864 it was argued that the Oldenburg claim was revived because the protocol of 1852 had been invalidated by the war.
[2] The silver lining to which the Queen here refers was the realisation that the cabinet was hardening against the Danes. On 25 June, Russell wrote to the Queen to say that the Cabinet had decided

1. Not to "engage in a war for the settlement of the present dispute, so far as the Duchies of Schleswig and Holstein are concerned".
2. If "the safety of Copenhagen, or the existence of Denmark as an

difference is now so small—it must be got over! I must tell you that Lord Clarendon praises poor Bernstorff so much, and says he is so very conciliatory and gentleman-like in the Conference. Tell Fritz so.

Alix is in very good looks again. The dear baby I think very backward and delicate-looking, though a dear good little thing. I can't help being anxious about it!

From the Crown Princess

PUTBUS, ISLE OF RUGEN, JUNE 26, 1864

Your dear letter by messenger [of the 22nd] reached me yesterday and gave me the greatest pleasure; a thousand thanks for all the kind things you say. I am still in perfect ignorance of what is going on in the world at large and of the result of yesterday's Conference—whether we are at war again or whether a peace has been concluded! Our whole fleet (small indeed) has anchored off a point a little way from here; I saw them yesterday from a piece of high ground overlooking the sea. A landing of the Danes here is quite possible though not likely as they are any thing but enterprising. If the war goes on again it will be their fault and not ours, and if their complete destruction is the end of it they will have themselves to thank for it.

My good excellent Baron is gone on a long leave of absence and I have on trial for six months a substitute for him in shape of an officer called M. de Normann.[1] I like him

---

independent Kingdom, be menaced, such a change of circumstances would require a fresh decision on the part of the Government".

Although the Queen does not refer to this she had been greatly heartened by a personal demonstration of the public's feeling for her in London. She went to Buckingham Palace for a Court on 21 June. Her return is described in the formal tones of the *Court Circular*—"The Queen, accompanied by Prince and Princess Louis of Hesse and Princess Beatrice, left Buckingham Palace at 6 o'clock and visited their Royal Highnesses the Prince and Princess of Wales at Marlborough House. Thence Her Majesty proceeded in an open carriage and four to the Paddington station for Windsor Castle." Writing to her uncle she said that the Park was full and crowds ran after her carriage cheering. *Letters of Queen Victoria*, Second Series, Vol. I, page 233.

[1] He was secretary to the Crown Prince and Princess for many years becoming Marshal to the Household in 1883.

very well; he seems so quiet and steady; clever and sensible he is—learned he is not, and seems a little slow, but a very good man of business and of agreeable manners. He is an ugly little man. He is married and I believe pretty well off.

From the Crown Princess

My time is unfortunately limited today and I must try and make my letter a short one which is difficult, as I have much to say. First many thanks for your dear letter. The letter from Lord Clarendon to you I forwarded to Fritz and translated for the King, adding what of your letter I thought might be of use.[1] Thank God! that a war with England is for the present averted! But I see with regret that no one—not even Lord Clarendon—completely understands our position to the question at issue. The aim of this war is to preserve the rights and integrity of a German state, that this German state should have been long under the lawful rule of a Danish Sovereign does not make it Danish and cannot excuse the King of Denmark for considering himself its Sovereign—when he has no longer the right. It would be no generosity on the part of a German power to allow even so small a part of what is German to become Danish again; we have no wish to dismember the ancient and respected though small Kingdom of Denmark; if it is too weak to support itself without keeping what does not belong to it, it is very sad for it but is a standpoint which can in no way influence our views on the subject of Schleswig-Holstein. As the Danes wish rather to sacrifice their army than relinquish their unlawful hold on German territory, we as the first German power have no other means than to resort to arms and take it from them by force—that is, defend at all hazards that part of our German Fatherland which is in danger of being wrongfully swallowed up by another nation.

That England should persist in turning the question up-

---

[1] He was the British plenipotentiary at the London Conference, and had set out for the Queen the varying points of view, including his own, at the Conference.

side down and in thinking that big Prussia wishes to eat up little Denmark is very lamentable. That the bad government we have been so long suffering under here in Prussia should have done much to complicate the case and to mislead public opinion in England as to the aims and cause of the war is sad enough. But to submit a second time to have conditions of an unjust and shameful peace dictated to us in order to prevent public feeling in England driving the country to war with us would be a crime—which we would not a second time be guilty of—and the first concession of which has sown the fruits of endless confusions and difficulties which we are now reaping!

What the calamity of a war with England would be no one knows better than I who lie awake half the night thinking of all the dreadful consequences with horror, but I would not have Prussia go one step aside from the right road in order to avoid it. The conquest of Alsen with such little loss to our troops is a great thing![1]

I left the dear Isle of Rügen with its green woods and sweet fresh air blowing across clover fields from the sea on Wednesday—the whole way to Stettin meeting express trains filled with troops that were singing and hurraying with a great deal of noise.

I have written to the King begging him to allow me to send Willie to Osborne and I hope to have the answer tomorrow, and in that case would send him next week. I am so grateful to you for receiving him; though he looks much better now—I am sure it will do wonders for him! Please let Dr. Jenner watch him attentively—as to his general health, then as to the position of his head, the weakness of his left eye, and the awkward position of his legs—his poor arm there is nothing to be said about; it has made no progress since December. The time is too short for any to be visible. I hope you will find him good and obedient. I think he is.

---

[1] The Armistice ended on 25 June and during the next few days the Prussians attacked and captured Alsen. This disaster compelled King Christian to make the best terms of peace he could.

He makes more noise than Beatrice of course, and as it only is a sign of health it is hardly fair to check it, the more he romps and runs the better for him.

From the Queen

In answer to your observations in reply to mine and Lord Clarendon's, I must observe that you entirely misunderstand what was meant regarding peace, and I will quote Lord Clarendon's own words:

"Her Royal Highness has entirely mistaken the meaning of Lord Clarendon, who considered that the whole of Schleswig was lost to Denmark, from the moment that the Conference came to an end, and hostilities recommenced; and his wish, rather than his hope, was, that Prussia might be induced not to push her conquests further, and to annihilate the Danish Monarchy.

"The only wish in England now, is that Prussia may be contented with the rights she has acquired by conquest, and not push these rights so far as to blot out Denmark from the map of Europe, and create a feeling here which it may be impossible to control."

This is all we are now so anxious about. Let Prussia, who is master of the position, be magnanimous. She can be so now so easily; she has obtained all Germany wished, viz. the severance of the duchies from Denmark and their release from a yoke which had become so hateful to them.

Let Prussia also show that she does not mean to keep them for herself, and I believe all will come right. The shameful attacks against her grieve every right-minded person; and they have brought on the equally intemperate abuse of England in the German Press. But this will wear off, if once peace is made, and there is no attack on Copenhagen, or anything of that kind.

You and I have but one common object, which was beloved Papa's, viz. the prospering of our two countries, and a good and friendly understanding between them. Let us therefore spare no pains to try and bring this about; and it is now in Prussia's power to do this.

Here the selection from this royal correspondence comes to an end. During the weeks that follow, the writers are largely concerned with domestic matters and with the Crown Princess's approaching confinement. After further defeats the Danes agreed to an armistice. In October 1864 King Christian renounced his claims to the duchies, but to the indignation of Queen Victoria the Augustenburg family was ignored and Prussia remained in possession of what they had seized. Whether this and the subsequent aggrandisement of Prussia proved that the Queen was right or wrong is a matter for argument. This is however indisputable. The crisis of 1864 was one of the few occasions—as John Morley noticed—when the Sovereign in alliance with public opinion in the great manufacturing districts pulled up a war-like minister at the eleventh hour. So far as the Queen was concerned this was not achieved without agitation to herself and risks to her popularity. Her inner feelings are revealed in a letter to a member of the Cabinet which was written by General Grey who was acting as her secretary at the time.

"I think I have never seen the Queen so completely upset as she has been these last few days, during which she has, for the first time, been made fully aware of all the attacks directed against her on the subject of her supposed German predilections. . . . She says, I believe most truly, that she doubts whether any one of her subjects, placed in a similar position, with all the ties of birth, relationship and education enlisting their sympathies on one side, would divest themselves so completely as she has done of all thought of those natural ties, and give themselves up to the one thought of what was for the interest of England. . . . There is not a line she has written to them [the members of her own family] that she would not wish laid before the world."[1]

---

[1] Lord Edmund Fitzmaurice, *Life of Lord Granville*, Vol. 1, pages 466–7.

INDEX

(Throughout this correspondence continuous references are made to the Prince Consort, the Crown Prince of Prussia, the Prince and Princess of Wales, Princess Alice and Prince Alfred. Only important allusions to them are included in the index.)

Demidoff, Princess Matilde, daughter of Jerome Bonaparte, 147

Denmark, Princess Alexandra of. See Wales, Princess of

Denmark, Prince Christian of, 91, 94, 103, 106, 126, 149; becomes King of Denmark as Christian IX, and proclaimed ruler of the United Danish Kingdom, 286, 294, 299, 352; renounces claim to the Duchies of Schleswig-Holstein, 354

Denmark, Princess Christian of, 41, 51, 54, 55, 57, 71, 75, 76, 82, 83, 94, 103, 106, 112, 113, 131, 149, 187, 221, 261

Denmark, Princess Dagmar of, 54, 55, 126, 186

Denmark, Frederick VII, King of, 16, 112

Denmark, Prince Waldemar of, 163, 169

Denmark, Prince William of, second son of Prince Christian, later George I of Greece, 186-7, 192

Denmark and the Schleswig-Holstein issue, 14–17, 91, 95, 280, 281, 286, 292, 294, 297, 298, 299, 310, 313, 319, 322, 323, 327, 330, 331

Derby, Lord (1799–1869), 14th Earl, statesman, 299, 340

Dietrichstein, Grafin von, 63

Disraeli, Benjamin (1804–81), Earl of Beaconsfield, statesman, 203

Dobeneck, Mlle Sophie, 74, 216

Duff, David, author of *Hessian Tapestry*, 152

Duncker, Professor Max, 228, 240, 241

Düppel, Danish stronghold—siege of, 310, 313, 319; falls to the Prussians, 322, 323

Eastlake, Sir Charles (1793–1865), President of the Royal Academy, 68

Elgin, Lady, daughter of 1st Lord Durham, 284, 301

Elgin, 8th Lord (1811–63), Viceroy of India, 284, 325

Ellenborough, 1st Earl of (1790–1870), statesman, 340, 343

Elphinstone, Sir Howard (1829–1890), tutor to Prince Arthur, 127

Ernest, Prince of Leiningen. See Leiningen

Ernest I, Duke of Saxe-Coburg. See Saxe-Coburg

Ernest II, Duke of Saxe-Coburg. See Saxe-Coburg

Essays and Reviews, 306, 307

Eugénie, Empress, wife of Napoleon III, 149

Farquharson, Mrs. of Ivercauld, 89, 90, 220

Farr, William, 267

Farre, Dr. Arthur, obstetrician, 193, 251

Feodora, Princess. See Hohenlohe-Langenburg

Ferdinand, King of Portugal. See Prince of Saxe-Coburg

FitzGeorge, George, son of George, Duke of Cambridge, 124

Fitzmaurice, Lord Edmund, author of *Life of Lord Granville*, 354

FitzRoy, Lord Charles, later 7th Duke of Grafton, 125

Flanders, Philip, Count of, 20, 62, 149

Frederick Augustenburg. See Schleswig-Holstein-Sonderburg-Augustenburg

Frederick of the Netherlands, Prince, 93

Frith, William Powell (1819–1909), painter, 311

Fürstenstein, Count, 88, 304, 305, 306, 308, 310, 315

Gallenga, Antonio, 317, 318

Garibaldi, Giuseppi (1807–82), visits England, 313, 316, 322, 324, 332

Geibel, Emanuel (1815–84), 58, 335

George, 2nd Duke of Cambridge. See Cambridge

Gibson, John (1790–1866), sculptor, 135, 147

Gladstone, W. E. (1809–98), statesman, 12, 31

Glücksburg. See Schleswig-Holstein

Graefe, Albrecht, 215

Graefle, A., 209

Grant, John, 59

Granville, 2nd Lord (1815–91), Liberal statesman, 31, 32, 54, 70, 78, 122, 139, 167, 290

Greece, 33, 152, 157, 158, 159, 160, 168; Prince William of Denmark becomes King George I of Greece, 186–7

Greece, King Otho of, 33, 127

Grey, Sir George (1799–1882), 31, 73, 254, 291, 303

Grey, General (1804–70), 49, 61, 63, 65, 79, 86, 114, 125, 142, 162, 182, 197, 201, 220, 223, 225, 226, 229, 253, 254, 354

Gruner, Ludwig, engraver and authority on Italian fresco painting, 27, 31, 32

Guest, Lady Charlotte, 9

HAGEN, Professor, 185, 188

Hahnstep, Countess, 307

Haig, Lt.-Colonel Arthur of Bemersyde (1840–1925), 325

Hamilton, 11th Duke of (1811–1863), 249

Hammond, Edmund (1802–90), afterwards 1st Lord, 337

Hanover, Princess Frederica of, (1848–1926), 56, 326, 328, 330, 331, 333, 344, 345

Hanover, King George V of, and Duke of Cumberland (1819–1878), 331

Harcourt, Mrs. William, 174

Hardenberg, Countess, 310

Hardenberg, Prince (1750–1822), Prussian statesman, 171–2

Hardie, Frank, author of *Political Influence of Queen Victoria*, 17

Hawkins, Caesar (1798–1884), president, College of Surgeons, 200

Helena, H.R.H. Princess (1846–1923), third daughter of Queen Victoria, 53, 72, 100, 125, 126, 127, 182, 187, 198, 217, 222, 233, 234, 237, 238, 249, 262, 291, 303, 311, 314

Helena, Grand-Duchess. See Russia

Hellner, Professor, 255

Helps, Sir Arthur (1815–75), Clerk to the Privy Council, 64, 99–100, 153

Hesse-Cassel, Princess Augusta of (1823–89), 51

Hesse-Cassel, Prince Frederick, later Landgrave of (1820–84), 51, 149, 215

Hesse-Cassel, Princess Anne of, daughter of Prince Charles of Prussia (1836–1918), 51, 149, 215, 218

Hesse-Cassel, Princess Louise Charlotte, Landegravine of (1790–1864), 51

Hesse-Cassel, Elector William II of (1777–1847), 43

Hesse-Darmstadt, Prince Alexander of, 152, 205

Hesse-Darmstadt, Princess Anna of (1843 65), daughter of Prince Charles of Hesse, 56, 312, 316

Hesse-Darmstadt, Prince Charles of (1809–77), 85, 90

Hesse-Darmstadt, Princess Charles, granddaughter of Frederick William II of Prussia (1815–85), 79, 80–1, 83, 85, 88, 90, 260

Hesse-Darmstadt, Prince Henry of (1838–1900), fought with distinction in Franco-Prussian war, 234

Hesse-Darmstadt, Grand-Duke Louis III of (1806–77), 64, 66, 67

Hesse-Darmstadt, Prince Louis of, later Grand-Duke Louis IV, married H.R.H. Princess Alice, 56, 59, 65, 77, 80, 81, 82, 83,

Prime Minister, 96; birth of son, Prince Henry, 14 August, 101; further political disturbances arising out of army reorganisation, 103–4; welcomes the news of the successful meeting between the Queen and Princess Alexandra in Brussels, 104; is pained to hear of the misbehaviour of Prince Alfred, 104–5; start of holiday with the Crown Prince and Prince of Wales, 109; visit to Hohenzollern, 109–11; embarks at Marseilles on royal yacht *Osborne* and visits Sicily, 115–16; arrival in the Bay of Tunis, 116; impressions of Tunisia and visit to the Bey, 117–20; at Malta, 123; from Malta to Syracuse, 124–5; is alarmed at the political atmosphere in Prussia and the influence of Bismarck, 128–129; visit to Naples, 129–30; sends an affectionate account of the Prince of Wales, 130, 134, 140–1; arrival at and stay in Rome, 132–3, 134–7; Prince of Wales returns home, 140; visit to the Sistine chapel, a Jewish synagogue and the German Roman Catholic church, 144; visit to Leghorn, Florence and Pisa, 147; in Venice and Milan, 149–153

1863:

Is astounded at the offer of the Greek throne to the Duke of Saxe-Coburg, 157; discusses marriage prospects for Princess Mary of Cambridge, 157–8; refers to the general indignation in Prussia caused by the publication of *Matinées royales*, 161; illness of Baron Ernest Stockmar, 161–2; does not agree with the Queen's suggestion of Prince Frederick of Schleswig-Holstein for the Greek throne, 163; expresses relief at refusal of the throne by the Duke of Saxe-

Coburg, 166; defends Sir John Acton's publication of *Matinées royales* as being of purely literary interest, 167; explains the disagreement which exists between the King and the Prussian Parliament, 170–1; illness of youngest son, Prince Henry, 175–6; visit of the Duke and Duchess of Württemburg, 177–8; return to Berlin from Osborne after the Prince of Wales's wedding, 181; apologises for her expressions of love for England, 183; at work on a bust of the Prince Consort, 185; reports that Count Bernstorff writes disparagingly of the English Court, 188; enquires about the proposed visit of the Queen of Prussia to England, 189; meditates on the past year and regrets her shortcomings, 191; refers to Dr. Colenso and the controversy over his book on the Pentateuch, 191, 194–5, 197; describes treatment prescribed by the German doctors to correct the physical defects of Prince William, 200, 203–4; arranges a garden for the children, 207–8, 210; further political uproar in Prussia, 211–12; regrets that she will be unable to visit Balmoral this year, 220–221; visit to Danzig, 224; where Prince Frederick in his speech disclaims all part in the recent press ban, 225; tours Lithuania, 231–2; assures the Queen that the proposed visit of Prince Albrecht to England has no connexion with Princess Helena, 234, 237–8; refers to the anti-Prussian articles in *The Times*, 240–1; and to the antagonistic attitude of the Kreuzzeitung party towards herself and the Crown Prince, 241–3; expresses anxiety about the health of Baron Christian Stockmar, 245;

Prussia, Crown Princess Victoria (1840–1901)—*continued* discusses possible marriage prospects for Prince Alfred, 265; attends Manœuvres, 268; writes to say that a visit to Balmoral is now possible, 271–2; tries to convince the German doctors that Prince William should receive electrical treatment for his arm, 282

1864:

Comments on the recent events in Denmark, 286; is delighted to hear of the birth of a son to the Prince and Princess of Wales, 288; in the absence of her husband asks if Countess Blücher could be sent to Berlin, 293; reports on the progress of the Prusso-Danish war and the capture of the Dannevirke, 298; lays the blame for the war at the feet of Lord Palmerston and the Emperor Nicholas of Russia, 299; accuses *The Times* of spite and hatred towards Prussia, 303; sends Count Fürstenstein to attend the christening at Buckingham Palace, 304–5; gives her opinion of the shortcomings of Count Bernstorff, 309; obtains permission from the King to have more rooms in the Neues Palais, 317; writes in praise of the Prussian troops who are denigrated by *The Times*, 317–318, 323–4; defends the bombardment of Sonderburg, which is violently attacked by the English press and Parliament, 320–1; is pleased by the visit of Prince Alfred to Berlin, 326, 327–8; is saddened by the anti-English feeling in Prussia, and the anti-Prussian tone of the English press, 332; is reunited with the Crown Prince at Hamburg following the armistice, 333–4; writes again of her uneasiness over the deterioration of English-Prussian relations, 336; suggests the removal of Sir Andrew Buchanan as British Ambassador in Berlin and the substitution of Lord Napier, 338; discusses the problems arising out of the final settlement of the Prusso-Danish war, 343–4; visit of the Emperor and Empress of Russia, 345–6; disagreement with Dr. Wegner over sea-bathing for Prince William, 346–7; fears war with England, thought by people in Germany to be a probability, 348, 349; is relieved to hear war is averted, but feels that the whole Prussian-Danish issue is not really understood in England, 351–2

Prussia, Prince Henry of (1862–1929), second son of Crown Prince Frederick, 7, 101, 175, 183, 188, 244, 272, 273, 277

Prussia, Princess Louise of, daughter of King William I. See Baden

Prussia, Queen Louise of (1776–1810), wife of King Frederick William III, daughter of Duke Charles of Mecklenburg-Strelitz, 170, 312

Prussia, Princess Marianne (1837–1906), daughter of the Duke of Anhalt-Dessau, 298

Prussia, King William I of (1797–1888), brother to King Frederick William IV; fled to England in 1848, 4; was considered by the Crown Princess as being "incapable of taking in the principles of constitutional government", 5; political interests predominantly military, 13; his reluctance to allow the Crown Prince to attend the 1862 Exhibition in London, 49, 54; permission granted, 57; sides with the Prussian reactionary party, 90; favours Bismarck, 96; makes imprudent speeches, 128; opposes the idea of Ernest II of Saxe-Coburg becoming King of Greece, 160; orders the Crown Prince to go to Poland, 221; urged by the Crown Prince not to give his consent to any unconstitutional measures, 223; reproaches the Crown Prince for his opposition, 224; rejects the Crown Prince's offer of resignation, 230; visits Queen Victoria at Rosenau, 259, 260; expresses a desire for an understanding with Austria, 264; birthday celebrations, 312; confers the Order of the Black Eagle on Prince Alfred, 326, 328, 330

Prussia, Prince William of (1859–1941), the future Kaiser, 7, 26, 36, 80, 165, 166, 168, 170, 177, 179, 180, 199, 200, 202, 203, 204, 206, 216, 252, 272, 273, 277, 278, 299, 321, 346, 352

Prusso-Danish war. See Schleswig-Holstein

Putbus, Prince William, 240, 252

RANKE, Leopold von (1795–1886), 171

Redern, Count, 283

Rhoades, James, 80

Richmond, 6th Duke and Duchess of, 273

Robertson, Rev. F. W., 319

Robertson, Dr., factor at Balmoral, 59

Roggenbach, M. de, 41, 42

Rokeby, 6th Lord, 291

Rollande, Mme, 150

Roon, Count (1803–79), 283

Ros, 24th Baron de, 58

Royal Order of Victoria and Albert, 27

Rulandt, Mr., 65, 77, 78, 138, 226, 253, 297

Russell, Lord John (1792–1878), 1st Earl, 17, 31, 96, 122, 232, 254, 296, 299, 320, 337, 338, 339, 340, 349

Russell, Odo, later 1st Lord Ampthill, 136, 144, 146, 308

Russia, Alexander II (1818–81), Emperor of, 54, 345

Russia, Grand-Duchess Constantine of, 265

Russia, Grand-Duke Constantine of, 341

Russia, Grand-Duchess Michael, 341

Russia, Marie, Empress of, wife of Alexander II, 345

Russia, Nicholas I (1796–1855), Emperor of, 299

ST. ALBANS, 10th Duke and Duchess of, 147

St. Germans, Lord (1798–1877), 3rd Earl, 202

Sahl, Hermann, 297

Salisbury, Lord (1830–1903), 3rd Marquess, 15

Samwer, Karl, 66, 98, 189, 248, 264, 267, 282

Saturday Review, 322, 348

Saxe-Altenburg, Agnes, Duchess of, 262, 271

Saxe-Altenburg, Princess Alexandra of. See Grand Duchess Constantine

Saxe-Altenburg, Prince Edward of, 56

Saxe-Altenburg, Princess Marie of, 56, 260, 262, 267, 271, 275, 325, 329, 331, 344, 346

Saxe-Coburg-Gotha, Prince Albert of. See Prince Consort

Saxe-Coburg-Gotha, Alexandrine, Duchess of, wife of Ernest II, 45, 65, 149, 159, 165, 168, 263

Saxe-Coburg, Prince Augustus of, 68

Saxe-Coburg, Princess Clementine of, 68, 175

Saxe-Coburg, Ernest I, Duke of, 134, 263

Saxe-Coburg-Gotha, Ernest II, Duke of, 5, 27, 33, 40, 41, 45, 52, 53, 62, 64, 65, 66, 72, 85, 94, 96, 104, 149, 157, 158, 159,